PLAY AND EARLY CHILDHOOD DEVELOPMENT

Second Edition

JAMES E. JOHNSON
The Pennsylvania State University

JAMES F. CHRISTIE
Arizona State University

THOMAS D. YAWKEY
The Pennsylvania State University

Photographs by Francis Wardle

D0220888

LONGMAN

An imprint of Addison Wesley Longman, Inc.

New York • Reading, Massachusetts • Menlo Park, California • Harlow, England
Don Mills, Ontario • Sydney • Mexico City • Madrid • Amsterdam

Acquisitions Editor: *Virginia Blanford*
Associate Editor: *Arianne Weber*
Marketing Manager: *Renée Ortbals*
Project Coordination and Text Design: *York Production Services*
Cover Designer:Kay Petronio
Cover Photo: Francis Wardle
Full Service Production Manager: *Richard Ausburn*
Electronic Page Makeup: *York Production Services*
Printer and Binder: *The Maple-Vail Book Manufacturing Group*
Cover Printer: *Coral Graphic Services, Inc.*

Library of Congress Cataloging-in-Publication Data

Johnson, James E. (James Ewald), 1947–
    Play and early childhood development/James E. Johnson, James F. Christie,
Thomas D. Yawkey.—2nd ed.
        p. cm.
    Includes bibliographical references and index.
    ISBN 0-321-01166-X
    1. Play.   2. Child development.   I. Christie, James F.   II. Yawkey, Thomas D.   III. Title.
HQ782.J63   1998
    155.4´18—dc21   98–8742
                                                                            CIP

Please visit our website at http://longman.awl.com

ISBN 0-321-01166-X

12345678910—MA—01009998

Contents

Preface

The purpose of this book is to combine theory and research knowledge on a number of relevant topics in the literature on children's play and to draw out implications for practical application in early childhood education. The focus includes the primary grades, but with emphasis on children 3–6 years old.

The role of the adult in children's play is a major theme of this text. When adults intervene in the play world of youngsters, they need to base their actions on knowledge and understanding of children and their play. Accordingly, we attempt to provide a balanced presentation of theory, research, and practical ideas found in the literature on children's play. In this endeavor, we base our discussion on what we know about child development and early education. We also combine research and theory in these fields with relevant information gleaned from the fields of anthropology, sociology, history, and even folklore. We further build on this sound foundation of research and theory by continually considering applied research and related theory in the areas of child development and early childhood education.

Developmentally appropriate practice (DAP), as defined by the National Association for the Education of Young Children (NAEYC), informs our recommendations (Bredekamp & Copple, 1997). Accordingly, we view adults who work with young children as decision makers who require three sets of information to guide practice: (1) the *developmental level* of the children, (2) the *individual differences* among children (including children with special educational needs), and (3) the *cultural backgrounds* of the children. Thus, another major theme of this book centers on diversity and individual differences as key concerns. These concerns interact with our major theme, affecting the roles of adults as they observe children and facilitate children's play, both through direct behavioral intervention strategies and through providing materials or playmates.

Chapter 1 grapples with the difficult matter of "what play is," by discussing various theories of play. Apparently, play, like love, is a "many-splendored thing." Subsequent chapters build on the theories, concepts, and definitions of children's play presented in this chapter. Chapter 2 presents both theory and empirical research showing the vital role of play in the development and well-being of children. Chapters 3 and 4 deal with developmental progressions and individual differences (gender and personality) with respect to play phenomena in early childhood. Chapter 5 addresses cultural diversity, and Chapter 6 focuses on the play of children who have special educational or therapeutic needs, including children in hospitals served by Child Life Programs.

The themes of the second half of the book chiefly answer the questions, "What qualifies as good play?" and "How can adults influence children's play to improve it?" Chapters 7 and 8 address two topics critical to successful adult intervention in the play of children: Chapter 7 discusses adult facilitation strategies, and Chapter 8 focuses on observation methods. Chapters 9 and 10 cover the applied literature in the field, particularly those aspects concerned with play environments (both indoor and outdoor) and play materials, including television and computers. Chapter 11, the final chapter, discusses play in relation to the curriculum and academic content areas, with reference to (a) emerging literacy and numeracy during the preschool years, and (b) literacy, other symbolic attainments, and knowledge mastery during the primary grades.

Although the topics in the chapters are diverse, a number of common themes run throughout the text. First, we have tried to provide even-handed coverage of controversial topics—such as the effects of federal deregulation of the television industry on the quality of play. We give both sides of opposing positions on various issues in the research literature.

Secondly, we have striven to address both diversity and inclusion concerns prominent in today's society. Interests in multicultural education often accentuates variability, while stakeholders in special education and related fields tend to emphasize the basic similarities and commonalties among all children. We believe that it is important to balance an emphasis on how children are different with an equal emphasis on the fundamental sameness among all children.

Throughout the text we have employed this dialectical mode of thinking to our treatment and attitudes about various polarizations or dichotomies that appear in the research and applied literature on children's play: educational play versus recreational play, theory versus practice, socio-emotional versus intellectual, social integration versus personal individuation, convergent thinking versus divergent thinking. These contrasts stand in a reversible figure-ground relation with each other and together make up a Gestalt whole. We recommend that these polarized constructs and other binary divisions that appear on the pages that follow (either explicitly or "reading between the lines") be "deconstructed" or "unpacked" so that variation along continua and associated nuances be appreciated and discussed.

Since the publication of the first edition of this text in 1987, the research literature on play, child development, and early childhood education has grown enormously. A play canon and ethos has taken firmer grip on a host of disciplines ranging from play therapy to occupational sciences and child life, to early intervention and special education, to children's library sciences, to child care and on to early and primary education. We want adults in various walks of life who interface with children at play to know that play is both a means to other ends as well as an end in itself.

Play can indeed serve developmental, socialization, enculturation, therapeutic, remedial, and educational purposes. But play also is a time-honored expression of being human and should be cherished in its own right. Respect for childhood and for play go hand-in-hand. In part, our purpose in writing this book is to contribute to improved understanding and communication across disciplines about core concepts and descriptive facts pertaining to children's play and development. We have also attempted to make sound recommendations and suggestions for practical application based upon extant theory and research on children's play. We hope that readers will benefit from this text's attempted integration of theory, research, and practice on children's play, and that those adults who work, or will work, directly with children find our suggestions and recommendations especially useful. All of us can and will continue to learn how to serve better the future of childhood.

For thoughtful review suggestions, the authors would like to thank:

Carol Bersani, *Kent State University*
LaVonne Carlson, *University of Minnesota*
Martha Taylor Dever, *Utah State University*
Jeffrey I. Gelfer, *University of Nevada, Las Vegas*
Andrew Gunsberg, *Oakland University*
Joan Isenberg, *George Mason University*
Marilynn M. Jones-Parker, *University of Oklahoma*
Mona Lane, *Oklahoma State University*
Carol Seefeldt, *University of Maryland*
Kevin J. Swick, *University of South Carolina*
Alice Whiren, *Michigan State University*

For co-authoring chapters with us and for photographic work we are extremely grateful for the contributions of Francis Wardle and Susan Welteroth. Thanks are also extended to Karen McChesney Johnson and to Georgia Mitchell for their help in preparing the index. We are most appreciative of the love and support of Karen and Mary for accepting our having to be away long hours working on this book, and others who have tolerated or assisted us in sundry ways while we did this book. Thank you all!

James E. Johnson
James F. Christie

Chapter 1

THEORIES OF CHILDREN'S PLAY

Preschoolers Wendy, John, and George are enacting a domestic scene in their classroom's housekeeping corner. John takes the role of the father, Wendy is the mother, and George, the youngest of the three, reluctantly agrees to be the baby.

WENDY: *Baby looks hungry. Let's cook him some food.*

JOHN: *Okay.*

WENDY: *(addressing George) Cry and say that you're hungry.*

GEORGE: *But I'm not hungry.*

WENDY: *Pretend that you are!*

GEORGE: *(using a babyish voice) I'm hungry.*

WENDY: *(addressing John) Father, what should we have for dinner?*

JOHN: *How about eggs?*

WENDY: *I'll go get some eggs from the 'frigerator. (She goes to a wall shelf and takes several cube-shaped blocks.)*

GEORGE: *Aah! I'm hungry!*

WENDY: *(pretending to scold George) Be quiet! (She puts the blocks in a toy pan and places the pan on the toy stove.) The eggs are cooking. Father, you'd better set the table.*

JOHN: *Okay.*

GEORGE: *Let me help, Daddy.*

JOHN: *No! Babies don't set tables! You're just supposed to sit there and cry.*

John then sets the table using miniature plates and cups. There is no silverware or coffeepot, so popsicle sticks and an empty can are used as substitutes. George pretends to cry from time to time, and Wendy continues cooking. Finally, Wendy puts a block on each child's plate, and John pretends to pour coffee from the empty can. The children then act as if they are eating the make-believe eggs and drinking the invisible coffee. ■

Everyone knows that children's play is fun and exciting. The smiles and laughter that accompany play attest to its enjoyable nature. Less obvious, however, is whether play is educational, as well as pleasurable. There are sharp differences of opinion on this issue. Some adults consider play trivial and nonessential, while others believe that play makes important contributions to all aspects of child development.

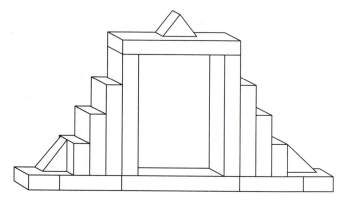

Figure 1.1

Megan's block structure

Two important types of play—sociodramatic play and constructive play—illustrate these contrasting viewpoints. Both types of play are common during the preschool and kindergarten years. *Sociodramatic play* occurs when two or more children adopt roles and act out a make-believe situation or story, as we saw in the preceding scenario. *Constructive play* involves using materials such as blocks or Tinkertoys to build something, as in the following scenario.

> *Five-year old Megan is playing with unit blocks on the floor of her bedroom. She first makes a base with a double-unit block in the center and with unit and half-unit blocks on either side. She then makes a bridge in the center, using three more double units. Next, Megan uses unit and half-unit blocks to make graduated steps up each side of the bridge. She finishes by adding small triangles to both ends and to the center of her structure. Megan admires her bridge for a few moments and then gleefully knocks it down. She then begins building a new, entirely different structure.*

Some adults would argue that the two preceding play episodes are unimpressive and of little importance. The children in the first example are only engaging in trivial make-believe, and the girl in the second example apparently thought so little of her block structure that she tore it down as soon as she completed it. People with such opinions regard play as frivolous and believe that it would be better if children spent their time in more serious activities, such as receiving academic instruction or playing organized sports. They oppose using school time for play activities because they feel that children spend more than enough time playing outside of school.

Other people would contend that the two episodes illustrate some of the important ways play contributes to child development. For instance, the three children in the sociodramatic play example must use precise language to plan and carry out their story lines. By dramatizing these events, they are also learning to use and interpret symbols (e.g., a block represents an egg). By enacting various roles, the children learn to view things from different perspectives, and they develop social skills such as cooperation and turn taking to keep the dramatic-play episode going. In the constructive-play episode, Megan has been gaining valuable experience with the concepts of symmetry and sequence. The deliberate manner in which Megan went about building the bridge structure implies that she may have been following a mental plan. Children in both episodes are learning to persist at the task at hand.

Since the late 1960s, research on play has increased dramatically. During the 1970s alone, more than 200 scholarly journal articles and dozens of research books were published on the topic of play (Sutton-Smith, 1983). Most of the studies in these publications have fallen into four categories of research: (1) *definitional studies*, which attempt to distinguish play from non-play behaviors; (2) *correlational studies*, which investigate the relationship of play to social, emotional, and cognitive development; (3) *individual-difference studies*, which examine how factors such as age, sex, and cultural background affect play; and (4) *ecological studies*, which investigate the effects of settings and materials on play behavior. The various chapters of this text offer many examples of studies in each of these categories.

More recently, Fein (1997) has described the voluminious research literature on children's play as occurring in waves. The earliest studies established that it is possible to scientifically investigate play and showed how children's play can be rendered empirically manageable. The second wave of research surged with training studies, and the third wave tossed up correlational studies using global categories of play (e.g., constructive and dramatic play). As those waves ebbed, the fourth wave flowed forth with more intensive qualitative observational studies. These studies included case studies and ethnographies with detailed codes for play text and context, giving attention to the sequence of play behaviors between interactive play partners, as exhibited in adult–child or child–child dyads or larger social groups. Further evidence of the field's accumulating knowledge base and increasing importance is the growing number of college textbooks summarizing information on play, early development, and early education (following the publication in 1987 of the first edition of this text).

In this chapter, we discuss the concept of play and value systems surrounding it. We review both the historical background and the recent developments in theories of play. These theories are important because they reflect changing attitudes toward—and understandings about—play, and they have motivated much of the research on play. We then examine the definition of play in order to better understand exactly what play is and what it is not. This is followed by a discussion of how modern theories have generated four contemporary metaphors for play, which can be applied to early childhood education and the role of the teacher.

CONCEPTUALIZING PLAY

Play is an extremely difficult concept to define—there are 116 distinct definitions listed in the *Oxford English Dictionary*! In addition to the many denotations of *play*, the connotations of the term are often vague and slippery, and even personal and idiosyncratic. Like love, play is a many-splendored thing. How can we get a handle on this very elusive concept?

Philosophers such as Ludwig Wittgenstein (1958) and Bertrand Russell (1912/1967), deft masters of such profound issues as the logic of meaning and the relation of experience to semantics, have suggested that we abandon hope of choosing the right words for a single precise definition of a broad, multifarious construct such as *game* or *play* (not to mention *love* again). Rather, we should think of such definitions as a "rope" comprising many intertwining strands and fibers. There is no one specific meaning but instead many interwoven threads giving shades of meaning to the concept and a sense of definitional clarity or strength in the unity of the whole. This whole is not reducible to the mere sum of its parts. In conceptualizing the phenomenon of play, scholars have sought to bring to light elements of both *convergence* (overlapping characteristics of play) and *divergence* (distinguishing characteristics). Others have rested content simply to define play by example ("I can't tell you what it is but I sure recognize it when I see it!").

Numerous lists of the essential or nonessential defining characteristics of play have been proffered by scholars conceptualizing play. Some definitional schemes have approached play by stressing its behavioral manifestations, others by highlighting internal states or dispositions (e.g., "playfulness"), and still others by emphasizing situational factors. It is safe to presume that all these approaches to the concept of play are valid and important to varying degrees and that some kind of holistic model is to be recommended, similar to Wittgenstein's rope analogy. A holistic model means that we think about play from many different angles, each one comprising many different possible ingredients—such as flexibility, quirkiness, spontaneity, nonliterality, freedom, process orientation, and the like. Play can perhaps best be conceptualized as a convergence or intertwining of relevant if not indispensable features or components. Which factor is most central in the sense that it best approximates "pure play" (whatever that is)? Do you think there is a central factor or ingredient? (The accompanying feature, "Telltale Sign of Play?" explores this question further.)

It is important both to acknowledge the conceptual difficulties associated with articulating the meaning of play and to recognize and make explicit the values surrounding play. In the United States and many other countries around the world, the "Protestant work ethic" has dominated the societal value system. This ethic leads to subconscious anxieties about play as a form of wasting time. Most of us have been socialized to feel guilty about indulging our lust for play when we should be adhering to productive work as a sign of our worth, if not even our salvation. We often view play as something we have to earn, as our language readily attests: "I deserve a break," "I need a vacation," "Finish your work before you play," and so on. Consequently, it is not surprising that educators who advocate play in the classroom come up against strong resistance from defenders of the status quo. Play remains subordinate to work.

Theory in Action

"TELL-TALE SIGN OF PLAY?"

Peter Smith and his colleagues at Sheffield University in Great Britain have undertaken research to discern which aspects or dimensions of play are the best "tell-tale sign" of the phenomenon (Smith & Vollstedt, 1985). In this research, adult subjects were shown a 30-minute videotape of young children's behavior, independently rated for the occurrence of play. Before being asked to code children's behavior as to whether it was play, each group of subjects was trained to use a particular characteristic of play as the sole criterion for choosing the play code. These behavioral characteristics included *intrinsic motivation* (undertaken freely, for its own sake), *positive affect* (expressing positive emotions), *flexibility* (involving quick changes in activity), *process orientation* (emphasizing means over ends), and *nonliterality* (pretending or otherwise assuming an as-if stance toward reality). In other versions of the experiment subjects were give more than one criterion to use in coding the children's behaviors (e.g., both intrinsic motivation and nonliterality).

The results indicated that "nonliterality" was the most reliable indicator. If the nonliterality criterion is used together with positive affect or flexibility, observers almost always agreed as to whether particular behavior being exhibited by the youngsters could be called play. Intrinsic motivation was the least helpful indicator when attempting to discern play: Many behaviors performed by children, such as going to the drinking fountain to get a drink of water, are intrinsically motivated but are clearly not play.

Perhaps the best litmus test for play, then, is the nonliterality standard. Within a playframe, internal reality takes precedence over external reality, and objects and actions take on new, play-related meanings.

THEORIES OF PLAY

The theories described in this section attempt to explain and, in some cases, predict play behavior. They help define what play is and what causes it. We have divided play theories into two groups:

1. Classical theories, which originated in the nineteenth and early twentieth centuries
2. Modern theories, which were developed after 1920

The relative sophistication of modern theories shows our progress in understanding the phenomenon of play.

Table 1.1 CLASSICAL THEORIES OF PLAY

THEORY	ORIGINATOR	PURPOSE OF PLAY
Surplus energy	Schiller/Spencer	Eliminate surplus energy
Recreation	Lazarus	Regenerate energy expended in work
Recapitulation	Hall	Eliminate ancient instincts
Practice	Groos	Perfect instincts needed for adult life

CLASSICAL THEORIES

The classical theories of play all originated before World War I. They try to explain why play exists and what purpose it serves. Ellis (1973) refers to them as "armchair" theories, based more on philosophical reflection than on experimental research. The four classical theories can be grouped into two pairs: (1) surplus-energy and recreation theories, which view play as a means of energy regulation, and (2) recapitulation and practice theories, which explain play in terms of instincts. It is interesting to note that the members of each pair have opposite explanations of how play affects energy or instincts. Table 1.1 summarizes the four classical theories of play. A more detailed discussion of these theories is presented in Ellis's (1973) book *Why People Play*.

SURPLUS-ENERGY THEORY   The surplus-energy theory of play can be traced back to two men: Friedrich Schiller, an eighteenth-century German poet, and Herbert Spencer, a nineteenth-century British philosopher. According to this theory, each living thing generates a certain amount of energy to meet survival needs. Any energy left over after these needs have been met becomes surplus energy. This extra energy builds up pressure and must be expended. Play, which is viewed as otherwise purposeless behavior, is how humans and animals get rid of this surplus energy.

The surplus-energy theory has a commonsense appeal that may explain why it is still popular today. Anyone who has seen young children run out to the playground after a long period of sedentary work in a classroom can see the element of truth to this theory. It also neatly explains why children play more than adults (adults take care of children's survival needs, leaving children with lots of surplus energy) and why animals higher on the evolutionary scale play more than lower animals (the higher animals meet their survival needs more efficiently, resulting in more energy being left for play).

RECREATION THEORY   In direct opposition to the surplus-energy theory, recreation theory postulates that the purpose of play is to restore energy expended in work. According to its originator, German poet Moritz Lazarus, work uses up energy and creates an energy deficit. This energy can be regenerated either by sleeping or by engaging in an activity that differs greatly from the work that caused the energy deficit. Play, being the opposite of work, is the ideal way to restore lost energy.

As with the surplus-energy theory, recreation theory shows a certain commonsense quality. If people get tired doing one type of activity, it helps to switch to something completely different. This theory explains the popularity of adult recreational activities. After a long day of stressful mental activity at the office, a period of physical activity (such as handball) or of mental activity of a different sort (such as a game of chess) can be rejuvenating. Early childhood educators have long recognized the principle behind the recreation theory, and the school day is structured so that periods of sedentary mental work alternate with periods of active play.

RECAPITULATION THEORY   Prior to the turn of the twentieth century, scientists discovered that as the human embryo develops, it appears to go through some of the same stages that occurred in the evolution of the human species. At one point, for example, human embryos have physiological structures similar to fish gills. This discovery led to the theory that *ontogeny* (the development of the individual) recapitulates or reenacts *phylogeny* (the development of the species).

G. Stanley Hall, an American psychologist, extended recapitulation theory to children's play. According to Hall, through play, children reenact the developmental stages he observed in the human race: animal, savage, tribal member, and so on. He held that these stages of play follow the same order that they occurred in human evolution. Thus, children climb trees (our primate ancestors) before engaging in gang play (tribal humans). The purpose of play is to rid children of primitive instincts that are no longer needed in modern adult life. For example, sports such as baseball enable children to play out and eliminate ancient hunting instincts such as hitting with a club.

PRACTICE THEORY   Philosopher Karl Groos believed that, rather than eliminating instincts from the past, play serves to strengthen instincts needed for the future. Newborn humans and other animals inherit a number of imperfect, partially formed instincts that are essential for survival. Play offers a safe means for the young of a species to practice and perfect these vital skills. The purpose of play is to exercise and elaborate skills required for adult life.

The best example of play as a means of practicing survival skills is the play fighting of young animals such as lions. Groos believed that his theory applied to humans, as well. For example, Groos would contend that when children take on roles as parents during sociodramatic play (as in the example at the beginning of this chapter), they are practicing parenting skills that they will need in adult life.

CRITIQUE OF CLASSICAL THEORIES   All of the classical theories of play have serious weaknesses. They are very limited in scope and explain only a small segment of play behavior. There are numerous exceptions to each theory. The surplus-energy theory offers no reason why children continue to play when exhausted. The recreation theory falsely predicts that because adults work more, they should have larger energy deficits and should therefore play more than children. The recapitulation theory cannot explain why children like to play with toys such as cars and spaceships, which reflect modern technology. All four theories are also based on outdated, discredited beliefs about energy, instincts, and evolution. For instance, the surplus-energy theory assumes that energy has hydraulic properties similar to those of water, and the practice theory contends that children inherit a knowledge of the specific skills they will need in adult life.

In spite of their limitations, however, the classical theories are still important. First, they give historical perspective to contemporary adult attitudes about play. Notice that the current debate about the importance of play is evident in these old theories. While the surplus-energy theory holds that play is purposeless, nonproductive behavior, the practice theory argues that play is vital for the survival of the species. Second, several of these theories are still very much with us. Many of today's adults believe in the surplus-energy theory, though they do not know it by name. Third, a number of the modern theories of play discussed in the next section have their roots in the early theories. For example, Hall's recapitulation theory stimulated interest in systematically observing children's play, and its proclamations about the stages of play heralded modern stage theories of play (e.g., Piaget's theory). Further, Groos's practice theory held that many play behaviors have adaptive significance, an idea that is reflected in the theories of play and evolution proposed by Bruner (1972) and by Sutton-Smith (1998).

MODERN THEORIES

Modern theories of play attempt to do more than simply explain why play exists. They also try to determine play's role in child development and, in some cases, to specify antecedent conditions that lead to play behavior (Ellis, 1973). These modern theories are summarized in Table 1.2.

PSYCHODYNAMIC THEORY   Sigmund Freud, the founder of psychoanalytic therapy and psychodynamic theory of personality development, believed that play has an important role in children's emotional development. According to Freud (1961), play can have a *cathartic effect*, allowing children to rid themselves of negative feelings associated with traumatic events. Play allows the child to suspend reality and switch roles from being the passive recipient of a bad experience to being the one who gives out the experience. For example, after being spanked by a parent, a child might spank a doll or pretend to punish a playmate. By reversing roles and becoming the active party, a child is able to transfer negative feelings to a substitute object or person.

Repetitive play is another mechanism through which children deal with unpleasant events. By repeating a bad experience many times in play, the child can divide the experience into small, manageable segments. In this manner, the child can slowly assimilate the negative emotions associated with the event. Brown, Curry, and Tinnich (1971) give an excellent example of the therapeutic value of repetitive play. Their preschoolers had the misfortune to watch a worker fall 20 feet to the ground and sustain serious injury. They

Table 1.2   MODERN THEORIES OF PLAY

THEORY	ROLE OF PLAY IN CHILD DEVELOPMENT
Psychoanalytic	Mastering traumatic experiences; coping with frustrations
Cognitive	
Piaget	Practicing and consolidating previously learned skills and concepts
Vygotsky	Promoting abstract thought; learning within the ZPD; self-regulation
Bruner/ Sutton-Smith	Generating flexibility in behavior and thinking; imagination and narration
Singer	Modulating the rate of internal and external stimulation
Other Theories	
Arousal modulation	Keeping arousal at optimal level by increasing stimulation
Bateson	Promoting an ability to comprehend multiple levels of meaning

watched while the man was given first aid and then taken away by an ambulance. Initially, many of the children were deeply disturbed by the incident. They frequently, almost compulsively, engaged in dramatic-play themes related to the accident (falling, death and injury, ambulances, hospitals). After many weeks the frequency of such play diminished, and the children no longer appeared to be bothered by the accident.

Erikson (1950) extended the psychoanalytic theory of play by examining its contribution to normal personality development. According to Erikson, play progresses through stages that mirror children's psychosocial development. Through play, children create model situations that help them master the demands of reality.

COGNITIVE THEORIES   Cognitive theories include those of Piaget, Vygotsky, Bruner, Sutton-Smith, and Singer.

Piaget's Theory   Swiss psychologist Jean Piaget (1962) proposed a detailed theory of children's intellectual development. According to Piaget, children go through a series of distinct cognitive stages during which their thought processes become increasingly similar to those of adults. Children engage in the type of play that matches their level of cognitive development (see Table 1.3). For example, children under 2 years of age can engage in practice play (e.g., repeated physical movements) and simple pretense activities. They cannot participate in more advanced dramatic or make-believe play because they do not yet have the necessary cognitive and social abilities (see Chapter Three).

In Piaget's theory, play does more than merely reflect a child's level of cognitive development; it also contributes to that development. Piaget stipulated that in order for learning to take place, there must be adaptation. Adaptation

Table 1.3 PIAGET'S THEORY OF PLAY

APPROXIMATE AGE	COGNITIVE STAGE	DOMINANT TYPE OF PLAY
Birth–2 years	Sensorimotor	Practice play
2–7 years	Preoperational	Symbolic play
7–11 years	Concrete operational	Games with rules

requires a balance between two complementary processes: *assimilation* (incorporating new information about reality even as this process involves some distortion, modification, or otherwise 'bending' of reality in order to fit existing cognitive structures) and *accommodation* (changing those cognitive structures to match, imitate, or otherwise conform with what is observed in reality). Piaget viewed play as an imbalanced state in which assimilation dominates over accommodation. Imitation also is an imbalanced state in which accommodation dominates assimilation. Imbalanced states in themselves do not engender genuine learning or development and are in this sense nonadaptive intellectually. Children do not learn new skills when they play. They do, however, practice and consolidate recently acquired skills. Although play is not the 'cutting ege' of cognitive development according to Piagetian theory, it makes an important contribution. Take, for example, the sociodramatic play episode described at the beginning of this chapter. When Wendy used several symbolic transformations (e.g., using a wooden block as an egg), she was not learning a new skill. She may have been practicing representational skills learned earlier in a nonplay context, however. Piaget considered this practice and consolidation role of play very important because many newly acquired skills would be quickly lost if they were not practiced and consolidated.

Vygotsky's Theory Lev Vygotsky (1976), a Russian psychologist, believed that play has a more direct role in cognitive development. According to Vygotsky, young children are incapable of abstract thought because, for them, meaning and objects are fused together as one. As a result, young children cannot think about a horse without seeing a real horse. When children begin to engage in make-believe play and to use objects (e.g., a stick) to stand for other things (e.g., a horse), meaning begins to become separated from objects. The substitute object, the stick, serves as a pivot for separating the meaning "horse" from the horse itself. As a result, children soon become able to think about meanings independently of the objects they represent. Symbolic play therefore has a crucial role in the development of abstract thought.

Vygotsky's views on play are holistic. He considered play to be important to the social and emotional development of children, as well as to their cognitive development; in his view, all three domains of development interrelate. Vygotsky distinguished two levels of development: "actual development" (independent performance) and "potential development" (assisted performance), with the *zone of proximal development* (*ZPD*) defined as the distance between the two levels of development. In Vygotsky's analysis, play is a self-help tool.

Children engaged in play often seem ahead of themselves developmentally; play may even promote further development by serving as a scaffold within the children's ZPD, to help them attain higher levels of functioning.

Potential development in the ZPD is a transitional state in which children need special help or scaffolding to grasp what is within their reach. Usually, we think of scaffolding as support from a more expert partner, such as a parent, teacher, older sibling, or peer. In play, children can create their own scaffold, stretching themselves in such areas as self-control, language use, memory, and cooperation with others (Bodrova & Leong, 1996). For example, suppose the following: A child who made a big fuss and cried when put to bed pretends to go to bed without crying during subsequent sociodramatic play. In play, the child can control the behavior because the child controls the play frame or imaginary situation. The child can pretend to cry but can stop in the play episode, unlike in real life. Better attention, memory, language use, and social cooperation also have been reported when children are playing, as compared with other situations. Vygotsky saw play as a kind of magnifying glass revealing potential new abilities before these same abilities became actualized in other situations, especially formal ones such as school lessons.

Bruner's Theory   Other cognitive theorists have emphasized how play promotes creativity and flexibility. Jerome Bruner (1972) pointed out that in play, the means are more important than the ends. When playing, children do not worry about accomplishing goals, so they can experiment with new and unusual combinations of behavior they never would have tried if they were under pressure to achieve a goal. Once children have explored these new behavioral combinations in play, they can use these to solve real-life problems. Behavioral subroutines that are practiced and overlearned in play can become integrated and useful as established patterns of behavior. Thus, play promotes flexibility by increasing children's behavioral options. Furthermore, play provides opportunities for exploring different possibilities in a buffered state that protects the child from experiencing real-world consequences for behavior and from making premature commitments. For Bruner, these outcomes demonstrate the adaptive usefulness of play during a time of immaturity in human development and evolution. That is, Bruner has championed *neogeny*, the value of holding back youth for potential subsequent higher-level functioning.

Bruner's earlier ideas on the significance of play stressed its differentiation and integration functions. More recently, Bruner has emphasized the importance of narrative modes of thinking. For Bruner, two modes of intelligence (defined as both knowledge and understanding) are the *paradigmatic* and the *narrative*. The former deals with organization of experience, logic, analysis, and problem solving, and the latter with meaning, reconstruction of experiences, and the imagination. Piagetian theory has been preoccupied with paradigmatic functions of the intellect and has neglected the narrative. Bruner has sought to address this imbalance by stressing the importance of narrative understanding in human development and education, as well as in life in general (Bruner, 1986, 1996). To Bruner, play is vitally linked to the narrative mode in how humans represent knowledge in human intentionality and consciousness (see Chapter 2, "Play and Development").

Sutton-Smith's Theory   Brian Sutton-Smith (1967) believes that the *symbolic transformations* (e.g., using a stick *as if* it were a horse) that occur in make-believe play facilitate children's symbolic transformations in cognition, thereby enhancing children's mental flexibility. According to Sutton-Smith, these as-if transformations allow children to break free from conventional mental associations and put ideas together in new and unusual ways. These transformations result in an enlarged collection of creative ideas and associations that can later be used for adaptive purposes. Thus, the theories of Bruner and of Sutton-Smith relate to Groos's classical practice theory, in that these theories argue that play prepares children for adult life. However, the two modern play theories contend that children do this either by developing flexibility or by conserving the potential for flexibility, rather than by practicing specific skills. Sutton-Smith's early theorizing used the metaphor of play as adaptive potentiation (Sutton-Smith, 1979). *Adaptive potentiation* means that play is the enactment of possibilities—that is, as a result of play, the child is more likely to consider various options or alternatives and to manage this increased flexibility well.

More recently, Sutton-Smith (1998) proposed a new theory of play as *adaptive variability,* in which he draws an analogy between play and evolution, based on both brain-development research from the neurosciences and evolutionary theorizing by Stephen Jay Gould. In this theory, the variability of play is the key to its function in human development, just as physiological and behavioral variability is central in evolution, according to contemporary biological thinking (Gould, 1995). Because one cannot predict the future, with its radically changing environments, one cannot predict the skills and knowledge needed in those future environments. Therefore, the adaptive potential of developing children (or evolving species) requires not exact and precise adaptations (which can lead to rigidity of behavior and response set) but great flexibility in behavior or, in the words of Gould (1995, p. 44), "quirkiness, sloppiness, unpredictability, and massive redundancy."

Play is significant in human development because it assures broad adaptive potential. Contemporary neurological research, using brain-imaging technology, shows that this adaptive potential is built into the early development of the human brain (Nelson & Bloom, 1997). Sutton-Smith (1998, p. 333), commenting on the drop in the number of synaptic connections from age 10 months to age 10 years (from 1,000 trillion to 500 trillion), has observed, "as the brain begins in a state of high potentiality, so does play. . . . Play's function at early stages might . . . be to assist the actualization of brain potentiality . . . to save in both brain and behavior more of the variability that is potentially there than would otherwise be saved if there was no play."

Singer's Theory   Jerome Singer (1973; see also Singer & Singer, 1990) has proposed what he calls a constructive cognitive–affective account of play, in contrast to what he views as the compensatory theories of play propounded by Freud and by Piaget. According to Singer, play and especially imaginative play is a positive force in development, not just a coping mechanism due to emotional immaturity (Freud) or a means of assimilation due to defective logic (Piaget). Singer's emphasis on both cognition and emotion was influenced by the work of Sylvan Tomkins (1962), concerning the relation of emotions with cognition. To Singer, play offers a way for a child to modulate the rate of incoming stimulation, both from the external world and from the internal world of brain activity (which is seen as constantly replaying and recoding experiences). Through play, the child can optimize the flow of internal and external stimulation, thereby experiencing pleasurable emotions—unlike the startle response associated with too much stimulation and the boredom response caused by too little stimulation. For example, a child lacking for things to do while waiting in an airport can engage in internally generated stimulation through an imaginative play episode.

Singer has accumulated considerable research support for an individual-difference variable he calls "fantasy-making ability"(see Chapter 4, "Individual Differences"). Although the ability to imagine is a developmental phenomenon that improves with age for all children, some children appear to have a greater tendency to fantasize than other children do, and this variation emerges early in ontogeny. Nature and nurture affect this fantasy-making propensity, and Singer and his associates (and especially his wife Dorothy) have argued for the important influence of parents in its early manifestions. They recommend specific encouragement of imaginative play during the early years. For the Singers and many others, play positively contributes to a whole host of important developmental processes and outcomes, from language development to divergent thinking, from empathy to impulse control, and so on (see Chapter 2, "Play and Development," for a discussion). These diverse processes do not have a direct cause-and-effect relation with play, however, not even with make-believe play. Instead, play is seen as influencing the general symbolic capacity of the developing child.

OTHER THEORIES

Arousal-Modulation Theory   Another theory that considers the relationship between stimulation and play is the arousal-modulation theory, which was developed by Berlyne (1960) and then modified by Ellis (1973). Unlike Singer who focuses on cognitive processes, arousal modulation theory focuses on the solitary player or explorer in relation to objects. This theory contends that play is caused by a need or drive to keep arousal at an optimal level in our central nervous system. When there is too much stimulation, arousal increases to uncomfortably high levels and causes us to engage in stimulation-reducing activities. For example, if arousal has been elevated because of the presence of a strange object, arousal can be reduced by exploring the object and becoming familiar with it. On the other hand, if there is not enough stimulation, arousal falls to unpleasantly low levels, and we become bored.

Ellis views play as a stimulus-seeking activity that can elevate arousal to its optimal level. Play increases stimulation by using objects and actions in new and unusual ways. If, for example, children get bored sliding down a slide in the conventional manner, they can increase their level of stimulation by going down (and up) the slide in as many unusual ways as they can imagine. To Ellis, play is therefore a stimulation-producing activity caused by low levels of arousal. As later chapters explain, this theory has important implications for the design and use of playgrounds and play materials.

Bateson's Theory   Play, according to Bateson (1955), is paradoxical. Actions performed during play do not mean what they normally mean in real life. When children engage in play fighting, the blows delivered denote something very different from actual hitting. Before engaging in such play, children must establish a play "frame" or context to let others know that what is about to happen is play, that it is not real. Children usually establish this frame by smiling and laughing. If a play frame is not established, the other children will interpret the mock blows as a real attack and will respond accordingly. When children play, they learn to operate simultaneously at two levels. At one level, they are engrossed in their pretend roles and focus on the make-believe meanings of objects and actions. At the same time, they are aware of their own identities, the other players' real identities, and the real-life meanings of the objects and actions used in the play.

Bateson's theory has stimulated interest in communicational aspects of play, prompting psychologists such as Garvey (1977) to examine the messages that children use to establish, maintain, terminate, and reinstate play episodes. This research has led to the discovery that children constantly shift back and forth between their pretend roles and their true identities while engaging in sociodramatic play. When problems arise during the make-believe portion of the play, children often "break frame" and resume their real-life identities to resolve the difficulties. Note that several frame breaks occurred in the play episode at the beginning of this chapter. For example, when George inappropriately asks to help set the table, John breaks the make-believe frame by reminding George that babies do not do that sort of thing.

For Bateson, play does not occur in a vacuum. *Play texts*, the play activities themselves, are always affected by *contexts*, the surroundings in which the play occurs. For example, in considering context, Schwartzman (1978) has demonstrated how children's social status affects their play. The fact that George (in the play episode) is low in the classroom pecking order helps explain why he had to take the role of baby and why the other two children order him around. It is important to realize the impact of context on play.

Bateson's text/context distinction has also stimulated interest in play texts. Fein (1975) and others have investigated developmental trends in the symbolic transformations that children use in make-believe. One consistent finding is that 2-year-olds must use symbols that physically resemble the objects they represent (e.g., a small, rectangular piece of wood may stand for a comb), whereas older children can use symbols that are increasingly dissimilar to what they depict (e.g., a toy car or rubber ball can be used to represent the comb).

Wolf and Grollman (1982) have focused on a different aspect of play text, examining age trends in the narrative organization of children's play. Their results showed that as children grow older, the scripts they enact become better integrated and increasingly complex. This type of research is adding greatly to our knowledge of play behavior and how it changes with age.

CONTRIBUTIONS OF MODERN THEORIES Modern theories of play have increased our understanding of play, both through the explanatory power of the theories themselves and through the research the theories have stimulated. For instance, in Chapter 2, "Play and Development," we examine a selection of studies from the wealth of contemporary research on play and child development. Most of this research can be traced back to the theories of Freud, Piaget, Vygotsky, Bruner, and Sutton-Smith. Research generated by Bateson's theory is discussed in Chapter 9, "Play Environments," and in Chapter 10, "Play Materials." Arousal-modulation theory has led to research on the distinction between play and exploration, reviewed in the next section.

DEFINITION OF PLAY

As previously noted, play is easy to recognize but very hard to define. Most adults have little trouble deciding whether children are playing. As Ellis (1973) points out, we can even recognize play in other species, such as dogs and chimpanzees. Defining play, on the other hand, has proved to be extraordinarily difficult. Some scholars have even considered the term undefinable and the concept so vague that it does not merit serious study (Schlosberg, 1947).

Fortunately, the current increase in play research has led to progress in defining play. The following section discusses how this research has helped us differentiate between play and exploration and has led to a clearer understanding of the characteristics of play. We end the section by clarifying how we intend to use the term *play* in this book.

PLAY VERSUS EXPLORATION

Research by Hutt (1971), Weisler and McCall (1976), and others has revealed that play and exploration are similar, in that they are intrinsically motivated behaviors, not directed by externally imposed goals. Recent research (S. Hutt, Tyler, C. Hutt, & Christopherson, 1989), however, has revealed some important differences between play and exploration. Exploration is a "stimulus-dominated" behavior, concerned with acquiring information about an object. It is controlled by the stimulus characteristics of the object being explored. Play, conversely, is "organism-dominated" behavior, governed by the needs and

Table 1.4   PLAY VERSUS EXPLORATION

	EXPLORATION	PLAY
Timing	Precedes play	Follows exploration
Context	Strange object	Familiar object
Purpose	Gain information about object	Create stimulation
Behavior	Stereotyped	Variable
Mood	Serious	Joyful
Heart rate	Low variability	High variability

Source: Based on research by Hughes & Hutt (1979), Hutt (1971), and Weisler & McCall (1976).

wishes of the child. Play is concerned with generating stimulation, rather than with gaining information about objects. Hutt (1971, p. 246) explains, "In play the emphasis changes from the question of 'what does this object do?' to 'what can I do with this object?'" When children play, they ignore the reality of how an object is supposed to be used and instead use it in any way they desire. Table 1.4 summarizes the major factors that differentiate play from exploration.

CHARACTERISTICS OF PLAY

Contemporary research has done more than simply differentiate play from exploration. It has also led to the discovery that play is usually characterized by a small number of dispositional factors (Garvey, 1977; Rubin, Fein, & Vandenberg, 1983), such as nonliterality, intrinsic motivation, process orientation, free choice, and positive affect:

1. *Nonliterality.* Play events are characterized by a play frame that separates the play from everyday experience. This essential characteristic applies across all play forms—sociodramatic play, solving a puzzle, building with blocks, or playing a game. Within this play frame, internal reality takes precedence over external reality. The usual meanings of objects are ignored, and new meanings are substituted. Actions are performed differently from when they occur in nonplay settings. In the play episode at the beginning of this chapter, for example, the children used wooden blocks as if they were eggs and used the motion of lifting a toy cup to represent drinking. This as-if stance toward reality allows children to escape the constraints of the here and now and to experiment with new possibilities.
2. *Intrinsic motivation.* Play is not externally motivated by drives such as hunger or by goals such as gaining power or wealth. Instead, the motivation for play comes from within the individual, and play activities are pursued for their own sake.
3. *Process (over product) orientation.* When children play, their attention focuses on the activity itself, rather than on the goals of the activity. In other words, means are more important than ends. This absence of

pressure to achieve a goal frees children to try many different variations of the activity and is a major reason play tends to be more flexible than goal-oriented behavior.

4. *Free choice.* Free choice is an important element in young children's
   conceptions of play. For instance, King (1979) found that kindergartners considered an activity such as block building to be play if it were
   freely chosen but considered the same activity to be work if it were assigned by the teacher. The free-choice factor may become less important as children grow older. A subsequent study by King (1982) revealed that pleasure, rather than free choice, was the key factor
   differentiating play and work for fifth-graders.

5. *Positive affect.* Play is usually marked by signs of pleasure and enjoyment. Even when it is not, children still value the activity (Garvey,
   1977). Sometimes play is accompanied by apprehension and mild fear,
   such as when a child is preparing to go down a steep slide. However,
   even this fear seems to have a pleasurable quality because the child
   will go down the slide again and again (Rubin, Fein, & Vandenberg,
   1983).

Freedom from externally imposed rules and active engagement are also
often listed as characteristics of play (e.g., Rubin, Fein, & Vandenberg, 1983).
However, we believe that these two characteristics are too restrictive because
they exclude two important forms of play: (1) games with rules and (2) daydreaming. Games, by definition, involve following preestablished rules. As
Chapter 3 explains, games are a form of play that becomes increasingly important as children grow older. Daydreaming also becomes more prevalent as
children approach adolescence. Singer (1973; Singer & Singer, 1990) contends
that daydreaming slowly replaces dramatic play as the major form of fantasy
activity. Adolescents mentally and internally play with ideas, rather than physically or externally playing with words and actions.

KINDS OF PLAY

In this book, we adopt a rather broad definition of play. We treat any activity
with most of the aforementioned five characteristics as play. In addition to the
traditional categories of play, such as practice, constructive, dramatic, and
game play, we include in our definition all activities, such as art and music,
that have an element of spontaneity (intrinsic motivation), nonliterality,
process orientation, free choice, and pleasure. Morover, we give equal concern
to *educational play* and to *recreational play.* We define the former as more under the control of an adult (e.g., classroom projects or free-play activities that
are initiated, paced, and terminated by the teacher) and the latter as being
more free from adult influence (e.g., recess time or break time on the playground). Nancy King (1986) has referred to these two types of play as *instrumental play* and *real play,* respectively, in her discussions of school play. We
treat both educational play (or instrumental play) and recreational play (or
real play) as important concerns for teachers and parents who interact with

*Positive affect—fun and enjoy-
ment—is perhaps play's most
important characteristic.*

the world of children's play. On the other hand, we do not examine in depth
King's third type of school play, *illicit play* (e.g., "throwing spitballs," "silly
laughing"), which has a deviant flavor or defiant bent to it. Although such play
is important to recognize, this book is directed toward drawing out implications based on theory and research connected with educational and recreational play.

APPLYING MODERN THEORIES OF PLAY

Early childhood educators are vitally interested in practical decisions regarding
how to equip preschools or child-care centers, how to organize play activities,
how to define appropriate use of play materials, how to structure adult participation and interaction with children, and how much to gear the curriculum to-

Theory in Action

CHILDREN'S PERSPECTIVES ON PLAY AND WORK

A continuing debate in early childhood education and in family life is how much young children need to become socialized into work habits and obligations to adhere to adult-generated strictures or reality demands in general which, of course, take them away from playing and their "house of make-believe." This debate assumes a split between what is play and what is work. Is it possible that the two are one and the same at times? Research would seem to indicate an affirmative answer to this query. For example, although traditional early childhood programs may encourage children to accept play as their work, and academic ones may try to convince youngsters that work is play, other programs built on the educational philosophy of constructivism may influence children's ideas about work and play differently.

For example, one university preschool program adopted as the curriculum the Projects Approach (Katz & Chard, 1989) in which children and teachers both decide what the projects and play themes will be. The children were interviewed *in situ* by their teachers while they were engaged in different classroom activities and were asked whether they were playing or working. Illustrative of the kinds of answers the children gave were: (a) alternating states of play and work with *working* on making something prerequisite to play (making sand pies to "sell" when later *playing "Bakery"*; (b) neither play nor work as children reject superimposing a label on what they are doing (e.g., I'm BUILDING with these); (c) fun work (e.g. when given a broom and dust pan upon their request, children persisted using these during clean up time for 15 minutes before the teacher asked them to stop); (d) both work and play (e.g., "the teacher want us to do it but we want to do the fun thing"). Sometimes the dichotomy between work and play seems inadequate to the children.

More research is needed to examine children's views on play and work in relation to the kind of program attended. Perhaps programs that rigidly exclude play lead to sharper but narrower definitions of play by children. Do children see a difference between educational play and recreational play and when can they verbalize this distinction? Many unanswered yet researchable questions remain for future study (including teacher-initiated action research) in the applied hybrid field of early childhood education/child development.

ward play activities. Are theoretical notions or metaphors about play of any use to teachers of young children? This section discusses four current metaphors for play influenced by modern theory and then suggests practical implications derived from each for use by preschool and primary-grade teachers.

FOUR METAPHORS FOR PLAY

PLAY AS TRANSFORMATION   This metaphor, inspired by Piaget, emphasizes the symbolic character of play in young children. In Smilansky's famous (1968) work on sociodramatic play among children assumed to be culturally disadvantaged, she considered the transformational aspects of play important for evaluating the level of play. (The extent of cooperation, verbal behavior, and persistence in play were other critical factors she considered.) To judge the quality of transformational behavior, she raised four questions: (1) Is the child pretending to be someone other than who the child really is? (2) Is the child pretending that others are different from who they really are? (3) Is the child pretending that objects are different from what they actually represent? (4) Is the child pretending that the situation is different from what it really is? These types of transformations were assessed further in terms of their degree of difference from the concrete or familiar experience of the child. For example, is the child engaging in object transformation with the help of replica miniature props, substitute objects, or pretend objects? Is the play theme and content close to, or far from, the child's normal everyday life?

PLAY AS METACOMMUNICATION   The ideas of communication, negotiation, and context are central in a second metaphor about the play of young children. In this metaphor, children must use interpersonal (when playing together) or intrapersonal (when playing alone) messages to establish, maintain, interrupt, reinstate, and terminate the play event. Ethnographic researchers characterize play events in terms of either frames and scripts or contexts and texts. Play cannot be divorced from its surroundings, and children quite easily enter and exit their play world, always cognizant of the real world.

In other words, children at play operate on multiple levels. While engrossed in a play episode, children are simultaneously aware of the real identities of their playmates—who they are and their standing in the peer group—as well as who they are within the play episode. Both the play itself and the negotiations around the play episode reflect and express the social relations that exist within the play episode, as well as outside of it. Duplicity of meaning is an inherent characteristic of play behavior. What takes place in the pretend world is the play proper, but play is always embedded in the actual world, revealing the dynamic relationship between the two worlds. Anything in the actual world can become play through the communicational message, "This is play." Children and adults are constantly framing and reframing their behaviors and experiences across this threshold.

PLAY AS PERFORMANCE   A related idea from Sutton-Smith (1979) is the notion that play actually involves a *quadralogue*. If an ordinary conversation is a dialogue, then play involves four sets of communicators—players and coplayers, directors, producers, and audience. Even during solitary play, the child often imagines coplayers and a pretend audience. Social play demands considerable coordination, as individual children have their own ideas for how the play should be done—or redone if the play does not go right the first time.

This quadralogue metaphor focuses on the fact that play is a staged event with multiple elements, as players interact in a pretend world set up for a real or imagined audience.

PLAY AS SCRIPT   The narrative or script metaphor is another recent perspective on children's play. According to this view, play content represents the child's attempt to make sense out of personal experiences. As preschoolers develop intellectually, they become better able to structure events based on experience. The content of children's play is an expression of their interpretation of their own experiences.

In this metaphor, knowledge structures activated from memory are called "scripts." A script represents the child's knowledge of a network of possible major subactions or "scenes," which make up a larger activity such as going to the grocery store or taking a trip to the beach. Scripts identify culturally accepted ways of behaving in situations that are commonplace in the child's experience. Components of scripts include scenes, subactions, roles and relationships, props (environmental objects) within scenes, variations of the script (e.g., going to a big supermarket vs. a small grocery store), and conditions in the social world that signal the beginning and the ending of the script.

When examining children's dramatic or imaginative play as script, an observer can analyze the level of narrative organization displayed in the enactments, thus gaining an indication of the child's cognitive and language development. Wolf and Grollman (1982) suggest three different levels: scheme, event, and episode. The *scheme level* is shown when children perform one or more brief actions associated with a single small event (e.g., putting a doll to bed). At the *event level,* children enact two or three schemes that are parts of pursuing one goal (e.g., bathing the doll and then putting it to bed). This level may also entail contoured events involving four or more different schemes all aimed at the same end (e.g., pretending to create a meal by cooking hamburgers, making coffee, baking a cake, and preparing a salad). The *episode level* occurs when children perform two or more events directed toward a single goal (e.g., baking a pretend cake and then serving it to a playmate). Episodes may also involve two or more contoured events (e.g., pretending to cook a variety of food, serving them to several playmates, and then washing the dishes). Hence, the play-as-script model permits the observers to witness, appreciate, and roughly gauge both personality and self-concept disclosure, and to estimate intellectual and linguistic maturity in young children.

IMPLICATIONS FOR TEACHERS

Teachers can apply the four preceding metaphors in a number of ways. The *play-as-transformation* idea has been around the longest and is widely incorporated within the early childhood field. With this metaphor in mind, teachers are able to discern the various types of transformational behaviors implicit within pretend play episodes. They are also able to measure each child's progress in verbal, imagery, and representational abilities, as shown through the child's use of realistic props, then less realistic props, and, finally, no props at all during pretend play. As a result, teachers are able to make appropriate changes in what is available in activity centers for children to use during play (such as removing or adding realistic props). Furthermore, teachers should respond sensitively to the apparent difficulty of enacting various roles and themes within make-believe play. For instance, children usually choose to enact themes close to their familiar everyday experiences before themes based on fictional roles and events (e.g., superheroes).

The *play-as-metacommunication* metaphor provides the adult with an additional lens with which to perceive play: Teachers realize that during play, children are engaged in communication on several levels. Children's enactments not only express the themes and plots of the play episode itself, but also reveal the social dimension of the play in context. Just as transformational theory makes the teacher more aware of the "vertical nature" of play (developmental sequences and ability levels in symbolic representation), metacommunication theory makes the teacher more aware of the "horizontal nature" of play, considering the social context. Social relationships within play reestablish and express social relations outside of play. By witnessing play in this way, the teacher has a sensitive barometer of interpersonal relations within the classroom or child-care center. Thus, this theory can be valuable in evaluating the peer status and the social development of each child, and it can be used to explain some of children's behavior during play.

The *play-as-performance* metaphor can offer a useful perspective on play in at least two ways. First, as with the previous metaphor, it highlights the fact that play is framed, consisting of both content and context. A practical suggestion for educators, which emerges from this metaphor, is to respect the play boundary that divides the child's pretend world from the actual world, either when seeking to enter the play world as an adult, or when attempting to help a child join an ongoing play group. Insensitivity can lead to unnecessary disruption of play.

For example, overmanaging or excessive structuring can weaken or destroy the child-initiated coordination among players, coplayers, directors, producers, and audience. If a teacher feels that children would benefit from some guidance, a helpful suggestion could be made in the character of an appropriate role within the play episode instead of as an outside authority figure. For example, if the children were enacting a store scene, the teacher might take the role of a customer and make suggestions while enacting this minor role. Likewise, children who have difficulty joining play groups can be coached to use appropriate social entry skills (e.g., offering to take a minor role) and to make smooth transitions between groups.

A second useful perspective offered by the quadralogue performance model is that play is more than what it may seem at first. Children are not only players, but also directors, producers, and audience members—real or imagined. The teacher can observe children's growing skills in these different areas. At a certain point, children may seek perfection in the performance—portrayals that most accurately express the child's imagined scenario. For instance, children may realize something new during their play and may want to start the sequence or cycle from the beginning again. As children mature, they develop increasing skills in directing and managing their play. These behaviors may then provide an additional index of intellectual and linguistic ability in children. Furthermore, given the inevitable individual differences in these skills, teachers who examine play in this way will be in a better position to promote these skills, as compared with those teachers unaware of this perspective.

The *play-as-script* metaphor helps the teacher recognize and analyze differences in intellectual and linguistic abilities, as well as differences in self-concept and personality. As such, this perspective enables the teacher to see the child in a new way. By observing what the child is doing during play, the teacher can evaluate what the child knows, how the child is organizing experiences and is able to express them, and what matters to the child. The teacher can then design lesson plans that will capitalize on special interests of selected children, such as by arranging field trips and supplemental activities. The effects of these lessons can then be observed in subsequent play scripts.

For example, a teacher might observe several children enacting a restaurant scene and notice that the children have rather vague notions about the roles of different restaurant personnel. A field trip to a nearby restaurant could be planned, followed by the introduction of theme-related props (e.g., menus). Observation of the posttrip play would reveal whether conceptual growth occurred as a result.

CONCLUSION

As we will see in the next chapter there is a great deal of research that indicates that certain types of play are linked to cognitive and social development. Correlational studies have revealed that sociodramatic and constructive play are positively related to a number of different cognitive variables including IQ scores and creativity and to social skills such as cooperation. Experimental and training studies have yielded evidence suggesting that these forms of play may actually promote cognitive and social growth.

However, these findings do not indicate that all forms of free play contribute to development. There is little evidence linking gross motor play or nonsocial forms of dramatic play with growth in intellectual or social skills. It should also be noted that, in the play training studies mentioned, it is not clear which component of the treatment sociodramatic play, adult involvement, or peer interaction caused the gains brought about by play training (Smith & Syddall, 1978). It is likely that the play itself was not totally responsible for the benefits. Adult and peer involvement may often be needed for play to have a developmental impact.

Our answer to the question "Is play nonessential or educational?" is that some types of play are educational. Play that is optimal for development is play that reflects or slightly stretches the current social or cognitive abilities of the child. Some play experiences devised by teachers and parents may do little more than amuse or entertain children; some play may actually bore or frustrate them. To contribute to the development and education of the child, play opportunities must be appropriate and challenging. The main objective of this book is to acquaint adults with strategies for providing this type of challenging play. In the chapters ahead, we discuss how adults can enrich play by provision of appropriate materials and conducive settings, by observation, and by direct participation. In so doing, we hope to make parents and teachers "play connoisseurs"who can help their children and students obtain the maximum benefits of play.

Chapter 2

PLAY AND DEVELOPMENT

So Jean, just what is *the purpose of it all? The words still haunted her as she made her way home after the first parent night of the school year. After she had taken a group of new parents around her kindergarten classroom—dutifully explaining the rationale behind each play-based activity center—Jean had been caught off guard by a mother who asked her "what's the purpose behind all your purposes?" Sure, it was a good question, she admitted, but she did not like being caught off guard like that. She had prepared well for the meeting and gave a good explanation of the benefits of each center. Play, learning, and development happen all around her well-planned room and its curriculum.*

Jean prided herself as being a play expert and was a respected veteran teacher. Both book knowledge and personal professional experience told her that yes, indeed, the large-block area fosters motor coordination, the book center emergent literacy, the dramatic-play center social perspective-taking skills, the art center creativity and imagination, and so on. Jean had tried to tackle the unexpected question but knew her answer did not quite convince several of the parents. Humming the tune "What's It All about, Alfie," from the old 1960s English movie title song, Jean became more determined than ever to reflect on her teaching, to brush up on the latest literature, and to be able to clearly articulate her beliefs about the developmental and educational significance of play. "I'll really impress them with an incredibly awesome answer when this comes up again," she muttered to herself, thinking about how she would bring up this challenging question first next time, assuming a parent did not beat her to it. ■

As we have seen in Chapter 1, the function of play in development and learning has received considerable theoretical attention over the years. In this chapter, we further discuss the importance of play in child development and provide in-depth coverage of research investigations on this topic. During the past decades, scores of studies have explored the relationship between play and child development. The focus has been on varied domains of children's growth, including, in addition to motor development, cognition, language, social, and emotional areas. This chapter reviews research done within each of these latter four domains, which we hope can provide, when synthesized, the kind of combined information that Jean and others can use to explain an integrative play approach to achieving educational and socialization goals during the early childhood years.

CHILD DEVELOPMENT AND PLAY: BASIC OBSERVATIONS

There are three ways to consider the relation of play with development. First, the play behavior of the growing child may serve as a "window" on the child's development, revealing the current status of the child in various areas. That is, play simply *reflects* development. Second, play may serve as a context and medium for the expression and consolidation of developmental acquisitions, be they behavioral skills or conceptual attainments—play *reinforces* development. Third, play can serve as an instrument of developmental change; play can generate qualitative improvement in the organism's functioning and structural organization. In other words, play can *result in* development.

All three of these views are correct to some degree; they are not mutually exclusive hypotheses about play and development. Before deciding which answer is best in a given situation, however, a great deal of additional information is required. We must know what kind of play is involved and which areas and levels of development are under consideration. If important practical matters are involved, we must also know the individual child and the context. Sometimes, play can result in development; sometimes, play reinforces development and learning; and at other times, play only mirrors or reflects development. We must not envision the role of play in development monolithically or praise its virtues indiscriminately. Some play is even detrimental to development and well-being, such as *illicit play,* which can lead to social disapproval and rejection, or, even more extreme, *dark play* (e.g., 'elevator surfing,' or jumping from tops of adjacent moving elevators, Russian roulette), which can lead to injury or even death.

Greta Fein's (1997) analogy of play to eating is helpful in this regard. We do not ask the simple question of whether eating is good for growth and development. We decompose eating into its constitutive nutrients (e.g., calories, vitamins, minerals). After such analysis, we may pose more specific and cogent queries about eating food—such as which ingredients and how much are good for whom, when, under what circumstances, and so on. Fein urges us to approach the general question of play and development in like manner and to be prepared to construct and reply to sharper questions such as these.

Theory clearly suggests that play has both short-term and long-term benefits for the child. *Short-term benefits* are positive effects of play, realized immediately or in relatively close temporal proximity to the play experience. *Long-term* (deferred) *benefits* are positive outcomes realized later, often cumulatively, over days, weeks, months, and sometimes years. A *sleeper effect* occurs when the value of prior experiences is not seen over considerable time periods but then emerges and is attributable to the earlier experiences. Beneficial effects take the form of play *contributing to* development or at least *cementing* it (i.e., play both *results in* and *reinforces* development, as noted previously).

Martin and Caro (1985) assert that play often has delayed, long-term effects on development, and that organisms tend to engage more in those behaviors that are adaptive and useful in development and evolution. Only with lengthy longitudinal research can such effects be determined with certitude. Researchers have usually extrapolated from short-term studies, even one-shot experiments, to make claims about persisting advantages of play. Many play-intervention studies, for instance, assume that any immediate effects of play training on positive child-development outcomes are sustained and even amplified over time, in interaction with subsequent experiences. Children may be more likely to benefit from these subsequent positive experiences because they were primed by the play intervention. This leads to a cumulative long-term effect. As an illustration, preschoolers who experience enriched literacy-based dramatic play at school, it is assumed, will probably acquire a greater tendency to explore and experiment with the structure of print at home and elsewhere, receiving helpful feedback from parents, older siblings, and peers. Over time, these experiences eventuate in writing and spelling (Christie, 1994).

Short-term benefits of play are argued on theoretical grounds, as well. These are said to occur across the various developmental domains. Empirical investigations back these claims. For example, within the Vygotskian tradition (El'Konin, 1978), a number of scientists in the former Soviet Union found that children's cognitive functioning appeared to operate at an elevated level when the children performed play, compared to nonplay, activities. Manujlenko (cited in El'Konin, 1978) found greater self-regulation during play than during other activities, as witnessed in a little boy who, when playing army, waited at his post and showed a great deal of concentration and attention to detail—more so than when his teacher wanted him to focus on something during school lessons!

As a second example, Istomina (1948/1977) tested preschoolers' memory under a play condition and in a traditional laboratory condition. He found that children could remember a list of grocery items better when playing store, relative to the usual experimental testing condition. At play, children seem ahead of themselves developmentally. They appear able to engage in a form of self-scaffolding behavior, within their zone of proximal development (see Chapter 1). Playing seems to enrich the *processes* of cognitive development in real time, in addition to leading to beneficial *consequences*, a perennial concern of Western researchers.

When positive developmental correlates or consequences are found and are attributable to play, we need to be concerned about the *epiphenomenon issue*—the possibility that it is not play per se, but confounding variables, such as peer interaction and conflict that go along with play, that are responsible for positive child development. When do we know that it is some aspect of play that is making a distintive contribution to child development, not some other factor co-occurring with play and the play context? Furthermore, even when an outcome is related to play and not to confounding factors, there is also the issue of equifinality. *Equifinality* means that specific positive outcomes can happen in multiple ways in an open system (Sackett, Sameroff, Cairns, & Suomi, 1981). For instance, later spelling and writing achieved by preschoolers who were in a literacy-enhanced dramatic-play program could also be traced to alternative developmental pathways such as teacher storybook reading or direct instruction. There is no one "royal road" (e.g., the play way) to literacy or any other positive developmental endpoint. Accordingly, we need to temper our enthusiasm for extolling the virtues of play.

Still, it would be a mistake to underestimate the importance of play in development on the basis of inconclusive and problematic experimental research. Research, broadly defined, includes a wide range of disciplined and systematic inquiry. For example, the following riveting testimony by psychiatrist S. Brown (1994, pp. 9–12) cannot be discounted:

> As a psychiatrist I have long studied the development of abused children who became violent adults. My first case was explosive.
>
> On August 1, 1966, I was at the Department of Psychiatry at Baylor College of Medicine in Houston, Texas where I was on the faculty. At about noon I was hunched over the radio, listening to a fusillade of gunshots broadcast live from the University of Texas in Austin. A 25-year-old student named Charles Joseph Whitman had hauled an arsenal of firearms to the top of the university's 27-story tower. He began firing at anything that moved on the campus below. By the time a policeman and a volunteer stormed the tower and fatally shot Whitman, 13 people were dead and 31 wounded.
>
> Governor John Connally ordered a full investigation. What had made Charles Whitman tick? I was charged with part of the behavioral study, and my team began interviewing everyone who had known him. Beneath Charles's Mr. Clean image—he had been a Marine, an Eagle Scout, an altar boy—we found a history of violence and brutality, with Charles and his mother often abused by his father.
>
> But another, more subtle revelation emerged from our interviews—the absence of a normal play pattern. Charlie's teachers recalled a frightened little kid who never played spontaneously, who often slumped against a wall in the schoolyard while the others had fun. Outside school, Charlie's father controlled him so completely that the boy had virtually no time to play, even by himself.
>
> After the investigation I began thinking more and more about Charlie's lack of play. The next year I helped conduct a study of 26 convicted murderers in Texas. The profiles of 90% of these young men showed either the absence of play as children or abnormal play like bullying, sadism, extreme teasing, or cruelty to animals. Another examination, of 25 drivers who had either killed someone or died in a crash—most were driving drunk—found that 75% of them had had play abnormalities.
>
> I wasn't thinking that problems with play are the causes of criminal or antisocial behavior. But the fact that it turned up so often in such individuals began to haunt me. It made me realize what a powerful, positive force play is. Play is an important part of a healthy, happy childhood, and playful adults are often highly creative, even brilliant individuals.

COGNITIVE DOMAIN

The play behaviors of children provide fascinating clues about what they are thinking and how they are thinking. All of us have paused one time or another to watch children at play and to wonder what might be going through their minds and how they might turn out as adults. We may remember ourselves at the same age and try to recapture how we used to experience and cognize the world from a child's perspective.

Beginning in the late 1960s—as the cognitive theories of Piaget, of Bruner, and of Vygotsky and others gained prominence in the United States—there was a resurgence of interest in play's role in cognitive development. Researchers began to investigate the relationship between play and a host of specific mental abilities. The methodology of most of the research was quantitative in nature and fell into three categories:

1. *Correlational studies*—These descriptive studies attempt to determine the extent of the relationship between play and various cognitive abilities. It is important to note that causality cannot be determined from this research. If a correlational study reveals that make-believe play is related to creativity, this does not mean that the play causes creativity. It is just as likely that creativity is responsible for high levels of pretend play or that play and creativity are both related to a third factor, such as home environment.

2. *Experimental studies*—These studies use experimental controls in an attempt to determine whether play has a causal role in cognitive development. Different groups of subjects are exposed to play and nonplay treatments, and then the effects of these treatments are monitored on different cognitive variables.

3. *Training studies*—In this special type of experimental study, adults attempt to teach children how to engage in different types of play (usually make-believe). If the training results in higher levels of play and enhanced cognitive performance, it can be assumed that the increased level of play is responsible for the cognitive gains.

Research on play and cognitive development in the 1970s and 1980s was quantitative in nature and influenced by Piagetian theory (linear and analytical). Variables and measures derived from Piagetian theory are discrete and productlike (e.g., object transformations), and they tend to emphasize child's play and other symbolic behaviors independent of the social context. In the 1990s, there has been a trend toward qualitative research, inspired by Vygotsky's sociocultural theory (interactive and holistic). Qualitative inquiry involves fewer children and greater attention to context. Examples include conceptual analyses, case studies, and anecdotal accounts. Constructs and assessments congruent with Vygotsky are more social and highlight process variables. They assume a more reciprocal connection among play, cognition, and language, which unfolds in an interpersonal and cultural context.

In the following sections, we briefly review the evidence linking play with six important clusters of cognitive variables: conceptual development, intelligence, operational thinking, problem-solving skills, divergent thinking, and metacognition. For a more complete review of this area of research, see Christie and Johnsen (1983); Creasey, Jarvis, and Berk (1998); and Johnson (1990). This section closes with a brief discussion of the emerging field of study, children's theory of mind.

CONCEPTUAL DEVELOPMENT

Certain forms of adult-guided social-pretense play activities have been found to relate to the development of symbolic abilities. *Sociodramatic play* occurs when two or more children adopt roles and act out a story. This advanced form of pretend play requires a considerable level of representational competence. Children must be able to build scripts and conceptual networks, which enable them to impose order and to establish predictable patterns across diverse arrays of experiences. For example, in order to act out a supermarket story, children must be able to reconstruct the correct order of events involved in grocery shopping: travel to the store, getting a cart, selecting food and putting it in the cart, paying the cashier, and taking the groceries home.

Smilansky (1968) has argued that sociodramatic play helps children integrate experiences that are separate and seem unrelated at first, such as selecting food and paying money to a cashier. Research supports her claim. Saltz, Dixon, and Johnson (1977), and Saltz and Johnson (1974) reported that sociodramatic play and *thematic fantasy play* (i.e., adult-facilitated role enactment of fairy tales) helped preschool children from impoverished backgrounds connect discrete events. Compared to control-group youngsters, those trained to engage in sociodramatic play and thematic fantasy play had significantly higher scores on sequencing and comprehension tests that required both a reconstruction of the order of pictures representing a story line and an explanation of the relationship among the pictures.

Children's storehouse of knowledge and basic concepts increase geometrically during early childhood, and play can greatly facilitate this process. Immature concepts of space, time, probability, and causality can be tested and revised during play. For example, the abstract concept of time comes to have meaning within the context of play. When children wait for their turn to use a toy or to perform their part in a script, expressions such as "in a few minutes," "a little while," "tomorrow," and even "next week" come to make more sense (Athey, 1988). Although time and space are often altered in make-believe play episodes, sequence and structure are often preserved and can become better understood. Children use their representational skills in play, transforming and transcending concrete reality, the *hic et nunc* (here and now).

INTELLIGENCE

General intelligence and cognitive growth is indicated by three mental skills: (1) the ability to discriminate information that is relevant from information that is irrelevant to a given purpose, (2) increased adeptness in using fewer cues to generate more information, and (3) higher levels of abstraction. These entail a number of different cognitive abilities, including memory, reasoning, abstraction, and understanding of language. As explained in Chapter 1, play behavior may contribute to these skills in several ways. According to Vygotsky, the use of symbols in make-believe play leads to the development of abstract thought. In addition, Piaget contends that play enables children to practice and consolidate newly acquired mental skills.

Research supports the possibility that play increases intelligence or general mental development. Correlational studies have revealed a positive relationship between IQ scores and two types of play: sociodramatic play and constructive play (Johnson, Ershler, & Lawton, 1982). Investigators have also found that play training positively affects children's IQ scores. Children who initially exhibited low levels of sociodramatic play were taught how to engage in this type of play. Results showed that the training resulted in gains in both play and IQ scores (Saltz, Dixon, & Johnson, 1977). Long-term studies have demonstrated that the gains in IQ brought about by play training are lasting (Christie, 1983; Smith, Dalgleish, & Herzmark, 1981). For more information about play training, see Chapter 7.

OPERATIONAL THINKING

Conservation refers to the understanding that certain properties of objects, such as quantity and number, do not change in spite of perceived transformations. For example, the amount of clay in a ball does not change even when the ball is flattened out like a pancake. Piaget discovered that most preschoolers are not capable of conservation. These children will be fooled by the change in the clay's appearance and will be convinced that the amount of clay has been altered.

Rubin, Fein, and Vandenberg (1983) have argued that the role playing that occurs in make-believe play involves two cognitive operations needed for conservation: (a) *decentration*, the realization that children can be themselves and enact a role simultaneously, and (b) *reversibility*, the awareness that they can change from their make-believe role back to their real identity at any time. Research has indicated that making children aware of the reversibility inherent in make-believe transformations can help some children perform better on conservation tasks (Golomb & Cornelius, 1977).

PROBLEM SOLVING

Bruner (1972) has theorized that play contributes to children's ability to solve problems by increasing their behavioral options. Children try lots of different behaviors in their play, and their behaviors can later be used in solving problems. Researchers have generally supported Bruner's theory. Several studies have found that play helps children's problem-solving abilities (e.g., Simon & Smith, 1983; Sylva, Bruner, & Genova, 1976). In these studies, children had to solve a problem that involved clamping sticks together to retrieve a marble or piece of chalk that was out of reach (see Figure 2.1). Results show that children who were allowed to play with the clamps and sticks did just as well at solving the problem as children who were directly trained to solve it.

It appears that the play–problem-solving relationship is affected by both the nature of the play and the problem being solved. Pepler and Ross (1981) made a distinction between *convergent problems*, which have only one correct solution, and *divergent problems*, which have a variety of solutions. They found that playing with puzzle pieces and form boards led to better solving of convergent puzzle problems. Non-task-related, divergent play (playing with puzzle pieces as if they were blocks) tended to interfere with the solution of

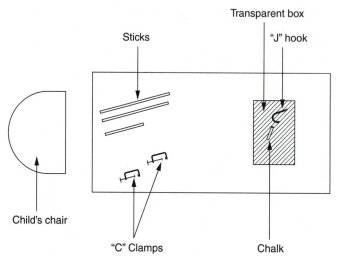

Figure 2.1

Schematic view of task posed by Sylva et al.
Source: Sylva, Bruner, and Genova (1976), p. 246.

puzzle tasks. Divergent play did, however, result in a wider variety of problem-solving strategies and facilitated the solving of divergent problems, such as using blocks to build a make-believe village.

It is important to note that some investigations on play and problem solving have reported negative findings. For example, Vandenberg (1990) tested the hypotheses that play promotes problem solving by providing the opportunity to observe features of the environment that are overlooked in more goal-oriented activities. He compared free play with two goal-oriented activities: (1) a *narrow-focus task* that required children to construct a puzzle and (2) a *broad-focus task* that required children to "save" a stuffed animal located in one corner of the room without crossing a line that went completely across the classroom floor. The correct solution required children to find one of several long, extended objects located in the room and to use it to retrieve the animal. Results showed that the broad-focus goal-oriented group recalled and recognized more features of the environment than did subjects in the free-play group. Vandenberg concluded that his findings, along with criticisms of experimenter bias in earlier lure-retrieval studies (Cheyne, 1982; Simon & Smith, 1985), raise "serious questions about the merits of play for enhancing problem solving" (1990, p. 271).

DIVERGENT THINKING

A number of correlational studies have established a positive relationship between play and various measures of creativity. Lieberman (1977), for example, found that kindergartners who were rated high in terms of playfulness scored higher on tests of divergent thinking than did other children. In addition to such correlational evidence, a series of experimental studies by Dansky and Silverman (1973, 1975) has yielded evidence that there is a causal link between play and creativity. These studies revealed that children who were allowed to play with objects were later able to find more creative, nonstandard uses for them. A series of play-training studies have provided further evidence that play promotes creative thinking (e.g., Dansky, 1980a). Dansky (1980b) discovered that free play helped divergent thinking only in children who regularly engaged in make-believe. This finding supports Sutton-Smith's (1967) contention that the symbolic transformations that occur in make-believe play are a key factor in play's contribution to creativity.

Findings of more recent research on the play–creativity connection have been mixed. On the negative side, Smith and Whitney (1987) repeated the Dansky and Silverman (1975) experiment, with tight controls for experimenter bias, and they failed to replicate the connection between play and creative use of objects. Dunn and Herwig (1992) did not find dramatic play to be related to estimates of divergent thinking in middle-class preschoolers attending mixed-age all-day programs. Dunn and Herwig suggest that ecological factors, such as attending a half-day versus a full-day early childhood program, may moderate play–creativity relations. All-day child care may be less than optimal for peer contact and social play. These investigations urged others to build an ecological view of play and learning by conducting research across early childhood contexts.

On the positive side, Fisher (1992) examined the impact of play on development, performing a *meta-analysis* (i.e., use of statistical methods to estimate the probability of relationships or differences among variables, synthesizing numerical information across studies on the same topic). He looked at 46 investigations done since 1974, dealing with cognitive, linguistic, and social–affective domains. An overall effect size of $r = .35$ was unearthed using Cohen's scaling methods, where .20 is considered modest and .40 a noteworthy finding. Effects of play on divergent thinking, in particular ideational fluency, was .39. As a characteristic of creative imagination, *ideational fluency* consists of the ability to produce flexible and original associations. Results focusing on sociodramatic play were most robust in Fisher's overall analysis, yielding a remarkable overall effect size of .60.

METACOGNITION

Metacognition is thinking about thinking. With age, children become more and more aware of their own cognitive processes. For Piaget, this was a central fact about cognitive development. When children make reference to their own memory state, how well it is working, and what factors influence it (e.g., I can remember better when my mother tells me twice), their behaviors are referred to as *metamemory*. When kids talk about their social interactions, including social dramatic or other forms of social play, their behaviors are referred to as *metacommunication*. Research has pointed to the importance of metacognition (and particularly metacommunication) in social-pretense play—where planning and negotiation over roles are necessary for smoothly flowing episodes characterized by children going in and out of scripts within play frames.

The link between metacognition and play is important for the conversational coherence of social interaction. This importance was shown to be age related in a study by Goncu and Kessel (1984). They employed interpretive–hermeneutic methods in analyzing videotapes of play interactions of 24 middle-class children. They scored children's social interactions for evidence of a variety of metacommunicative behaviors—planning, inviting, negotiating, and acceptance statements—which were part of the play frame or context, separate from the play script or text itself. These metacommunications proved indispensable for linking players' intentions and actions during the play, with older children having a significantly higher incidence of linked utterances than younger preschoolers had. As we show in Chapters 3 and 8, Carollee Howes considers metacommunication to be the distinguishing feature of her highest level of peer play, "complex social dramatic play" (see the accompanying sidebar, "Metacommunication in Play.")

THEORY OF MIND

This relatively new area of research on play and development is closely related to both metacognition and perspective taking, which is discussed in the following "Social Domain" section. Human consciousness and thought requires a model of one's own mind and those of others. During early childhood, the child develops a model of mental states called *theory of mind* (Leslie, 1987). This theory is an implicit and rudimentary awareness that even young children possess about their own and other people's internal psychological states. Before 4 years of age, most youngsters seem insensitive or oblivious to their *privileged information* (knowledge that they have but that another person lacks), thereby preventing them from realizing that another person who lacks this privileged information might have a false belief. As children develop their "theory of mind," they become more sensitive to the fact that other persons have their own minds and perspectives, which often are at odds with the children's own points of view. Significantly, when engaged in pretense play, children often seem precocious with respect to having a theory of mind (Lillard, 1998). Pretending is held to be instrumental in fostering a theory of mind.

Singer and Singer (1990) provide a useful modification of Leslie's original work on the theory of mind. Based on Leslie's work, Singer and Singer maintain that a major step in development occurs when children can "de-couple" or cordon off pretense representations from primary-level mental representations, such as being able to pretend that a telephone cord on the floor is a "snake." When children or adults engage in this type of pretending, it does not create a distortion or disregard of reality that causes their representational systems to come crashing down. This is because they have developed their own systems of metarepresentations by which they can manipulate, modify, transform, or otherwise flexibly characterize and use their primary

Theory in Action

METACOMMUNICATION IN PLAY

Observational research by Garvey (1977) and others has revealed that children use two types of verbal exchanges while engaging in sociodramatic play: pretend communications and metacommunications. *Pretend communications* occur when the children adopt roles and make comments appropriate for those roles. During these exchanges, children address each other by their pretend names (or at least attempt to do so). For example, if two children are enacting a hospital scene, one child might say, "Doctor, I'm very sick. Can you make me better?" Pretend communications are made within the play frame that the children have established.

Metacommunications, on the other hand, occur when children temporarily break the play frame and make comments about the play itself. When making these comments, children resume their real-life identities and address each other by their actual names. In the foregoing hospital scene, if the child acting as doctor made an inappropriate action or comment, the other child might say, "Suzy, doctors don't do that." Such exchanges are used to resolve conflicts over roles, rules, the make-believe identity of objects, and the course of the story line—conflicts that arise during the course of a dramatization. Rubin (1980) contends that these conflicts are responsible for much of play's positive effects on social development.

Sawyer (1997) points out that metacommunication can be either explicit or implicit. He gives the following examples (p. 35):

Explicit metacommunication
A   Let's play teenage mutant ninja turtles.
B   OK!

Implicit metacommunication.
A   I'm Donatello! [a character in a TV show about teenage mutant ninja turtles]
B   I'm Raphael! [another character in the show]

Note how the implicit metacommunication is also pretend communication because the players are speaking from pretend roles. However, because the character Donatello is known within the peer culture to be a teenage mutant ninja turtle, player B realizes that player A has adopted a role and is engaging in make-believe play. Player B's response implicitly communicates that he has joined the make-believe. Thus, the distinction between pretend communication and metacommunication becomes blurred in the complexity of actual play activity.

(continued)

Theory in Action *(continued)*

The following transcript from a study by Giffin (1984) illustrates the extent to which some children engage in explicit metacommunicative exchanges and conflicts during the course of sociodramatic play. In this episode, Heather (age 5), Andy (age 4), and Kathy (age 3 ½) are enacting a story about a wedding (Giffin, 1984, pp. 96–97):

"Bad Mother"
[Heather (H.), Kathy (K.), and Andy (A.) are playing in the dress-up room of a preschool]

H. (to K.) You're crying in the wedding place. Make the crying sound.
(K. "cries.")

H. What's the matter? You want to get married is why?
(to A.) She wants to get married so she's crying. You should get married. Let's say you guys were already married. OK?

A. No! I'm going to put on the song.
(The play stove becomes a disco booth.)

H. Andy has to put on the song and then he'll dance with you.
(to A) Give me the song.

K. You have to come and dance with me Andy.

A. No I . . . Dad.

H. And he can't dance.
And you say what's the matter with me, Andy.
(H. "cries").

H My mother yelled at me.
Let's say you gave me a spanking, Kathy O'Neil.

K. No, my name is Annie.

H. Annie, let's say you gave me a spanking. And I call you Mom.
(to A.) Daddy, I'm crying 'cause my mother gave me a spanking and she yelled at me.

A. I'll kill her!

Notice how Heather uses metacommunication to structure the story and to prompt the other players. Andy and Kathy each use metacommunication to rebuff other players for not using their pretend names. Through such exchanges, children gain valuable experience in solving social problems, and they also learn a lot about rules and roles in the process.

representations of information from their perception of ostensive reality. As shown in Figure 2.2, pretend play differs from reality play in its reliance on metarepresentation.

Recent research has examined pretend play and theory-of-mind-development, the latter usually operationalized as passing the false-belief task. In the *false-belief task*, a child is shown "Maxi," a doll, who conceals candy in a blue cupboard. Maxi goes away, and during his absence, his mommy arrives and moves

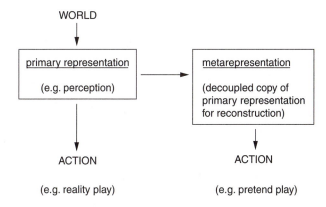

Figure 2.2

A general model for pretend play
Source: Copyright © 1987 by the AmericanPschological Association. Reprinted with permission.

the piece of candy from the blue cupboard to an adjacent white one. The mommy then leaves the scene and Maxi comes back. The cupboard doors are shut closed, so that the candy is not within the child's field of vision. The child is assumed to have been successfully led to believe that Maxi did not see his mother move the candy by the way the dolls were moved in and out of the scene by the researcher. The child is asked, "Where will Maxi look for the candy?" The correct reply is the blue cupboard because that is where Maxi put it, and he does not know that his mother moved it. Research shows that youngsters less than 4 years of age tend to assert that Maxi will look in the white cupboard, egocentrically failing to suppress their own privileged information about what has transpired. Youngblade and Dunn (1995) report that those children who did more role-enactment play at age 33 months performed better on this task at 40 months of age than did other children, who exhibited significantly less pretending at 33 months of age. Similarly, Dockett (1994) found that children trained to engage in pretend play pass the theory-of-mind task earlier than do control-group children. Astington and Jenkins (1995) found pretend-play person transformations significantly correlated with false-belief understanding in 3- to 5-year-olds, controlling for language ability and verbal intelligence. This new body of research supports the hypothesis that pretending is a causal agent in social cognitive development and in the theory of mind young children are developing (Lillard, 1998).

LANGUAGE DOMAIN

Observational research has revealed that young children frequently play with the different forms and rules of language (Weir, 1962). Young children play with sounds (phonology) by repeating strings of nonsense syllables, with syntax by systematically substituting words of the same grammatical category, and with semantics by intentionally distorting meaning through nonsense and jokes. This language play helps children to perfect newly acquired language skills and increases their conscious awareness of linguistic rules (Cazden, 1976).

There is persuasive evidence that symbolic play and language are associated during toddlerhood (Bornstein, Vibbert, Tal, & O'Donnell, 1992; Tamis-LeMonda & Bornstein, 1991, 1993). Toddlers were observed during 15-minute free-play sessions alone and with their mothers at home, with toys such as a clown doll, cups and saucers, a toy telephone, a book, blocks, and other materials available. Two indexes of play are typically used in these studies: *quantitative measures* (frequency and duration) and *qualitative measures* (level of sophistication). Results showed that pretend play is associated with language development, particularly syntactical complexity. Tamis-LeMonda and Bornstein (1993a) reported that frequency of symbolic play at 13 and 21 months was related with semantic diversity at 21 months, but not with productive vocabulary or grammar (mean length of utterance). They hypothesize that play–language links reflect an underlying core component of representation in the child. These links do not appear to depend on maternal mediation, in that mothers' contributions in these studies were partialed out in the statistical analyses.

Older preschool and kindergarten-age children also gain valuable language practice by engaging in play (Garvey, 1974). For example, remember the sociodramatic-play episode depicted at the beginning of Chapter 1, in which Wendy, George, and John acted out a meal-preparation story. The children followed the rules of conversation (e.g., turn taking) and used language precisely to plan story lines and to designate the make-believe identities of objects and actions.

Bruner (1983) contends that "the most complicated grammatical and pragmatic forms of language appear first in play activity" (p. 65). In addition to being complex, the language that children use during play is decontextualized (Pellegrini & Jones, 1994). *Decontextualized language* is marked by its use of adjectives, pronouns, and conjunctions to carry meaning, relatively independently of nonverbal means and reliance on context. Explicit and intentional use of lexical and syntactical features of language enables children to signify person, object, and situational transformations in pretense play, and to identify and elaborate on play themes as they unfold during the play episode. Play can strengthen children's representational competence and can help children to overlearn skills needed for comprehending and producing decontextualized texts in later academic reading and writing lessons.

The relationship between play and language, communication, and emergent literacy persists as children continue to develop during the early childhood years. For instance, in addition to evidence that sociodramatic play is associated with preschool children's language-arts skills, correlational studies by Wolfgang (1974) and Pellegrini (1980), conducted years ago, revealed a positive relationship between levels of sociodramatic play and reading and writing ability. Other researchers also reported that children's story comprehension was enhanced by dramatic-play activities (Pellegrini & Galda, 1982). Research on this topic has continued unabated to the present (for reviews, see Pellegrini & Galda, 1993; Roskos & Neuman, 1998).

For example, Pellegrini, Galda, Dresden, and Cox (1991) studied 12 preschool children attending a university-affiliated program for 2 years. Children's symbolic-play transformations and linguistic verb usage were assessed from free-play observational notes and audio recordings. Children were given additional tasks to tap their receptive vocabularies (Peabody Picture Vocabulary Test) and other literate behaviors (e.g., children were asked to tell, dictate, and write about two different series of pictures from the books *Daddy Makes the Best Spaghetti* and *Maybe a Bandaid Will Help*). Symbolic play and linguistic verbs predicted emergent reading and writing.

Longitudinal research by Sara Smilansky and her associates has linked sociodramatic play activity in kindergartners with their scholastic achievement in second grade. Total sociodramatic play correlated .40 with standardized reading scores and .45 with arithmetic scores. Make-believe play with objects, one of the criteria of sociodramatic play, correlated .41 with these test scores, the highest correlation found. Smilansky (1990) concluded that make-believe play with objects and situations during kindergarten accounted for 23% of the variance in reading achievement in second grade. The study did not control for the effects of intelligence, although Smilansky did point out that earlier work (Smilansky & Shefatya, 1979) showed that Stanford-Binet IQ in kindergartners only correlated .36 with the children's reading achievement at the end of the first grade. She urged more research, especially cross-cultural replication.

Other longitudinal research has demonstrated that pretend play and cognitively challenging talk in preschool influence language and literacy skills in elementary school (Dickinson, 1994). Research suggests that object substitutions in pretend play may predict academic achievement in writing, but less so in reading. Researchers have concluded that the relation between play and literacy, from a strictly psychological perspective, remains problematic. The development of young children's identities as literate persons requires attention to cultural and ecological factors in general, and to the interaction of person and context variables in particular (Roskos, in press).

SOCIAL DOMAIN

Play, a major activity of childhood, is intricately involved in the socialization process. There is a two-way relationship between play and social development. The social environment is an important influence on children's play. Children learn attitudes and skills needed for play from their parents and from other children. Parents and peers may also encourage certain types of play behavior and discourage others. At the same time, play acts as an important context in which children acquire social skills and social knowledge. The social practices of parents, peers, and teachers can affect children's play. Conversely, play has a key role in social development by providing a context in which children can acquire many important social skills such as turn taking, sharing, and cooperation, as well as the ability to understand other people's thoughts, perceptions, or emotions. Thus, while the social environment influences play, play also affects children's ability to get along in the social environment.

SOCIAL COMPETENCE

Studies by Garvey (1974) and others have provided detailed descriptions of the social abilities underlying group play. The most fundamental of these is the ability to understand the rules of play. All social play is rule governed. Even simple parent and infant games such as peekaboo require the establishment of the rule that participants take turns. In sociodramatic play, the rules become much more complex. For example, once children adopt a role, their behavior must be consistent within that role. If their behavior becomes inappropriate, such as a baby acting like an adult, the other players will usually issue a sharp reprimand. Unlike formal games with rules, rules for role play are not set in advance; rather, the rules are established by the players during the course of the play. This conscious manipulation of rules provides an opportunity for children to examine the nature of rules and rule making. Therefore, play is a context in which children not only learn specific rules such as turn taking but also learn about the meaning of rules in general.

Children must also be able to construct and vary the theme of the play activity together (Garvey, 1974). This joint planning ability is particularly important in sociodramatic play. To successfully engage in group dramatizations, children must first agree on who will adopt each role and on the make-believe identities of objects and actions. For example, they might agree that Janice will be a doctor, Judy a nurse, and Joey a sick patient. It might then be decided that a pencil will be used as if it were a thermometer, and a narrow cylindrical block will be a syringe. The children must also make cooperative decisions about the story sequence. Janice, Judy, and Joey might agree that first, the doctor will take the patient's temperature; next, the nurse will administer a painful injection; and finally, the doctor will perform an operation. These initial plans can also be altered during the course of the play. The children may decide, for example, that a second injection is needed before the operation can be performed. This type of joint planning requires cooperation and give and take. Children who do not go along with the group's consensus are often excluded from the play. On the other hand, cooperation is rewarded by inclusion in a successful dramatization.

Descriptive studies have provided evidence that social play requires a number of abilities, such as turn alternation and cooperation; these findings suggest that play may have a role in the acquisition or consolidation of these social skills. This possibility has motivated researchers to investigate further the relationship between play and social competence. Several studies have reported significant correlations between levels of group dramatic play and measures of peer popularity and social skills (Connolly & Doyle, 1984; Rubin & Hayvern, 1981). Both teachers and peers rated children who frequently engaged in sociodramatic play as more popular. These children were also rated as more socially skilled by their teachers. In addition, the high-sociodramatic-play children exhibited more positive social actions toward peers.

Other play forms have been related to social competence and peer status, as well. Rough-and-tumble play (running around, chasing each other, engaging in mock fighting on the playground) has been studied longitudinally in older children and has been found to positively correlate with social cognitive ability and popularity (Pellegrini, 1995). Parallel constructive play (e.g., sitting on the floor with other children, independently playing with blocks) has also been found to correlate significantly with peer popularity, teacher ratings of social competence, and a measure of social problem solving (Rubin, 1982).

Given the high social demands of group dramatic play, the relationship between this form of play and measures of social competence is hardly surprising. A high degree of social skill may be required for children to engage in this advanced form of play, or group dramatic play may help children acquire these social abilities. (Note that because of the correlational nature of the aforementioned studies, the causal direction of the relationship cannot be determined.) Likewise, the connection between rough-and-tumble play and social competence seems easy to understand. Social flexibility, affect regulation, and perspective taking are involved in this form of play.

However, the finding that parallel constructive play also seems related to measures of social skill is less easy to explain. Rubin (1982) speculated that the relationship may be based on the fact that parallel constructive play closely resembles the group activities that commonly occur in preschool and elementary-school classrooms. Children who frequently engage in parallel constructive play may be better able to adjust to school activities and therefore be rated as socially competent and popular by their teachers.

To investigate causal relationships between play and social competence, several researchers have conducted training studies in which children were taught or encouraged by an adult to engage in sociodramatic play. Results showed that the training not only resulted in gains in group dramatic play but also led to increases in positive peer interaction and cooperation (Rosen, 1974; Smith, Dalgleish, & Herzmark, 1981; Udwin, 1983). These findings both indicate that play training enhances social development and support the position that engaging in group dramatic play promotes the acquisition of social skills. However, as we discuss in the sidebar, "Play: A Causal Agent?" (shown later in this chapter), other factors associated with the training, such as adult or peer interaction, also may have been responsible for the gains in social competence.

PERSPECTIVE TAKING

Perspective taking is the ability to see things from other people's points of view. It involves understanding what other people see (visual perspective taking), think (cognitive perspective taking), and feel (affective perspective taking or empathy). These abilities have an important role in social and moral development and social competence. For example, children are better able to solve interpersonal problems if they accurately understand one another's thoughts and feelings. Altruistic behavior such as generosity is motivated by an understanding of other people's distress and the joy they experience as a result of a generous act. In addition, perspective-taking ability has been found to be positively related to children's level of moral reasoning (Selman, 1971).

Research by Piaget and others has shown that young children have great difficulty with all forms of perspective taking. This difficulty is generally attributed to the egocentric nature of their thought. For young children, self and nonself are not differentiated, which leads them to assume that their own points of view are the *only* points of view. As children mature, the self gradually decenters and becomes separated from the environment. This process of decentration makes it possible for children to realize that other people can have perceptions, thoughts, and feelings that differ from their own.

Sociodramatic play may have an important role in the development of children's perspective-taking abilities and social competence. While engaging in group dramatizations, children act out a variety of roles. A child might, on different occasions, take on the role of a baby, parent, grandparent, firefighter, and superhero. In order to portray such characters accurately, children must be able to mentally put themselves in other people's places and experience the world from others' points of view. This act of consciously transforming their own identities into a variety of make-believe identities may hasten the decentration process, thereby promoting perspective taking and a number of other cognitive skills (Rubin, Fein, & Vandenberg, 1983).

Research has generally supported this proposed relationship between sociodramatic play and perspective taking (Creasey, Jarvis, & Berk, 1998). Levels of group dramatic play have been linked to children's perspective-taking abilities (Connolly & Doyle, 1984; Rubin & Maioni, 1975). Other studies have shown that sociodramatic play training resulted in gains in children's performance on visual, cognitive, and affective perspective-taking tasks (Burns & Brainerd, 1979). However, as was the case with research on social skills, methodological limitations—including problems with assessment instruments and the confounding effects of adult and peer interaction—have prevented these training studies from providing conclusive evidence that dramatic play causes growth in perspective-taking ability (see the accompanying sidebar, "Play: A Causal Agent?").

Recently, Sawyer (1997) has provided a fresh theoretical lens and accompanying research pertaining to the connection between play and social cognitive development during the early childhood years. Sawyer develops the metaphor of group pretense play as a jazz band that engages in a great deal of improvisation. Pretense play scripts are shared in a social context in sociodramatic play. Not only the immediate play context, but also the peer culture from which the children come, help the players forge mutual understanding in their play episodes. Children's *play motifs* (shared collectively from the children's local peer culture, such as the names of the characters in the latest Disney movie) are akin to jazz musicians' "riffs" or "figures," which are employed to reach shared understanding—and to afford opportunities for variation, repetition, and embellishment during the play episode.

Theory in Action

PLAY: A CAUSAL AGENT?

Past research has shown that training in group dramatic play can result in gains in social skills and perspective taking. However, there is some controversy over which aspect or component of the play training is primarily responsible for these gains in social development. There are three possibilities:

1. *The play itself*—object and role transformations that occur in dramatic play may hasten the decentration process.
2. *Adult instruction*—the adult–child interaction that occurs during the training may directly or indirectly teach the children new skills.
3. *Peer interaction*—the conflicts among children that occur in sociodramatic play may cause cognitive imbalance or disequilibrium, resulting in new learning.

Peter Smith tested the first two possibilities by carefully monitoring and controlling the adult–child interaction in a large-scale training study (Smith, Dalgleish, & Herzmark, 1981). Results indicated that adult instruction may have been responsible for many of the *cognitive* gains brought about by the training, including higher scores on measures of intelligence, creativity, and perspective taking. However, the play itself appeared to be responsible for the increased positive *social* interaction resulting from the play training. Thus, it is possible that the two components of play training have an impact on different areas of development: Adult instruction primarily affects cognition, and play itself primarily affects social competence. This hypothesis is purely speculative and needs to be confirmed by further research.

Observational research by Garvey (1977) and others has revealed that children often engage in conflicts during the course of group dramatic play. They argue over roles, rules, the story line, and the make-believe identities of objects (see the section on "Metacommunication," presented earlier in this chapter, for an example). These conflicts do not occur during the dramatic play itself; rather, they occur during *frame breaks,* in which the children temporarily leave their make-believe roles and assume their real-life identities. Once the conflicts are resolved, the children resume their make-believe roles and the play continues.

The peer conflicts that occur during sociodramatic play are undoubtedly responsible for some of play training's impact on perspective taking and social development. Rubin explains:

(continued)

Theory in Action *(continued)*

Rule understanding, the comprehension of obligations and prohibitions, and the ability to consider reciprocal role relations may be less a function of non-literal social play per se and more the outcome of peer interaction and conflict. . . . When children beg to differ concerning issues of importance to them, cognitive disequilibria are likely to ensue. Since such mental states are not pleasurable, conflict resolution is necessary. Often, when disequilibrium is provoked by social conflict, compromise results. Suffice it to say that compromise is accommodative and adaptive. In short, given conflict, the child comes to realize that: (1) survival in the social world, as well as (2) popularity among peers are marked by compromises and socialized thoughts. (Rubin, 1980, p. 80)

Because peer interaction and conflict are integral parts of group dramatic play, their effects are difficult if not impossible to separate from those of other aspects of play. It may be best to think of play training as a context in which make-believe role enactment, peer conflicts, and adult instruction all combine to promote children's social–cognitive development. Perhaps some day, researchers may be able to untangle the separate contributions of each component of play training, but for now, the fact remains that such training appears to be effective in the development of perspective taking and social competence.

A great deal of mutual tacit knowledge is possessed by the players in the early childhood setting—just like in a jazz band of accomplished adult musicians. Play script and frame are merely tips of the iceberg, according to Sawyer. Underneath the surface of overt social behaviors, there is a great deal of potential material for mutual play, due to the shared peer culture. The challenge is for players to integrate individualistically inspired performances with the ongoing group performance. Here is an opportunity for children to learn to balance their budding individual creativity with their improving social radar to be able to blend in with the group play, as well as to be able to do "their own thing." For Sawyer, skill at group pretense in childhood may foreshadow skill as a conversationalist later in life. His conceptual analyses and descriptive data add to our appreciation of the relation between play aspects and social and cognitive aspects of development.

Rough-and-tumble play has also been linked to social competence (Creasey et al., 1998). How are the two related? Pellegrini (1995) has suggested that rough-and-tumble play be unpackaged into its component parts, with each part, studied in connection to specific areas of the developing child's competencies. For example, there are locomotive aspects, physical vigor aspects, verbal aspects, and so on. *Flexibility*—the use of a variety of behaviors—is the aspect of rough-and-tumble play that may be responsible for the connection of rough-and-tumble play with social competence. Each part

Children tend to use objects in nonstandard, creative ways during play.

shares this flexibility component. Pellegrini (1995) recommends longitudinal studies to explore such specificity hypotheses. Pellegrini holds that high-quality rough-and-tumble play should be viewed as reinforcing social cognitive development, if not contributing to it.

EMOTIONAL DOMAIN

From 1930 until the mid 1960s, psychoanalytic theory was the dominant theory of play. Most of the research and writing on play during this period dealt with psychoanalytic topics such as play therapy, use of play for diagnostic purposes, and its role in emotional development. The research was primarily nonexperimental, consisting mainly of case studies of individuals. Axline (1964), for example, detailed how play therapy helped a young boy named Dibs solve his emotional problems. The little experimental research that was conducted suffered from methodological weaknesses such as inadequate controls and unreliable or invalid instrumentation (Rubin, Fein, & Vandenberg, 1983). As a result, findings were inconsistent and often contradictory. A number of doll-play studies were conducted to investigate the *displacement hypothesis,* which says that people tend to shift negative emotions onto a substitute. This hypothesis predicts that children who have been severely punished by their parents will be more aggressive in their play with dolls. While half of the doll-play studies supported the displacement hypothesis, half did not (Levin & Wardwell, 1971).

The disappointing results of past research, combined with the rising influence of cognitive theories of play beginning in the 1960s, resulted in a sharp drop in research on play and emotional development. Sutton-Smith (1983) reports that only 5 psychoanalytically oriented articles on play were published during the 1970s, as compared with 69 studies during the 1950s.

Although few direct experimental data back up the contention that play has an important role in emotional development, indirect data from other sources do provide such support. For example, Guerney (1984) reported that play-therapy studies improved and became more sophisticated, and Barnett and Storm (1981) showed physiological evidence linking play with anxiety reduction. Moreover, retrospective accounts and clinical case studies, such as the work in Texas by Brown (1994) cited at the beginning of this chapter, further suggest how important play is in emotional development. In addition, there are experimental animal studies, such as Harry Harlow's work with rhesus monkeys, in which early play deprivation was shown to lead inevitably to profound disruption in the social–affective sphere in adulthood. Finally, anecdotes by various child observers—such as teachers, therapists, and hospital child life workers—add still more supporting documentation about play's role in emotional development (see Chapter 6). For instance, after culling examples from Rosalind Gould's (1972) excellent book containing a wealth of richly descriptive nursery-school free-play vignettes, Singer and Singer (1990, p. 151) state the following about the importance of play for children's selfhood and emotions:

> We believe that those children who have less opportunity, encouragement, and (possibly in the case of autistic children) less constitutional predisposition towards regular make-believe play miss an important phase of becoming fully human, developing complex self-schemas and learning how to express emotions.

SELF-CONCEPT

Views about play and development can be divided into two general camps: (1) the belief that play serves important purposes in child development within specific domains; and (2) the view that play is expressive behavior that does not affect development directly in any positive or constructive manner. In this second camp, play is seen as serving general ego-building functions and is not reducible into component parts to be linked to other developmental phenomena. What is most important to understand about play, according to this second view, is that the phenomenon of play is holistic and integrated within the individual personality and self-identity of the player. This position is reflected in the theoretical writings of Erikson (1940), Peller (1952), Sutton-Smith (1980), and Vandenberg (1998).

Erikson, for example, addressed the ways in which the psychosexual conflicts of children are reflected in the spatial configuration of their play with toys. While controversial, his ideas deserve some consideration, in that they have reinforced the development and use of play as therapy to help children cope with emotional and behavioral difficulties. The belief that play can enable children to better cope with traumatic events, for example, led to a groundswell of sentiment for providing pediatric patients with play experiences to help alleviate anxieties associated with hospitalization (Lindquist, Lind, & Harvey, 1977).

According to Erikson (1963), the adaptive resolution of each stage of psychosocial development (for example, trust vs. mistrust at 1 year of age) involves the successful integration of social and biological functions. Play creates "a model situation in which aspects of the past are relived, the present represented and renewed, and the future anticipated" (Erikson, 1977, p. 44). Therefore, play helps to solve ego conflicts, such as anxieties, by allowing these conflicts to be dramatized and played out. For example, playing with toys is a behavior in which children explore and reduce concerns about their competence. Erikson has also noted the expressive value of play. He explains that the themes children enact during play are often associated with working through a traumatic experience, but they also express playful *renewal*. "If they seem to be governed by some need to communicate, or even to *confess*, they certainly also seem to serve the joy of *self expression*" (Erikson, 1972, p. 131; emphasis in original).

Hence, Erikson moved beyond a narrow view of the part play takes in anxiety reduction and compensatory wish fulfillment to a more positive holistic view of play in childhood. Erikson considered the sense of hope as a "prime mover" in human development. Play, and particularly future-oriented role play, reinforces children's intrinsic faith in the future of the human race, as well as hopefulness about their own developing personal identities.

Peller (1952) presented a more traditional psychoanalytic view about play, highlighting the diversity of essentially compensatory reasons a child plays. For Peller and other Freudians, play seems to be a substitute for reasoning and, as such, is a "crude kind of test action" (p. 124). Nevertheless, because play enables the child to reexperience past personal events with accompanying moods and emotions, playful repetition is seen as an essential step toward concept formation, including the concept of self.

Sutton-Smith (1980), a scholar who has written extensively on play and relation to the self, has highlighted the way role reversal in play can foster a sense of control and autonomy in the child. Given that children operate from a position of weakness in relation to adults, it is important for children to know that they have opportunities to turn the tables on adults and on aspects of living that make them feel inferior because of their immaturity and size. Play is a medium that is self-enabling. Play and fantasy give the child a chance to be powerful and the master of circumstances.

Consider how young children might feel, for example, about routine events forced on them by adults who may or may not think about the consequences of those events for children. Take a child who is dropped off at school or a child-care center day after day by a parent who hurries off to work. The child has no choice in the matter. The parent decides what happens and is virtually in total control of the entire situation. In play, however, the child can reverse roles and pretend to leave dolls or teddy bears at a pretend child-care center or nursery, thereby recapturing a little of the loss of control experienced in the actual occurrences.

Playing, then, is intimately related to the expansion of a sense of self as an autonomous and functioning person who can influence surrounding events. Through play, the developing identity of the child emerges. The child forms a secure position and from this position of strength is able to achieve empathy for others. Playful reciprocity is first seen in adult–infant and adult–toddler interactions. From this base, and through later adult-mediated peer role play, the child is able to engage in social play with peers. This process reflects and expresses the child's understanding of self and others, and the relationship between the two.

In a provocative essay, Vandenberg (1998) has pointed out that, with development, children are more and more able to partake in intricate imaginative play alone and with others, and they also become capable of making increasingly complex and nuanced distinctions between the *real* and the *not real*. He speculates that this task is more difficult for young children than is differentiating their *play* from *nonplay* experiences. Vandenberg's perspective on the significance of play is best described as existential; in play, children operate on the border between the real and the not real, being and not being in the world. Moreover, there is great personal freedom and power in play. Children learn about the fluidity and fragile nature of social constructions—how simply saying "it's play" can change the whole experience and meaning of an event for self and others (i.e., the Batesonian "this is play" signal discussed in Chapter 1). Children at play can venture forth numerous actions without having to worry about the consequences. Play reflects the past but also projects the future. Linked to children's play are children's hopes and their anticipations of becoming who they are.

Vandenberg cautions us about educational play, with its implicit or explicit adult agenda. Unfortunately, educational play can easily be reduced to an activity that is no longer playful. This robs children of the joy, freedom, and zest realized at the boundary of real and not real—where they are when they are really playing. Vandenberg argues that recreational and expressive play must be preserved for children, especially as they are introduced to formal institutional life (e.g., child-care, preschools) at younger and younger ages.

STRESS AND COPING

Elkind (1981) has stated that play is an antidote to hurrying. Children play to release the stress they build up from all the pressure exerted on them by socialization agents in today's fast-paced society. Children, according to popular current views, are under pressure to grow up fast. Parents, the schools, and the media conspire to pressure children to perform tasks and meet demands earlier than did previous generations. Elkind defined *hurrying* as "the pressure on children to make social accommodations at the expense of personal assimilations" (p. 195). In other words, children are hurried and forced to learn new things, when the time would be better spent playing to reinforce or digest past experiences. Play and work are separate but complementary activities.

Elkind is highly critical of the dictum "play is child's work" because of the way it sometimes gets translated into teaching practice. He gives a poignant example of the inappropriate use of the spokesperson-for-reality intervention strategy. A teacher interrupted children playing with various toy dinosaurs to try to point out their different sizes. As a result, the children drifted off into other activities to avoid the teacher. Dinosaurs have great symbolic significance—they are big and strong, but as toys, they are small and easy for children to use. Such play gives children a safe way of dealing with the giants in their world—adults. Elkind believes that adults should avoid interrupting this type of play.

Similar examples of inappropriately turning play into a teacher-oriented lesson plan are all too numerous and well known. Typically, in a classroom or child-care center, teachers are eager to have children learn. It is easy to become overly enthusiastic. For example, a teacher interrupted a young child during a so-called free-play period when the child, who played alone most of the time, was finally beginning to play with other children. The teacher wanted to help the child learn how to spell and write her name! For more information about appropriate and inappropriate forms of adult involvement in play, see Chapter 7.

According to Elkind, children's personal assimilations should not be turned into social accommodations. Elkind argues that the real work of children is not play but to meet the countless socialization demands placed on them (remembering their phone numbers and addresses and how to get home from school, learning how to brush their teeth, learning to read, learning to deal with conscious and unconscious fears and concerns, etc.). To complement this real work of childhood, children need opportunities to play and use toys for full personal expression. Accordingly, Elkind emphasizes the value of the arts in the elementary schools for obtaining a balance between work and play. In preschool environments, the premium certainly should be on play and toys that give the greatest scope to the child's imagination—toys that allow for personal expression. This not only permits personal and autonomous activity and interpretation, but also is assumed to be appropriate cognitive enrichment that prepares the child for later school and life challenges. (See the accompanying sidebar, "What Good Is Play?")

SUMMARY

In this chapter, we have explored the research literature on the relationship between play and child development. Three positions were first noted—play (1) *reflects,* (2) *reinforces,* or (3) *results in* development. Possible benefits of

Theory in Action

WHAT GOOD IS PLAY?

ELAINE SELFRIDGE

In response to one of the questions on a midterm for an undergraduate course on play, as a Penn State University student, I wrote the following:

What good is play?

One of the reserved readings stated that play is "worthwhile in its own right as a potentially empowering, integrative, joyful, aesthetic, and humanizing experience" (Fromberg, 1997, p. 55). I wholeheartedly agree. More specifically, I agree with Vygotsky that play is the "zone of proximal development" for children. To demonstrate, allow me to introduce you to two students, Ronald and Tracy.

Ronald is a fourth grader. He wears many labels, including "learning disabled," "noncompliant," and "passive–aggressive." In the classroom, Ronald refuses to read aloud and will not answer questions; he barely looks at or speaks to the teachers or his peers. However, while playing basketball, Ronald teases his peers and jokes with a friend from class. While waiting for a ride home with a group of his peers, this boy, who refuses to read or speak in class, pretends to speak in a high brow English accent. Ronald's teachers are amazed. Where did this come from? They never knew Ronald had the capacity to tell jokes, to play with language (a very sophisticated skill for this language disabled student). This boy who has been labeled as a learning and behavior problem is indistinguishable from his friends when they are playing.

Tracy is three and a half years old. She has no label—yet. She has little intelligible speech, and it is strongly suspected that she is learning disabled and has a language disorder. Yet in Tracy's home, I observed this sequence. Tracy grabs the Barney doll and hugs him. Then shouts, "Oh no, oh no," and throws the doll to the floor. She leans over him mumbling. I cannot understand her words, but her tone is soft. Then she puts her hand to her forehead and like the best Hollywood actress, says, "Oh go, oh go (oh god)." And proceeds to give Barney CPR, and finally to lift him, hug him and pronounce that he is okay. She repeats this sequence several times. Even showing Barney to me so I can make sure he is really better. Her mother says, "She plays like this all the time, you wouldn't believe the things she comes up with." This child who is seen only for her inability to speak, is able to communicate an elaborate plot through her play. Play is indeed good.

Play not only demonstrates children's development as can be seen in the above descriptions, play also promotes development in all domains. Play promotes physical development, both fine and gross motor skills. When children play outside, they practice a wide range of motor skills, running, jumping, throwing. When they play with toys, they use fine motor skills, putting puzzles together, coloring, pretending to cook, dressing and undressing dolls.

(continued)

Theory in Action (continued)

Play enhances cognitive development. Rich play correlates with creative (divergent) thinking. Play improves imagination and creativity. According to Vygotsky children develop the "ability to separate thought from actions and objects" through play. They develop symbolic thought, an important part of Piaget's theories of play. Play also promotes memory and use of memory strategies. It promotes storytelling and fosters reasoning abilities.

Play promotes communication development. An important part of play is the metacommunication skills involved. Metacommunication refers to the negotiation and planning that takes place during play. Children learn how to communicate their ideas and intentions to one another and how to verbally resolve disputes. For example, "Just give me one and I'll be your friend, okay?" (*The Boy Who Would Be A Helicopter,* Paley, 1990, p. 90). They learn how to use language.

Play also promotes social development. In play, children practice skills like getting along with others, entering groups, sharing, and taking turns. According to Vygotsky, they also learn to follow social rules by making and choosing to follow their own rules during play. According to Vygotsky, in play children develop the "capacity to renounce impulsive action in favor of deliberate, self-regulatory activity."

Play also helps children to develop emotionally. They develop self-esteem and their own self-concept. The child is in control of the play. They learn to deal with fears and stress in a non-threatening situation, project feelings during play, and learn to identify their emotions. By playing with others and taking on various roles, children learn empathy and decenter. They learn to take another person's point of view. Role-playing leads to role-taking; children learn about their own and others' roles. (class notes, 2/2)

My answer here is comprehensive—but it is my anecdotes that capture the essence of play. Ronald and Tracy are able to function a lot better in the play mode. This is very typical. Why? Is it because children are less threatened and inhibited or uptight? Is it due to the close connection between development, behavior, and context? What do you think?

play for child development and well-being can be immediate or delayed—even operating as "sleeper effects." These possibilities fall under the second and third positions. When linking play with development, the *epiphenomenon* and *equifinality* principles lead to difficulties in discerning verifiable connections. The former principle posits that other factors often occur along with play, such that play per se is not responsible for the purported benefits of play; the latter principle posits that, even when play is convincingly shown to be implicated in an important child outcome such as literacy attainment, there are always presumed to be other pathways to the same developmental endpoint.

The chapter covered play in relation to the cognitive, language, social, and emotional developmental domains. We saw qualitative research has become more common, in addition to quantitative work, in determining the significance of play in child development. Considerable empirical research is consistent with theories of the role of play in development covered in Chapter 1. At a minimum, play reinforces cognitive development with respect to representational competence, operational thought, and problem solving. Play seems even more strongly connected with decentration and perspective taking and also appears to be a causal factor in the development of divergent thinking, metacommunication and other metacognitive abilities, and theories of mind. Language development is closely associated with cognitive development, and we saw that play has an important role in the child's use of language, emergent literacy, and narrative competence. Research suggests that play in early childhood can have valuable outcomes later on in school in the areas of reading and writing.

Finally, we reviewed the literature showing the importance of play for social development and emotional development. Play is related to social skills and social cognition (perspective taking and theories of mind) and is vitally important in self-awareness, emotional differentiation, and emotional regulation. The child's sense of reality and being, and of trust and hope in the future, as well as the child's management of stress, were all discussed in connection to play behavior and experience. Implied throughout the chapter is that a holistic, integrative approach to play and child development enables us to best appreciate play's significance, thereby improving our theories of practice with respect to the roles of the adult in children's play, and our abilities to explain to others the place of play in children's lives and in early childhood programs.

Chapter 3

DEVELOPMENT OF PLAY

It's been like this before—having to break in a new teacher midyear, after the program is solidly in place and the kids and teachers know each other pretty well. At the first staff meeting, new teacher Sal wants to know about the curriculum and, when told it is play based, expresses some dismay over how to teach in such a program. Sal's background lacks coursework in children's play and early childhood education, so Sal shows eagerness to do any catch-up reading or in-service training necessary to better the program.

An interesting discussion ensues, with the director and more experienced teachers sharing an overview of their program's philosophy and foundations. One of the first things they try to get across to Sal is that their program does not view or treat all forms and levels of play the same way. The staff members are "play connoisseurs," who promote and value particular certain forms of play. Sal wants to know how these forms of play are determined—and how you recognize them. The staff members explain that it depends on the child and the situation, the developmental status of the child and where you are in a situation as it is unfolding. Sal ponders what might be the meaning of this—"think, think, think—just like Winnie the Pooh," Sal muses to himself as he makes plans to head to the nearest listing of workshops and to the library after work. ■

In Chapter 1, we discussed definitions of play and classical and modern theories about the role of play in development, and in Chapter 2, we discussed theoretical and empirical evidence concerning the relation of play with development. We have sought to answer the questions "What is play?" and "What good is play in the child's development and early education?" We have seen that there are different ways to begin to answer these important questions. Now in this chapter, we devote ourselves to another major aspect of the research literature—the development of play behavior in its own right. Obviously, this is an important topic, from a practical point of view. Information about dimensions and normative sequences of play development position us to better appreciate the meaning and significance of play within the context of the growing child. Teachers and parents are able to answer the questions "What is good play?" and "How can we make it better?" only by knowing about the developmental processes and sequences of play during the early childhood years.

In this chapter, we first discuss the concept of play development and then trace the development of play behaviors from infancy through the preschool years within four domains: (1) play with people, (2) play with objects, (3) play with symbols, and (4) motor play. Second, we discuss developmental changes in play as children make the transition from the preschool years into the primary school years up to age 8. Here, we include extended discussion on the preceding four domains, as well as coverage of additional play or play-related activities relevant to this older age group. This material is organized around what the Consumer Product Safety Commission calls "cognitive play" and "creative play" (Goodson & Bronson, 1985). Cognitive play is the label given for projects and activities in which convergent thinking and epistemic mental activity seem more prevalent than divergent thinking and ludic mental activity. In general, games with rules, use of educational toys and materials, and books and other receptive forms of play are subareas of cognitive play. We define creative play as activities and projects that emphasize imagination and divergent thinking over reasoning and convergent thinking. Arts and crafts, Legos and blocks, narrative and pretense as constructed in microworlds, and musical expression are subareas of creative play.

CONCEPT OF PLAY DEVELOPMENT

Systematic change in play behavior can be discerned over very small periods of time within a single event. For example, we learn from play observational studies that children often explore single objects before combining or transforming objects. Tempo, intensity, variability, and style of behavior can also change drastically over time—as demonstrated in Hutt's (1966) classic study of specific and diffuse exploration. Here, children's responses to a novel toy were systematically observed for 10 minutes over 6 consecutive days. Children's action patterns and postures and expressions were stereotyped and rigid at first, but usually by the fourth day, children exhibited a more relaxed playful approach to the novel toy and demonstrated considerable response variability. Subsequent work by the late Corinne Hutt and her associates examined children's use of different preschool materials (e.g., dry sand or water) over time, measured in seconds and minutes (Hutt, Tyler, Hutt, & Christopherson, 1989). Studies such as these describe sequential patterns and temporal fluctuations in play behavior or experience over very brief periods of time. The term *microgenesis* refers to these short-term developmental changes.

Developmental change also means shifts in play behavior over much longer periods of time—as in age-related developmental stages of play. The term *ontogenesis* applies in this case. What are recognizable stages and substages of play that unfold over months or years of the child's life? Qualitatively different kinds of play are known to emerge in a stagelike fashion, such as the Piagetian play stages of sensorimotor play, symbolic play, and games with rules. Long-term developmental changes occur *within* each play category, as well. The symbolic play exhibited by toddlers, for instance, is much less developed than the symbolic play displayed by the average kindergarten child. Play ontogenesis occurs within each play behavior category, while different play forms emerge sequentially, forming larger developmental patterns.

These ideas of play microgenesis and play ontogenesis are important both as discrete concepts and as concepts working in tandem for aiding theoretical understanding about children's play behavior development. Information about play microgenesis or about the likely phases or cycles within and across relatively brief play episodes (e.g., examine–reexamine–combine–transform—examine–...) assists in anticipating play behaviors and in making situational arrangements or adjustments to optimize children's play in a given circumstance. For instance, during ongoing play, teachers may judiciously introduce new props or remove play props consistent with where children seem in microgenetic exploration-play cycles.

Similarly, information about developmental norms and milestones in play development is indispensable for creating developmentally appropriate play environments and for making accurate predictions about how children will play. Both kinds of information together enhance even further our ability to comprehend and evaluate what takes place sequentially within a play episode, either for an individual child at a certain developmental level (microanalytic level), or for a group of children of a given age composition (macroanalytic level). How children go through microgenetic play phases or cycles varies as a function of their developmental level (i.e., ontogenesis).

Play-development information is crucial for adults who work and play with growing children. However, this necessary information is not sufficient for achieving adequate working knowledge about children's play or for assuring competence in play interactions with children. Traditional theories of the development of play are quite linear, unidimensional, and decontextualized. As such, they are isolated from the cultural setting. Recent thinking about play development applies conceptual frameworks that are recursively interactive and multidimensional (Monighan-Nourot, 1997). For example, Corsaro (Gaskins, Miller, & Corsaro, 1992) proposes a reconstructive, as opposed to linear, view of social-play development, in which there is a recursive relation (or feedback loops) between developing children's social play and the continual creation and re-creation of *peer cultures,* evolving cultures that in turn affect the social play of individual children. A European root to this line of thinking can be traced to the French play theorist Chateau, who considered play a means for self-affirmation (*l'affirmation du moi*) for younger children. As these younger children grow up, they encounter the "challenge of the elder" (*l'appel de l'aine*) and are motivated to play and behave in such a way as to be accepted into (and, in time, to modify) the play culture of older girls and boys (cited in van der Kooij & de Groot, 1977).

Indeed, most of the play literature in the past saw the development of play as simply unidirectional quantitative and qualitative change in play skill or ability over time. A second criticism of these linear accounts of play development is that they are further limited by being decontextualized and unidimensional. Nowadays, play scholars have reacted by becoming increasingly sensitive to the ecocultural context that surrounds and engulfs the developing child. More common now is using a multifaceted perspective to view play development. Such a perspective allows us to consider "developmental time," as noted by Monighan-Nourot (1997), in relation to "many contextual factors, including situation, culture, language, and social relationships" (p. 132). (See Chapter 5 in the present volume, "Play in Diverse Cultures.").

Furthermore, knowledge about developmental trends with respect to play behavior and change must be integrated with information and understanding about individual differences (Chapter 4), cultural and social-class contexts (Chapter 5), atypicality (Chapter 6), and environmental factors of various sorts (Chapters 7, 9, and 10). For actually working and playing with children in particular situations, adults need to continually construct and reconstruct their "theories of practice," based on their book knowledge and on their practical knowledge gained from their experiences with children. Theories of practice relating to children's play, to be sure, rest first and foremost on an understanding of the developmental foundations of play—but also on an appreciation of other relevant considerations. We need to have multivariate theories of practice. Both the quality and the rates of development of various play behaviors show wide interindividual variability, due to different social and physical environments, as well as to maturation. Context effects prevail, as exemplified in commonplace observations that although play quality generally improves with development, children of a given developmental status exhibit different levels of play in different social contexts.

DEVELOPMENT OF SOCIAL PLAY

By kindergarten age, children normally possess an array of social play skills. They are expected to be able to engage in complex social exchanges during play. Children must learn to assert their wills to achieve personal goals, using behaviors that are acceptable within the peer group. Social competence is required to engage in positive interactions with peers, to become involved in relationships, and to nurture budding friendships. The parent–child "primary socialization system" gradually becomes joined with the "secondary socialization system" of peers, as the home and family become integrated with the microsystems of child care or school, the neighborhood and community.

French ethnologist Hubert Montagner (1984) learned from his extensive observations of young children that socially competent youngsters appropriately combine five types of actions: (1) *actions to produce attachment or to pacify*—behaviors that fall into this category include offering toys, caressing another child, and moving or vocalizing in a nonthreatening way; (2) *actions that generate fear, flight, or tears*—examples are frowning, loud vocalization, showing clenched teeth, and raising an arm; (3) *aggressive actions*—examples are grabbing objects, shaking another child, and hitting or kicking; (4) *gestures of fear and retreat*—for instance, a child might widen the eyes, blink, run away, or cry; and (5) *actions that produce isolation*—such behaviors include thumb sucking, lying down, tugging at the hair, or standing or sitting apart from other children. These behavioral and social actions and interactions are expressions of the child's cognitive abilities and problem-solving skills. Children who are simply dominant and aggressive are not the most socially adept.

In fact, such children tend to become unpopular. The best-liked children, the ones who become social leaders, use affection and power to persuade other children. To what extent are these competencies acquired as a result of social play? How do such social and play skills form? What does the research literature indicate?

Social-play development from infancy through the preschool years has been examined in longitudinal research (e.g., Howes & Matheson, 1992). In addition, a scattering of cross-sectional and short-term studies covering narrower age ranges helps us piece together a fairly comprehensive view of the development of social play.

In general, researchers agree that as a child grows older, there is an increase in interactive play. Interactive play skills develop along with a number of other social skills within the changing social situations of the growing infant, toddler, and preschooler. For example, as the child's social play becomes more complex, specific social behaviors become more pronounced, such as being able to take turns or to initiate, maintain, or end social interactions. Use of language in socially appropriate ways also becomes more elaborate.

Two different research traditions on the social aspects of play have developed. One examines how social play fosters specific social skills; the other focuses on the extent to which social play depends on and reflects these skills (Strayer, Mosher, & Russell, 1981). Although it may seem that this distinction is merely academic, in fact, the two offer rather different approaches for fostering play and development. The acompanying sidebar, "Practical Approaches to Promoting Social Competence in Children," illustrates these approaches.

The social world of the infant is very important for the development of play. Through interacting with caregivers, the child acquires several abilities needed in early games and pretend activities. Ross, Goldman, and Hay (1979) conducted a program to identify the characteristics and purposes behind the social play of infants and their caregivers. These researchers point out that because any interaction between the young child and another person can include mutual involvement, alternation of turns, and repetition, those interactions that highlight the difference between literal and nonliteral events are especially important. Often, simple repetition such as rolling a ball back and forth signals nonliterality or pretense; that is, what is taking place is separate from the usual things that come up in everyday life. After all, why roll a ball back and forth?

Our typical indications that social interaction is to be taken playfully, not literally, include gleeful vocalization and other exhibitions of pleasant feelings or levity. Positive affect often is caused by doing something unexpected, in an exaggerated manner, or not otherwise according to the usual routines. For example, instead of holding onto an object, we drop it; instead of approaching the oncoming person, we run away; instead of opening our mouth to receive food, we close it tight. Pretense in each instance is defined by the social context. Research shows that playful children have playful mothers who are sensitive to changes in their developing children's play skills (Damast, Tamis-LeMonda, & Bornstein, 1996; Fiese, 1990).

Theory in Action

PRACTICAL APPROACHES TO PROMOTING SOCIAL COMPETENCE IN CHILDREN

Sally's parents are concerned about her. She is almost 5 years old and wants to play with other children in the neighborhood. However, when Sally goes next door to play on the gym set or in the sandbox, other children ignore her. She wants to play with other children but does not seem to know how to do so. Her parents and teachers want to help her play and get along better with other children. How can they help?

Teachers and parents can provide ample opportunities for play, as well as specific learning activities and coaching to encourage children to make better use of play time. A number of techniques are possible, based on different views of the relationship between social-skill development and the development of social play.

From the point of view that play fosters the development of social skills, it follows that through opportunities, encouragement, and support for play, the child will become more skillful in social situations. Adult-guided play and adult coplaying with the young child and infant are important for play development, as are making playthings and peer play partners available in structured situations. Smilansky (1968) refers to two types of identification—general and specific—that are important for play development. Children in their home environment need to form positive attachment with parents or other adults to establish basic trust. Beyond this, however, young children also need to be shown specifically how to play and to be encouraged to play with parents in the home. Social skills emerge through playing in social situations.

On the other hand, it is possible that there are social-skill prerequisites to being a good play partner. Teachers and parents may have to model and encourage divergent thinking and various social and language skills to improve the child's play skills and foster her or his acceptance by other children. A certain amount of learning and development may be needed to engage successfully in different types of play. For example, children could be taught to perform communication or perspective-taking tasks outside of play to help them in subsequent situations. Exercises in inferring what the other person sees on the other side of a two-faced card, for example, could be helpful. Learning outside of play—through reading, listening to records, watching television, and other shared activities—can help make the child more playful with others in play situations. Parents can help by pointing out good social behaviors in others, as well as by rewarding the child for good social behaviors, such as greeting others, sharing, and "using your words" instead of physical aggression in social conflicts.

(continued)

Theory in Action *(continued)*

In extreme form, neither of the preceding two approaches is effective. Undoubtedly, the relationship between social skills and play is complex and reciprocal. Positive play experience promotes the acquisition and use of social skills; possessing these skills makes the child more likely to achieve satisfying and enjoyable play experiences. What is critical from a practical point of view is to recognize when a negative cycle exists and to attempt to change it for the better as soon as possible, using any number of possible techniques.

Because children differ from one another both developmentally and individually, it is obvious that the same technique will not be effective for all children. Perhaps Sally needs to be taught how to listen to and observe what others are playing and then be coached to enter ongoing play gracefully and not disruptively, by assuming an appropriate role for herself in relation to what others are doing. For example, instead of asking "Can I play?" perhaps Sally will learn that it is more effective to assume a complementary part in a pretend episode, such as acting the part of another pupil or the principal in a situation in which others are teachers and students. Perhaps puppet play depicting these strategies would help Sally learn. On the other hand, maybe Sally will learn best from storybooks or discussion with her parents or from some kind of reward system aimed at shaping her overt behaviors through reinforcement and praise.

Both Damast et al. and Fiese demonstrated that mothers adjusted their play level to be at or one notch above their toddlers' play level. In general, mothers support more sophisticated play as their children get older. In addition, mothers tend to support the child's autonomy by being less directive and by offering fewer play suggestions as children develop. Damast et al. examined play at home in a sequential analysis of 50 mothers and their toddlers (mean age = 22 months). They found that mothers were sensitive and responsive to their children's play behavior on a microlevel episode-by-episode basis within play sessions. These researchers also estimated maternal knowledge about play development using their Empirical Play Scale (see Table 3.1). Mothers were asked to rank, in order of developmental appearance, 24 actions of infants and toddlers, as shown in the right-hand column of Table 3.1. Mothers who were more accurate on this task tended to appropriately stretch the skills of their playing toddlers to engage in behaviors a bit ahead of their ongoing play.

Singer and Singer (1973, 1990) ditto the idea that the early social context is all-important in the development of play. They emphasize the importance of games such as "This Little Piggy Went to Market" and peekaboo for the baby to get the feel of the special world of make-believe. Such encounters promote not only pretend play skills, but also social skills and social-play skills. The three are interrelated. Learning to communicate the play intent or

Table 3.1   EMPIRICAL PLAY SCALE

LEVEL	ACTION ON MOTHERS' QUESTIONNAIRE
EXPLORATION	
1. Mouthing	1. Suck block.
2. Simple manipulation	2. Hold spoon and look at it.
NONSYMBOLIC	
3. Unitary functional	3. Turn wheel on toy car.
4. Inappropriate combinations	4. Put toy dish on car.
5. Combinations based on perception	5. Stack toy plates.
6. Combinations based on function	6. Put toy lid on teapot.
SYMBOLIC	
7. Self	7. Feed self with toy spoon
8. Agentive animate	8. Wash mom with toy sponge.
9. Agentive inanimate	9. Rock doll.
10. Sequenced self	10. Stir in toy cup, and eat from toy spoon.
11. Sequenced agentive animate	11. Pour into toy cup from toy teapot, and feed mom.
12. Sequenced agentive inanimate	12. Cover doll with blanket, and pat to sleep.
13. Vicarious	13. Make doll wave hi.
14. Self substitution	14. Use block as sponge and wash own face.
15. Agentive animate substitution	15. Put toy plate on mom's head as hat.
16. Agentive inanimate substitution	16. Use spoon as brush and brush doll's hair.
17. Sequenced vicarious	17. Make stuffed bear walk to toy car and drive away.
18. Sequenced self substitution	18. Stir in toy pot with comb as spoon, and eat from comb.
19. Sequenced agentive animate substitution	19. Wash mom with block, wipe her mouth with toy sponge.
20. Sequenced agentive inanimate substitution	20. Wash doll with block as sponge, and dry with towel.
21. Vicarious substitution	21. Make toy person drive away in nesting cup as car.
22. Sequenced vicarious substitution	22. Put toy bib on doll as coat, and make her walk.
23. Self-removed	23. Make one doll kiss another doll.
24. Emotive	24. Make doll fall down and cry.

Source: Infant Behavior and Development (1994), What do mothers know about the developmental nature of play? pp. 341–345, Table 1.

the make-believe attitude through play signals is an important accomplishment and is a forerunner to later play development.

Social features of play during infancy and toddlerhood involve an interaction with an accommodating play partner. This is usually a parent or an older sibling, a relative, or an unrelated but familiar older child or adult. The infant and this other person become engaged with each other, attending to and responding to the other. From this mutual engagement comes alternating turns—waiting for the partner to perform an act before reciprocating. Communicational signals such as standing up, shaking a toy, or waving arms often show that one is waiting for a turn.

As the work cited earlier by Damast et al. (1996) would suggest, usually the infant or toddler plays with others who are aware of the child's limitations and abilities and who help assure that the play flows smoothly. Repetition extends the sequence of interaction and maintains mutual engagement and attention. These playful early interactions provide the foundation for social development in general, and social play development in particular. The purpose behind these early games, routines, or exchanges is simply to be involved in a social interaction with another person.

Researchers have concluded that play with objects is a major factor in the development of social play during infancy and toddlerhood (Mueller & Lucas, 1975). Toys can serve as "social butter," facilitating interactions particularly between peers who, unlike adults, are unable or unwilling to make special accommodations or concessions to keep play going. Toys often serve as entry mechanisms as two toddlers go from parallel to interactive play. Toys mediate social interaction. Another view is that social interaction increases in its sophistication as a result of accumulating social experiences and that the use of toys with other people is but a by-product of this experience-based increase in sophistication. Studies of social play during the second year of life suggest that children progress to more advanced forms of social play through both the use of toys with peers and other interactions with peers (Jacobson, 1981).

During the preschool years, we witness continued increases in interactive play skills as children mature and gain experiences in a variety of social situations. Although there has been general agreement on this point since Parten's (1932) classic observational studies showing a progression from solitary (2 to $2\frac{1}{2}$ years) to parallel ($2\frac{1}{2}$ to $3\frac{1}{2}$ years) to associative ($3\frac{1}{2}$ to $4\frac{1}{2}$ years) to cooperative ($4\frac{1}{2}$ years) play, recent studies have questioned the developmental status of solitary and parallel play and have shed some doubts on the validity of Parten's stages, asking whether it is even helpful to picture changes in play in such broad terms, and recommending a finer analysis of play changes in specific social situations.

In a longitudinal study of social play during the preschool years, Smith (1978) found that while many children followed the trend suggested by Parten, others did not. Older children alternated between solitary and interactive play as they outgrew a tendency to engage in simple side-by-side or parallel play. In fact, with development comes an increasing capacity to use parallel

Parallel play occurs when children are close to each other and engage in similar activities but do not interact socially.

play strategically to initiate or terminate play with particular play partners (Bakeman & Brownlee, 1980). Other researchers have reported that perhaps parallel and not solitary play is the least mature social form of play (Moore, Evertson, & Brophy, 1974; Rubin, 1982; Rubin, Maioni, & Hornung, 1976).

Howes and Matheson (1992) followed 48 children longitudinally from infancy through preschool, focusing on social-play development and social pretend-play development. Beginning when the children were 13–15 months of age, the children were observed at their centers during free play every 6 months, on two consecutive days by two observers, which yielded 4 hours of observational data per child at each time of measurement. Observations were coded using a system for observing and coding the social play of toddlers and preschool children, which had been originally developed by Carollee Howes (1980). This system, described in Chapter 8, was revised to include two measures of social pretend play: cooperative social pretend play and complex social pretend play, with the latter marked by the appearance of metacommunication about the play (Howes, Unger, & Seidner, 1989).

The Howes and Matheson results showed that parallel play and parallel aware play (levels one and two) decreased over time, and that complementary and reciprocal social play, cooperative pretend play, and complex pretend play increased over time (levels four and five). Level three, simple social play, did not vary as a function of age. Emergence of higher play forms were perfectly consistent; not a single child reversed the sequence of the five levels in the Howes scale. In this study, 33% of the children did not exhibit any complex social pretend play until after their fourth birthday. There were stable individual differences reported—those children who showed earlier signs of high play levels when they were younger had higher play levels when they were older. For example, children who engaged in a higher proportion of cooperative social pretend play at age 30–35 months had earlier emergence and a greater proportion of complex social pretend play at 44–60 months.

Howes's system analyzes social play, particularly parallel play, in a more fine-grained manner than Parten's original formulation of parallel play. Table 3.2 presents categories of social play developed by various authors, including Howes. Howes's system is recommended and detailed further in Chapter 8 which discusses play observation and assessment.

In a provocative conceptual analysis of the early precursors of the development of peer social play, Whaley (1990) inverted the original Howes's scales in discussing changes in mother–child social play during the first years of the child's life. According to Whaley's analysis—which is supported by research, as well as by relevant theory on attachment (Winnicott, 1971)—the starting point for mothers and infants resemble Howes's fifth stage, and the end point for the dyad is like Howes's first stage! At first, the mother–child "play dance" is highly fused, with a great deal of support and scaffolding by the mother to maintain the play bout. The mother and infant are in a relative state of undifferentiation, akin to peers who are playing intently on a cooperative level (Stage 5 on the Howes Peer Play Scale). Progressively, the mother does less and less as a way of better accommodating the increasing play skills of the developing child, giving the child more psychological space by separating and engaging the child in a more parallel play fashion, which then resembles the lower levels of the Howes Peer Play Scale. Whaley's proposed developmental sequence of infant–adult social play, which *reverses* the peer play scale of Howes (1980), captures an important essence of the transition from the child's primary socialization system of the family into the secondary socialization system of peers.

DEVELOPMENT OF OBJECT PLAY

The typical kindergarten child shows a great deal of versatility in using objects during play. The typically developing child is able to use tools, participate in supervised cooking activities, and create elaborate constructions from blocks and other materials. The child can finish rather complicated puzzles and can display considerable problem-solving strategies using objects in play. Furthermore, these skills are frequently exhibited in social settings requiring additional capabilities. Such behavior reflects and requires considerable development—cognitive, social, affective, physical, and linguistic. How does the kindergarten child obtain this level of proficiency in using objects?

Table 3.2 Categories of Social Play

Parten (1932) Developmental stage	Erikson (1950) Categories refer to broad stages of development	Seagoe (1970) Play report based on structured interviews with child
Solitary play—plays alone and independently; different activity; no reference to others	*Autocosmic*—world of self; explores own body and the body of mother; repetition of activity	*Informal–individual*—self-directed; not imitative of adults; not formally patterned
Parallel play—plays independently but near or among others; similar toys or activities; beside but not with	*Microcosmic*—world of small, manageable toys and objects; solitary play; pleasure derived from mastery of toys	*Adult-oriented*—adult-directed; formally patterned; not imitative of adult life
Associative play—plays with others; conversation is about common activity, but does not subordinate own interests to groups	*Macrocosmic*—world shared with others	*Informal–social*—self-directed; imitative of adult life; not formally patterned
Cooperative play—activity is organized; differentiation of roles; complementing actions		*Individual–competitive*—formally patterned; directed toward individual victory
		Cooperative–competitive—formally patterned toward team victory

Source: Based on Frost and Klein (1979).

IWANAGA (1973) *Categories pertain to how an individual child structures the play situation in regard to other children*	HOWES (1980) *Categories show increases in reciprocity, complexity of interaction within dyads*	HOWES & MATHESON (1992) *Categories show increases in reciprocity, complexity, and communication and metacommunication in dyads*
Independent—no involvement of peers in play	*Parallel–engaged*—in similar activities but not paying any attention to one another	*Parallel play*—in proximity and in similar activities but without notice or awareness of each other
Parallel play—with peers; undifferentiated roles; roles enacted independently; close physical proximity; awareness of activity of others	*Mutual regard*—similar activities plus eye contact and awareness of each other; no verbalization or other social bids	*Parallel aware play*—in proximity and in similar activities with eye contact and mutual awareness
Complementary—Differentiated roles, enacted independently; some cooperation but each child engages in a different activity; little adjustment to others' behavior	*Simple social*—similar activities along with social bids such as talking, smiling, offering toys	*Simple social play*—Engaged in similar activities with eye contact and presence of social bids—talking, giving, holding, etc.
Integrative—roles enacted interactively; intense awareness of others; adjustment of behavior to shifts in others' complementary roles	*Complementary*—collaborating in the same activity with mutual awareness but no social bids	*Complementary and reciprocal play*—Presence of social bids plus "action-based role reversals," e.g., hide-and-seek, run-and-chase.
	Complementary reciprocal—collaborating in the same activity with social bids	*Cooperative social play*—Enactment of organized constructive or sociodramatic play with complementary roles and communication
		Complex social play—Engagement in organized constructive or dramatic play with play communication and communication about the play or metacommunication

As we saw in Chapter 1, the arousal-modulation theory of play focuses on motivating factors inherent in the external world, which prompt the child to play. This theory is particularly useful for understanding play with objects in a particular situation at a given time. Stimulus properties such as novelty, complexity, and manipulability motivate the child to interact with objects. This interaction can take several forms. For example, based on Berlyne's work on arousal and motivation, Hutt (1966), distinguishes between exploring and playing with objects. *Exploration* occurs when the child seemingly asks the question "What does this object do?"; *play* happens when the child seemingly asks the question "What can I do with this object?" In either case, there is intrinsic motivation to learn about objects and what can be done to or with them. Important behavioral changes occur in how objects are used in exploration and in play during the first 6 years of life.

How many objects are played with at one time and how they are played with are two dimensions of object play that have been investigated developmentally. Quality of play has been judged according to how discriminant, sequenced, and appropriate the activity is. Object play has been studied in children before and after the emergence and consolidation of children's symbolic capacities, thus making it important to distinguish between presymbolic object play and symbolic object play.

During the first months after birth, there are great changes in how babies play with objects. The newborn is equipped with reflexes and sensory capacities but does not know how to play with objects. Play actions develop as a result of experience. There is widespread agreement that object play during the first year progresses from repetitious and undifferentiated activity to more organized and sequenced action patterns. Piaget (1962) traced the development of presymbolic or mastery or exercise play while advancing his theories about cognitive development during the sensorimotor period. For Piaget, objects direct the infant's actions at first and then come under the control of the infant—providing the child with an opportunity to employ action schemes. Infants repeat actions on objects and generalize these actions to other objects. Piaget uses two categories of assimilation: (1) *reproductive* or *functional* (repeating actions on an object) and (2) *generalizing* (extending these actions to additional objects) to describe this behavior. While not goal directed, these early behaviors are pleasurable, and they define the essence of play for Piaget. During the second year, the child is able to construct new schemes from combinations of past experiences. Ritualization and conventional uses of objects increase in frequency.

Rosenblatt (1977) has described major shifts in how infants and toddlers use objects between their first and second years. The use of single objects decreases in frequency. Whereas the child less than 1 year old typically uses only one toy at a time in an unpredictable manner, the child older than 1 year of age is much more likely to use many objects in play. In addition, the toddler uses toys in a much more predictable way. That is, the toddler uses toys in appropriate or stereotypic ways, paying greater attention to the physical characteristics of playthings and showing knowledge of how different objects are used in daily life.

Several researchers have investigated the developmental transition of object play into symbolic play or presymbolic to symbolic action schemes. For example, Fenson, Kagan, Kearsley, and Zelazo (1976) compared the object play of 9½-, 13½-, and 18½-month-old children. Motor schemes such as mouthing and banging objects predominated in the youngest infants. By 13½ months, infants used objects functionally, grouping or sorting similar objects and making simple pretenses that were self-directed. Like Piaget, these researchers concluded that object play in infancy becomes decentered and more integrated. They also found an increase in combinational play and change from functional or motor use of objects to conventional applications.

Similarly, in Belsky and Most's (1981) study of 7- to 21-month-old children, the authors noted consistent developmental trends in exploratory and manipulative play behaviors. Tasting, mouthing, and handling of materials were replaced as children matured with *correct functional play* (e.g., pushing a toy car along the floor). Then came *enactive naming* (i.e., giving names to things), *pretending with self,* and *pretending with others.*

Social environmental factors influence play development. For example, Tamis-LeMonda and Bornstein (1991) in a longitudinal study examined the nonsymbolic and symbolic play of mothers and toddlers in the home setting, at toddler ages 13 months and 20 months. Mother and child play were correlated in these dyadic free-play interactions ($N = 45$). There was considerable variability in patterns of behavior. Slightly over half the sample of toddlers ($N = 23$) showed increases in symbolic play, contingent on maternal symbolic play. Transitional behavior between nonsymbolic and symbolic (e.g., puts telephone receiver to ear without vocalization) was commonplace at 13 months (44%) and at 20 months (57%). This study suggests that children's maturing play behaviors and cognitions are mediated by their more mature partners' promotion of play.

During the preschool years, object play progresses from the simple to the complex, as children gain increasing ability to order objects and actions in time and space. Smilansky (1968), influenced by Piaget (1962), has defined two types of play: functional and constructive. Together, they are the dominant cognitive forms of play involving objects during the preschool years. *Functional play* refers to manipulative play, motor exercise with or without objects, or the use of objects in a stereotyped manner. This form of play decreases as children develop. *Constructive play* is organized, goal-oriented play and increases in frequency as the child matures. For instance, Hutt et al. (1989) reported that 3-year-old children often engaged in playing with water and dry sand in an active and functional way, at best; they often performed uncontrolled actions such as splashing. Four-year-olds often simply avoided these materials and younger playmates when this happened, preferring instead more productive activity. An interesting example of this contrast, 4-year-olds used only half the number of brush strokes that 3-year-olds did while painting over a comparable period of time. By age 4, constructive play becomes the most prevalent form of play, occupying more than 50% of free time in preschool settings (Rubin et al., 1983).

The typical preschool classroom or child-care center is equipped with interest centers and other play areas designed to encourage more constructive and imaginative play by young children as they grow older. The simpler functional play is seen less and less. Preschoolers become increasingly capable of building complex structures and of producing recognizable products through drawing, painting, arranging designs, and making small constructions. Moreover, toys and play equipment and more recently computer-related activities (discussed in Chapter 10) are used more and more in preschools and child-care centers to challenge young children to interact creatively with the world of objects. Trageton (1997) proposes a general developmental shift from divergent types of play to convergent types of play. Constructive play of preschoolers transforms into arts and crafts creative play in primary school, just as their dramatic play transforms into drama and performing skits as they get older.

DEVELOPMENT OF SYMBOLIC PLAY

During the second year, as children begin their conventional uses of objects, their representational abilities emerge. There is a transition from the mastery play of the infant to the symbolic play of the preoperational child. The infant becomes able to evoke images or symbols derived from imitative activities. This enables the infant to engage in beginning pretense or make-believe play. This new ability is an outgrowth of the infant's use of objects and the adult–infant game and play routines previously discussed (Damast et al., 1996; Tamis-LeMonda & Bornstein, 1991). The origins of symbolic play are in the interpersonal context (e.g., Whaley, 1990) and in the individual context of the developing child's autonomous encounters with the physical world. Piagetian accounts of the origins of symbolic play, while stressing the latter, also include the former.

Children's earliest symbolic transformations involve realistic toys that closely resemble their real-life counterparts.

Piaget (1962) discusses the relationship between mastery play and symbolic play: "In mastery play the schemas follow one another without any external aim. The objects to which they are applied are no longer a problem, but merely serve as an opportunity for activity. This activity is no longer an effort to learn, it is only a happy display of known actions" (1962, p. 93). "In pretense the child is using schemes which are familiar, and for the most part already ritualized games . . . but (1) instead of using them in the presence of objects to which they are usually applied, the child assimilates to them new objectives unrelated to them from the point of view of effective adaptation; (2) these new objects, instead of resulting merely in an extension of the schema (as is the case in the generalization proper to intelligence), are used with no other purpose than that of allowing the subject to mime or evoke the schemas in question. It is the union of these two conditions—applications of schema to inadequate objects and evocation for pleasure—which characterizes the beginning of pretence" (1962, p. 97).

Piaget (1962) defined three kinds of symbolic play. The first type involves the application of one symbolic scheme to new objects. For example, a child says "cry, cry" to a doll and imitates the sound. What is imitated is taken from the child's own experience. This represents the emergence of symbolic play. The second type involves again only one symbolic scheme, but an object may be substituted for another or the child may act like another person or object. Imitated behaviors are borrowed from other models. For example, the child pretends to shave like daddy. The third kind of symbolic play involves planned combinations of symbolic schemes and a sequence or pattern of behavior. For example, a child takes a doll on a stroller ride, saying, "You see this, you see that." According to Piaget's theory, during the preschool years, there is a continuing trend toward more coherent and orderly symbolic play, often resulting in a replication of reality that is, most important, performed in a social context (termed "collective symbolism"). Piaget's general account covering individual and social factors in symbolic-play ontogeny has inspired many researchers who have sought to understand the origin and development of nonsocial and social pretense during the early years. Dimensions or components of symbolic play studied include (a) pretend actions and objects and (b) role enactments and themes.

PRETEND ACTIONS AND OBJECTS

Researchers of infant and toddler play—such as Bornstein and O'Reilly (1993), Fenson et al. (1976), Lowe (1975), Rosenblatt (1977), and Watson and Jackowitz (1984)—have traced the development of presymbolic action schemes. Play becomes less imitative and more generative. Sequences of actions in pretending are analyzed in terms of agent and object substitutions. Infants as young as 12 months have been observed engaging in the simplest type of pretend play involving self as agent.

Examples of the earliest forms of this behavior include pretending to be sleeping, drinking, eating, or talking on the phone. In pretending to sleep, for instance, the infant does not merely touch its head to a pillow. Instead, the behavior seems to replicate in gestures the fine details of such behaviors as they would occur in ordinary life. The behaviors are not related to real needs and are not characterized by confusion or overgeneralization. Instead, the behaviors are selective and representative of customary practices but are independent of needs. During the second year of life, the toddler becomes increasingly able to pretend and uses a variety of substitute objects (such as a toy banana or a block for a telephone). These simple pretense activities, although unrelated to real needs or wishes, are all self-directed. Thus, they do not represent genuine symbolic play, according to Piaget (1962).

It is only after the child is capable of outer-directed symbolic activities, at around 18 months of age, that we see genuine symbolic play sequences unfold, according to Piaget's meaning of the term. Here, the child can make a mother or a doll pretend to drink from a cup or talk on the phone. Transformation of so-called recipient objects (telephone, banana, block) occurs developmentally before the ability to transform agents of pretending (e.g., self as agent, mother as agent, doll as agent). Within each type of transformation, it is important to note the level of symbolic substitutions required to judge the relative difficulty of the pretend act (Watson & Jackowitz (1984). Self as agent and a realistic or representational toy such as a prototypical toy phone as the recipient object are simplest, in that no real transformation is needed.

The form and function of substitute objects, as opposed to each real object, are important to note to judge further the complexity of the pretend actions. For example, a toy banana has a shape similar to that of a toy phone handset, suggesting its use as a substitute object for the phone. Substituting a toy car for a toy phone would clearly be a greater symbolic leap because of dissimilarity in both shape and intended function. A third dimension that determines the difficulty of the pretend act is the content of the objects and actions. Jackowitz and Watson (1980) suggest that real telephones may be off limits to children in some homes, and hence, pretend play with phones may be inhibited in the same children who may find pretending with cups and dolls relatively easy. Social conventions that promote sex-typing of toys may be viewed in this vein as limiting the play development of children, as we explain in Chapter 4.

In summary, pretend action ranges in degree of difficulty, according to the type of object transformation, level of transformation, and content. Self-directed or self-as-agent behaviors are the first signs of symbolic play in infancy (pretending to eat, talk on a phone, put on a hat, drink from a cup). Outer-directed pretense occurs when other objects or persons are made the agent of the pretend actions performed on different recipient objects—for example, pretending that toy cows are eating straw. Within both agent and recipient object transformation, transforming things similar to or not conflicting with the thing (either in appearance or intended use) is an easier task for the child than transforming things dissimilar to or conflicting with the real object. The nature or content of the pretend play is the third factor to consider to determine whether the child has had positive or negative experiences with the objects involved, which would either facilitate or inhibit the pretend play actions.

Thus far, we have kept to single pretend-play actions or simple combinations. The older infant or toddler becomes able to engage in more complicated and involved pretend-play sequences (Piaget's third type of symbolic play) in which actions are linked meaningfully while objects are used conventionally and consistently (Fenson et al., 1976). During the second and third years of life, the child is able to perform two or more consecutive acts that reflect a similar theme or topic, such as pretending to serve tea to dolls or teddy bears seated around a table. A child may at first place each cup on a saucer, then put a spoon in a cup, then pour tea from the pot into the cup, and then place the cup in front of one of the dolls. The variety and diversity of such pretend-action sequences increase as the child leaves toddlerhood. The content of such play is always familiar and comfortable for the child, and the child usually does not interact with a playmate in any reciprocal sense. However, the play can and often does involve a teacher, parent, or other older person who is able and willing to adjust to the child's needs for support and scaffolding of the make-believe experience; these experiences, taken together as we have implied, can be viewed as a critical foundation rock for social competence and, indeed, for the child's later mental health.

A good review of early symbolic play development is available in a *Young Children* "Research in Review" article by Jean Gowen (1995). Her review of research supports our claim that the child's maturation, the individual child's actions on the physical world, and social action all have a role in the emergence and consolidation of symbolic play. Vygotsky's (1978) constructs of the zone of proximal development and the importance of the interpersonal sphere for development (i.e., the interpersonal becomes intrapersonal) are stressed. Nine categories or stages in the development of symbolic play are given, based on her synthesis of the research literature (see Table 3.3, "Stages in the Development of Symbolic Play").

ROLE ENACTMENTS AND THEMES

Until now, we have been examining pretend-action–object development and have seen that it becomes more elaborate and organized as the child matures. During the third year, for most children, an important change occurs. The child engages in pretend activities while adopting the role of another person—a person with whom the child is intimately familiar. Typically, it is the child's mother or another primary caregiving or significant person. *Role enactment*, adopting the role of another, differs from the earlier pretend activities with objects, in that now the child is able to infer and imagine the role identity behind the pretend actions. This new capacity lends greater coherence, enjoyment, and meaning to the pretend activities of the child. The adoption of the role dictates and controls the actions. Role enactment guides the pretend play. The pretending that results is more planned and persistent.

Role enactment (role play) is significant because it indicates not only awareness of others but also the child's knowledge of role attributes, role relationships, and role-appropriate actions (Garvey, 1979). Role-enactment behaviors are influenced by cognitive development and by personality factors (see Chapter 4), as well as by the social situation—the other persons (children, as well as adults) who form part of the play or the events surrounding the play. Garvey and Berndt (1977) distinguish four types of roles: (1) *functional roles* (pseudo-role enactment), which are organized by an object or activity (e.g., pretending to cook dinner, triggered by the presence and use of a toy oven or mixing bowl); (2) *relational roles* (e.g., family roles that suggest real complements,

Table 3.3 STAGES IN THE DEVELOPMENT OF SYMBOLIC PLAY

CATEGORY	DESCRIPTION	EXAMPLES
Prepretense	Child engages in approximate pretense but gives no confirming evidence of pretense	Child briefly touches telephone to ear; briefly puts bottle to doll's mouth
Pretend self	Child engages in pretense behavior, directed toward self, in which pretense is apparent	Child raises cup to lip, tips cup, makes drinking sounds
Pretend other	Child engages in pretense behavior directed away from child toward other; pretends the behaviors of other people	Child feeds doll with toy baby bottle or cup; pushes truck on floor and makes truck noise
Substitution	Child uses an apparently meaningless object in a creative or imaginative manner, or uses an object in a pretense act in a way that differs from its usual use	Child feeds doll with block as "bottle" puts piece of play dough on plate and calls it a hamburger
Imaginary objects or beings	Child pretends that an object, substance, person, or animal is present	Child tips empty teapot over cup and says "coffee," child moves around the room making motor sounds, as though riding an imaginary motorcycle
Active agent	Child animates a toy (e.g., doll, toy animal) that represents a being so that toy becomes an active agent in the pretend activity	Child hops toy animal across rug as though it were running, puts doll's hand to its mouth as though it were feeding itself, talks in a high voice as though the doll were talking
Sequence, no story	Child repeats a single pretense act/scheme with multiple receivers	Child gives mother a drink from the cup, then gives doll a drink from the cup
Sequence story	Child uses more than one related scheme in pretense activity	Child stirs in cup, drinks from cup, and says "Mmmm, tastes good"
Planning	Child engages in pretend play preceded by evidence of planning	Child says that she will feed the baby before putting toy baby bottle to doll's mouth

Source: Gowen (1995).

such as mother–child, wife–husband); (3) *character roles*, which are either stereotypic (e.g., firefighter, witch) or fictional (characters with proper names such as Aquaman, Hercules, Megan, or the Big Bad Wolf); and (4) *peripheral roles*, which are discussed but not enacted (e.g., real or imaginary friends).

Role enactments typically suggest the theme of the play episode. The development of symbolic play during the preschool years moves away from an exclusive preoccupation with highly familiar themes, such as playing house or doctor, and toward a greater interest in play themes that are more out of the ordinary. Over time, children become more interested in enacting the roles of characters from fiction, as opposed to familiar occupational roles. Potential themes for role enactments become more numerous as children begin to possess greater linguistic and cognitive abilities and social cognitive abilities and social skills, as well as greater knowledge about the world they live in—both the real world of everyday living and the events transmitted through media, which children experience vicariously.

OTHER ASPECTS AND CONSIDERATIONS

The end point of symbolic-play development is seen in the older preschool child, who is able to imagine with no objects at all, who is versatile in improvising with props and substitute objects of all types, and who can evoke imaginary situations through words. High levels of symbolic development are seen in the child's being able to take on a variety of diverse roles in collaboration with peers (Goncu, 1993), engaging innovatively and with great enjoyment in socio-dramatic and fantasy themes, ranging from the most commonplace to the most extraordinary. Concentration, persistence, attention to detail, and seeing the play episode as a whole are other manifestations of symbolic development.

Metacommunication, improvisation, and multivocality (i.e., speaking in different 'voices') characterize complex social pretense (Howes & Matheson, 1992; Sawyer, 1997). Children at this level will repeat play sequences or start them over again to make them follow a plan. Children commonly talk about their imaginative play, decision making about props and space markers, role negotiations, and the like. Interest grows in directing and codirecting a play sequence while playing and coplaying the roles in front of real and imagined audiences. Children engaged in complex social play have been characterized by Sawyer (1997) as an improvisational jazz band, fitting in and doing one's thing simultaneously, applying different voices in their play—actor's voice, political voice, director's voice, and so on.

Finally, concerns with reality and peer pressure reduce overt make-believe play, as children move toward an interest in games with rules, sports, arts and crafts, and other activities appropriate for school-age children. Piaget (1962) and Singer (1973), among others, speculate that overt make-believe play goes underground and becomes internalized at this stage of development. There is the speculation that a residual of the preschooler's earlier active fantasy social life persists in exerting a beneficial influence on the child's creativity, imagination, divergent thinking, and operational thinking abilities. Decentration and the duality of pretend play and operational thought and social reciprocity all seem interconnected, as discussed in Chapter 2. Moreover, as we show later in this chapter, continuing outlets for make-believe play exist in the form of videogames and the like for the older child. The disappearance (or "going underground," if you will) of overt pretense may be an artifact of the location of one's play observations—in classrooms and on school playgrounds, overt pretense play may be missing or reduced drastically, but not at home or in the neighborhood.

DEVELOPMENT OF MOTOR PLAY

By their sixth birthday, children possess considerable motor-play skill. They may be a far cry from Olympic champions who have reached a zenith in the development of gross- and fine-motor strength and coordination, but children have progressed a great deal since birth. They can ride bicycles, pull wagons, and construct snow forts. What are the motor-development milestones as children progress toward this level of maturity?

Newborns possess rudimentary grasping movements; they can blink and throw out their arms. Newborns also possess a number of motor reflexes, such as the rooting reflex. That reflex is evoked by touching the baby on the cheek near the mouth, causing the baby's head to turn in that direction. Motor abilities of newborns form two general categories: (1) the general ability to move body parts in an uncoordinated and random way (waving arms or turning the head), and (2) the automatic and involuntary swift and finely coordinated reflexes. Healthy human babies progress to gain even better control over their bodies, enabling them to be upright, mobile, and able to explore their surroundings. Often, while there is considerable individual variation in the rate of development, the order of acquisition seems fairly constant.

From ages 1 to 3 months, infants become able to lift their chins and heads while lying on their stomachs. At ages 4–6 months, infants gain control over their neck muscles and can pull themselves into a sitting position, with head remaining erect. The body trunk obtains more muscle control, and at age 6–7 months, infants can sit up for a minute or so.

In the second half of the first year, considerable motor development takes place. Many babies begin to stand, holding onto supports such as chairs; they can roll and repeat actions. (As we discussed earlier, playful repetition is significant in many play theories.) Infants play by themselves with body parts and objects. From age 7 months on, infants begin to have some mobility. From a prone position, they can wiggle forward. As babies approach their first birthday, some can walk or stand alone and can easily pivot from side to side while sitting. After the first birthday, most begin walking. At first, they are shaky and fall frequently. They have to concentrate on what they are doing. Very soon, though, they can walk without having this motor skill be the focal point of their awareness. They can use this new skill as a means to other ends, such as reaching places and exploring objects. By age 2 years, the toddler can run. The sequence of major motor milestones in becoming mobile from birth up to age 2 includes crawling, creeping or the bear walk, standing, walking, and running.

Progress in gross-motor behavior involved in sitting and walking is accompanied by steady improvement in hand skills. To be able to grasp and manipulate objects requires considerable fine-motor or small-muscle strength and coordination. At birth, there is virtually no small-muscle control. During the first month of life, the limbs, including fingers, act in unison, much like a fin. Even at age 1 month, infants cannot grasp objects in front of them. In the second month, they might hold an object, but only briefly.

Babies begin to pick up objects at ages 4 through 6 months, with great effort, often using two hands to trap an object. When they hold a small object, it is often between fingers. By the seventh month, objects are held between the thumb and several fingers; in the eighth month, babies can transfer objects from hand to hand. Hand skills involving grasping and manipulation make play with objects possible and also help babies acquire informal, practical, or intuitive understandings of objects, actions, three-dimensional space, and cause–effect relations. From ages 1 to 2 years, then, infants can walk well and even run, and they can turn a few pages of a large picture book.

During toddlerhood (ages 2–3 years), there is continual motor-play development. This is evinced both in gross-motor activity involving large objects and use of large muscles for mobility and in fine-motor activity involving hand muscles, hand–eye coordination, and the use of small objects. During this period, the child walks easily, runs, needs no help in going up or down stairs, and can hold a cup in one hand and a cookie in the other. All of this motor progression depends on physical development, experience, and practice. Motor play occurs in play with objects, people, and symbols.

Preschoolers from 3 to 4 years of age demonstrate further developmental progression in motor/physical skills and motor play. They can walk and run easily, surely, and with good balance. They can tiptoe and stand on one foot. Tricycle riding and playing with other vehicles gives them great pleasure. In climbing stairs, children at this age can put one foot on each step. From 4 to 5 years old, children achieve further motor mastery, allowing for greater varieties of play. They can skip, climb, hop, and run. They enjoy chasing games and almost any kind of athletic activity, including rough-and-tumble play. Some children are even able to ride a small bicycle equipped with supportive training wheels. Children can button clothing and put puzzles and simple constructions together.

From 5 to 6 years of age, further physical development makes possible new forms of motor play—jumping rope, doing acrobatics, and performing trapeze tricks. Because their fine-muscle development has advanced, children can string beads, cut, trace, draw, and paste. Many children can use a knife, although they cannot cut very well.

Motor play often occurs with the other forms of play. It overlaps with object play to a great extent. Nonetheless, it is more distinct in play that involves only body parts—such as in running, hopping, and skipping. In this case, a body part becomes an "object" of play.

Rough-and-tumble play is motor play that overlaps with social play. In rough-and-tumble play, parts of the bodies of playmates and the actions of playmates become a focal object of play. Rough-and-tumble play as a special subcategory of motor play also overlaps with symbolic play or pretense. That is, rough-and-tumble play is play fighting, not actual fighting. In rough-and-tumble play, children engage in a form of make-believe in which the body parts and actions of themselves and others take on a symbolic significance, which becomes the object of play. This form of play aggression may involve physical movements such as mock wrestling, running, chasing/fleeing, kicking, pouncing, piling on, pushing, open-hand hitting, and poking, as well as loud noises (Sutton-Smith, Gerstmyer, & Meckley, 1988). In the play aggression or rough-and-tumble play episode, typically several children are involved, and there are role reversals—from being the bad guy to being the good guy to being the bad guy again, allowing children to share powerful roles, as well as being the hapless victim (Pellegrini, 1991). Gender differences are sharp, as is discussed in Chapter 4. Criticisms of rough-and-tumble play are discussed in the accompanying sidebar, "Rough and-tumble Play: Some Issues."

Theory in Action

ROUGH-AND-TUMBLE PLAY: SOME ISSUES

Why do many teachers frown on rough-and-tumble play and even forbid it? After all, many researchers who have studied the phenomenon suggest that this form of play is valuable in many ways. For one thing, physical contact is important to young children. They need a chance to exercise and release energy. Second, because rough-and-tumble play occurs with other children, it is a form of social communication. It has been noted that rough-and-tumble play is instrumental in children's learning to handle feelings. Children filter out negative from positive feelings and learn to control impulses so as to be able to participate appropriately within a group. Furthermore, pretense saturates the phenomenon. Rough-and-tumble play is play fighting, not real fighting. One special value of this form of play, then, may be that children so engaged, although perhaps especially tempted to cross over the threshold into real fighting, usually hold back because of peer pressure. Why, then, is this not good for children? What are the objections, if any?

First of all, criticisms of rough-and-tumble play often arise because of failure to adequately define the phenomenon. Many researchers have linked inappropriate acts of aggression with playful aggression to create composite categories, which then invariably show that children who engage in rough-and-tumble play are also unpopular with their peers and seem to be deficient in social skills. However, when rough-and-tumble play is distinguished from real fighting or from physical exercise play in general, the behavior can be judged more positively. That is, when properly defined, rough-and-tumble play does not appear to lead to statistically significant negative behavior. Such play may even have some developmental virtue.

Nevertheless, many teachers no doubt will remain unconvinced that such play has value. Some may even hold the view that it is downright unethical to permit, let alone encourage, rough-and-tumble play in young children. Why? The most common answer tends to be that one cannot take any chances that play fighting might turn into real fighting. Accidents can easily happen. Children may fall onto a hard or sharp object and hurt themselves, or they may unintentionally hurt another child. Thus, it is much wiser to forbid rough-and-tumble play.

Second, many teachers hold to an implicit threshold theory. Sooner or later, children will begin fighting seriously as the intensity increases. As an illustration, Tim, John, and Paul were observed recently in the block area, wrestling and roughhousing, playing "Power Rangers." During one episode, Tim's arm unintentionally swung and hit Paul on the nose, hurting him. To retaliate, Paul deliberately poked Tim hard, and John joined in creating a fracas. The teacher quickly separated the children.

(continued)

Theory in Action *(continued)*

A third reason teachers object to rough-and-tumble play is that it symbolizes violent acts of aggression and thereby goes against many teachers' accepted values. Thus, for the same reason teachers outlaw toy guns and knives in their classrooms, they forbid play fighting. As such actions and objects are desensitizers to violence (making aggression seem more natural or commonplace), teachers certainly do not want children exposed to such influences, just as they do not approve of children's exposure to acts of violence in the media.

To summarize, we have surveyed some important findings from research and some important theoretical ideas about developmental trends in play from birth to age 6 years. We examined trends in social, object, symbolic, and motor play. Table 3.4 depicts some specific behaviors teachers and parents can look for to trace development in each of these four related categories of play.

PLAY DEVELOPMENT FROM AGES 6 TO 8 YEARS

Considerable play development continues in the social, object, symbol, and motor domains beyond the preschool years. Developmentally giant strides are being made from 6 to 8 years of age in children's social and cognitive competence; their ability to regulate attention, activity, and affect; and their capacity to engage in sustained high-level play episodes alone or with others. As the social ecology of the home becomes ever more meshed with the cultures of school, child care, and various neighborhood and community institutions, new play and recreation possibilities open up and are supported. (See the accompanying sidebar, "European Research on Play Behavior.")

SOCIAL DOMAIN

Children in this age group normally possess considerable skill in social interaction. Their levels of social cognitive abilities enable them to take the perspective of others in terms of perceptions, thoughts, intentions, and feelings. Impulse control and the ability to plan and delay gratification are better established, and children usually have more differentiated self-concepts, leading to more social competence and more mature friendship relations, compared to when they were younger. Their social play is characterized by more intimate peer relations, as well as enhanced group membership. There is a rampant rise in peer-group formations during these so-called "bubblegum years" (Thornburg, 1979).

Children typically navigate a more complex social world, interacting with a wider range of people in diverse roles. They often engage in some

Table 3.4   PLAY DEVELOPMENT PROGRESS SCALE

MANIPULATION/CONSTRUCTIVE	SYMBOLIC
1. Plays with body parts (fingers, toes)	1. Imitates in play: (a) imitates sounds; (b) imitates gestures; (c) imitates facial expressions; (d) deferred imitation (imitates words/actions that have been heard/seen previously)
2. Swipes at objects playfully	2. Uses sounds in play
3. Plays with other person's body parts (face, hair)	3. Uses words in play
4. Plays with water	4. Make-believe use of objects, ascribing meaning to objects (e.g., block becomes truck, clothespin becomes doll)
5. Obtains objects in play	5. Functional use of symbolic toys (phones, cars, dolls, tea sets, etc.)
6. Releases objects in play	6. Acting out make-believe situations using adult clothes
7. Brings both hands together, such as in clapping or banging objects together	7. Acting out single make-believe events (as drinking cup of tea, driving car down road)
8. Repeats actions that affect environment (e.g., hits object that makes noise)	8. Acting out make-believe situations (sequence of events) (one role for less than 5 minutes) (having a tea party, driving around town to store or gas station, etc.)
9. Stacks objects	9. Acting out make-believe situations (one role for more than 5 minutes)

SOCIAL	PHYSICAL
1. Touches image in mirror	1. Sits without support while playing
2. Smiles at image in mirror	2. Stands alone well while playing
3. Laughs during play	3. Crawls or creeps
4. Participates in social games (e.g., pat-a-cake, peekaboo)	4. Walks well during play
5. Solitary independent play (the child plays alone and independently with toys that differ from those used by the children within speaking distance and makes no effort to get close to other children)	5. Throws ball overhead
6. Independently plays with toys for 15–30 minutes	6. Climbs in and out of adult chair
7. Parallel play (independently but the activity chosen naturally brings the child among other children; play with toys that are like those the other children are using, but the child plays with the toy as he or she sees fit and does not try to influence or modify the activity of the nearby children, with the exception of taking toys away)	7. Kicks ball forward
8. Associative play (The child plays with other children. Interest is as much in association with other children as it is in the objects used in the activity. There is communication. Children engage in a common activity. There is no organization of the activity of several individuals around a common goal or product.)	8. Makes whole-body rhythmic response to music
9. Cooperative couples play (Two children organize around a common goal or product. These common goals may be dramatic situations, competitive and non-competitive games, and/or making material products. The efforts of one child are supplemented by those of another.)	9. Pedals tricycle

(continued)

Table 3.4   *(Continued)*

MANIPULATION/CONSTRUCTIVE	SYMBOLIC
10. Scribbles spontaneously	10. Acting out make-believe situations (plot line organized)
11. Pulls toys	11. Acting out make-believe stories (plot line organized)
12. Empties containers	12. Make-believe play with other children
13. Organizes objects in rows	13. Child requests to play with another child
14. Manipulates sand (filling, patting, smoothing, piling, dumping)	14. Bragging and name calling
15. Plays with puzzles: (a) piece form board (circle, triangle, square); (b) 4 pieces, which are separate (nontouching); (c) 4 pieces, which are touching; (d) 7 pieces, which are touching; (e) 12 pieces, which are touching	15. Plays with one person frequently and refers to him or her as best friend
16. Fills containers	16. Observes rules and takes turns in games
17. Puts on lids in play	
18. Clay: (a) clay is crudely shaped, squeezed, and rolled; (b) uses tools with clay; (c) simple representation through clay and/or sand (constructs recognizable object and/or labels object)	
19. Blocks: (a) constructions without representations; (b) constructions with representation	
20. Scissors: (a) tears with scissors; (b) snips; (c) cuts on line: (d) cuts out simple shape; (e) cuts out picture except for small details	
21. Simple representation through drawing or painting (draws recognizable picture and/or labels picture)	
22. Results of a play construction become important	
23. Makes craft assemblies	
24. Uses coloring books (coloring in lines)	
25. Uses stencils and tracing	

Source: Golden and Kutner (1980).

SOCIAL	PHYSICAL
10. Cooperative group play (Three or more children organize around a common goal or product. These common goals may be dramatic situations, competitive and non-competitive games, and/or making materials or products. The efforts of one child are supplemented by those of another.)	10. Jumps in place (both feet off ground)
11. Share while playing	11. Jumps from a chair 10 inches high
12. Can wait turn while playing	12. Catches a large ball
13. Performs for others	13. Runs easily (without falling)
	14. Climbs ladder on low play equipment
	15. Jumps rope (two or more consecutive jumps)
	16. Daredevil play (somersaults, jumping, swinging, skating, jungle-gym play)

Theory in Action

EUROPEAN RESEARCH ON PLAY BEHAVIOR

A great deal of research and theory on play continues in Europe but seldom reaches American shores. Nevertheless, our theories and concepts about play are heavily influenced by European tradition. Many of the major modern play theorists from Europe—such as Freud, Erikson, and Piaget—are well acknowledged, but others—such as Buhler and Chateau—remain less well known on this side of the Atlantic. Play-behavior categories derived from European theory sometimes are unfamiliar to American audiences. For example, another name for role play is *fiction play*. Another name for functional play is *repetition play*. Construction play has been called *material-formation play*. Object or other-person transformation pretense (e.g., playing with a stuffed animal or a pet animal as a good friend) is referred to as *illusion play* by some European play scholars. In this chapter, we used the term *reception play*, which is uncommon here; this term is common in Europe.

In 1959, the International Council for Children's Play (I.C.C.P.) was launched in Ulm, Germany, devoted to research on children's play and toys. Biennial meetings have been held ever since, bringing together researchers from around the world. An illustration of current research from Europe on the topic of the development of play is work done by one of the founders and leaders of I.C.C.P.

Rimmert van der Kooij (1998) reports descriptive cross-sectional data showing the percentage of different kinds of play or nonplay activity occuring from 3 to 9 years of age (see Table 3.5). In this study, the 3-, 4-, and

Table 3.5   INDIVIDUAL PLAY BEHAVIOR (IN % OF PLAYING TIME) AT DIFFERENT AGE LEVELS

AGE	*N*	I	II	III	IV	V	VI
3;0	29	0.8	1.6	64.2	29.3	3.9	—
4;4	56	—	7.0	41.5	35.6	10.9	4.8
5;0	31	—	4.3	35.1	36.9	20.0	4.1
6;0	42	—	6.0	27.4	45.5	7.0	14.0
7;0	99	—	7.9	29.2	32.6	8.7	21.8
8;1	80	—	5.1	25.2	40.9	8.1	20.6
9;0	80	—	8.5	26.3	32.9	7.0	25.4

Note: Age = Years; months. N = Frequency. I = No play activity. II = Cleaning up. III = Repetition play. IV = Imitation play. V = Construction play. VI = Grouping play.

Source: R. van der Kooij (1998). Spiel (Play). In D.H. Rost, *Handwörtenbuch Pädagogische Psychologie* (Dictionary of Educational Psychology). Weinheim: Psychologie Verlags Union.

(continued)

5-year-olds were observed at home, while the remaining older children were observed in the play laboratory of Groningen University. A standard set of toys was used in both settings to determine the highest play form. Children of 5 years and older were observed for 1-minute intervals, using time sampling, for a total of 45 minutes. Younger children were observed for a total of 30 minutes, using 30-second samples. Independent observers agreed in 92% of the cases as to the kind of play or nonplay exhibited. The data shown in Table 3.5 reveal age differences. Repetition (functional) and construction (constructive) play declines with age, while grouping (cooperative) play increases. Imitation (symbolic, fantasy, fiction) play or role play stays fairly stable over the ages studied. Note that these findings differ from those of many American studies that have reported a decline in imitation play (i.e., pretend play). Perhaps this discrepancy can be traced to context variables (e.g., the laboratory setting used in van der Kooij's study) or to cultural differences.

group or organized play-related activity, such as classes on developing some physical or aesthetic ability (e.g., ballet, tap dance, ice skating, tennis, karate lessons, swimming, or gymnastics). Adult-supervised individual competition, as well as team competition, while often starting in the preschool years, becomes more prevalent as children enter elementary school. Little League baseball, Pop Warner football, hockey, soccer, and other adult-organized and adult-supervised group games enter the social landscape for children.

Adult involvement in organizing and structuring children's leisure time has been on the rise in today's postmodern society and has been the target of some sharp criticism (e.g., Elkind, 1994). For example, Elkind argues that many adults justify their intrusions into the lives of children by overestimating children's competence and underrating childhood as a time of innocence and freedom. He speculates, in his thoughtful and well-documented book, that many adults today are meeting their own needs more than children's needs through these forms of involvement. When an adult agenda is present and important (and events scheduled and structured accordingly), the experience for children may be at best an aberrant form of play—but one cannot question that the social lives and play of children are affected. Children's play activities away from adults require increasing independence and skills in getting along with peers.

OBJECT DOMAIN

Kindergarten and primary-grade schoolchildren's use of objects in play becomes increasingly complex and elaborate. Higher levels of constructive or product-oriented play or activity are exhibited as children work on different projects, either alone or with others in various settings, including home, school, or the community. Constructive play in this older age group is distinguished from the play of preschoolers, not only by its enhanced sophistication, but also by the higher levels of social collaboration and pretense. Moreover, older children at the kindergarten level, compared to preschoolers, more often build props and engage in elaborate planning and negotiation as a prelude to sociodramatic play, consuming considerable time and effort in setting the stage just right for playing a particular theme, such as playing grocery store or putting on a country fair.

Block play continues to be popular among children in this age group, who have mastered the use of toys such as Lego blocks, Lincoln Logs, and other assorted playthings, including activities with materials such as interlocking cogs, snapping together objects, pressing tubes or bricks together, and the like. Many children who are 7 and 8 years old enjoy tiny screws, nuts, and bolts, and playing with battery-powered construction sets (Goodson & Bronson, 1985). They are becoming increasingly scientific and experimental as they enter what Piaget calls the stage of concrete operational thinking and what Erikson calls the stage of industry. They classify objects, using multiple criteria in combination, and they measure and balance materials—and in general solve problems—in their object play. Children's use of objects and materials in building activities, experimentation, and problem solving at times assumes gamelike qualities, as well as being part of role playing.

SYMBOL DOMAIN

Pretense is a major form of play during childhood, emerging in the second year and increasing during the preschool years, reaching a high-water mark in 4- and 5-year-olds in a form of overt make-believe play called sociodramatic play. Typically, there are declines in overt social make-believe play after age 5 or 6 years, at least in the school classroom or on the school playground. In other social contexts, however, children remain keenly interested in imaginative play. They share make-believe in home and neighborhood settings and engage in various forms of related storytelling, with themes and content often related to the popular culture and the media (see Chapter 10, "Play and the Electronic Media"). This make-believe storytelling becomes a form of social glue that facilitates the formation of early peer groups during this age range (Singer & Singer, 1990).

Kindergartners and primary-grade schoolchildren show pretense play with richer texts, more contoured scripts, and more elaborate plots than preschool children do. Play episodes are more differentiated and organized for this age group. They also show higher levels of metacommunication in their complex role play. A lot more stage managing and directing and redirecting occurs, as seen, for example, when 6- to 8-year-olds put on a puppet show or do some skit, or dramatize a battle or a circus. They very much enjoy costumes and props for a variety of pretense activities but also like to make their own props out of blocks, cartons, or other manipulatives (Johnson, 1998).

In addition, children in this age range express their interest in play with symbols in a variety of other ways. Some ways seem more continuous with symbolic play during the early years, while other ways are more discontinuous. These are discussed later in this chapter, under the headings "Cognitive Play" and "Creative Play."

MOTOR DOMAIN

As children make the transition from preschool into school they possess considerable fine- and gross-motor ability and can be expected to rapidly achieve more mastery in these domains. Their developing large-muscle strength and coordination and sense of balance, together with their increasing skill and dexterity in the use of small muscles, allows for the emergence of additional and more varied motor activity.

Primary-grade schoolchildren are better able to use small objects, writing and drawing utensils, and the computer keyboard. Children 6–8 years old exhibit remarkable fine-motor skill in hand games and snapping fingers and the like. Their fine-motor development is used in play activities such as constructing model cars, working with train sets, and collecting stamps and coins and other artifacts. With gross-motor maturation and experience, many children in this age range learn to ride a two-wheeler, jump rope, climb trees, and do trapeze and acrobatic tricks. Rough-and-tumble and other forms of physical play, including daredevil and risky play, can be seen. Capture and escape, hide and seek, and tag and its variants (dungeon tag, frozen tag, etc.) are displayed. Children's gross-motor development is used in rollerblading, ice skating, dancing, gymnastics, swimming, and other forms of sports and athletics.

COGNITIVE PLAY

Cognitive play and creative play often blend or go together. In a sense, all play is cognitive and creative. Two important dimensions of cognition are divergent thinking and convergent thinking. Elements of each apply, to varying degrees, in any play episode. Consider musical play, for instance. Clearly, learning to play musical instruments is highly convergent, but musical expression and especially improvisational activity can be highly creative and certainly involve a great deal of divergent thinking. Creative play and cognitive play are not rigidly set apart from one another, but rather stand in a complementary or dialectical relation. When convergent thinking dominates, play is called *cognitive;* when divergent thinking dominates, play is termed *creative.* Labeling activities a priori is somewhat arbitrary, but we refer to games with rules, use of educational toys, and books as cognitive play.

(1) GAMES WITH RULES   Sports and various physical games, board games, and computer and video games become increasingly popular during the primary-grade school years. Although younger children are known to partake in these activities, when they do, the rules are much simpler or are simplified, and

adult support and scaffolding is usually available. Even for the 6- and 7-year-olds, the games must remain rather simple and easy to follow, with few rules and little skill or strategy required for entry-level participation. For 8-year-olds and other children who are younger but who have reached the age of reason or what Piaget called concrete operational (logical) thinking, more sophisticated games (e.g., chess) entailing greater cognitive and social demands are possible. Strategic planning and genuine cooperation are important ingredients in game play among primary-grade schoolchildren and are undergirded by Piagetian concrete operations.

(2) EDUCATIONAL TOYS   Primary-grade schoolchildren often encounter educational or skill-development materials in home, school, or community settings. Cognitive play in this subcategory consists of using educational toys and games and materials. These include a great deal of what comes from the electronic medium (see Chapter 10, pp. 300–312), such as computers and educational software, electronic toys, and games, including teaching toys and science toys. For example, science toys for preschoolers and older children include magnifying glasses, flashlights, magnets, color mixes, rock and shell collections, clocks, calculators, and other materials. Older children also use microscopes, chemistry sets, field binoculars, and more challenging software in their cognitive play. Use of these materials in projects at school or at home can engage children in exploration, discovery, and problem solving, ideally in an open-ended, playful, and creative manner. Sports and athletic equipment and electronic sports games foster skill development, too.

(3) BOOKS   Books and other printed matter elicit cognitive play, or what in Europe is called *reception play* (van der Kooij & de Groot, 1977). Reception play also includes looking at pictures; being attentive when someone is drawing, building, or otherwise modeling something for the child to copy; listening to (or reading aloud) fairy tales, other stories, songs, or verses; watches videos, movies, puppet shows; and so forth. In all these cases, mental activity is assumed, but not physical activity, to any great extent. Children are passive in appearance but very much alive and attentive intellectually. Books play a predominant role in this so-called reception play. While children ages 5 and under love books with silly stories, wild adventure, fantasy, and everyday life stories, from 5 years old on up, children increasingly enjoy credible stories, poetry, holiday and seasonal stories, and comics. Children ages 6 to 8 are also known to also find pleasure in stories about magic, fears, catastrophes, nature and the elements, and the supernatural. Book reception play and other forms of cognitive play are readily incorporated into academic programs centered on educational play and projects (see Chapter 11).

CREATIVE PLAY

The laurel of "creative" is bestowed on the child's play when it is imaginative but also possesses the qualities of directed thinking and self-regulation. This rules out free association or nondirected thinking or random or stimulus-dominated types or patterns of behavior. A child scribbling on a page, for example, is not engaged in creative play, even for a very young child—unless the child says he or she is writing or drawing something.

Creativity implies originality, as well as aesthetic or technological usefulness. Unlike for adults, for whom societal standards apply, for children, personal standards apply—is the play original and useful for this particular child? As children mature, social norms of creativity are increasingly used, replacing individualistic norms for deciding whether the term *creative* is an apt descriptor for characterizing the activities or products of children. Although not limited to the following, we discuss creative play as exhibited by 6- to 8-year-olds in terms of the following categories: (1) arts and crafts, (2) microworlds and narratives, and (3) musical expression.

(1) ARTS AND CRAFTS Children 6, 7, and 8 years of age are capable of making elaborate and creative representational products using a variety of expressive media and materials. Like the younger preschool child, they can create products with paints, beads, strings, crayons, paste, scissors, and the like. They can go well beyond the preschooler in what they can do with these materials. Kindergartners and especially primary-grade children can engage in a variety of new activities, as well. They enjoy model building, woodworking, sewing, and working with craft kits such as leatherwork, papier-mâché, simple jewelry, and enameling.

(2) MICROWORLDS AND NARRATIVES The microcosms or microworlds that children make or enter represent a second kind of creative play commonplace with preschoolers and older children. An important and popular form of creative play during the early and middle childhood years is imaginative play involving miniature worlds with small toys of various sorts (e.g., toy soldiers, dolls, stuffed animals, or a farm set) or unstructured materials (e.g., pipe cleaners, blocks) set up on tabletops, bed sheets, or rugs. Computer and video games (see Chapter 10, pp. 305–311) provide additional means for make-believe play of this kind, involving simulated microworlds on the screen. Creative play in either two-dimensional or three-dimensional miniature worlds entails children acting on objects (or pictures and icons) to construct various configurations, as well as producing narratives or stories about the play scenes. This can be solitary or group pretense, which typically lasts some time, with considerable manifest interest. Children 6–8 years old exhibit preferences for very detailed and realistic models in their creative play with miniature worlds. Their plots and products are much more intricate than are those of preschoolers.

(3) MUSICAL EXPRESSION Creative play with tunes, melodies, and songs are perennial childhood favorites. Rhythm and musical instruments are appropriate throughout the early childhood years. Creative language play includes inventing songs and rhymes, while creative body play includes inventing dances and movements. Primary-grade children begin to learn to play real instruments and to read music; they do group singing and dancing. Creative music play is helped by recording with audio- or videocassettes, using CDs and tape players, and mixing and reconstructing musical events. Musical creative play is often fanciful and combined with, or part of, narrative and pretense.

SUMMARY

In this chapter, we conceptualized play development as comprising microgenetic (short term) and ontogenetic (long term) change over time in play behavior and experience. This distinction and the idea of contextualizing play development within a multivariate framework (culture, gender, physical environments, peers) help edify our play practices and policies. Decontexualized linear accounts of play development were deemed insufficient but important foundational knowledge.

Four basic dimensions of play development (social, object, symbolic, and motor) were described over early childhood. *Social play* has its origins in the first infant games or routines involving an accommodating partner who compensates for the child's limitations. Objects inspire infant and toddler play but are less important for preschoolers and older children. Social-play skills improve with experience in the peer group, where mutual accommodations are required. *Object play* develops from simple and repetitive motor and functional play routines to constructive play combinations.

Symbolic play advances from earliest imitations of self (and then of others) toward more coherent and orderly symbolic play entailing planning and patterning in a social context. Genuine pretense, according to Piaget, commences when the infant displays outer-directed, as opposed to self-directed, play behavior. Dimensions of symbolic play were traced: pretend actions, use of objects, role enactments, and themes. By the end of the preschool years, children engage in highly developed sociodramatic or thematic fantasy play characterized by a great deal of metacommunication, a variety of roles with peers, and concentration, persistence, and attention to detail. *Motor-play* development from birth to age 6 years is marked by numerous major motor milestones as children grow physically, become more mobile, and gain greater control, balance, and coordination using their large and small muscles.

Finally, we discussed social, object, symbol, and motor play of children beyond the preschool years. Children 6–8 years old form peer groups and enter into adult-supervised activity; their use of objects becomes more elaborate and instrumental for collaborative and pretense activities; symbolic play takes on additional forms and reaches new heights in sophistication; motor play advances remarkably, allowing for new play activities using fine- and gross-motor skills. Cognitive play occurs with games, educational toys, and books. Creative play is seen in arts and crafts, children's pretense and narration using small objects, computers and videogames, and musical expression.

Chapter 4
INDIVIDUAL DIFFERENCES IN PLAY

The issue was finally resolved, at least for now. With the teachers' help, the children had explored various ways to stop the bickering between boys and girls over the use of the large blocks. It seemed that some of the boys had monopolized the large-block area for days on end, justifying the exclusion of girls on the basis that, as one boy piped up, "Girls aren't strong enough." The teachers, despite their reservations, were going to allow the children to implement their own consensus solution: To alternate days when the large blocks were off limits to one gender or another. Although time alone would tell the general wisdom of this decision, the boys soon did learn that, indeed, the girls were strong enough to play with the large blocks. The teachers also noticed a pattern they had already seen in the boys—some of the girls would build carefully constructed configurations, exhibiting considerable interest in details about the objects themselves or their physical properties, whereas other girls subsumed the blocks and other objects into their usual ongoing dramatic play. ■

The previous chapter discussed the concept of the development of play; described changes in social play, object play, symbolic play, and motor play from birth to age 8 years; and covered cognitive and creative play during the primary-grade school years. By understanding the development of the different kinds of play over long periods of time (play ontogenesis) and over short periods of time (play microgenesis) in particular contexts, we can better anticipate and guide the play of children. Play development knowledge by itself, however, even when tempered with a prudent appreciation for different rates of development, is an insufficient base for constructing theories of practice. Contextualized and multivariate working models need to encompass a whole host of factors that moderate and mediate play development and individual differences among children.

Play development and individual differences are two key constructs required for an adequate conceptual framework. Development, or the developmental function, refers to the sequence of qualitatively distinct behaviors that mark the child's progress in a particular domain, such as play or exploration. Developmental functions are normative aggregate explanations for when milestones or stages are generally achieved in a population. Individual differences, on the other hand, refer to variability in the rate of growth or the shape of the developmental function (Wohlwill, 1973). For example, across age-group comparisons for simple social play (Howes, 1988) can be used to describe the developmental function for that construct, but within age-group comparisons would reveal individual differences.

We maintain that the force of development, which is a confluence of nature and nurture (the pull of the future), interacts with situational determinants (influences occurring in the present) and with individual-difference variables (factors shaped in the past) to affect play behaviors and experiences. Each of these three dimensions comprises numerous variables, which can enter into complex interactions within and across dimensions. Constructing comprehensive and useful models of children's play and adult roles is a daunting task requiring all of the aforementioned factors and possible interactions to be entered into a working formula.

Now suppose you were asked to predict how a particular child would play in a randomly selected situation. You know absolutely nothing at all about the child. What would you predict—a random guess? Suppose instead that you could ask two questions to learn specific facts about the child. Which facts would be most helpful in predicting the child's play behavior? Having read the preceding chapter, we hope that you requested to learn the child's chronological or developmental age. In additon, however, what would be the other fact about the child you would like to know? Would you want to know the child's culture, social class, family structure, or preschool experience? All of these variables are indeed relevant.

We maintain, however, that next to chronological age as an estimate of developmental level, gender is the best single predictor of how a child would react in a randomly chosen situation. Throughout life, age and gender account for more of the variability in a person's general behavior than any other pair of personal attributes. Gender is a social marker and a crucial individual-difference variable that is responsible for a lion's share of the variance in how all of us behave and think over the course of our lives, including our play.

In this chapter, we examine gender and personality as two individual-difference variables that must be incorporated into any comprehensive or functional theories of practices, with respect to children's play and adult roles. The first half of this chapter is devoted to gender differences in play. The second half of the chapter is devoted to personality differences in play during the early childhood years.

GENDER AND PLAY FORMS

By the time children enter the preschool classroom or child-care center, they show extensive gender differences, as well as similarities, in play behavior. Both similarities and differences are noted in the following sections, dealing with general behavior in our four major domains of motor or physical play, social play, object play, and pretense play.

MOTOR OR PHYSICAL PLAY

Physical or *motor play* is defined as gross- and fine-motor activity or the use of body parts in play. As noted in Chapter 3, objects are not the focus of this form of play, but outdoor or indoor play equipment—such as large mats, climbing frames, or trampolines—are often used. Natural features of the environment may also be involved. For example, children can walk along a fallen log, skip across a grassy area, or fall and roll down the slope of a hill.

Gender differences in physical-activity level do not emerge prior to age 4 or 5 years (Fagot & O'Brien, 1994). Once boys reach this age, they have been found to be more active and boisterous than girls are. Holmes (1992) found this distinction to be true even during snack time in a middle-class kindergarten class, where participant observations were conducted, along with ethnographic interviews with 10 boys and 11 girls. All children pretended and told jokes during snack time, but only the boys, not a single girl, showed the boldness to fool around (e.g., using taboo humor) or goof off (e.g., hiding someone's milk or pulling a chair from under someone).

In New Zealand, Smith and Inder (1993) observed $3\frac{1}{2}$- to 5-year-olds in a kindergarten and a child-care center. Kindergarten boys appeared to be involved in more physical contact. In both the kindergarten and child-care settings, boisterous play was more likely in boys and mixed-gender groups. Girls' groups tended to be quieter and more passive. Choice of play environments was related to gender in this study, as well. Outdoor play was more prevalent by boys in kindergarten; girls were more often seen playing inside. In neighborhood settings in Australia, this same pattern emerged–boys preferred outdoor environments, and girls preferred indoor environments (Cunningham, Jones, & Taylor, 1994).

Research shows that preschool boys are more vigorous and active than preschool girls, in both indoor and outdoor play environments. For example, for 2 years, Harper and Sanders (1975) recorded the total amount of time and use of space by middle-class 3- to 5-year-old boys and girls. Boys spent more time outside than did girls. (There was no difference between girls who wore dresses and those who wore jeans.) It was common to see boys playing outside and in sand, on a climbing structure, on a tractor, and around an equipment shed, and girls inside, at craft tables or in the dramatic-play kitchen. Although there were no sex differences in the percentage of time spent farther away from school buildings, boys used 1.2 to 1.6 times as much space and entered significantly more play areas.

A prevalent type of physical play appearing in early childhood that is gender related is rough-and-tumble play. *Rough-and-tumble play* is not real fighting but one major form of play fighting (other forms include *superhero* and *war-toy play*). Boys tend to engage in this form of play much more often than girls do (Carlsson-Paige & Levin, 1987; Goldstein, 1992; Humphreys & Smith, 1984; Smith, 1997). They chase one another, wrestle, and struggle, often while pretending to be fictional characters (which then can overlap into superhero play aggression, with or without war toys).

Peter Smith (1997) has been conducting a series of investigations in England, employing teacher interviews to obtain estimates of the frequency of occurrence of rough-and-tumble play and real fighting. His own research and his review of the literature in this area lead him to conclude that when direct playground observations are made, real fighting is a rarity. In contrast, rough-and-tumble play is typically reported to be occurring between 5% and 10% of the time, with a maximum of 20%. Boys have been observed engaging in real physical fighting and play fighting at twice-to-thrice the rate, relative to girls.

An interesting difference has been found in the types of aggression in which boys and girls engage. In general, boys tend to exhibit more *instrumental aggression* (e.g., hitting, grabbing, pushing, or otherwise using physical force to obtain a desired object, territory, or privilege during social conflicts), whereas girls score higher on measures of *relational aggression* (i.e., indirect or verbal aggression or "indirect bullying," as seen in ostracism, breaking contact, gossiping, and intending to harm peer relations). For example, McNeilly-Choque, Hart, Robinson, Nelson, and Olsen (1996), in a large multimethods study of 241 preschoolers in Head Start or university-affiliated programs, reported that girls were more relationally aggressive than boys on playgrounds. However, boys exhibited significantly more instrumental aggression than did girls. Both kinds of aggression are significant correlates of lessened peer acceptance. Crick and Grotpeter (1995), among other researchers, corroborate these findings. Note that these studies are dealing with real aggression, not play aggression. Unexplored to date is whether girls do more verbal or relational play fighting than boys do. Perhaps they do, but at a later age than the peak season for physical play fighting so common among the boys during the early childhood years.

The transition from the preschool to the grade-school years is marked by gender-linked developmental transformations of physical and motor play into sports, athletics, and other activities. There is a basic continuity in boys' tendencies to be more aggressive and adventuresome and to be keenly interested in the power and speed of performance. Girls tend to remain less boisterous and more cooperative and interested in aesthetics and grace in their physical play. For instance, while far more boys join PeeWee ice-hockey teams, more girls pursue dance groups. *Gender linked* does not mean being *gender exclusive*, however. Many girls engage in more boylike activities, and boys in more girllike activities.

In summary, considerable support exists for the assertion that boys, compared to girls, engage in more rough-and-tumble play, do more real fighting (instrumental but not relational), and more strongly prefer to use outdoor space. Research is less conclusive concerning level of physical activity, especially at younger ages (Fagot & O'Brien, 1994). Gender differences do not appear in total activity level prior to age 4 or 5 years. Marked variation occurs at each age, making generalizations difficult (see the accompanying sidebar, "Do Boys and Girls Really Play So Differently?"). During the grade-school years, gender-linked trends in physical play are manifested in sports, athletics, and other organized physical activities. Boys' play, compared to girls' play, is marked by larger-size play groups and by more competitiveness, interdependence, role differentiation, and rule-governed team play.

Theory in Action

DO BOYS AND GIRLS REALLY PLAY SO DIFFERENTLY?

Although many research studies have led to the conclusion that boys and girls play differently along various dimensions, it is important to avoid simple generalizations or overstatements. How common it is to hear anecdotes from teachers and parents, sometimes with some concern, about a child playing in a way some may think is totally opposite from what one would expect, based on the child's gender. Take the following illustration.

On the third floor of an urban school, a rooftop served as an outdoor play area for preschool-age children. Because the roof's surface was hard, little if any rough-and-tumble play occurred, although a great deal of highly charged activity involving Big Wheels or other large toy vehicles was regularly observed. Also available were a climbing frame and other outdoor playground equipment. Cindy, a lively 3-year-old, was one of the spunkiest of the youngsters in gross-motor activity, which many times involved "Superhero" themes. The toy vehicles became Ram Chargers or Wind Raiders, as superheroes and villains raced around the area chasing one another. Cindy always looked forward to play time and was a frequent participant in such play.

Cindy also was one of the most athletic in climbing and swinging. One day, unbeknownst to her teachers, who were momentarily distracted by an altercation involving other children, Cindy pushed a slide, which had become unbolted from the roof, to the wall surrounding the rooftop playground and used the slide's ladder to climb to the top of the wall, on the edge of a three-story drop to the parking lot. Imagine the fright of the teacher who saw her there. Fortunately, that teacher had the good sense not to shout to Cindy or make a hurried move toward her. Instead, she quietly and calmly approached the child, slowly extended her arms, and Cindy jumped safely down to her. Cindy soon resumed her active play and the teachers, shaken, discussed safeguards against a repetition of the incident.

SOCIAL PLAY

Overall, sociability does not differ greatly across genders in the play of young boys and girls. Parten (1933) found that the play scale she developed showed age-related but not gender-related differences. However, she did find that two thirds of the play groups that children chose were same-gender groupings and that each child's preferred and favorite playmates were usually the same gender as the child. Findings of more recent studies generally support Parten's findings regarding the lack of gender differences in the sociability of play. For example, Johnson and Roopnarine (1983), in their review of research, concluded that the social-play differences between preschool boys and preschool girls were not significant. However, one large-scale study in England found that girls are ahead of boys in social play during the preschool years (Tizard, Philps, & Plewis, 1976).

Others who have researched the social play of young children concur with Parten's observation that same-gender playmates are more common and more compatible than opposite-gender playmates. Preference for same-gender groupings have been noted by numerous researchers (Fishbein & Imai, 1993; Hartle, 1996; Powlishta, Serbin, & Moller, 1993; Ramsey, 1995; Shell & Eisenberg, 1990; Urberg & Kaplan, 1989). Findings from these studies suggest tentative generalizations.

First, gender cleavage begins in earnest during the fourth year. However, this bias against the opposite sex is more apparent in self-reports (stated preferences) than in actual behavioral observations (Ramsey, 1995). Apparently, even if a child shows a tendency toward gender-based exclusion in self-reports, the child may show much less of this bias in actual behavior because attraction to an activity may overrule the child's nascent sexist tendencies. An alternative interpretation for this finding is that children overstate their bias in an interview, to conform to some perceived social norm operating in their lives at this time (e.g., it's cool not to like the opposite sex or at least to admit it). Second, while girls might start to show a preference for same-gender playmates at an earlier age than boys do, once this bias is established, it seems more consistent and rigid in males (Powlishta et al., 1993; Shell & Eisenberg, 1990). Third, this bias exists across Euro-American, Asian-American, and African-American children (Fishbein & Imai, 1993). Fourth, constructive-play activity appears somewhat immune to this bias, relative to other play forms (Hartle, 1996; Urberg & Kaplan, 1989). Perhaps this finding reflects the fact that constructive play is usually more structured and more closely monitored by the teacher.

In a 3-year study of children ranging in age from 1 to 6 years, LaFreniere, Strayer, and Gauthier (1984) found that girls typically preferred playing with same-gender peers at an earlier age than boys did. However, at later ages during the preschool years, boys' tendencies for same-gender interaction increased, while those of the girls leveled off (see Figure 4.1). More recent work confirms that children's preference for same-gender peers tends to increase during the early childhood years (Diamond, LeFurgy & Blass, 1993; Maccoby, 1990; Ramsey, 1995).

Children tend to play with same-gender play partners perhaps because of a combination of abilities, sex-role stereotypes, and compatible interests (Hartup, 1983). Moreover, contrastive behavioral and social interactional styles have been implicated as responsible for the gender cleavage in social play during the early childhood period. For example, some girls may dislike assertive and aggressive behavior in the classroom and may avoid boys unless a teacher is there to mediate the activity, as in typical constructive play.

Research has examined gender differences in interactional style during early childhood, both as a phenomenon in its own right and as an avenue for finding explanations as to why gender segregation is so pronounced in young children. Ideas generated from the research also may turn out to be useful to teachers. In their field-based research in New Zealand, Smith and Inder

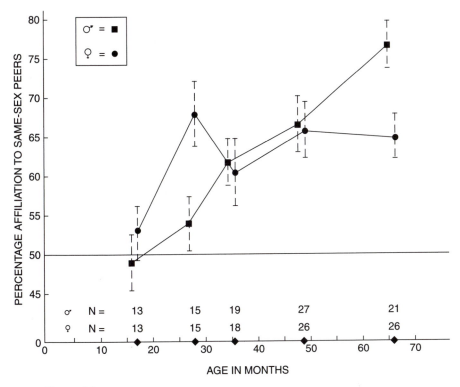

Figure 4.1

Mean affiliative activity directed to same-sex peers, as a function of age and sex
Source: From LaFreniere, Strayer, and Gauthier (1984).

(1993) compared the free play of younger children in child care with the play of older children in kindergarten. Observations revealed mixed-gender play groups in operation one third of the time and same-gender play groups during the remaining observations, with the former type of play group larger in size. The authors surmised that perhaps this was because children bring same-gender friends with them to combine with the opposite-gender groups. Boys tended to dominate the play in mixed groups, and more conflicts and rejection incidents occurred in these groups, relative to homogeneous groups. Higher rates of physical conflicts happened particularly in the kindergarten setting, whereas rejection and withdrawal occurred more in the child-care setting. The researchers saw these patterns as evidence of incompatible styles of interaction between boys and girls.

Black (1989) observed same-age, same-gender triads of 3- and 4-year-old preschoolers playing in a university-affiliated preschool laboratory. Various toys and materials were available for free play by the triads. Social skills differed solely as a function of sex. Girls, in general, used a smooth style of turn taking in their play interactions. Behaviors were related to each other interactionally and topically. Girls anticipated each other, seemingly valuing smooth and continued interaction more than the boys did. Girls' episodes were longer lasting and more coherent. Boys appeared more interested in having their own play suggestions adopted by the group, causing their play to become more fragmented and having to be started anew. Black suggests that her study's results are consistent with Carol Gilligan's (1982) notion that girls are socialized to adopt roles of nurturance, and boys to assume roles of dominance.

Other researchers have investigated gender differences in the directness of play interactions. An example of a direct or explicit strategy would be as follows: Child A—"Let's play doctors"; Child B—"Okay!" An implicit strategy would be this one: Child A—"Pretend I am a nurse now"; Child B—"My sick baby is sleeping over there." Sawyer's (1997) research involving 8 months of naturalistic observations in an indoor free-play preschool setting (see Chapter 2, p. 42) revealed that boys used twice as many direct verbal strategies to enter play. However, both boys and girls used a similar number of indirect play-entry strategies. Sachs (1987) found a similar pattern. She compared pairs of boys and girls between 24 and 64 months of age playing "doctor" with an assortment of the usual play paraphernalia (syringe, stethoscope, etc.) related to this theme. Although the amount of pretend play was the same for boys and girls, boys assigned themselves to the dominant role 79% of the time, compared to 33% for girls. In play negotiations, new roles were assigned, using both imperatives ("You're the patient") and questions ("Will you be the patient?"). There were no significant differences in use of questions as a function of gender, but there was in the use of imperative: 72% of the boys' proposals were imperatives, whereas only 20% of the girls' were.

In summary, while there is little evidence suggesting significant gender differences in levels of social play or sociability, there is considerable support for the hypothesis that gender preferences and interactional styles in social play are different for boys and girls. Same-gender playmates are usually chosen, beginning around age 4 years and growing steadily in frequency during early childhood. Conflicting play styles are implicated. Girls tend to be less direct and explicit. Boys are more assertive and dominant. As they move into the primary-grade school years, girls and boys often do not share the same peer culture. Boys' social worlds are more extensive, individualistic, and competitive, while girls' tend to be more intensive, affiliative, and subjective.

OBJECT PLAY

Researchers have found significant differences in the kinds of toys young boys and girls use in play. Young boys tend to prefer to play on the floor with pushing and pulling toys, blocks, or wheeled toys, while girls like to play on a tabletop, coloring, doing puzzles, or playing with their dolls (Wardle, 1991). The way children use toys also is linked to the child's gender. Preschool-age females show a strong propensity toward constructive play, while their male counterparts display a greater tendency for functional play. In other words, girls are more likely to use objects according to a plan that has a goal, such as completing a puzzle or coloring a page. Boys are more likely to handle toys

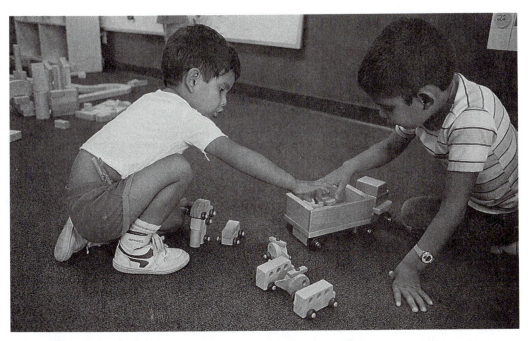

Blocks and wheeled toys are among boys' favorite playthings.

and materials in ways that are appropriate but somewhat stereotyped and repetitive, such as pushing a small vehicle, blowing bubbles, or cranking a mechanical toy (Johnson & Roopnarine, 1983).

One possible explanation for this gender difference in tendencies toward functional or constructive play is the difference in active involvement required. Research has shown that preschool girls move objects less and use them more educationally and quietly than do boys (Moore, Evertson, & Brophy, 1974). Tabletop activities that encourage constructive play tend to involve females predominantly (teachers, as well as children) and entail sedentary behaviors, while functional play is typically associated with more active movement.

Between the ages of 6 and 8 years, new expressions of object play arise in the form of arts and crafts. Many of these emergent activities are gender linked, but there is great overlap. During the preschool and the primary-grade school years, boys and girls differ not so much in *how* objects are used, but in *what* objects are used in play. Thematic content but not structural properties of the play are usually different for boys and girls. This is seen in sharpest relief in pretend play.

PRETEND PLAY

In general, research has shown that during the early childhood years, boys and girls do not differ in total amounts of pretend play or in their general level of fantasy-making ability (e.g., Connolly, Doyle, & Reznick, 1988; Sachs,

1987). Nevertheless, gender differences have been reported in certain aspects of pretend play. In addition to differences in interactional style, described previously, perhaps an even more reliable gender difference exists with respect to the content or theme of pretense play. Research presents a less convincing case for gender differences in *structural* aspects of pretense play—such as its organizational complexity, narrative richness, or transformational quality.

OBJECT TRANSFORMATIONS One child may use realistic or representational toys in pretend play—dolls, miniature farm animals, toy soldiers, or toy superheroes. A second child may play with substitute objects that bear little concrete similarity to the imagined object—for instance, a large rectangular block may be used as a make-believe computer. A third child may imagine a missing object and may use language and internal imagery to sustain the make-believe play episode. What is the probable gender of each child?

Research suggests that preschool girls may be ahead of preschool boys in object transformational abilities, as studied in semicontrolled laboratory settings. Matthews (1977) reported that 4-year-old girls were ahead of 4-year-old boys in initiating fantasy play without relying on concrete props. Boys gradually became less dependent on objects in make-believe play episodes over successive trials, while girls began at a lower level than did boys and at first maintained a balance among all three types of object transformations, but later on, they preferred substitute and pretend transformations. McLoyd (1980), in her study of low-income African-American preschoolers, found that girls made significantly more substitute and pretend object transformations than did boys. Fein, Johnson, Kosson, Stork, and Wasserman (1975) found that girls seemed to pretend more than boys during toddlerhood and to become less dependent on realistic concrete props at an earlier age than did boys.

These gender differences in object transformation favoring girls tend to disappear in free-play situations. Johnson, Ershler, and Bell (1980), in a free-play observation study, found that preschool girls and boys did not differ significantly in their use of objects during pretend-play episodes. In fact, Black (1989) reported that triads of preschool boys appeared *less* dependent on props to instigate imaginative play than did triads of girls.

In summary, it is difficult to say with conviction that girls are ahead of boys in object transformational skills. The extent to which this may be the case during the early years probably reflects girls' accelerated linguistic and cognitive development. In the second half of the preschool years (ages 3–6), however, and certainly during the so-called bubblegum years (ages 6–10), differences in modes of pretend play are probably more a matter of preference than of cognitive maturity. Neither gender is behind the other in the transformational qualities of their play. Girls and boys have the same symbolic representational capacities, a cognitive parity that also accounts for the apparent lack of gender differences along other structural features of pretend play, such as its narrative script organization (Wolf & Grollman, 1982) and integration (Goncu & Kessel, 1984).

ROLE ENACTMENT AND PLAY THEMES Research and anecdotal evidence suggest that during pretend play, girls show a preference for home-centered interests involving dolls, dress-up clothes, and domestic items, whereas boys are more inclined to adopt more villainous and dangerous themes and plots and to make more use of vehicles and guns (Sutton-Smith, 1979). In other words, while girls tend to portray family characters and to select themes based on everyday experiences, boys tend to participate in adventure themes and to enact superhero roles, and boys seem to be more physically active in pretend play (Levin & Carlsson-Paige, 1994; Paley, 1984).

Matthews (1981) investigated gender-role perception, portrayal, and preferences in the fantasy play of 16 four-year-olds who were observed in pairs with a playmate of the same sex. The two roles most often played were those of mother and father. Based on how they enacted the roles during the episodes, it appeared as if boys perceived mothers as homebound and concerned with housekeeping and child care. In the role of the wife, boys seemed to suggest that wives are inept and helpless. In the role of fathers or husbands, boys enacted leadership roles, and their participation in housekeeping involved only 30% of their role play. In the girls' play, mothers were nurturant, generous, and highly managerial. Again, however, wives were portrayed as being helpless and incompetent. Apparently, the role of the mother is viewed in a positive light, while the role of the wife is not. Girls saw the male role as being masterful and also nurturant, although they showed little desire to play the male role and spent almost 75% of their role play in housekeeping.

Given freedom to choose roles, preschool children usually prefer to enact roles that are stereotypical for the child's gender. Grief (1976) found that in almost all cases, boys performed the roles of fathers, husbands, sons, and firefighters, whereas girls usually assumed the roles of mother, daughter, wife, baby, and bride. Parten (1933) found that preschool boys acted only in male roles while playing house and that boys would not enter the housekeeping corner of the nursery if dolls were present. On the other hand, Bergman and Lefcourt (1994) report a case of a child attempting to integrate both masculine and feminine identifications into the same role play. A little boy, who was under 3 years of age, enacted the role of a repairperson (his father was in the construction business), yet the boy included in his tool kit a vacuum cleaner, which was used by his mother. At times, there is not a sharp dichotomy—play enactment can occur within an appropriate gender role but also blending masculine and feminine traits.

Boys and girls choose different kinds of activities during pretend play in part because of differences in interests, temperament, and available shared scripts. Boys soon elect to go beyond the familiar and realistic themes of house, doctor, and school and into the more unfamiliar and fantasy themes of space explorers, superheroes, and different creatures; girls appear more content to stick with the themes and roles popular with all children initially.

For example, Howe, Moller, Chambers, & Petrakos (1993) studied the play of 3- to 5-year-old preschoolers at a university-affiliated child-care center. Their purpose was to examine the children's social and pretend play in the housekeeping center and in other novel dramatic-play centers, which were constructed by early-childhood-education majors. Examples included hospital, office, bakery, pharmacy, pirate ship, and fruit and vegetable store, among others. Although these new centers were very well done and were attractive to the boys, the girls still preferred the traditional housekeeping centers. Because the study took place over just a few days, perhaps girls would express more interest in the novel play centers over a lengthier period of time. Weinberger and Starkey (1994) also reported that preschool girls exhibited strong ties to the housekeeping center. Their study involved observations of play behaviors of African-American children in different play centers in a Head Start program. The only statistically significant gender-related result was that girls liked playing in the housekeeping center more than boys.

A developmental trend exists in pretend play themes going from being proximal to *distal* (removed from children's everyday experience) (see Chapter 3, pp.72–73). However, it would be a mistake to infer that boys are more cognitively advanced than girls because they show greater interest in remote or distal roles and themes in pretend play. The quality of play can never be evaluated in terms of one aspect in isolation. Organization, freedom from concrete props, use of language, and originality are all important as indicators of cognitive maturity in play, and, as we have argued, girls and boys seem equal on these structural dimensions.

Fantasy aggression play is characterized by the presence of images or themes of violence and aggression, with or without the use of objects. *War play* is when imaginary battles are waged or war toys are used. War toys may be commercially made or constructed by the child (e.g., using Lincoln Logs as a rifle). This form of play appears in children as young as 2 years old and continues throughout childhood and even into adolescence and indeed adulthood. Virtually unanimous is the view that boys do a lot more of this type of pretend play than girls do.

As discussed in Chapter 10, under the section "Electronic Media and Play," very often, fantasy aggression play in preschoolers seems almost a direct imitation from aggressive television shows and their related store-bought products that kids use in this controversial form of play. Levin (1995) feels that this form of play is very narrow and stereotypic and inhibits creative play—and may even promote sexism, racism, and xenophobia through its incorporation of imitative components of the TV shows that can breed not only acceptance of violence, but also intolerance and suspicions about differences among people.

Goldstein (1995) and others on the alternative side of this controversy would argue back that television and toys are used in fantasy play but do not determine it—war toys and media are not play scriptwriters, and children are not "walking tape-recorders." In children's aggressive fantasy play, they go beyond the surface inputs and features of the toys and the violent television programs and create new and original play content. They are thereby able to work through various psychological issues.

Whatever your opinion on this issue, remember our earlier discussion about girls sticking to housekeeping themes. Just because boys gravitate to fantasy aggression play does not, ipso facto, make their play inferior, just as girls' choice of housekeeping roles does not make their play inferior. From the overall corpus of the literature on children's play, harping on single dimensions or aspects is perhaps a disservice comparable to doing a selective and biased research review. Research studies, or single issues, lifted out of context, unfortunately, can and do serve adult-centered academic arguments or sociopolitical agendas. Keeping in focus a holistic, contextualized view of the evolving play canon, together with maintaining an open-minded scientific attitude, is always desirable. It is especially critical when approaching controversial areas—less rhetoric prevails. More light and less heat can be generated in our scholarly debates on the issues when additional high-quality—and preferably longitudinal—empirical research is done on these topics.

As children move into later periods of early childhood and their overt dramatic play transforms into more covert imaginative or creative play expression appropriate to the primary-grade school-age group, certain gender-linked pretense play patterns persist. The overall sophistication and complexity of pretense play, which increases with age, does not favor either gender. Nonetheless, the content and the themes vary in line with the developmental and socialization goals of each gender. There is a continuation of girls' pretend play themes and play content, reflecting their primary concerns and interests relating to nurturance and inner connection with others, and boys' concerns with autonomy and power. Play themes in videogames, books, and toys, or from movies and television, can be viewed as varying along a continuum from more boylike to more girllike. Each gender tends to gravitate to its own kind in picking play activities to do, songs to listen to, parts in classroom skits to perform, arts and crafts to make, or hobbies to cultivate.

In addition, children from 6 to 8 years of age come into their own as affecting and effective storytellers. Children's narratives reveal gender-linked concerns. Tarullo (1994), using case-study methods and analysis of play narratives of 7-year-olds, demonstrated that a central developmental task for children in this age bracket appears to be how to balance (a) intimacy and identity, (b) being connected and being autonomous, and (c) conforming in a group and being creative as an individual. Tarullo's case studies of Eddy and Maggie and their respective stories illustrate how children's stories anticipate the human need to eventually outgrow a polarized gender schema, which pits masculinity against femininity. Eddy tells about a neighborhood bully and Maggie in her story about confronting her friends over a grievance. Eddy fears admitting his anxiety, as much as dealing with the bully. His manifest concern is whether he is macho enough, and his latent worry has to do with feelings and vulnerabilities. Maggie fears what might happen if she stops blaming herself and instead asserts herself in public. The manifest issue here is confrontation and potential damaged relationships with friends; the latent issue for Maggie, according to Tarullo, would seem to be coming to realize on a personal level that newly achieved individual assertiveness and feelings of self-reliance can be equal in importance to caring about relationships with others.

Singer (1995) similarly argues that an important developmental task, which is assisted by gender-linked pretense in its various forms, is to come to grips with the inherent male–female dichotomy within each of us. Boys and girls, men and women, all of us, are always battling to balance affiliation needs with autonomy needs. The make-believe play of preschoolers and older children, in its content and themes, reflects the child's efforts to master achievement- and power-related needs with affiliation needs. In practice, there is consensus that achievement and affiliation needs must both be met in human development. Theoretically, less consensus exists as to whether these clusters are opposite ends of one bipolar dimension or are better conceptualized as two separate unipolar dimensions.

Singer maintains that all humans are motivated to make sense of the world and to assign meanings. The *structural features* of pretense play (kinds of transformations, complexity of scripts, organization of the play, etc.) are helpful in achieving this goal of integrating the strange with the familiar and new knowledge with existing knowledge (i.e., accommodation and assimilation). The *content* of the pretense, on the other hand, reveals the child's attempts to cope with these gender-related anxieties concerning linkages and attachment versus power and assertion of individuality. Play themes relating to war (primordial male creature anxiety?) and having babies (primordial female creature anxiety?) may stem from polarized opposites etched in the human psyche from our past as a species on earth (i.e., Jungian collective unconscious). Be this as it may, humans, in their life course, often do seem to seek convergence along the continuum connecting these extremes—both privately (intrapsychically) as represented in fantasies, and publicly (interpersonally) as represented in their ongoing attempts to meet and master real-world tasks. Developmental precursors of these strivings for balance may be seen increasingly in the play and narratives of boys and girls growing up.

GENDER DIFFERENCES IN OTHER PLAY-RELATED BEHAVIORS

Boys and girls can be compared not only in terms of the general play forms of physical or motor play, social play, object play, and pretend play; they also exhibit differences in the play-related areas of toy preferences, team or group activities, and imaginary companions.

TOY PREFERENCES   Many objects and toys are gender-typed in our society. Gender-role stereotyping of materials and activities appears as early as age 12 months and is responsible in part for the fact that many young boys and girls show toy preferences that are well ingrained by 3 years of age (Sutton-Smith, 1979). The finding that some materials are more consistently preferred by either males or females has been consistently reported in the play literature for more than 60 years (e.g., Parten, 1933). Girls tend to play more frequently and longer with dolls and art materials, while boys prefer blocks and wheeled vehicles.

The literature also indicates that girls seem to enjoy a greater variety of play materials and activities, due to the *gender asymmetry* in toy selection by boys and girls: Whereas girls use both so-called boy toys and girl toys, boys are far more likely to shun certain so-called girl toys. This generalization is reflected in Liss's (1981) study of kindergarten children's play with traditional female, male, and non-sex-typed or neutral toys. Children were observed and rated on appropriate use of a toy, enjoyment, aggression, movement, and nurturance. Boys

Theory in Action

ANALYSIS OF PRETENSE-PLAY PROCESSES

In evaluating pretense play as a process, teachers can use classification schemes such as the one proposed by Smilansky (1968) or other schemes that analyze transformation, communications, performance, and script.

Teachers need to distinguish two independent dimensions when characterizing the play scripts or themes of children to determine the sophistication level of the play. One dimension is the extent to which imaginative play reflects content close to the child's everyday existence or content removed and distant from the child's familiar, actual experiences. The second dimension is the extent to which play behavior is stereotypic and repetitive versus varied and unusual. Teachers can plan environments with judicious use of props and interventions to promote play diversified in terms of content (adventuresome and domestic themes), and to promote high-level play in terms of process (innovative, rather than stereotypic, behaviors with materials). By being sensitive both to the varied levels of play scripts used by children and to the children's ability, personality, and situational antecedents to their play behavior level, teachers and parents can encourage the transition from more to less dependency on realistic toys by implanting in the play environment inexpensive materials suggesting a variety of pretend actions and themes.

seemed more familiar with, enjoyed, and played more appropriately with male and neutral toys, while girls played with toys in each category. Girls showed more nurturant behavior than boys, and boys were higher on noise production. (See the accompanying sidebar, on evaluating pretense play as a process.)

The hypothesis that asymmetry exists in gender-linked toy and activity preferences is supported by numerous research studies. For example, Carter and Levy (1988) asked young children to sort line drawings of a kitchen, a doll, a sewing machine, a gun, a bat, a truck, a balloon, a drum, and a telephone on the basis of which ones they would like to play with. The children were then to sort again within the groupings, as a measure of flexibility. Boys' preferences were more stereotyped and consistent. Powlishta, Serbin, and Moller (1993) observed children who were almost 3 years old using masculine (e.g., vehicles, balls, manipulative toys) and feminine (e.g., dolls, dress-up, art) toys. While the girls were inconsistent in their attraction to the male toys, the boys displayed stable differences favoring the masculine items. Interestingly, the girls who played most often with so-called boy toys tended to be seen most frequently with girls—perhaps avoiding boys made it easier to play with their toys because cross-gender peers tend to inhibit gender-inappropriate play. These trends with respect to toys and play themes (e.g., Smith & Inder, 1993) persist through the early childhood years (Sutton-Smith, 1979).

TEAM OR GROUP ACTIVITIES   During the early childhood years, boys and girls initially appear to have similar interest and participation in games and group activities. As children get older, marked gender differences appear in group and game participation. Boys are much more likely to become involved in large-group competitive play than are girls, who seem more comfortable within a smaller group of children or best-friend dyads (Maltz & Borker, 1982; Sutton-Smith, 1979; Tarullo, 1994). Although girls are more likely to play inside or in the confines of their own yards and to engage in activities that are less likely to be rule-governed, they are as concerned about fairness and have as many conflicts as boys. However, girls' interactions are more subjective and focused on the nature of social relations per se, whereas boys tend to focus more on the activity itself. As precursors to things to come, these trends give boys the edge in certain activities where hard-nosed and objective legalistic formulas and social algorithms hold sway, while girls are favored when a caring mode of social participation is called for. Again, these are extreme contrasts, and a great deal of overlap or convergence can be expected with specific girls and boys.

IMAGINARY COMPANIONS   Partington and Grant (1984) reported that children who create make-believe playmates are most likely to be 3–6 years old, with more girls than boys having such companions. More than half the time, imaginary companions are about the same age and the same sex as the children who have them. Best estimates are that approximately 25% of children enjoy this fantasy, and children who have imaginary friends tend to be brighter and to manifest more stable and creative behavior than children who do not. However, these conclusions are tentative and have not always been supported with other research that has been done more recently on this topic.

Dorothy and Jerome Singer (1990) suggest a gender cleavage in the general incidence of imaginary companionship but also note that this difference is not statistically significant. The Singers have reported that for boys, imaginativeness and positive affect during free play are positively linked to having an imaginary companion (which is negatively correlated with watching television cartoons). For girls, having an imaginary companion was associated with persistence during play and with fewer negative emotional outbursts of anger, fear, or sadness. Both boys and girls who had an imaginary companion were more likely to help and share with peers (Singer & Singer, 1990).

Boys were more likely to have animals as make-believe playmates, while girls were significantly more likely than boys to have a female imaginary companion. Only 13% of the boys with imaginary friends included any female ones, while for girls, this figure is 42%. One-third of the time, the children with imaginary companions named them after real people, even friends. Sometimes the children take their imaginary friends from the media. Again, girls were interested in both male and female characters, such as Bionic Woman or Wonder Woman and Superman or Batman. Boys selected only male characters (Singer & Singer, 1990). While bemoaning this asymmetry (which they see as an expression of what perhaps can best be described as a "stalled sex role liberation movement"), the Singers are pleased to note that having an imaginary companion bodes well for a happy childhood in general, and for rich imaginative play in particular.

Research by Taylor, Cartwright, and Carlson (1993) and by Gleason, Sebanc, McGinley, and Hartup (1997) is consistent with the Singers' findings linking imaginative play with imaginary companions. Taylor et al. (1993) found that 4-year-old boys with imaginary companions were more likely to engage in fantasy play than in reality or object play, while Gleason et al. (1997) reported that role play was related with having imaginary companions. Gleason et al. differentiated between invisible friends and relationships with personified objects and found that children with imaginary companions in the form of personified objects showed significantly higher levels of role play than children without imaginary companions. Invisible friends functioned as peers that provided a controllable relation and a solitary forum to rehearse social skills, whereas personified objects (often stuffed animals) were known by others more and used by the child across a greater variety of situations, perhaps serving dramatic-play purposes to a greater extent than invisible friends. Partington and Grant (1984) have speculated that imaginary-companion fantasy may provide an important initial link between fantasy and reality. During their early years, if children have difficulty with roles and rules that frame play episodes with real children, they may gain valuable experience practicing these skills with invented playmates they can control. Having imaginary playmates in the primary grades is not considered a positive sign or a negative sign, unless corroborating data suggest emotional difficulty.

ENVIRONMENTAL FACTORS AND GENDER

Teachers sometimes comment that the initial school experience is a great homogenizer of individual differences among children. *Homogenization* means that children behave more and more similarly and predictably as they get used to classroom routines and as they affect one another during the school year. However, at first there is considerable individual variation in children's reactions to the demands placed on them by other children and teachers.

Patterns that emerge in sex-differentiated preschool play in the classroom or child-care center follow the general homogenization tendency. The groundwork for these patterns is, of course, laid in the home environment; family influences are the source of both the variation among children that exists at first and the consistency in play interests and behavior that grows during the school years.

PARENTAL INFLUENCES

The initial shaping of gender-differentiated behavior occurs within the family. Parents and other individuals significant in the child's home punish gender-atypical activities and reward gender-typical ones (Maccoby & Jacklin, 1974). Social-learning theorists have attested that parents treat their sons and daughters differently. They may ignore doll play by their sons, while encouraging nurturant and submissive behavior in their daughters.

Home influences on gender-based play interests and behavior begin immediately after an infant enters the family. Parents have almost immediate gender-typed expectations of their children. Fathers describe newborn daughters as soft, small, and delicate; fathers of newborn sons describe their offspring as large and active (Rubin, Provenzano, & Luria, 1974). Children may not actually differ in these dimensions at birth, but parents apparently believe they do.

How these parental expectations influence the socialization of boys and girls is illustrated by the way parents dress their sons and daughters differently and provide them with different toys early in life. For example, a study by Rheingold and Cook (1975) surveyed the bedrooms of 48 boys and 48 girls, examining furnishings and toys. The boys' rooms contained more vehicles, educational and art materials, sports equipment, machines, and military toys. The girls' rooms contained more dolls, dollhouses, and domestic toys and were decorated with ruffles and floral prints. These children, between the ages of 12 and 71.6 months, all had their own rooms. Not only did the boys have more toys at every age, but they also had more classes of toys. The boys were given toys that encouraged activities away from the home; girls' toys encouraged home-centered activities.

Parental expectations are also transmitted through their interactions with their children. Caldera, Huston, and O'Brien (1989) observed mothers and fathers as they played with their toddlers. *Female-typed toys* were identified as dolls and a kitchen set; *male-typed toys* were identified as trucks and blocks; and *neutral toys* were identified as puzzles and shape sorters. Although parents did not openly encourage the use of one type of toy over another, the parents' initial nonverbal responses to the toys were more positive when the toys were stereotyped for the child's gender, and they were more likely to become involved in their children's play.

In addition, there is evidence that fathers make themselves more available to their sons and interact with them differently than do mothers of sons, mothers of daughters, and fathers of daughters. Lamb (1977) found that fathers engaged their sons in more vigorous and physically stimulating infant games or play routines. Mothers were more likely to engage their infants in conventional activities such as pat-a-cake and to stimulate their infants with toys and other objects. Fathers held their infants primarily to play with them, while mothers usually held their children for caregiving purposes and to restrict the children's exploration. These parents' actions maximize the possibility for their children to acquire same-sex behavior patterns. These findings lend further support to the contention that parents strongly influence the development of gender-differentiated play activities.

PEER INFLUENCES

It should not be surprising that there are considerable and extensive gender differences in children's play by the time they are 3 years old. These differences are accentuated when children come under the influence of teachers and peers in a classroom or child-care setting, in addition to the continuing effects of parents and siblings on their behavior.

Gender differences in group play have been observed in relation to subtle forms of social behavior. Research suggests that gender-differentiated play may be determined in part by responses of peers to children's activities during free play. For example, Serbin, Connor, Burchardt, and Citron (1979) investigated the effects of peer presence on the gender-typed toy choices of 3- and 4-year-old boys and girls. The experiment consisted of testing the children alone, in the presence of a same-gender peer, and in the presence of an opposite-gender peer. Male- and female-typed toys were presented to the children. Results indicated that the probability of play with cross-sex toys was highest for both boys and girls when they were alone and was lowest when they were with an opposite-sex peer. Girls were more likely to play with cross-gender toys than were boys.

Other researchers have found similar tendencies in preschool children. Observations have shown that boys who engage in male-typed behavior receive more positive responses from peers than do girls who engage in female-typed behavior. Peer reinforcement, particularly same-gender peer reinforcement, is also effective in changing children's behaviors to become gender typical (Lamb, Easterbrooks, & Holden, 1980). The male peer group during the preschool years is especially potent in shaping stereotypically male behavior (Fagot, 1981). Children, especially boys, risk ostracism if they fail to conform to peer-group standards for play and toy use.

TEACHER INFLUENCES

As noted, there is overwhelming evidence to suggest that the early channeling of children toward traditional gender-typed activities is based on children's experiences as family members. Parents, siblings, and peers lay the foundation for the gender differences observed in the classroom or child-care center. By the time they come under teachers' influence, children already seem to possess well-formed notions about gender-stereotyped behaviors sanctioned by our society. The media and popular culture provide another incessant influence on children. What responsibility, then, does the teacher have? What can a teacher do?

Research has shown that there is a tendency for teachers to spend more time with children who engage in female-sex-typed activity, such as arts and crafts, and doll and kitchen play. Teachers of young children are usually females; preschool-age girls and their teachers tend to focus on the same activities. Typical male-sex-typed play behavior, such as vehicle or truck play, tends not to attract much teacher attention or reinforcement. Girls are often seen as being closer to the teacher than boys are, and girls seek structured or constructive play activities far more than boys do (Carpenter, Stein, & Baer, 1978).

Serbin, Tonick, and Sternglanz (1977) explored the effects of teacher presence in the vicinity of play activity and the effects of teachers' modeling play with male and female gender-typed toys. The gender of the teacher was systematically varied, in order to examine the influence of this factor on the free play of boys and girls. The results showed that both boys and girls increased their rates of play participation in response to teacher presence in gender-typed activity areas. The boys were more responsive to teacher involvement in male-preferred activity areas, especially when the teacher was male. These findings suggest that teacher presence and involvement in different locations in the classroom or child-care center can influence children's gender-related play patterns.

Modification of the spatial organization of the classroom can change children's sex-typed play behavior. For example, a number of researchers have suggested that the block areas and the housekeeping areas should be linked, so that the areas can be used together; this arrangement may lead to more social interaction with opposite-gender companions. Children's play experiences would be enriched by increasing the range and type of toys available. Kinsman and Berk (1979) demonstrated that removal of a divider between the housekeeping area and the block area significantly increased play between boys and girls who had been together 1 year or less. The removal of the divider also encouraged children to play with toys traditionally used by the opposite sex. Older preschool children, or those who had been enrolled in the same center for 2 years, however, did not change their patterns of play. Instead, some of these children attempted to replace the divider! Old habits die hard, even for young children. Nevertheless, this study does suggest that teacher modification of the physical environment can influence play patterns.

ADULT ROLES

What, then, is the role of the adult with respect to gender differences in play? Should parents and teachers support these patterns, tolerate them, or try to change them? Answers to these questions depend on individual values. Some authorities have found trends away from traditional sex typing in children's play over the past decades (Sutton-Smith, 1979). Fueled in part by growing feminism in society, a unisex movement arose in the late 1960s and early 1970s, in which early childhood educators were encouraged to put more emphasis on nonsexist activities in the classroom (Simmons, 1976). However, questions can be raised about whether teachers' values correspond or compete with the value systems of families. Different ethnic groups and residents of certain geographic regions of the country, for instance, may be strongly opposed to any move away from traditional sex-role socialization. Parents may not want their children to engage in play behaviors that they do not deem appropriate for their children's sex. Some teachers who are more flexible about sex roles than parents may be overzealous in encouraging such families to be open to change.

Certainly there have been great changes during the past decades in the play behavior of girls (Sutton-Smith, 1979). Throughout early and middle childhood, the sexes share many more forms of play and games than was the case 30 years ago. Furthermore, girls today participate more and more in organized sports as soon as they are old enough to compete in them. Finally, there are a growing number of popular books on the role of games in the lives of today's working women (e.g., *Games Mother Never Taught You* by Harragan,

1977). These books vary in emphasis, but all advocate that the play and games of children are critically important for learning social skills and finesse useful in later life in corporate America. Mothers are told either to help their daughters learn to beat the male-dominated system, or to try to humanize the working world. In any case, the message is clear: Gender-typed play patterns lead to important consequences in life, and parents and teachers should be cognizant of those patterns and take countermeasures if deemed appropriate. For example, if parents favor change, one recommendation would be to help girls become better team players.

We recommend that mothers and fathers make every effort to treat sons and daughters equitably by providing them with toys and other play materials, including storage and space for play. Expenditures of time and money should be about the same for boys and for girls. Time devoted to playing with sons and daughters should be equal, and both mothers and fathers should play with sons and with daughters. Finally, and most importantly, parents should engage their children in both traditionally masculine and traditionally feminine kinds of play. This means, for example, that fathers not only wrestle with their daughters and play baseball with them, but also sew with their sons and bake cookies with them. No play form or activity should be precluded on the basis of tradition. In the process, not only will parents model and reinforce novel play content and contexts, but they will also show children a fresh approach to play.

We recommend that teachers attempt to display the same versatility outlined for parents. In addition, we urge teachers to reexamine and expand children's play options. That means providing more opportunities for different kinds of play. Messages from encouraging research reports should be heeded; for example, Kinsman and Berk (1979) found that while fixed patterns of gender-differentiated play were the rule, preschool children's play patterns could be changed through careful teacher intervention and environmental manipulation. We strongly recommend this kind of enterprising teacher-led experimentation. Teachers should also review and expand dramatic-play options. Unfortunately, what passes for a dramatic-play interest center in some classrooms is sometimes nothing more than the customary domestic-play area— limited to the kitchen at that. If playing house must be the theme, why not at least provide props representing other rooms, such as the family room or garage? Certainly, such efforts will be rewarded by enriched group play, benefiting preschool girls and boys alike. Also, through such efforts, we may help girls and boys balance inner needs for achievement and affiliation and become the kind of men and women who will have successful and productive, as well as happy and fulfilling, lives in the twenty-first century.

PERSONALITY AND PLAY

The term *personality* is often cited to explain a wide range of diverse phenomena. What do we mean when we use the term? Within psychology and education, the notion of personality has taken on the meaning of consistency in certain features of an individual's behavior, which persist across a wide range of situations. In addition, these differences in personal qualities and behavior must be stable over time and not be caused by differences in cognitive maturity.

We typically employ the concept of personality to attempt to account for some specific social or personal behavior. Social and personal behaviors vary in their expression from individual to individual. How much of this variation in behavior stems from individual personality factors? How much of the behavior is caused by situational influences? Finally, how much is based on an individual's level of developmental maturity?

As we traced in Chapter 3, play behavior is a developmental phenomenon. We have seen this developmental progression in examples of object-dependent play evolving toward increasing independence from props—and in the shift from object manipulation to object transformation and then to object-independent play and internalized fantasy. Yet, by definition, play is open to unlimited forms of expression and is subject to a wide range of influences. Children in the same situation and at the same level of cognitive maturity play differently as they attempt to make sense of their worlds and as they grapple with internal psychological conflicts and states. Children express their idiosyncratic preferences and unique personalities in their play. (See the accompanying sidebar, "Theory-Guided Observation.")

Consider how Anais and Petula engage in the following pretend play. They are from the same family backgrounds and are similar in development level. Each is 5 years old. The theme is pirates and princesses, and the play occurs during a free-play period at nursery school within a larger group of children (C).

ANAIS: Yeah, let's finish this meal and go to the shore. Pirates are near.
C: Where are the pirates? On the shore?
      (Anais and C go and crawl on a rug and pretend to watch for pirates.)
ANAIS: Do you see any pirates?
C: Yeah, they are on the boat!
      (C points to gym frame laden with boys.)
ANAIS: We can hide in the cave.
C: OK.
ANAIS: Watch for mountain lions up on the hill.
      (Anais and C walk across the room.)
ANAIS: Look at Jessie, she is injured. Let's help her.
C: Bring her here.
ANAIS: Put her on this rug.
C: OK.
ANAIS: I'll start warming some soup.
      (Anais goes to the domestic center to get some pots and pans, and a new play theme begins.)

In contrast, here is a subplot of the same theme in which Petula was involved the same day, but with different children (C).

PETULA: Where is the treasure? Did the pirates get it?

THEORY-GUIDED OBSERVATION

Keeping track of how each individual child plays and behaves in a variety of classroom situations is not an easy task, but it is nonetheless the responsibility of every teacher. Each child expresses a unique and budding personality. It is fascinating to see such individual variation in the early years. Noting this individuality becomes particularly important when the time comes for conferences between parents and teacher or in less formal situations when a parent can be informed of a child's progress at school. Often, teachers collect some examples of the child's artwork, constructions, and other products for the parent. Long-term projects such as audiocassette logs, diaries, or books of drawings collected over time may also be included. In addition, observations and anecdotes are a common basis of information about a child. Some teachers also keep systematic play records to offer more objective and quantitative information.

The source and kind of observations or information are not as important as what a teacher makes of them regarding a particular child, when considering what information to pass on to parents. It is at this point that comprehensive models of child behavior can become useful to analyze what is going on in the classroom. Such models enable teachers to view children through a discriminating lens to acquire a more sophisticated understanding of each child. Thus, the teacher is able to give a more thoughtful and valid account or appraisal of how each child is doing in the classroom.

Consider the following case. Innocently—but harmfully—a teacher told a parent that the parent's child was very shy at school. This surprised the parent to some extent because the child was not shy at home and in other situations. The teacher's remarks troubled the parent. Such labeling, as we know, can influence others and have long-range effects on children. Personality-trait labeling should be used sparingly. The important point about this example is that the teacher used a simple model of the child's behavior in deciding what to say to the parent. It was a one-factor model. That is, the child's behavior was explained by one factor, the individual difference notion of shyness. It would have been much better if the child's behavior had been considered in terms of a host of factors. It happened that the child was the youngest in the class. Tendencies to withdraw or avoid others, in other words, could be seen as reflecting relative social immaturity or the child's developmental status, as much as anything else. It would also have been smarter for the teacher to have noted situational variation in the child's behavior. That is, are there times in the daily schedule of class events when the child appears to enjoy social commerce? When and under what circumstances does the child seem to avoid social interaction or seem to display passivity? Theories and models of child development may seem at times a bit too remote or abstract to be practical, but understood and applied properly, they can be used to great advantage, enhancing the well-being and development of children.

> C: No, not now.
> PETULA: Bring me the box of gems.
> (C bring a box of old jewelry discarded by the teachers and student teachers.)
> PETULA: I better get my purse, too.
> (Petula carries over purse.)
> PETULA: Let me see what is in here.
> (Petula takes out a number of items and discards them.)
> PETULA: I need room for the diamonds. Give them to me.
> C: Here.
> PETULA: Let's see, these are bigger and these are smaller.
> C: Oh.
> PETULA: This one is the prettiest one of all. This is gold. This is silver.

Anais and Petula are well-matched in developmental level and background and are playing in the same social and physical situation. Still, their play behavior differs considerably. Anais conjures up a narrative relatively independent of objects. She uses words to transform time and space, and her physical surroundings are less important to her than her social surroundings. Petula, in contrast, seems much more dependent on her physical surroundings and is more likely to shift attention to particular physical objects during social pretend play.

OBJECT-VERSUS-PEOPLE ORIENTATION

One major individual difference in play concerns object-versus-people orientation. Some children are more attracted to activities where there is a lot of interaction with people. Others prefer solitary activities, where the focus of attention is on objects.

Jennings (1975) investigated the relationship between preschoolers' cognitive abilities and object-versus-social orientation. He found a significant difference in children's abilities to perform cognitive tasks involving physical manipulations of materials. Children who spent more time playing with objects performed better on tests requiring organization and classification of physical materials. Social knowledge, but not simple preference for social interaction, correlated positively with effectiveness of social interaction. Jennings suggested that object orientation and social knowledge are established early in life and serve to reinforce cognitive skills related to these orientations.

COGNITIVE STYLE

Other researchers have examined the relationship between a child's orientation to objects and people as a measure of cognitive style. *Cognitive style* refers to individual variations in ways of responding to a cognitive task. The most widely researched and generally accepted measure of cognitive style has been field independence–dependence (Witkin, Lewis, Hertzman, Machover, Meissner, & Wapner, 1954). The child who is more *field-independent* has an easier time finding a simple figure within a complex design. The child's attention and perception, it is assumed, do not get lost in the total design (field). The *field-dependent* child apparently gets distracted by elements in the total design and often cannot find the hidden figure.

Coates, Lord, and Jakabovics (1975) found that children who were more field independent sought out objects to play with, while field-dependent children were more people oriented. The field-independent children's greater success at finding the figure in a design may be due to an analytic style that may make them more likely to learn through observing and responding to physical aspects of the environment. Field-dependent children, because of their more global approach, may pay more attention to the social aspects of the same situation.

Saracho (1998) has summarized the literature on the play of field-dependent (FD) and field-independent (FI) children. Studies generally favor FI over FD children in play and social competence and peer status. However, there are some conflicting results. Some studies indicate that FI children play more than FD children (e.g., Saracho, 1995), while other studies suggest that FD children engage more frequently in different forms of play than FI children (e.g., Saracho, 1991). Obviously, firm conclusions cannot be drawn about play in relation to cognitive style in young children. Perhaps these mixed findings are partly due to methodological problems—it is difficult to obtain stable estimates of this trait in young children—and partly due to the conceptual issue of distinguishing cognitive style from developmental progression. Children in general become more field independent with development (i.e., less diffuse and global and more articulate and differentiated). Higher-quality play and peer status found in this research in FI children may be due to their advanced cognitive development, rather than to their field independence.

PLAYFULNESS

Researchers have also studied general playfulness as a personality dimension contributing to observed variations in play behavior and divergent thinking. *Playfulness*, according to Lieberman (1977), can be understood in terms of five traits: physical, social, and cognitive spontaneity; manifest joy; and a sense of humor (see Table 4.1). Lieberman, using rating scales for scoring the play behavior of 93 kindergarten children, found that four of the five playfulness traits were very highly related, with the remaining trait (physical spontaneity) less related. Lieberman concluded that playfulness is a single personality dimension defined by these traits. She found that playfulness was correlated with divergent thinking scores, mental age, and chronological age (see Chapter 2).

Barnett (1991) has researched playfulness in kindergarten children in relation to the five dimensions proposed by Lieberman and in relation to other personality traits and individual characteristics of the children, including gender, number of siblings, and birth order. Seven child-care programs in the

Table 4.1   LIEBERMAN'S PLAYFULNESS CONSTRUCT: FIVE ASPECTS

TRAIT	MANIFESTATION
Manifest joy	Laughter, expressions of happiness and enjoyment
Sense of humor	Appreciation of comical events, recognition of funny situations, gentle teasing
Physical spontaneity	Exuberant, coordinated movement of the whole body or parts of the body
Cognitive spontaneity	Imagination, creativity, and flexibility of thought
Social spontaneity	Ability to get along with others and to move in and out of groups

Source: Based on Lieberman (1977).

Midwest, serving a white middle-class population, provided a total of 271 children in this study. The Children's Playfulness Scale (see Chapter 8) was used to assess the five dimensions of playfulness, and a second questionnaire was used to assess various other personality traits. Correlational analyses revealed a complex set of correlations between the five dimensions of playfulness and the other personality traits. Only one personality trait—being confident—was a statistically significant correlate of all five dimensions of playfulness. Boys were rated higher in physical spontaneity and manifest joy, with girls higher on the cognitive spontaneity dimension. Boys from larger families were most physically active, while girls from larger families were rated lowest for manifest joy. More research is needed on the construct of playfulness and its antecedents and consequences.

Truhon (1979, 1982) has argued that there appear to be two aspects of playfulness and that it is not the unidimensional construct proposed by Lieberman. One aspect is a cognitive component that may lead to creativity and to the understanding of a joke. The other aspect is the affective component, which is seen in the joy of play and the laughter in a joke. Truhon used a modification of Lieberman's playfulness scales to observe 30 kindergarten children in solitary play. Each child was also given a battery of creativity tests. Truhon's statistical procedure (path analysis) supported a distinction between affective and cognitive components of playfulness—a playfulness–fun cluster and a playfulness–intelligence cluster. The two related aspects of playfulness (cognitive and affective) had different impacts on play. The playfulness–fun part of the playfulness scale measured manifest joy and sense of humor, while the playfulness–intelligence part measured intelligence and cognitive spontaneity. Truhon concluded that playfulness is a reasonably good predictor of play activities, but that playfulness and play are weakly related to creativity.

FANTASY-MAKING PREDISPOSITION

A third individual-difference variable concerning play was originally proposed by Singer (1973). Fantasy-making predisposition and playfulness are related but different concepts. *Fantasy-making predisposition* refers to playfulness that takes primary expression in overt pretend play activity or in internalized fantasy; playfulness is more general and can be expressed in more reality-based forms of play (e.g., constructive play), as well as in fantasy play. Research on this individual-difference variable has used observation, projective tests, and oral interviews to estimate children's propensities toward fantasy making. Children high in fantasy-making abilities display higher levels of imaginativeness, positive affect, concentration, social interaction, and cooperation during free play than children with low fantasy-making tendencies. Moreover, children high in this predisposition are also more likely to report seeing movement in ambiguous stimulus cards (the Barron Movement Threshold Inkblot series) and to report in a play interview (Singer's Structured Interview) that they see "little pictures in their heads" and that they have imaginary companions. Their favorite games and play activities reported in the play interview typically involve some make-believe or transformational behavior.

Children high in fantasy-making tendencies have been reported to be better able to pass long periods of enforced waiting or delays in activity. Thus, these children are less likely to become disruptive or to interfere with others. Instead, they are able to engage in some form of imaginative play or to otherwise entertain themselves without overt acting out. High fantasy is associated with the ability to control impulses and delay gratification (Singer, 1961).

Pulaski (1970), among others, has used fantasy making as an individual-difference variable in "aptitude-by-treatment" research. She found that 5-year-old children already high in fantasy making generally scored higher than age-mates low in fantasy making on various measures of imaginative play with unstructured, as well as structured, playthings. Less-structured toys generally elicited a greater variety of fantasy themes. She suggested that perhaps at younger ages, during the preschool period, different kinds of playthings may influence imaginative behavior and its underlying fantasy-making predisposition. Both Pulaski (1970) and Singer (1961) suggested that fantasy making is linked to cognition and creativity (see Chapter 2).

Just as was the case in research on playfulness as an individual-difference variable, the early work on fantasy making seemed to indicate that the trait was an isolated one. However, subsequent studies have suggested otherwise. Singer and Singer (1980) analyzed a set of 33 variables relating to imaginative play, language, social interaction, affect, and home television viewing. Three factors emerged: One indexed general good-humored playfulness across a number of behavior domains; a second identified aggressive interaction associated with television viewing; and a third measured inner imaginative tendencies and prosocial behaviors. This factor structure was stable over the 1-year period of observations. The Singers suggested that manifestations of fantasy-making tendencies, both through play and through more inner-directed channels, are the result of a generally positive relationship the child has with the social and physical environment. Like Nina Lieberman's construct of playfulness, Dorothy and Jerome Singer have developed the idea that the individual-difference variable of fantasy-making predisposition is a life-span personality trait (Singer & Singer, 1990; Singer, 1995).

IMAGINATIVE PLAY STYLES

Research conducted at Harvard's Project Zero indicates individual styles of symbolic play in early childhood (Wolf & Gardner, 1979; Wolf & Grollman, 1982). In a long-term study of children's symbolic play, these researchers have delineated *styles of symbolic play*, or "modes of behavior remaining consistent across a range of materials and situations" (Wolf & Gardner, 1979, p. 119). *Symbolic play* is defined as the "ability to represent actual or imagined experience through the use of small objects, motions, and language" (Wolf & Gardner, 1979). Two styles of symbolic play are *object-independent fantasy play*, in which the child creates imaginary worlds by invoking nonexistent events, roles, and props; and *object-dependent transformational play*, in which the child creates an imaginary world by ably transforming existing objects and arrangements in the environment (Wolf & Grollman, 1982). Earlier in this chapter, Anais and Petula exemplified these contrasting patterns.

Wolf and Grollman (1982) propose that these two styles refer to the quality of an individual's behavior, rather than the child's developmental level. In addition, these individual styles are stable across time and are not instances of particular periods within developmental levels. Finally, analysis of free-play behaviors of preschool children support the notion that these stylistic differences persist and characterize children's interactions with materials.

What, then, are the characteristics of each of these play styles? By defining the imaginative elements in play, Wolf and associates were able to categorize the elements into those that were object independent and those that were object dependent. *Imaginative elements* were defined as "vocal or gestural schemes through which a child altered the pragmatic or actual constituents of the ongoing situation" (Wolf & Grollman, 1982, p. 55). Object-dependent instances of imaginative play involved existing or actually present events, objects, or persons. *Object-dependent* children constructed arrangements or patterns with objects and substituted items where actions required props. On the other hand, *object-independent* children evoked nonexistent elements, often incorporating actual events and objects, but in nonappropriate and far-fetched substitutions. For example, Anais incorporated a teacher's coughing into play, making it the roar of a mountain lion in the pretend cave. These two styles involve persistent and characteristic modes of play, which the researchers inferred are based on earlier investigations of symbolic development.

In their earlier work, Wolf and Gardner (1979) reported consistent patterns of preferences and characteristic ways of organizing responses with materials and tasks in both free-play and test situations. These consistent patterns were the basis for the object-independent and object-dependent styles. "Patterners" displayed considerable skill and interest in making patterns, structures, and orders with objects and materials. These children were interested in an object's mechanical and design possibilities, rather than in communication or interpersonal events. "Dramatists" exhibited a strong interest in human surroundings: what others did, felt, and how they could be known. Dramatists preferred and did well in games, sociodramatic play, and storytelling. These children often performed poorly when engaged in tasks demanding close attention to the physical properties of objects. Patterners, however, excelled in visuo-spatial tasks and in physical relations between objects. According to Wolf and Gardner (1979), these two distinct styles of play and problem solving are part of children's overall personalities and underlying mental structures.

Matthews (1977) supported the notion of individual differences in play style. In her investigation of transformational modes in make-believe play, Matthews pointed out two modes: *material* and *ideational*, which are direct parallels of object-dependent and object-independent play styles. A *material transformational mode* was characterized by the child's active manipulation of and transformation fantasy reference to actual material in the play environment (Matthews, 1977, p. 214). An *ideational mode* involved references, ideas, or mental images of things not physically present to the senses. In her study, Matthews stated that familiarity with the play situation had increased the use of ideational modes, and that girls shifted to ideational modes more quickly than boys did. This evidence suggests that individual differences in cognitive style may be developmental and gender related, rather than stylistic.

A review of the literature concerning individual differences in play styles indicates the need for further study to ascertain whether there indeed exist two persistent and characteristic styles of imaginative play. Research on the symbolic play of 2-year-olds failed to detect divergent styles during this developmental period (Frankin, 1985). Perhaps teachers and parents should expect variability within the same child across different play situations and should recognize that most children will exhibit behavior characteristic of each style.

ENVIRONMENTAL FACTORS AND PERSONALITY

Environmental factors, such as child-rearing styles and family structural characteristics, may influence not only the rate by which children progress through stages of play development, but also children's individual play styles and expression. Why is it that some children are more playful than others, or that different children acquire different play predispositions? Some children prefer fantasy-based play, while others prefer reality-based play; whereas some children are more interested in dramatic play and storytelling, others may find drawing and clay constructing more to their liking. What do we know about the sources of individual variation in play expression?

HOME FACTORS

The home-life experiences of the young child are vitally important in the development of play behaviors. We know that in general, parents and other significant adults in the child's environment exert very important effects on the child's play. Smilansky (1968) and Singer (1973) have both made the case that young children not only need a generally positive home environment and positive relations with parents to flourish in their imaginative play development, but also require specific modeling and encouragement to engage in make-believe play. Others, such as Dunn and Wooding (1977) and Feitelson and Ross (1973), have elaborated on these arguments. Certainly, distinctive play styles, such as being high versus low in fantasy-making predisposition, as well as the quantity and quality of play a child exhibits, emanate in part from patterns of child-rearing, and availability of play space, toys, storage areas, and places for privacy.

Bishop and Chace (1971) and Barnett and Kleiber (1984) are two pairs of investigators who have also sought to identify home-background factors in the emergence of playfulness in children, adapting Lieberman's (1977) use of the term. Both studies used the measure of the "home-as-a-play environment," developed by Bishop and Chace (1971): an interview and questionnaire method, which assesses such things as whether parents allow their children to play in unusual ways or in unusual places. Bishop and Chace reported that mothers' but not fathers' conceptual level of beliefs, measured on a scale from concrete to abstract, related positively and statistically significantly to the home-as-a-play-environment measure. In other words, children deemed more playful in performing specially devised tasks came from home environments that encouraged playfulness, their mother having a more abstract or differentiated belief system.

Barnett and Kleiber (1984) found a similar connection when examining each parent in the family separately, but not when looking at them in composite. In general, these investigators found gender differences when examining additional family-structure variables and parental background characteristics. For instance, when birth order, family size, and sex of sibling were analyzed to determine their influence on a child's playfulness in free-play periods at school, the investigators found that, for males only, later-borns were more playful and that children from larger families were more playful (again, males only). Having no sisters reduced the difference between boys' and girls' manifest playfulness, all other things being equal. That is, males with no sisters were less playful, but females with no sisters were more playful. Fathers' socioeconomic status was positively and significantly related to playfulness in children; maternal age was negatively and signficantly correlated with daughters' playfulness.

These results are complex, and research is needed that would evaluate more thoroughly the contribution of family-structure variables to play quality, quantity, and style. There is less evidence to suggest the importance of such variables than research evidence pointing to the importance of parental practices, particularly during the first and second years after birth, when the mother or father provides "scaffolding" that enables the child to engage in play to the margins of her or his ability (Bruner, 1974). At the preschool level, however, there is little or no evidence suggesting a direct positive link between parental playfulness and the preschool child's playfulness (Barnett & Kleiber, 1984; Johnson, 1978). Parental permissiveness and less family unity may, however, somehow be beneficial to the development of creativity during childhood (Miller & Gerald, 1979). Finally, a number of studies suggest an inverse relationship between anxiety and playfulness. Individual difference in play may be the result of underlying anxiety. Events in the home and the nature of parent–child relations, it is well-known, are related to anxiety in children. Barnett (1991) reported that confidence—the antithesis of anxiety—was a significant correlate of children's playfulness.

ADULT ROLES

Given that adults have important roles in the development of play in general, what part do they play in the child's adoption of specific play styles? Very little research has specifically focused on this question. Most of us would agree, however, that just as adults influence personality development in general, they can affect or change to a great degree play styles or a child's personality as expressed through play. For example, if a parent provides a child with a steady diet of reality-based object and puzzle play, at the expense of other kinds of play, we would expect the child to develop an object-based style of play. If a parent enjoys and conveys enthusiasm for music and dance, we would expect that preference to be mirrored in a child's play. If a parent enjoys pretending and sharing a world of make-believe, it is safe to assume that this would influence the child accordingly. Parents continually influence the styles of play behavior of young children, even if by the time the children are preschool age, parents no longer play an exclusive major role.

As we have seen, researchers have tried to classify play styles and styles of children's personal expression during the preschool years, using dichotomies such as visualizers versus verbalizers, patterners versus dramatists, configurational players versus narrational players (see Figure 4.2). Most children in varied settings no doubt show consistent patterns of play styles representative of each of these opposites. Thus, the divisions are artificial and probably are better interpreted as forming a continuous dimension, with children somewhere in the middle of each.

Valid questions remain nevertheless: Should teachers and parents attempt to foster in a child a particular type of play style? Is it better to be a dramatist than to be a patterner? Although it is quite possible that deliberately promoting a certain style of play is doomed to fail or to backfire in any case, there are at least two reasons for arguing against attempting to modify a child's style of self-expression in play.

First, as we have noted, leading play scholars have cogently stated that play is an ego-building process, the importance of which should not be reduced or tampered with by play theorists and play practitioners. Children at play need to be in control in order for the activity to be playful, enjoyable, and beneficial. The sense of power, mastery, control, and autonomy accompanying play is too integral to play, and too critical to a child's development and well-being to jeopardize through deliberate intrusions by adults trying to cultivate a particular play style.

Sutton-Smith (1979) has discussed the subtlety with which this kind of intrusiveness can take place. For example, a parent may want a child to be more aggressive, domineering, or assertive in play—perhaps particularly if the child is a girl and if the parent seeks to raise a daughter able to succeed in today's corporate, competitive America. This parent may deliberately allow the girl to assume domineering roles in complementary role play with the parent (a child is the doctor and a parent is the subordinate patient). However, a closer examination of what is taking place reveals that the parent is calling all the shots about the play context, even if the child is in control of the play text or what occurs within the script. Given the nature of communication as involv-

*Patterners*_____ *Dramatists*

Visualizers _____*Verbalizers*

Configurationalists _____*Narrators*

Object-dependent _____*Object-independent*

FIGURE 4.2

Imaginative play styles continua

ing multiple levels, even though the parent may feel that one particular play style is being promoted, quite a different one may be the result, which may become obvious in situations when the child is with peers. The child may be getting the message from the well-intentioned parent that others are to be in control of the play situation, although the child is allowed by others to pretend to be in control once the play episode gets rolling. The point is that it is extremely difficult, if not impossible, to infer what the child is experiencing in play, what it means to the child, and what the predicted outcomes may or should be. Hence, any programmatic effort by adults to subtly or not so subtly manipulate play situations and events to foster a particular personality trait in a child cannot be recommended and should probably be avoided.

A second case against deliberately trying to influence personality or play styles is derived from work done on symbolic development and multiple intelligences (Gardner, 1983). According to Gardner's theory of multiple intelligences, each child is endowed at birth with specific genetic predispositions that evolve in interaction with environmental events to produce differing levels of talent in specific intellectual domains, or frames of mind, as he calls them. He identifies the following intelligences: (1) logical–mathematical; (2) linguistic; (3) spatial; (4) kinesthetic; (5) musical; (6) intrapersonal; and (7) interpersonal. The main educational implication he draws from his theory is that each child, in early life, becomes "at risk" or "at promise" in each domain, depending on the amount of opportunities and encouragement for each category of intelligence found in the environment in which the child is developing. He recommends that because one cannot prejudge in which areas a child may have latent talent, assuring a general exposure to all kinds of stimulation relevant to each type of intelligence is wiser than providing more limited but intensive exposure only to factors selected to affect a particular intelligence. Purposely attempting to foster a particular style of play in young children could preclude the child's finding the intellectual, expressive, and creative ways of being that are most natural. This is too much to risk, given that spontaneous playfulness in children appears to be so critical for later adjustment and creative expression.

SUMMARY

Research has documented that boys engage in more rough-and-tumble play than do girls, and they are more aggressive during play. Beginning around age 4 years, boys are more active and girls more sedentary during play. Boys and girls do not differ in social-play development. However, there are significant differences in interactional style and in choice of playmates and materials. Boys are more direct in interaction, while girls are less rigid in their play selections. Girls are more likely to engage in constructive play and other table activities during early childhood. Moreover, while boys and girls do not differ significantly from one another in imaginative play interest and structural skill, considerable evidence shows that thematic content is gender typed, with boys more likely to exhibit individualistic and adventuresome themes, and girls relational and nurturant ones.

Parents, peers, and teachers influence gender-based patterns in play from birth to age 8 years. Parental expectations concerning gender-typed play are revealed in different situations provided for boys and girls in the home environment and in interactive patterns. Teachers' presence, play involvement, and modification of play areas can alter established patterns of play. Wanting to change traditional gender-based play patterns is a matter of an individual's value system, but parents and teachers are urged to treat girls and boys equitably in toy and time expenditures and to encourage a variety of activities through their interactions with children. Adults are encouraged to examine how their own values and biases influence play options for children, particularly play involving role enactments, as children learn social norms.

In addition to gender, individual differences in play during early childhood have been researched in terms of personality. Four personal-style variables are (1) people-versus-object orientation, (2) playfulness, (3) fantasy-making predispositions, and (4) imaginative play styles. Aspects of playfulness include a cognitive component that may lead to creativity and humor comprehension and an affective component that is seen in the joy of play and the laughter in response to a joke. Aspects of fantasy making include overt imaginative play tendencies and inner forms of fantasy. Styles of imaginative play are object-independent versus object-dependent orientations. Dramatists are less focused on objects in make-believe play than are patterners. Individual differences in object play relate to variation in action–object combinations, play tempo, elaboration, organization, complexity, and attention span or play persistence. All these differences are related to overall personality and underlying mental structures. Adults must recognize the ubiquitous effects they have on young children's personality formation and the importance of remaining sensitive to the child's striving for independence and personal fulfillment. In recognizing these effects, adults must provide broad support to help children find their own unique talents and preferences.

Chapter 5

PLAY IN DIVERSE CULTURES

It is June and the beginning of summer, with temperatures already in the 80s a bit past noon. The new season has begun at the city's outdoor swimming pool as the very first "Beginners One" swimming lesson has ended. Leaving the large pool, many children linger on, stopping to wade in a shallow pool for toddlers and young preschoolers. Acquiescing parents sit on the benches around the shallow pool as their 4- and 5-year-olds enter the water for an impromtu extension of their lesson. There are two Taiwanese parents, two Hispanic parents, one African-American, one Native American, one from Korea, one from Saudi Arabia, and three European-Americans. Much glee permeates the atmosphere as laughter and splashing sounds abound. Soon the children are chasing one another, growling and pretending to be dinosaurs. Most of the children go along with this activity, but a few wade away for their own quieter play in the water. The lack of conversation by the children does not seem to slow down the momentum and flow of events—chasing, retreating, splashing, giggling. Parents display very little intervening, watchful for falls in the water but otherwise laid back, relaxed, and occasionally nodding and smiling to other adults present, without speaking to them or their children. The children seem ready to continue their play forever, but soon the children are beckoned one at a time to go home with their parents to have lunch.

Remarkable about this scene is not the cultural diversity that is commonplace in today's society, or the lack of any conflict produced by that diversity. Rather, it is the ease with which the children, who are barely acquainted with each other, launch into group play that has clear elements of shared pretending and cooperation. The youngsters rely on gestures, voice intonation, and context to sustain a shared script about dinosaurs in the water. Mutual understanding quickly emerged without oral communication or adult facilitation in this case. Clearly, we should not underestimate the power of play to serve as a social bridge connecting people from diverse cultural backgrounds. Play can be a valuable tool for fostering many important social, psychological, and educational goals that are multicultural in nature. ■

This chapter is about multicultural play and early childhood education. We seek to understand play, culture, and child development and to apply this knowledge to educational ends. In previous chapters we studied play and development and the individual characteristic variables of age, gender, and personality. Here we focus on the variables of culture and socioeconomic status (SES).

Two major points to remember throughout this chapter are that (1) within-group variation is as important as between-group differences, and (2) play behavior and culture are best conceptualized as standing in a dynamic transactional relationship with each other. Play behavior both transmits culture and can modify culture, where *culture* is defined broadly as any social group consciously sharing, sustaining, and seeking to preserve itself over generations. Although culture offers some cross-generational stability, it is nonetheless dynamic. Cultural and subcultural identities are open to change and evolve over time, with each generation of children and youths leaving its stamp on culture.

In addition to cultural factors, many other contextual and psychological factors affect children's play patterns and choice of play topics and themes. Therefore, we must remain extremely cautious about making generalizations about the influence of culture. By focusing on each child as an individual, we may avoid stereotyping cultural groups.

There are three sections in this chapter:

1. In the first section, we examine important concepts and research concerning the variables of culture in relation to children's play. We give attention to different cultures around the world, as well as to immigrant groups and other minorities in the United States.
2. In the second section, we discuss ideas and research relating to the topic of social class (SES) and play.
3. In the third section, we discuss implications for educators and others who are involved with children's play. We suggest both overall concepts, attitudes, and skills needed by teachers and particular ideas for curricular adaptations.

CULTURAL DIFFERENCES

Increasingly, researchers have been conducting work on children's play in relation to cultural variables. As educational research and the social sciences in general have attempted to respond to the cultural imperative, play researchers and theorists have tried to integrate their studies of play and development with culture. A growing body of literature documents wide cultural variations in the play expression of young children, as well as cultural differences in childrearing and in early childhood educational beliefs and practices related to play and associated behaviors, such as sports, games, projects, and so on (Roopnarine, Johnson, & Hooper, 1994). Contributions have been either (a) conceptual, analytical, and theoretical; or (b) empirical. Empirical work has involved quantitatively oriented studies within the positivist tradition, as well as qualitative research within the emerging interpretive voice or hermeneutic tradition.

CONCEPTUAL WORK

In recent years, helpful frameworks and conceptual distinctions have been made, which provide background for our discussion of play and culture. Two main ideas are covered here: (1) the relation of culture to learning and development; (2) the importance of time as a variable of cultural context.

RELATION OF CULTURE TO LEARNING AND DEVELOPMENT   A decade ago, White (1987) dramatically asserted, "The sad fact is that cultural factors are treated as exotica rather than as creative, generative influences" (p. 186). Although this may be true of some research and educational practice, which follows the "tourist approach" to multiculturalism, the sentiments expressed in the White quote decidedly do not fit the work of Lev Vygotsky (1978), James Wertsch (1985), Beatrice Whiting (1980), Charles Super and Sarah Harkness (1986), and many other contemporary researchers. We discuss their work in this section.

Vygotsky   For example, the so-called 'Vygotskian triangle' of (a) individual/ self variables, (b) other person variables, and (c) cultural/context variables speaks to the need to integrate the cultural dimension into accounts of person and environment transactions as an important force influencing human development and learning. Vygotsky's influence is implicit in current critical reconceptualizations of early childhood education away from overreliance on child development theory or on curriculum theory. According to this view, we must fully appreciate the cultural context as the foundation of both child development and early childhood curriculum (Jipson, 1991). To Vygotsky, cultural context is also the source of our ideas about play and the role of the adult in children's play.

Wertsch   Wertsch (1985) further underscores the challenge for us to learn to understand the forces of development and the forces of culture as operating "in tandem"—not additively, but in a dynamic integrated fashion. To illustrate: We should not view children in general (and children at play in particular) in the context of culture *and* of *either* the family *or* the school *or* the neighborhood. Rather, we need to appreciate the embeddedness of all these contexts (family *and* school *and* neighborhood *and* culture) within a culturally pluralistic milieu. The conceptual challenge is daunting but critical for proper understanding and action. We must observe how well future theory construction and related practice builds on this important mandate.

Whiting   Among the various conceptions of culture and children's play, one widely employed framework for studying development and culture is the cultural–ecological model (Whiting, 1980). According to the cultural–ecological perspective, child development and behaviors, including play behaviors, are related to three sets of factors: distal factors in the broad cultural milieu, physical opportunities and settings, and proximal social networks and environments.

1. Broadly defined, distal influences of cultural, economic, historical, political, societal, and technical factors are outside children's direct experiences but nonetheless exert a powerful influence on children by constraining their experiences to a subset of all possible settings and to a subset of people within these settings.
2. Important effects on play result from the physical opportunities available to children within the immediate settings in which they live and play. These opportunities involve play terrain, the climate and its seasonal variations, natural objects and culturally defined human artifacts for play, danger from roadways, and so on.
3. Play behavior is a function of both the social networks and environments children encounter directly with adults and with other same-age and mixed-age peers, and the resulting experiences, interactions, and relationships that children have with others people (Bloch, 1989).

Super and Harkness An extension of Whiting's cultural–ecological perspective on the relation of culture with human development is the "developmental niche" model of Super and Harkness (1986). Like many other theorists, they do not limit culture to a variable added on after considering other factors; rather, they view culture as a pervasive dimension intertwined with all other variables contributing to behavior and development. For instance, Super and Harkness propose that peer interaction and play behavior cannot be understood apart from the settings in which they occur. These settings also include both the material and the psychological aspects of the actors. In this model, three major dimensions are included in any analysis of culture and play: (1) the physical and social settings; (2) the "inner psychology" of the participants (especially the mental representations of the caregivers concerning child development, socialization, and education); and (3) the cultural customs concerning care and educational practice.

What distinguishes Super and Harkness's model from other cultural–ecological theories is the importance given to systems of representations (the second dimension their model) as integral parts of contextual variables. Obviously, play behaviors are influenced not only by the immediate social and physical context, but also by the beliefs, attitudes, and values (inner psychology) concerning play that are held by the parents, teachers, and other caregivers. Do these caregivers believe that play is important for development and learning? Children will engage in more fully developed play if the adults within their culture support and encourage it. The adults will do so if they believe that the play behavior is important for children's future success in the culture.

Adult representations about play and development and learning in children help determine the kinds of play settings and experiences children will have. At the same time, these representations are connected to cultural customs (the third dimension in the model). These cultural customs are largely unconscious but have pervasive effects on the inner psychology of the participants in a culture. In addition, the effects of these customs are mediated by the culture's working models or blueprints for action, which in turn are based on cultural customs or deep-seated beliefs, values, and norms.

For instance, in our dominant United States culture, autonomy and independence (as opposed to dependency or interdependency) are basic cultural values. For us, these values are so fundamental that we take them for granted. For example, we do not think twice when parents or teachers encourage individualism and competition in children at every turn, at every chance. Like other basic cultural beliefs, this value has pervasive yet unconscious influence on the members of this culture.

The third dimension of Super and Harkness's model, cultural customs about care and education, must be factored into every analysis of children's play, with every culture or subculture yielding a different result. As we have seen in earlier chapters, children's play expresses the interaction of unique children and their distinctive environments. Thus, the individually defining characteristics of each child (e.g., gender, personality, and developmental status) interact with the child's immediate stimulus situation, comprising the social, psychological, and physical environmental factors at hand. The Super and Harkness model suggests an additional level of analysis of play, identifying both the obvious and tangible aspects of culture (e.g., indigenous play materials or the cultural makeup of a peer group, which help form the immediate stimulus field), and the more subtle and abstract aspects of cultural and social structure (e.g., cultural beliefs and values).

Sociocultural variables must always be considered when seeking full understanding of children's play. This broadened view of play accords with the tenets of the relatively new social scientific discipline of *cultural psychology* (Schweder, 1990), which seeks to transform questions of cultural influence or transmission into statements about interactional and psychological processes. Perhaps this new discipline can help teachers think about and base their practices on descriptive and explanatory multicultural findings relevant to early childhood education, particularly to children's play.

TIME AS A CONTEXT FOR CULTURE   In addition to considering culture in relation to learning and development, a second key idea for early childhood educators is the recognition that time (expressed in years, months, or generations) is a potent variable interacting with cultural influences. In current discussions within cultural psychology, child development, and education, scholars and practitioners recognize the need for a contextualizing temporal factor to gain better understanding of cultural contexts (Greenfield & Cocking, 1994; Ogbu, 1991; Slaughter & Dombrowski 1989). In this section, we focus on the work by Ogbu, which discusses historical and generational influences of time, and by Slaughter and Dombrowski, which highlights continuous and discontinous features of temporal experience.

Ogbu   Ogbu (1991) contrasts voluntary immigrant minorities (e.g., Italian, Polish, and Irish Americans) and involuntary minorities (e.g., African-Americans, Native Americans, and Mexicans who became Americans via U.S. conquest of Mexican territory). In particular, he highlights their differences in terms of their acquiescing (voluntary) or oppositional (involuntary) relation to the dominant American culture. Immigrants who come to this country voluntarily accept language and cultural differences and are willing to adapt, at least initially, to the demands of the formal educational system and to our society at large. On the other hand, involuntary minorities who were enslaved or conquered many years ago retain a residue of mistrust and skepticism about the status quo. Social injustices have led to alienation and to frustrated dreams of upward social mobility they have suffered within family lines across generations. For example, Ogbu speaks about the glass ceiling through which racial minorities can see as they watch white middle-class males in America get ahead at their own expense. Similarly, a "job ceiling" refers to employment barriers and truncated career opportunities that make the American dream unrealistic for them as they suffer the effects of institutional and personal racism.

On the other hand, immigrant minorities also may lose their idealism after they have been within the dominant culture a second or third generation and witness and feel social oppression and alienation. For example, in some immigrant families, the parents are more conforming and achievement oriented than are their discouraged sons and daughters, who, upon reaching adolescence and young adulthood, are struck with how unlevel the playing field really is for them as they try to compete for their share of the American dream (Gibson & Ogbu, 1991).

Ogbu's typology of voluntary and involuntary minorities and his concept of a job ceiling helps us better understand patterns of behavior and the adaptation of different minority groups, defined by ethnicity and by how long a group or family has been in the United States. Many people do feel marginalized and want their voices heard and faces seen as affirming both their distinctive identity and their right to be accepted into the mainstream culture. For example, while parents from certain ethnic or racial groups may demand civil, economic, and political rights in the public arena, on the domestic front, they may create a segregated and exclusionary school (e.g., highlighting Afrocentric ECE curriculum) to foster in their children pride in their own heritage. Moreover, even when ethnic minority groups consciously seek to accommodate to the dominant society, connections to the past and to the culture of origin remain important and often exert lasting influence on childrearing beliefs and practices (Greenfield & Cocking, 1994).

For example, immigrant or visiting international families may share distinctive games, crafts, songs, toys, and play activities with their offspring. At the same time, immigrant parents and their children are gradually acquiring a new play-behavior repertoire and some accompanying play attitudes and values. Over time, these families find means for both cultural preservation and cultural adaptation in response to the new cultural milieu. Continuities and discontinuities are in a dynamic state for each and every family, and educators must realize and respect this as they forge partnerships with parents. Culture is not a static variable, frozen in time. Educators can help children deal with competing forces from school and peers by being sensitive to this reality.

Slaughter and Dombrowski   Slaughter and Dombrowski (1989) have provided a helpful vocabulary for discussing various differences among changing families in changing contexts. Their typology is important for early childhood education in general, and for adults who are responsible for children's play in particular. According to these play scholars, *culturally continuous contexts* generally mean that the child's family has lived in the same broad socio-eco-logical context for at least two generations. *Culturally discontinuous contexts* refer to situations in which the child's family has changed socio-ecological contexts within the preceding two generations. Children in culturally discontinuous contexts include those whose families are migrants, refugees, immigrants, or visiting or studying from abroad.

Slaughter and Dombrowski have added to this continuous–discontinuous dimension a second dimension concerning whether the family, cultural, or subcultural group is assimilated or unassimilated. *Assimilation* usually is defined with respect to how well adjusted a group is in relation to the mainstream dominant majority. The disenfranchised are often *continuous* but *unassimilated*—as is the case with some involuntary minorities, with the oppressed, with the homeless, or with the so-called underclass in general. For many, if not most, unassimilated but culturally continuous individuals, their plight is seemingly endless: They expect never to taste the fruits of success in America. Many *discontinuous* and *unassimilated* cultural groups, such as new immigrants who came to the United States voluntarily, endure alienation also—but only temporarily, or at least they hope. Their goal is to become assimilated without eradicating their own cultural selves.

ASSIMILATION AND ADAPTATION   There is much current debate about the "unum" in our country's motto "e pluribus unum." Do we focus on the center or the boundaries, our samenesses or our differences, the whole or the parts, in working through our present national identity crisis? Stressing the whole can produce stifling conformity and stagnation in our nation's cultural evolution. Stressing the parts can lead to separatism and societal fragmentation.

We need to find a way to balance the whole and the parts. We need to avoid the extremes of too much meshing with or too much pulling away from the mainstream in defining our yardstick for judging an optimal degree of assimilation and cultural adaptation. Perhaps teachers and others who work with young children and their families from diverse cultural groups can learn to become more sensitive and responsive to intragroup, as well as intergroup, differences. Teachers need to understand the needs and interests of the many groups of children who are undergoing cultural change and who must adapt to multiple cultures as they seek to acquire more inclusive or transcultural identities (Angell, 1994).

EMPIRICAL WORK

In addition to the conceptual and theoretical work on culture and play, there has been extensive research on children's play in other countries around the world. In the past, such research has been undertaken to test the universality of stage theories of play development or the prevalence or even existence of certain play states, such as symbolic or pretense play. Ethnographic anthropological research, such as that compiled by Schwartzman (1978), has proven useful for dispelling certain prevalent myths. For instance, research has shown that children's early integration into the adult world of work does not preclude their having a play life or engaging in dramatic play with other children; social pretense does not depend on having play materials or toys designed for pretense play and having same-age peers. Cross-cultural differences in themes, content, and style are manifested in children's imaginative play expressions.

Research studies are helpful for broadening our knowledge base about the enormous variation across cultures in the content and style of children's play and on how play affects and is affected by cultural context. Three kinds of research studies contribute to our understanding:

1. Some investigations have described play and related behaviors in specific cultures (e.g., deMarrais, Nelson, & Baker, 1994). This kind of research has a rich tradition (Schwartzman, 1978).
2. Some studies have examined samples of children at play in other countries and have compared these data with observations of American preschoolers (Pan, 1994; Tobin, Wu, & Davidson, 1989).
3. Increasingly, empirical work has focused on the play of immigrant children attending preschools or child-care programs in the United States (e.g., Farber, Kim, & Lee, 1995).

EMPIRICAL STUDIES OF PLAY WITHIN SPECIFIC CULTURES   As a recent example of the first kind of research, consider the work of deMarrais et al. on Yup'ik Eskimo girls. This study, based on ethnographic interviews and participant observation, illustrated the importance of a particular play activity for the enculturation and development of 6 to 12-years-old girls living in villages along the Kuskokwim River in southwestern Alaska: storyknifing in mud. In *storyknifing*, makeshift mud palettes are used for drawing various icons and symbols as the girls tell stories, erasing the earlier scenes that they created by smearing the mud in order to make room for the new ones as they continue their stories. As the researchers noted, while the afternoon sun warmed the muddy banks of the river, girls would engage in storyknifing for up to 3 hours at a time. Their play took place far away from the buildings in the middle of town and away from the boardwalks that connected village buildings and were used by pedestrians and bicyclists.

Although much less common than before the advent of television and videos, storyknifing is still seen (ideas from the new media have even become incorporated into storyknifing) and provides an activity forum that helps the girls (a) learn from older peers cultural knowledge about kinship patterns, gender roles, and community norms and values; and (b) consolidate through play and story expressions their understandings and feelings about their culture and their own identities. Moreover, storyknifing promotes the learning of skills, habits, and attitudes relevant to the culture in which they live. It should be noted that, by tradition, women engage in pottery making, berry picking, and cooking, and men fish and hunt. Perhaps this is why boys never have done storyknifing. Only the girls stood to gain from the physical aspects of the play as practice for a later women's activity within this culture. The researchers reported that this tradition is now changing, as some women go off to college or hold jobs, and some men cook fish or pick berries. Current narratives by these girls, off to themselves by the riverbank using the mud palettes, reflect these changing gender roles in village life.

CROSS-CULTURAL COMPARISONS OF CHILDREN'S PLAY   A recent example of the second kind of research was done by Pan (1994), who compared the play of 62 kindergartners in Taipei with the results of Rubin, Watson, and Jambor (1978), who observed children of preschool and kindergarten age. Pan also explored her data set in relation to American data sets with respect to cognitive and role-taking correlates of different play forms (Rubin & Maioni, 1975), and in relation to maternal attitudes toward play (Johnson, 1986). The observation procedures and the way the play behaviors were coded were similar across the Pan and the Rubin studies.

Constructive play was commonplace in both Taiwan and America, but interactive dramatic play was more prevalent in the United States sample (twice as much in preschool and thrice as much at the kindergarten level), while parallel constructive play and interactive games with rules were more prevalent in the Taiwanese sample. Interestingly, in the United States samples, interactive dramatic play was positively correlated with intelligence and role-taking ability, but in the Taiwanese sample, it was not. In Taiwan, participation in interactive games with rules was positively and significantly correlated with mental age (.42) and with role-taking (.28). The mothers of these children did not endorse games with rules but did prefer constructive play and academic activities to a greater extent, relative to the United States sample.

Pan's findings are consistent with the *Preschool in Three Cultures* study by Tobin, Wu, and Davidson (1989). This study compared children in early childhood settings in the United States, Japan, and China, using multivocal visual ethnographic techniques. Through these techniques, teachers discuss their reactions to videos of programs in the other countries, as well as in their own. It was found that the U.S. responses fell between those of Japan and of China on dimensions of play and academic values for young children. For example, in response to the question "Why should a society have preschool?" 70% of the Japanese, 42% of the United States, and only 25% of the Chinese sample gave "opportunities for playing with other children" in their top three reasons.

Academic goals were within the top three choices of 67% of the Chinese sample, 51% of the United States sample, and only 2% of the Japanese sample. Japanese respondents fear educational burnout before the educational rat race is over and prefer to emphasize *kodomo-rashi kodomo* ("childlike children") during the early preschool years, while the Chinese favor preschool as a place for serious learning. The Chinese respondents were less likely to agree that "play is the child's work," than that "work (academics) is a form of child's play." For Chinese respondents, even using blocks must be according to *order*. In the United States, the picture is mixed, with many teachers and parents of young children torn between wanting to give young children a head start and worrying about inducing stress and achievement anxiety by hurrying them. Many of these U.S. parents and teachers unfortunately seem confused or uninformed about the value of play for giving young children an academic head start in a developmentally appropriate way.

STUDIES OF U.S. IMMIGRANT CHILDREN   Typical of research of the third kind is a recent study of cultural differences in 48 Korean- and 48 European-American 3- to 5-years-olds' social interaction and play behavior (Farver et al., 1995). Data sources included direct observations of the children within their respective preschool activity settings (which were markedly divergent), parental reports of home play, and teacher ratings of social competence. While the Korean-American children were observed to engage in social pretend play at less than half the rate this play behavior was seen in the Anglo-American sample, unoccupied states were coded twice as often and parallel play almost thrice as often in the Korean-American sample, relative to the Anglo-American sample of preschoolers. On the other hand, Korean-American children proffered objects to initiate play and were more cooperative than their European-American counterparts, a finding consistent with their cultural value of interdependence and field sensitivity. Teachers rated Korean-American children as more hesitant and less sociable, compared to the Anglo-American children.

These cultural differences displayed at school made sense in terms of what the preschool activity settings were like for these two groups of children. Although each setting had teachers and same-age peers together for the purpose of school readiness, the way this was carried out was quite different. In the Korean-American activity setting, the nature of the activities performed included memorization games, tasks requiring persistence and effort and passive learning centered on academic achievement. In the Anglo-American setting, the aim was to foster social and cognitive skills in the youngsters by means of active involvement in imaginative and other more convergent types of problem-solving situations where individual expression counted for more than group harmony. Parents of the Anglo-American children prized play and especially pretense play as a tool for cognitive and language growth and school readiness, and they reported that their children did a lot of it at home. In contrast, the Korean-American parents did not share this belief and instead saw play as basically for the child's entertainment and as a way to escape boredom.

INTEGRATING THE FINDINGS   Cultural group differences in the play abilities or preferences of young children have been documented in a number of studies, supporting our belief in the important role of environmental factors in play development (Feitelson, 1977; Finley & Layne, 1971; Murphy, 1972; Seagoe, 1971; Smilansky, 1968; Udwin & Shmukler, 1981; Whiting, 1963). Sociocultural variables are not explanatory in themselves, however, but are umbrella

There is considerable variation and overlap in play activity among children in different cultures.

variables under which related specific factors or proximal variables exert their more immediate influence on play behavior and development (e.g., the availability of play materials, adult encouragement). A basic premise of this book is that these specific factors, rather than the sociocultural umbrella variables, affect the rate and level of play behavior and development. The Farver et al. (1995) study is a good illustration of this point, as the cultural influence was seen to be mediated by the makeup and teaching philosophy of the classroom activity settings.

There is considerable variation and overlap in play expression among children across cultures. One generalization that has emerged from research may be that educational forms of play (see Chapter 1) take on a more homogeneous flavor, whereas recreational or expressive play retain more cultural specificity (Lasater & Johnson, 1994). Another is that children are more likely to engage in a particular form of play if the form is supported by the adults of the culture. For example, soccer is a favorite sport in most countries of the world, and preschool children as young as 2 years of age engage in this activity, even though it is a game with rules, which—according to Piagetian theory—makes it more developmentally advanced than symbolic play. On the other hand, sociodramatic play is not seen in many of the same cultures, even though it requires similar levels of cooperation and rule following. Clearly, then, such play variation is not due to cognitive limitations or strengths of the players but to differences in cultural influence.

In earlier studies, underdeveloped play skills have been observed in children growing up in countries where poverty exists (Ebbeck, 1973; El Konin, 1971). Sutton-Smith (1977) suggested that perhaps the critical determining factor of play is whether children are an economic asset and therefore forced to participate in early survival training and work, circumstances that would compete with play before age 4 or 5 years.

Children perform or fail to perform certain kinds of play because of environmental conditions. Physical space and time for play are important for the development of play skills. Children also need objects, including natural ones such as stones, twigs, cornstalks, and so on as play props to trigger and sustain their imaginations. Adults' attitudes about play and their behavior toward children at play are critical. A number of play scholars have noted the importance of having adults or older peers or siblings actively encourage and model play, to help young children develop a knack for certain kinds of play, such as make-believe play (Feitelson & Ross, 1973; Singer, 1973; Smilansky, 1968). If learning conditions are missing in a sociocultural group, then the play form may be absent or severely underdeveloped.

Earlier cross-cultural research on play behavior suggested that imaginative play was virtually absent in some societies (e.g., among Russian and East African children—see Ebbeck, 1973; El'Konin, 1971; Whiting, 1963) but very rich and diversified in others (e.g., among New Zealand and Okinawan children—see Seagoe, 1971; Whiting, 1963). According to Feitelson (1977), there are great differences in the quality of imaginative play among children growing up in different societies, and in some societies, imaginative play is almost nonexistent. She cites Ammar's (1954) description of childhood in rural Egypt and Levine and Levine's (1963) description of Gusii childhood in Kenya. These children were viewed as lacking in conditions for play, and adults in these societies were shown actively trying to prevent children from playing. Children were seen as passive and quiet observers of adults' doings. In her own research on Kurdish Jews, Feitelson found that an all-pervasive attitude of adults was that little children should be seen but not heard. She inferred that this attitude was responsible for young children's extreme passivity and lack of play.

Although these cultural distinctions may be legitimate, independent effects of social class and culture on children's play must be recognized. Udwin and Shmukler (1981), for instance, in examining low- and middle-class children in Israel and South Africa reported significant social-class but not cultural differences in imaginative play. These authors noted that the apparent deficits in imaginative play among lower-class children were not created by a lack of experiences or stimulation, but by the failure of lower-class parents to help their children with the integration of diverse stimuli that confronted them in the course of everyday life. We might expect social-class factors to

Theory in Action

RANDOM OBSERVATIONS ON PLAY

Francis Wardle

When I lived in the Highlands of Guatemala, I had the opportunity to observe young Mayan children in their natural setting. Although I was ostensibly building houses after the 1976 earthquake that devastated the area, as an educator, I was fascinated by the children. The young boys played a game with pop-bottle caps. (Water there was too polluted to drink, so everyone drank pop.) Children as young as 5 and 6 years old delighted in this game, where they threw the caps against a wall and scored points, depending on the position in which the caps landed.

I also played soccer with the boys in the small village. I marveled at the skill, knowledge, and teamwork that even the 5- and 6-year olds possessed. Anyone who has traveled in Third World countries has seen youngsters playing soccer in empty lots, plazas, streets, and backyards. Soccer is a universal game that has been passed on from generation to generation. Younger boys learn the game by playing with older boys and men.

While the boys were playing soccer on our highlands field, the girls were usually washing clothes in the stream. The girls seemed to make a game of it, though, by laughing and giggling, splashing each other, and throwing the soap. I often observed children accompanying their parents in work-related activities such as washing clothes, building fires for a barbecue, attending meetings, and caring for the corn and bean plants. In every instance, these children would develop a game to play while their parents worked: splashing the water, using sticks for swords, drawing in the sand, and playing with the leaves of the bean plants.

During the year I taught kindergarten there, I had a young student from Lake Titicaca (Bolivia). Her family belonged to an indigenous tribe in the area. She spoke no English but soon became fully immersed in all the classroom activities. Her favorite learning-center choice was the dramatic-play area. She usually played by herself or with one other student. She spent a lot of time caring for a large doll by dressing her, combing her hair, and putting her to bed. Even when she was engaged in other classroom activities, however, she carried the doll around the room on her back, tied with an imitation shawl or poncho.

My kindergarten children spent a great amount of time outside, exploring the natural world. We dammed streams, skated on frozen wetlands, built forts, and caught tadpoles and crawdads (Wardle, 1995). We jumped into piles of leaves, climbed trees, and went fishing. When I took

(continued)

them to use swing sets and playgrounds (climbers, slide, tunnel, swivel swing, etc.), however, they did not seem very interested. It was as if these human-made structures could not compete with the "real thing."

Another interesting setting I observed was an Amish school in rural Pennsylvania. I was surprised to see no playground equipment on the small patch of grass outside, not even old pieces of farm machinery, tires, or tree stumps. What did the children do at recess? Did they even want to leave the classroom for recess? Then I watched a small group of children engaged in a game with a broomstick. Two children held the stick at each end, parallel to the ground. Each child in the group, both girls and boys, jumped over the stick. Then the stick was raised. The object of the game was to see who could jump the highest. Apparently, their lack of equipment did not deter their enjoyment of outdoor play.

weigh more heavily than cultural factors in contributing to the frequency and quality of children's play. In this view, the content of play would differ by culture, but the level of play within each culture would vary as a function of socioeconomic level.

An opposing position has been advanced by others—primarily ethnographers, folklorists, and anthropologists—who have argued that all young children can engage in make-believe play, regardless of their cultural and social-class membership (Schwartzman, 1978; Sutton-Smith & Heath, 1981). According to this position, the reason that play deficiencies have been attributed to certain groups of children is because of ethnocentric or class bias in researchers who display their ignorance by using narrow research tools and who fail to recognize imaginative play in children who come from cultural or socioeconomic backgrounds different from the researchers'.

Schwartzman (1978), in her comprehensive book *Transformations: The Anthropology of Children's Play,* provides ample ethnographic data about the play of children from non-Western, less technologically and economically advanced societies. She notes that ethnographic studies that have reported a paucity of play among children in rural Egypt and Kenya and among the Kurdish Jews in Israel (Ammar, 1954; Feitelson, 1959; Levine & Levine, 1963) did not have as their primary focus children's play, let alone types of play. She warns that the absence of evidence on play from these studies is not evidence of the absence of such play. According to Margaret Mead (1975), "Students should be warned that one can never rely on a negative statement that any toy, any game, any song is absent just because it is neither witnessed nor recalled by adults" (p. 161). Indeed, recent ethnographic accounts (Roopnarine et al., 1994) suggest that children around the world participate in a wide variety of play forms, play which is often combined with work (e.g., Bloch & Walsh, 1983).

In his early work, Sutton-Smith (1972) developed the thesis that differences in imaginative play between Western and traditional (developing non-Western) societies may well relate to what he calls differences between "ascriptive" and "achievement" cultures. Children who belong to an ascriptive culture engage in play that (a) is imitative or copied but not transformational or creative and (b) relies on the use of realistic toy representations rather than improvised ones or none at all. In other words, children in ascriptive cultures imitate the behavior of their elders; they replicate but do not transform. In contrast, the imaginative play of young children in achievement cultures is replete with make-believe transformations that are more flexible and diversified (subject–object, object–object, and self–other transformations).

In later work, Sutton-Smith and his colleagues turned their attention to describing differences in imaginative play style related to cultural factors. Ethnographic work by Sutton-Smith and Heath (1981) analyzed two styles of imaginative behavior, which they call "oral" and "literate." The *oral style* of imagination is usually of a rhetorical type that is embedded in verbal communication between the central performer and the group. In cultures in which the *literate style* predominates, imagination is often used in solitary situations and stresses detachment from the mundane world and the conjuring up of things not present. Sutton-Smith and Heath suggest that what appear to be developmental deficiencies in imagination may be differences in imagination style.

Sutton-Smith and Heath (1981) went on to show that these cultural styles can be detected in the stories told by children as young as 2 years of age. They compared a sample of stories told by working-class black children in the Piedmont Carolinas with a sample of stories told by middle-class white children in New York. Stories told by the working-class African-American children tended to be relatively personal and to be taken, for the most part, from real-life experiences. White middle-income children, on the other hand, tended to tell stories in the third person, which were fantasy-like in content. Of the New York stories, 95% were in the third person, but only 30% of the stories by the African-American children were. In each collection, however, clear evidence of imagination, albeit of different types, was seen. Piedmont children were more likely to show their talents in a collective rather than in an individualized context.

Sutton-Smith and Heath suggest that children from cultures that are more oral than literate will often appear most imaginative and playful when words are the center of the activity. Still, the question remains whether certain kinds of play experiences (i.e., literate style) are more useful in preparing for modern technological and informational society.

SOCIAL CLASS

In her book *The Effects of Sociodramatic Play on Disadvantaged Preschool Children*, Sara Smilansky (1968) not only sparked interest in play training (see Chapters 1 and 7) but also helped to promulgate the belief that the play of children who come from low-income families is deficient in a number of respects (McLoyd, 1982). Many researchers and practitioners took to heart Smilansky's words that "children from the low sociocultural strata play very little and most of them do not participate in sociodramatic play at all" (1968, p. 4). Because of the commonly accepted connection between imaginative play and symbolic development, there resulted an eagerness to link social-class differences in pretend play to disparities in symbolic competence in general (either as a source or as an effect) and to devise remedial play tutoring to compensate for this supposed social-class gap (Freyberg, 1973; Saltz & Johnson, 1974).

Smilansky and other researchers influenced by her work have characterized the pretend play of economically disadvantaged children, compared to that of middle-class children, as less frequent and of lower quality. Typically, descriptions of their play include such adjectives as "unimaginative," "repetitive," "simplistic," "desultory," "dependent on objects," and "concrete." We might add that these terms are not far removed from the kinds of qualifiers that have been applied in the past to the play of young children with autism or mental retardation, qualifiers such as "personalized," "ritualistic," "less likely to combine toys" (Weiner & Weiner, 1974). Numerous researchers reported that middle-class preschoolers engaged in more sociodramatic play than did disadvantaged preschoolers (Fein & Stork, 1981; Rubin, Maioni, & Hornung, 1976).

To what extent can it be fairly stated that young children with a low-socioeconomic status do not develop their imaginative play as fully as middle-class children? Is there a delay in the rate at which children from impoverished backgrounds perform make-believe play? Is there a critical period during which children need to exhibit symbolic play or have their psychological development impeded? Instead, are the foregoing conclusions derived from research studies that used questionable methodology? If researchers had observed lower-socioeconomic-status children at play in locations other than school—such as in their homes, back lots, and backyards—maybe what appeared to be play deficiencies would have turned out to be play strengths.

RECENT RESEARCH

The 1990s has seen a sharp slowdown in research on play and social class, compared to the considerable attention paid to this variable in the previous three decades. An important reason behind the decline in interest has been the general consensus that it is less productive to continue researching social class as a macrolevel environmental variable in comparative investigations and more productive to focus on more specific microlevel contextual factors influencing children's play behavior. Furthermore, it is problematic to investigate the relationship between social class and play; the extant literature is fraught with technical difficulties having to do with the operational definition of social class and the ecological validity of the research, among other methodological issues (McLoyd, 1982). In general, it is now believed that any so-called "play deficits" related to low social class are differences in motivation or in opportunity for certain kinds of play and are not due to differences in ability.

For example, Doyle, Ceschin, Tessier, and Doehring (1991) examined social pretend play in relation to social class while also measuring children's cognitive and symbolic abilities. The sample included 51 boys and girls attending kindergarten and 67 boys and girls in the first grade in a suburban elementary school near a large Canadian city. Approximately half the children were categorized as lower SES, with the remainder in the middle SES group, based on parental education and occupation. Over a 5-month period of time, these children were observed at play and were given an individually administered test of a number of cognitive tasks. The tests and the observations were conducted by different researchers, to control for tester effects. Measures included scores on seven tests of conservation, verbal symbol substitution, and symbol use, together with observation scores for mode of play and types of transformation during pretense play (substitute objects, imagined objects, role transformations, etc.). Middle-class children spent, on average, 25% more time in social pretend play than did lower-class children, and their play episodes were 17% longer. They also scored higher on the conservation tasks and on the tests for verbal symbolic skills. However, amount and duration of social pretend play were unrelated to the cognitive task measures and did not increase with age, leading the authors to conclude that for older preschoolers and early elementary school children, social-class differences in pretend play are more probably due to motivational factors than to cognitive factors. Criticisms of earlier work involving younger children from lower social classes (Rubin et al., 1976; Smilansky, 1968) likewise suggest an underestimation of their play "ability," relative to middle-class standards (McLoyd, 1982).

FOCUS ON SPECIFIC PLAY BEHAVIORS   Another feature of more recent research dealing with children's play and social-class factors is the attempt to be more specific in the identification and assessment of play behaviors and more contextualized in characterizing the environments in which play occurs. Fantuzzo, Sutton-Smith, Coolahan, Manz, Canning, and Debnam (1995), for example, used observations and ratings of play of low-income African-American preschoolers attending Head Start programs. Rather than employing a priori global normative play categories—such as for parallel play, for constructive play, and so on, as has been done in previous research—they opted for an inductive strategy and operational specificity to capture finer details about children's behaviors.

In this sample of preschoolers, the many behaviors exhibited were first summarized and then interpreted, based on a factor-analysis statistical technique. Three major dimensions they found were (1) Play Interaction, (2) Play Disruption, and (3) Play Disconnection. Examples of specific behaviors under the first dimension included leading others, helping to settle disputes, directing others' play, showing creativity, adding details to others' make-believe play, and sharing ideas. Examples of specific behavioral items that were highly correlated, loading on the second factor of Play Disruption, included: does not take turns, tattles, grabs other things, is physically aggressive, verbally assaults, and does not share toys. Exemplifying the third factor, Play Disconnection, were: withdraws, wanders aimlessly, confused in play, seems unhappy, not invited into play groups, and needs teacher's direction.

A primary purpose behind the Fantuzzo et al. study was to create an assessment tool for play observation in a center-city Head Start population, which would be useful to teachers in their curricular planning and in individualizing their teaching (See Chapter 8 for further discussion of this study and the assessment scale.) The three dimensions are supported by psychometric evidence presented in this study, but the authors strongly warned that these dimensions represent behaviors of particular children at certain developmental levels within specific classroom ecologies. They are not static traits of children or decontextualized classifications to be misused, for example, as a basis for labeling children or for educational placement (e.g., this child is "disruptive," "not ready for kindergarten").

IN-DEPTH QUALITATIVE STUDIES   Other recent studies of children's play and social class and related variables (migrant children, homeless children, resilient children, etc.) are qualitative (e.g., case study or ethnographic in orientation) and examine circumstances and behaviors in depth, including the play of a small number of children. These studies are quite different from quantitative comparison studies, which have sought empirical generalization of the findings and have often led to unfair comparisons with an idealized middle-class referent group, adding to arguments about play deficiencies and the label *culturally disadvantaged*. Instead, today's qualitative studies tend toward providing localized knowledge consisting of rich contextualized descriptions of particular children in particular life circumstances. While researchers have no pretensions concerning the generalizability of findings in a statistical sense, these studies have deepened the understanding of children's play and SES variables. The meaning readers take from them often apply to other settings with which readers are familiar and are personally involved.

An example is a recent qualitative study of the English language acquisition of three Spanish-speaking children enrolled in a bilingual preschool (Orellana, 1994). Carlos, Veronica, and Elisa, all about 3 years old, were observed during free play for a total of 20 hours each. Field notes and audiotaped transcriptions were coded for pretense play, other kinds of play, and conversations during play. Pretense was further coded for playacting real people and for playacting characters from children's popular culture. Language use was coded for all analyzable units, and a count was made for children's choice of English or Spanish within and across each episode of play. The study also provided rich descriptions of the children's home and school contexts.

Among the findings was children's strong preference for English when enacting superhero roles, a very popular form of play reported in this study. One interpretation connected the play and language choices by the children to identity formation and the power of the dominant culture. All the children used English as part of the superheroic powers possessed while in character. Carlos noted that he would only use English when he grew up. Implications of the study included the potential value of pretense play to foster English language acquisition, and the possible need for extra effort by teachers to balance language use for facilitating bilingual, biliterate development in young children. Despite these suggestive findings, the researcher cautioned the reader not to overgeneralize the findings of this qualitative investigation.

Research generalization remains critically important, but ideally, it is the consumer of research who decides what is personally and professionally applicable, not claims about the research's validity and generalizability, based on the design and analysis of the study. A major lesson learned from qualitative studies is that they demonstrate the tremendous disservice that may have been done by some of the earlier quantitative studies in leading some readers to underestimate the full richness and importance of play in the lives of all children. Qualitative studies often offer a useful corrective lens through which to view some of the ethnocentric and myopic research instrumentation and choice of variables employed in the past.

SOCIAL-CLASS VERSUS SCHOOL-RELATED FACTORS   Depending on their immediate circumstances, children are developmentally "at risk" or "at promise" for school readiness, for positive growth and development in general, and for having rich and vibrant preschool play experiences in particular. There are gross inequities in the affordances and opportunities for play in the early environments of today's children, related to their family income. Over 20% of today's children are poor; according to the annual statistics released by the Children's Defense Fund, one child in nine is born into a family living at less than half the poverty level, which was $6,079 in 1995 (*The State of America's Children Yearbook,* 1997). Human services personnel and educators recognize and bemoan the material resource deprivations afflicting so many of America's children. Many social workers and educators actively seek to enhance the well-being and development of children and their families by providing technical and moral support through parent education and play interventions. Furthermore, today's informed social and educational policies and practices eschew the deficit model and embrace the difference or empowerment model, which is based on mutual respect and collaboration with parents and children from diverse social class, cultural, or ethnic group backgrounds.

Many previous studies confounded social-class factors with classroom and school factors. It is unfortunate when observations of spontaneous play are done exclusively in preschool or child-care settings. The problem is to determine whether such settings are fair locations to witness the imaginative and creative play of youngsters who are not from white middle-class backgrounds. The failure to see rich imaginative play in these settings, designed for middle-class children and adults, does not imply that other children are not capable of rich imaginative play in other less biased settings. Contrasts in values and social behaviors between children's home settings and their school or child-care settings may make children generally less comfortable in spontaneously expressing high levels of playfulness and imagination. Moreover, the activity centers and thematic play materials found in middle-class-oriented

Research on social class and cultural differences in play needs to be conducted in home and neighborhood settings, as well as in schools.

schools or child-care centers are less familiar to lower-class children than they are to middle-class children. If young children are not familiar with objects, they tend to explore them initially, only later using them in imaginative play. If children suspect that their behavior will lead to adverse consequences, they tend to be inhibited and reluctant to externalize their fantasies—fantasies they do have. One mother, when told by a teacher that her young son did not engage in sociodramatic play at school, emphatically retorted, "If you knew my son's fantasies, it would blow your mind." Moreover, some parents may want their children not to reveal their imaginative play at school, for fear that it will be misinterpreted (Phillips, 1996). Children may develop a countercurriculum for play in the home, to offset the lack of culturally acceptable play opportunities at school.

Several thoughtful recommendations have been made to help researchers more accurately calibrate the imaginative play abilities of low-socioeconomic-status children and children from different cultural backgrounds. McLoyd (1982) has suggested examining the spontaneous play of young children in a broader context, including home and neighborhood settings. If such observations are not available, then researchers may set up special playrooms; perhaps two-room mobile laboratories (although this will have schoollike associations) can be set up at school but away from the regular classroom. Children could be made familiar with the setting and helped to view it as a safe place where they play and have fun as they please, without wariness about a teacher's or a strange researcher's presence.

For example, McLoyd, Morrison, and Toler (1979) found that under such conditions, pairs and trios of preschoolers exhibited much richer sociodramatic play in their adult role enactments than did preschoolers aware of the presence of an adult. McLoyd recommends that coding systems be devised and employed to capture some of the play and communication patterns of lower-class or ethnically diverse children who were ignored in previous research. She notes that among African-American children, especially from low-income families, verbal communication is laced with affect and expression. Researchers need to codify degree of involvement or depth of role play, shown by components such as change of voice to represent changes in feelings or psychological states, if they are to evaluate adequately the quality of sociodramatic play in these children.

ADDITIONAL CONSIDERATIONS   Other scholars who have made excellent suggestions for observing children's play are Fein and Stork (1981), who are also concerned that we build a more adequate descriptive database to assess the spontaneous play abilities of different groups of children. Fein and Stork found a statistically significant difference in a composite score for play quality in favor of middle- over low-socioeconomic-status children enrolled in a heterogeneous child-care center. However, additional analyses indicated that for any specific play score assessing aspects of pretense that were *age sensitive* (showing a statistically significant difference between older and younger children), lower-socioeconomic-status children were not significantly different from their middle-class peers.

Fein and Stork went on to build a case for distinguishing between children's "typical" and their "best" display of pretend behavior. *Typical* play behavior is defined as the kind of play that occurs most frequently, compared to other kinds of play that are of interest to the researcher or practitioner observing a group of children. *Best* play performance is the highest level of play, in terms of a specified coding scheme, that a given child displays. If children from different socioeconomic or cultural groups show substantial discrepancies between typical and best play in a given situation, then we have to infer that certain environmental or motivational factors were operating.

Perhaps only in a very few areas of the classroom or child-care center is a targeted high-level behavior such as sociodramatic play likely to occur with low-socioeconomic-status children. In contrast, more advantaged children may feel comfortable exhibiting such play in a variety of contexts. We could conclude that lower-socioeconomic-status children have fewer opportunities to display the high-level behavior that they are quite capable of performing. Underdeveloped play goes hand in hand with play that is not supported by adults. Group differences in high-level make-believe play are differences in play performance (typical play), not differences in play competence (best play). Social class or cultural differences, then, are seen as motivational differences and not ability differences.

IMPLICATIONS FOR EDUCATORS

Most adults who frequently deal with young children—be they teachers, parents, or other child-care or human-service specialists—are coming into contact with an increasingly heterogeneous generation of young people as we enter the third millennium. What responsibilities do we have as we face this challenge? We strongly believe that educators must be informed of empirical studies and theoretical ideas and the key issues and controversies surrounding children's play, culture, and SES. This awareness offers an important initial step in trying to understand the relationships among cultural, subcultural, and social-class factors and children's play behavior. We hope that this chapter has given an adequate initial sampling of this important and developing area of the play literature. We now discuss practical applications of this information, including some recommendations for teacher attitudes and behaviors and for developing appropriate curriculum.

ATTITUDINAL RECOMMENDATIONS

Adults have a responsibility to cultivate positive attitudes toward children from diverse backgrounds. In a pluralistic society such as ours, we must model positive attitudes for our children by showing not only tolerance and acceptance but also respect for and enjoyment of group differences. All of us are unique individuals, as well as members of a social or cultural group. To center on the group at the expense of the individual or vice versa in perceiving or relating to others belies a certain primitive mode of social reasoning. Fortunately, most of us recognize and appreciate both individual and group variations.

As we hope is clear by now, it is unwise to make broad generalizations about the relations among culture, social class, and play. Repeatedly, the history and current state of research shows that generalizations based on differences in culture or social class inevitably give way to more refined conclusions after more detailed studies are done. Use of such dichotomies as lower- versus middle-socioeconomic status, for instance, usually leads to recognition of the need for more differentiated categories and to the realization that children's play involves many factors simultaneously. We all must remember this historical trend in the social sciences and not allow researchers to perpetuate stereotypes and misconceptions through preliminary studies of complex topics. As McLoyd (1982) noted, these stereotypes or "pejorative notions persist long after qualifying, if not outright contradictory, evidence has been proffered" (p. 26).

Labeling children as deficient in language use, academic skills, or imaginative play skills based on limited information, even as the prelude to remediation, often does more harm than good. Also, if apparent deficiencies do appear in certain individual cases (whether due to personal or environmental risk factors, as expressed in a specific range of situations and behavioral domains), the sensible person will remember that the problem pertains only to the present. For all we know, a 180-degree turn for the better may occur the next day. What is demanded is not to condemn the child's future as hopeless. Rather, the teacher must respect the great potential of all children and seek to rectify the situation in which underdeveloped play (or some other related apparent deficiency) seems to exist.

All of us should seek to develop a global perspective aimed at improving the quality of life for all children. This does not require constant cultural comparison or trying to be a walking storehouse of facts about other lands and other peoples. Having a cultural perspective does mean, however, that we realize and appreciate, both intellectually and affectively, the special qualities of each unique child and the cultural and specific situational forces working within the child's life space. We need to continue to cope with the complex equation involving nature and nurture, biology and culture, and how these broad sets of determinants interact and are manifest within each given context.

We then use this multicultural awareness to optimize the play experiences and development of children. Having a cultural perspective means that we are always open and ready for new learning about cultural diversity, and that we avoid rigid notions but seek instead *adaptive* intellectual and social habits. In this way, teachers and others who work with young children can be flexible and creative in meeting their needs and interests in our ever-changing pluralistic society.

BEHAVIORAL RECOMMENDATIONS

In addition to maintaining a positive and open attitude toward diversity, children, and play, there are a number of practical things we must realize to enhance children's development and enjoyment of play.

Fein and Stork (1981) have advocated that teachers who believe that pretend play in the classroom will aid children's development should plan encouragement sessions for those youngsters who seem reluctant to participate in sociodramatic play sessions. They point out that play performance can be improved fairly easily and swiftly by systematic effort on the part of adults who are friendly and encouraging (see Chapter 7). The long, intensive play training used by some researchers in the past (e.g., Saltz & Johnson, 1974) may not be necessary.

This practical suggestion is consistent with the interpretation of social class or cultural differences in play as motivational or performance differences, and not as deficiencies in cognitive functioning or symbolic competence (Saltz & Johnson, 1974). According to our current understanding, many children may be quite capable of high-level imaginative play but may require adult prompting and perhaps some encouragement to overcome initial shyness. To illustrate, many teachers have remarked that some children seem to need a second chance to shine when performing expressive behaviors in front of others. The first time around, a child may not sing, dance, or perform dramatic play as well as he or she could have, but given time perhaps to think about it, the same child might relish the additional opportunity to demonstrate expressive behavior. This is shown by marked improvement in performance when a similar expressive play situation comes up again in the classroom.

Before expecting high-level play, teachers are encouraged to make sure that children have sufficient time to become familiar with materials and routines in the child-care center or preschool classroom. For children whose primary language is not English, or for any child who comes from a home environment that markedly contrasts with the school environment, such familiarity is particularly important.

The teacher's example of a program underscoring the critical importance of play helps send an important message to those parents for whom the idea of the value of play is new (or old but rejected). Many immigrant parents need information and encouragement as they adjust to new sociocultural norms. Others who are members of oppressed minorities (i.e., continuous but unassimilated) need assurances that nothing at school will interfere with their children's later ability to compete in the job market (i.e., by having a play-based program and not a traditionally academic one).

Teachers should use newsletters (ideally in different languages, if needed, and devoid of jargon), parent meetings, conferences, and the like to explain why play is necessary for children and that educational play and related behavior (such as doing projects) are often quite different from children's play at home. Many parents went to school themselves starting at 6 years old and falsely assume that the same curriculum they remember experiencing back then also applies for their children, even though their own children might be as young as 3 years old when starting school. Such erroneous generalizations and misconceptions cannot be ignored by teachers. Parents need to be encouraged to try to adjust their inner psychologies, which are known from theory and research to have important consequences for children's play environments, behaviors, and development.

The form and content of children's play are influenced by cultural and social-class factors and furthermore express either children's interpretation of or their commentary on the social environments in which they grow up. As play advocates interested in having all children play to their fullest potential, we must always remain cognizant of the content of each child's own real-life experiences and provide play opportunities in line with children's backgrounds. In addition to carefully observing and listening to children playing at school to learn directly from their behaviors, teachers can use partnerships with parents to better understand children's diverse backgrounds. Parents can help teachers set up culturally appropriate play activities at school, which will resonate with children's experiences outside the school's walls. An enriched, culturally appropriate program can facilitate play, peer relations, and friendships among diverse children, teachers, and parents.

Furthermore, by welcoming input from parents and creating working relations with them, teachers foster, as an added bonus, greater multiethnic perspective-taking skills (Hyun & Marshall, 1997). Teachers must also go beyond getting accustomed to the idea of many lifestyles, languages, cultures, and so on and attaching positive value to this. In addition, teachers need to promote empathy and perspective-taking ability, both in themselves and in children, in order that all might successfully navigate together the diverse cultural landscape of today's pluralistic society. Communication and empathy go hand-in-hand, leading to detailed, up-close knowledge of the whole child and the family. These skills usually translate into a better understanding of intragroup variation; such understanding acts as an antidote to stereotyping and is a critical ingredient of any curriculum purporting to be antibias (Derman-Sparks, 1989).

CURRICULUM CONSIDERATIONS

Here we provide recommendations for multicultural curriculum in early childhood education, with primary attention to curricular matters that deal specifically with children's play. We begin with a couple anecdotes.

The need for curricular adaptation is exemplified by an anecdote of Curry (1971) involving a group of Navajo children. Apparently these children were not familiar with all the props available for dramatic play in the housekeeping corner of their middle-class-oriented preschool center. Teachers found that these children did not engage in sociodramatic play. Many of the children came from homes where there was no running water and the cooking was done over an open fire. These children did not use the domestic corner as it was usually set up for free play. One day, not by teacher design, the toys were left against the wall after cleaning. The Navajo children then vigorously engaged in sociodramatic play. The props were in the position where they were used to seeing them in their circular hogan homes!

A second anecdote, from Patricia Monighan-Nourot (1995), is about Sysavath, a little girl newly arrived from Laos, who enters her preschool classroom with a baby carrier on her back. Her baby doll has Asian features. All day long, Sysavath takes along her "baby" as she participates in program activities with the teachers and the other children—from easel painting, to water-table activities, to blocks, and so on. The opportunity for Sysavath to mother her doll this way helped her to acclimate to the program and to find a sense of belonging and mastery. It gave her peer-group recognition, too. Sysavath's mom was asked for replicas of the cloth baby carrier, so others may share in this new play in the classroom.

Multicultural early childhood education integrates play throughout the program, much as it does multiculturalism itself—neither are "add-ons" but essential dimensions of the inner workings of overall curriculum. Creating mutually directed activity in which adults negotiate and share power with children is integral to culturally responsive teaching (Stremmel, 1997). It is not surprising, then, that the teachers accommodated to Sysavath or to the group of Navajo children in the illustrations noted here. Children's knowledge, culture, and life experiences are taken seriously and are allowed to af-

Theory in Action

WORKING WITH PARENTS

Parents and teachers can work together as partners in the classroom and in the home setting. Parent involvement is heightened when parents see family-like activities regularly occurring in the classroom, such as cooking, washing clothes, taking care of pets, churning butter, and so on. Parents' input is vital to ensuring the authenticity of cultural experiences in the curriculum. A second way parents can become involved is through family education programs and home-based learning. The home becomes more schoollike to serve some important purpose in early childhood education. There are many ideas afloat as to how to do this. For example, family–child play was a critical element in a former Title VII project used to help culturally and linguistically diverse parents improve their interactions with children in home settings. A home visitor served as a parent educator and helped families use a parent–child play-mastery cycle, which had five components.

Component 1: Summarizing and Reporting from the Previous Week (5 minutes)

The play-mastery cycle began with the parent orally reporting to the home visitor concerning the settings in which play was used and how it was used in those settings. This component provided the parent with the opportunity to review the previous week's use of the play-mastery cycle and to ask questions that arose about its use in home and home-related settings. In addition, the home visitor was able to see whether the parent used the play-mastery cycle, determine whether it was used properly, and see the settings in which it was employed.

Component 2: Explaining the Current Session's Play Action Plan (10 minutes)

In this component of the play-mastery cycle, the home visitor explained and described to the parent the action plan to be used with her or his child this particular week. Each play action plan was phrased in specific behavioral terms and identified the set of behavioral routines that the parent was to use with her or his child and the toys or other play materials needed to carry out the plan. Each play action plan provided the parents with specific roles and actions to be used with their children. The number of play action plans introduced by the home visitor each week varied from one to three. The toy and other play materials used in play action plans were common and easily found in the homes.

(continued)

Component 3: Modeling the Play Action Plan for the Parent (15 minutes)

In this component, the home visitor modeled the play action plan (described in Component 2) for the parents and demonstrated the "whats" and "hows" of this plan. The parent observed the home visitor while the play action plan was modeled. The home visitor again repeated the modeling of the play action plan for the parents and urged the parents to repeat it several times with their child, depending on his or her interests and attention.

Component 4: Modeling of the Play Action Plan by the Parent (15 minutes)

After observing the modeling of the play action plan, the parent was encouraged to imitate the same routines and use the same toys and other play materials in ways similar to those of the home visitor. The parent practiced the plan based on the modeling without the child present, and the home visitor determined how effectively the parent matched the criterion episode and operationalized the play action plan. The parent's errors and misunderstandings in performing the routines in the play action plan were corrected, appropriate ones reinforced, and questions about the routines answered.

Component 5: Extending the Play Action Plan from Home to Home-Related Settings (10 minutes)

The play action plan explained, modeled, and practiced in Components 2 through 4 of the play-mastery cycle used situations in the home setting. Component 5 attempted to show parents how the play action plan could be used with children in other situations outside the home setting. The home visitor guided the parent in selecting, at minimum, one home-related setting in which the particular play action plan was to be used during the week.

Examples of home-related settings and different situations where the play action plan might be utilized included a relative or friend's house, a grocery store, or the car, or while walking down the street. In these settings, the parent used the play action plan where applicable and picked up on the youngster's incidental activities and actions outside the home. In extending the play action plan from home to home-related settings, the parents learned that it was usable, generalizable, and transportable (Yawkey, 1986).

fect curriculum and teaching. Children tell us about themselves and their backgrounds and cultures in play. According to Doris Pronin Fromberg (1995), (p. 59)

> Young children's pretend play . . . represents children's own social contexts, multiple perspectives, and attribution of significance to personal experiences growing out of their event knowledge. In effect, young children integrate their psychological and cultural experiences by negotiating and merging personal representations with shared symbols.
>
> In other words, play helps integrate meaningful learning, and is a "dynamic representation" of multiculturalism. (p.60)

Play and curriculum can come together in numerous ways, including in the form of *free play, structured free play,* and *play tutoring* (see Chapters 7 and 11). When implementing play-based multicultural education, responsive teachers should always seek to support the self-image and confidence of all children. Children learn a great deal from each other in heterogeneous groupings, and play interactions are vital to the process. Play can become a "social bridge" par excellence.

In general, *free play* should have available objects and symbols in the environment that show each child that his or her own culture is respected and validated. Parents can be consulted and invited to share materials and accessories useful for free play: items such as jewelry, costumes, scarfs, clothing, props for foods, music, and so on. A certain number and kind of multicultural toys, artifacts, books, photographs, magazine pictures should always be present—although specific items should be changed through rotation on a regular basis. Moreover, games and small manipulatives, puzzles, and other activities that are the staple of any program can be adapted with words, numbers, and pictures signifying the content and themes of various sociocultural groups. Such items should be available for children during free play.

Also, teachers must be ready to intervene whenever needed to foster multicultural competencies and attitudes during free play. For example, if the teacher sees children who are playing with restaurant dramatic play express a cultural stereotype such as "all Chinese like rice and all Mexicans like beans," they would suggest that some Mexicans do not like beans more than rice, that some Chinese people like beans, and so forth (Boutte, Van Scoy, & Hendley, 1996). Teacher interventions are required to counteract in children or other teachers any biased behaviors or words, as well as any expressions of the superficial "tourist approach" that fails to recognize intracultural variation and individual differences.

For *structured play,* multicultural theme boxes can be employed (Boutte et al., 1996). Theme or prop boxes (see Chapter 7) contain toys and other objects related to a particular theme, such as "Hair-Care Shop" or "Bakery." For example, a multicultural theme box for "Bakery" would contain simulations of baked goods representing different cultures (e.g., tortillas, baklava, pita bread, challah), with cookbooks and magazine recipes and pictures used for reinforcing diversity, as well as different kinds of cooking and eating utensils from different countries. Travel posters and folders could also be on display to augment a play atmosphere related to specific cultures or subcultures.

For constructive play, teachers can set up classification activities with various sociocultural content. Family pictures, artwork, stories, important family objects, and so on can be brought in from home and compared and contrasted. Educational constructive play can include matching or memory games using culture-specific items (types of dwellings or buildings, clothing, musical instruments, etc.). Favorite culturally related playthings and games can be a lively stimulus for group discussion, and even the start of an extended project on toys and play activities from different lands and eras. Play becomes richer and more cooperative when children are respected and encouraged to reflect on their own and each other's backgrounds. Constructive play materials and activities, including drawing and building-block activities, can set the stage for this to happen and are accordingly important components of a multicultural early childhood curriculum.

Play tutoring also has a place in the multicultural curriculum—whether the teacher is interested in implementing Smilansky's sociodramatic play training techniques, or the storytelling and enactment techniques that are part of Vivian Paley's narrative curriculum (Wiltz & Fein, 1996), or some other variation of it, such as thematic-fantasy play training (see Chapter 7). Depending on the needs and interests of the children, for instance, the teacher can select a distinctive sociodramatic play theme with a cultural focus, such as role enactment of a bus trip to an ethnic festival, or a meal at an ethnic restaurant. Instead, a folktale or fairy tale from a certain culture or a favorite story with a certain social group could be chosen for group dramatization. Alternatively, a teacher can prompt and direct role play of families in different cultures. Furthermore, teachers can use Paley's technique for recording stories the children create themselves and can later use those recordings for story reenactment and discussion in a large group. All these curricular adaptations exemplify what Fromberg means by saying that play is a "dynamic representation" of multiculturalism in early childhood education.

The role of the teacher is critical in making the curriculum work to achieve multicultural ends through play-related means. Teachers must remain vigilant and know when and how to intervene during play and at other times of the day, to promote empathy and friendships among children. Teachers need to be ready to facilitate and to guide different kinds of play, which serve various socio-emotional needs of the children and foster cognitive and language growth (see Chapter 3).

A significant although controversial programmatic teacher intervention is described in Paley's *You Can't Say You Can't Play* (1992). Here, she reports the happenings within an early childhood program in which the teacher imposed the classroom rule that one is not permitted to exclude peers from one's play. The rule evolved 'organically' about three months into the school year as a result of conflicts among the preschoolers concerning inclusion and exclusion in play groups. This teacher intervention is controversial because many early childhood professionals consider forced inclusion in play groups as unnatural and as detrimental in children's developing normal understanding of friendship and peer relations.

CURRICULUM FOR CULTURALLY AND LINGUISTICALLY DIVERSE CHILDREN

To extend the cultural content of their curriculum, teachers can ask parents and community members to lend cultural materials and ideas to their programs. Teachers can also tap published resource books relating to the curricular areas of literacy, folktales and folklore, music, songs, dance, drama and movement, and international foods.

Folktales and Folklore Across Countries

Folktales and folklore across countries can come alive as children listen to, learn, and role play these stories. Sharing folktales and folklore from various cultures provides a living context that children can experience and ponder. Such opportunities become windows to cultural and linguistic diversity. The following examples can provide international play experiences, using folklore and folktales as bases.

> *Anansi the Spider: A Tale from the Ashanti* (McDermott, G.) Henry Holt (Landmark Production), 115 W. 18th St., New York, NY 10011
> *Peter's Chair* (Keats, J.) HarperCollins, New York, NY 10032
> *Nine Days to Christmas: A Story of Mexico* (Ets, M, & Labastida, A.) Penguin Books, 375 Hudson St., New York, NY 10014
> *Arrow to the Sun: A Pueblo Indian Tale* (McDermott, G.) Viking Penguin, 40 West 23rd St., New York, NY 10010

Music, Song, Dance, Drama, and Movement Across Countries

Music, songs, dance, drama, and movement are useful for appreciating and understanding diversity. They can form a social context for nurturing linguistic and cultural understandings. The following examples are recommended.

> *El Toro Pinto and Other Songs in Spanish* (Rockwell, A.) American Economo-Clad Services, Box 1777, Topeka, KS 66601
> *The Music Teacher's Almanac: Ready-to-Use Music Activities for Every Month of the Year* (Mitchell, L.) Parker Publishers, West Nyak, NY 10995
> *Shake It to the One That You Love the Best: Play Songs and Lullabies from Black Musical Traditions* (Mattrox, C. W.) Warren-Mattox Productions, San Pablo Dam Road, El Sobrante, CA 94804
> *Arroz con Leche: Popular Songs and Rhymes from Latin America* (Delacre, L.) Scholastic Inc., Broadway, New York, NY 10003

(continued)

Theory in Action   *(continued)*

All Night, All Day: A Child's First Book of African-American Spirituals
(Bryan, A.) Maxwell MacMillan Publishers, New York, NY 10022
A Moving Experience: Dance for Lovers of Children and the Child Within
(Benzwie, T.) Zephyr Press, Box 13448 Tuscon, AZ 85732
A Handbook of Creative Dance and Drama (Lee, A.) Heinemann Publishers, Hanover Street, Portsmouth, NH 03801

Food Across Countries

A common and useful mode for developing positive views of various cultures is through cooking and food. This mode is especially meaningful in English-as-a-second language (ESL) and bilingual classrooms, where the emphasis is not only learning languages but also understanding cultures and customs. Also, these appreciations include food and its preparation and then sampling the products of children's directed play experiences and activities. Different clothing can be worn, which characterize the cultural and linguistic varieties as the children make and sample these country-specific foods.

The Multicultural Cookbook for Students (Albyn, C., & Webb, L.) Oryz Press, 4041 North Central at Indian School Rd, Phoenix, AZ 85012

Indeed, as Paley reported, the rule created a certain amount of turbulence for the children as well. Arguments and discussions followed its imposition. Although less radical measures may be seen as preferred, Paley's "You can't say you can't play" did serve as a catalyst for getting the kids to go "meta" and think about what they were doing, the trade off of receiving the benefits of being an 'insider' and the costs of causing hurt to the excluded 'outsider'. In a way this rule gave all the preschoolers their first lesson in 'equal protection under the law' according to Jerome Bruner (1996), who further commented how valuable it is be aware of what and why and how one enters into discriminative practices:

> It is through this process of becoming aware of practice that the good school and the healthy classroom can provide even the child of poverty, even the outsider immigrant child, some working vision of how a society can operate. In the instance of Vivian Paley's young nursery schoolers, her "rule" against mindless exclusion of other kids from your group does not assure that there will be an "even playing field," but (perhaps just as important) it gives children a lively sense of what an even playing field means and how one's praxis affects its "tilt." It is an antidote to mindlessness. And mindlessness is one of the major impediments to change. (p. 79.)

We might add that it is just this mindlessness, together with ignorance or the fear of the unknown, that forms the brew in the cauldron of hate leading to prejudice, intolerance, discrimination, and segregation found in our society. We can help change this by trying to nip the problem in the bud with early childhood education that is multicultural and antibias in its approach. With the power of play as our social bridge, the gold at the end of the rainbow might turn out to be the rainbow of cultural diversity itself.

SUMMARY

Theoretical frameworks help us understand the embeddedness of environmental settings and the relationships among social and physical situations, cultural influences, human development, behavior, and play. The developmental niche notion includes teacher and parent beliefs and attitudes as 'inner psychology' variables impacting play. Variation within sociocultural groups are mediated by these 'ideational' variables. Time also interacts with cultural influence. Residual effects of cultural roots influence play and adjustment to the society. 'Cultural-deficit' notions are rejected in light of these new concepts generated from within the cultural-ecological frameworks, as research on play of children in other countries, international comparative studies, and on immigrant groups in the United States demonstrate strong support for a 'cultural-difference' hypothesis. Nowadays researchers are interested in descriptions of play and contexts and are less interested in play training to compensate for any presumed 'play deficits'. Cultural and social class factors influence play expression with differences exhibited in play content and theme but not children's level of performance. Play is rich and important in the lives of children from all sociocultural groups.

Teacher are important for achieving the goal of having all children play up to their potential. Sensitivity to children's diverse home backgrounds assures better continuity between home and school and parent education is urged when play is undervalued in the home. Specific modifications of the curriculum in free play, structured play, and play tutoring can stimulate multicultural play in children. Classroom play policies can be valuable to build social bridges serving early childhood education that is multicultural.

Chapter 6

PLAY, SPECIAL CHILDREN, AND SPECIAL CIRCUMSTANCES

with Susan Welteroth

Sandra, a second-grader, was seeing a school psychologist regularly because of her disruptive behavior in the classroom, her low self-esteem, and her inability to make friends or to enter into productive social interactions with other children. The school psychologist attributed Sandra's difficulties to a high level of stress in her family (primarily centered around the separation and divorce of her parents) and to her speech delay caused by an undetected hearing impairment brought on by otitis media in her preschool years. Sadly, Sandra seemed to benefit very little from various behavioral interventions employed by the school.

The school psychologist then decided to intensify the intervention and to add a new twist. Two classroom peers nominated by the teacher were brought into special play sessions twice a week to play with Sandra under the supervision of the psychologist. Various board games were used to strengthen Sandra's underdeveloped perspective-taking skills. The peers served as role models and play tutors for Sandra, helping her to learn various social skills. They helped Sandra learn to take turns, to share, and to take the viewpoint of others. The school psychologist remarked that the peers genuinely and caringly tried to help Sandra learn to play and get along with others.

Progress was made even in the first week of this play-based intervention program, but several months passed by before an incident occurred that demonstrated the full impact of the program on Sandra's social skills. Sandra's mother told of how Sandra had a friend come over to play with her at home. The girls played together successfully for more than 2 hours. Given Sandra's long history of peer rejection and loneliness, her mother could hardly believe it! Teachers also reported significant improvement in Sandra's classroom adjustment and well-being. The school psychologist, who at one time had held to a behaviorist orientation, became a firm advocate for the power of play to help special children cope and learn. ■

Accounts such as the preceding one are becoming increasingly commonplace now that adults who work with children with special needs (or in special circumstances such as child-life programs or play therapy) are discovering the effectiveness of play-based interventions. This chapter examines three areas—special education, child-life programs, and play therapy—and attempts to summarize information that is useful for teachers and developmental facilitators in regular early and elementary education. We examine both how play is affected by different disabilities and how play can be used to help children with special needs relating to these disabilities.

PLAY AND SPECIAL EDUCATION

Teachers and others in the field of education are responsible for all children. Recent landmark civil-rights legislation, the Americans with Disabilities Act, requires that early childhood programs be prepared to serve children with special needs. Including all children in education is a philosophical and a moral mandate, and now it is also a legal one. Teachers are expected to meet this challenge. The words of Safford (1989, p. xi) are worth remembering: "The fields of early childhood education and special education have a great deal in common because of their stress on children as individuals, and their recognition of every child's right to an education that is appropriate to individual and developmental needs."

We begin with a general look at traditional conceptions of play in special education and with an overview of the effects of disabilities on play. After discussing inclusive education, we move to the topics of play in special-education curriculum and instruction. First, however, some background is needed so that the reader can evaluate to what extent philosophical and conceptual differences between early childhood education and special education linger, even in the most current formulations about play in the field of special education.

TRADITIONAL CONCEPTIONS

Misconceptions about play have beset the field of special education over the years, due to the dominant influence of behaviorism. As an educational theory or philosophy of how children behave, learn, and develop, behaviorism falls under the general rubric of the *cultural-transmission* model. Inherent in this model is the tabula rasa view that children are blank slates or empty vessels that get filled up by environmental inputs in general and by behavioral conditioning in particular. Alternative philosophical traditions in child care and education are (a) the *romantic* view, which stresses inherited traits and potentialities, as well as maturation; and (b) the *progressive-developmental* view, which holds that learning and development are due to predetermined structures and stages and specified interactions with the physical and social environment. According to DeVries and Kohlberg (1987), these three contrasting traditions or models represent complete worldviews encompassing psychology, ideology, and pedagogy. They also believe that these models are incompatible with one another. For instance, the endorsement of behaviorism requires educators to see children as passive learners, whereas a commitment to the progressive-developmental position requires educators to view children as active constructors of their own knowledge.

Historically, special education emerged from the behaviorist model and early childhood education from the progressive-developmental school of thought, resulting in sharply contrasting educational objectives and teaching methodologies. Special education has been highly pragmatic and has stemmed more from a medical or deficit model, which puts a premium on interventions that are highly structured, directive, and aimed at specific educational or behavioral objectives. The overriding concern has been to remediate problems and to prevent further decline in an ability or a prescribed behavior so that students with special needs do not fall farther behind their normally developing peers.

In contrast, early childhood education has been more idealistic in its orientation. A premium is placed on providing open-framework opportunities for learning, consistent with the metaphor of the child as an active constructor of knowledge or as an inquiring learner along a developmental path. Educational objectives are defined broadly in terms of general developmental considerations. For example, the Bank Street or developmental interactional model (so called because it emphasizes both *peer interaction* and the *interaction* of social, emotional, physical, and cognitive developmental domains) is an example of the progressive tradition in early childhood education (Zimiles, 1993). This model, which derives from the educational philosophy of Dewey—in addition to child-development views influenced by Bruner, Erikson, Piaget, and Freud—holds that the purpose of education is the optimal development and fulfillment of the whole person within a democratic society that values the intrinsic worth of each unique individual. Here, concepts such as self-actualization and respect for diversity apply, instead of the deficit-model orientation that has historically dominated special education.

The divergence in worldviews or models of human development underpinning the historical foundations of early childhood education and special education is seen in stark relief when considering how these related subfields of education have viewed children's play. Early childhood educators view play as a curricular core and as a critical context for learning. For them, play fuels the engine of developmentally appropriate practice within a progressive-developmental or constructive framework of education (Bredekamp & Copple, 1997). In contrast, play has been viewed by special educators as off-task behavior or as a reward for compliance with adult strictures. The relatively low status of play in special education is attributable to the fact that other behaviors and skills are seen as much more urgent for mastery.

Theoretically, the goals and functions of play and those of special education conflict because play is an intrinsically motivated, process-dominated behavior (see Chapter 1), while special education is preoccupied with overt behaviors governed by external contingencies. Special education places value on having the teacher be effective and efficient in instruction. It prizes the acquisition and expression of the *products* of learning (not the *processes*). Not surprisingly, a narrow and limited definition or theory of play is associated with the behaviorally governed tradition of special education. For example, in the past, play has been defined by special educators as down time, use of a toy, activity in a certain time and place, responses to adult commands or suggestions, and the like.

Play-based teaching strategies, curriculum, and assessment represent real progress in special education, and we applaud the growing recognition of the importance of play in much current early childhood special education practice. However, we also must remain alert to areas where refinement is needed to better integrate our most current play theories and related research with the policies and practices of special education. Residues of earlier impoverished conceptions of play can still be detected even to this day in various formulations of children's play in curriculum, instruction, and assessment in special education. We return to this issue later in this chapter, under the section entitled "Contemporary Conceptions."

EFFECTS OF DISABILITIES ON PLAY

Play behavior shows systematic variation due to age, gender, and other individual-difference variables and to culture and social class (see Chapters 4 and 5). A child's disability (both its nature and intensity) can affect a child's approach to play, the child's play activity, and what the child gains from a play opportunity or experience. Children with disabilities often require play tutoring or assistive technical devices (or both) in order to learn or to perform specific play skills or to meaningfully engage others during play and to benefit in general from the play experience.

To appreciate the challenge of inclusive educational practice in general, as well as to understand educational programming for children with special needs in particular, educators must examine the general effects of disabilities on play and social relations. Unfortunately, the research literature shows that little is known about the play of children with special needs. Teacher's lore and clinical case studies add some knowledge, but this area is less well understood than many other topics covered in this book.

Part of the difficulty lies with the great variety of disabilities and needs (e.g., physical, sensory, cognitive, social-emotional), plus the fact that many children have multiple disabilities. The proliferation of labels has also created a barrier to research on the play of children with special needs. For example, a child can have a *developmental delay* in one or more domains, a *potential disability*, or a *permanent disability*. Other distinctions concern biological, psychological, and social factors in defining children with special needs. For example, one view that is sometimes advanced is that *disorders* are biological or neurophysiological conditions, *disabilities* are psychological or functional conditions (often induced by biological factors), and *handicaps* refer to sociological conditions. That is, one can only be viewed as handicapped in relation to a specified social context and goal, much as anyone might encounter in a bowling or golf match. Researchers have varied in their use and interpretation of these labels, making it difficult to compare studies.

This proliferation of labels also imposes a deficit model on children with special needs. All too often, children with special needs are known basically for what they cannot do, rather than in terms of what they can do. This deficit orientation tends to devalue play, which is seen as less important than more pressing areas of children's development. Professionals and practitioners alike have shown more interest in stimulation and remediation of social and intellectual functions that have been mistakenly viewed in the past as detached from children's play.

It is a valid and nontrivial truism that children are more alike than they are different. As we survey the effects of disabilities on play in the sections that follow, try to keep this sameness in mind while examining all of the differences in the play of children with special needs.

Physical Disabilities   Physical impairments (such as those caused by cerebral palsy or spina bifida or injury due to accident) can influence play in a variety of ways, depending on how the physical disability restricts movement. Diminished fine-motor or gross-motor physical play are the most obvious effects of a physical disability. For instance, a child may have difficulty moving to the areas or the materials available for play, or the child may have difficulty manipulating materials in ways required for functional play or constructive play. Certain kinds of physical conditions, such as cerebral palsy, may even adversely affect the use of speech. The resulting speech impairment restricts children's abilities to engage in social play (see the subsequent section, "Communication Difficulties").

Sensory Disabilities   Sensory impairments, such as hearing or vision ability below the normal range, are known to affect play preferences and abilities of young children. Auditory impairment tends to reduce social skills and communication abilities and to interfere with cooperative and sociodramatic play. Visual impairment is more likely to reduce fine-motor and gross-motor play skills involved in exploratory functional play and in more complex constructive-play activity. Just getting play started is much more difficult for a child with impaired hearing or limited vision. A deaf child may not be able to respond to other children's verbal play-initiation signals and thus may be perceived by others as indifferent to play. Blind children often lack play skills because of their more limited abilities to explore their environments or to imitate others. Limited experience in watching models or in manipulating objects may prevent visually impaired children from understanding the use of toys or the full extent to which play materials can be made to operate. Consequently, opportunities for social interaction and productive engagements are reduced, and all forms of play can be impeded.

Communication Disabilities   Difficulties with speech and language likewise adversely influence social play. Children with these disabilities are less able to share their thoughts, interactions, and wishes with others. Children with speech delays or communication disorders find it much more challenging to frame play episodes and to negotiate play. As a result, they often show more inhibition when entering into or initiating play with others. These children have trouble being understood by others when attempting to describe, extend, or control play with others; they often have limited success expressing play likes and dislikes in terms of different activities.

PERVASIVE DEVELOPMENTAL DISORDER The diagnosis of Pervasive Developmental Disorder (PDD) or autism can extensively impact upon children's understanding of their social world, including their involvement in play. Autistic behaviors are characterized by significant impairments in communication. Children with autistic behaviors may engage in repetitive, stereotypical play and may use toys in an inappropriate manner. They are also less likely to engage in symbolic play (Baron-Cohen, 1987).

COGNITIVE DISABILITIES Cognitive disabilities can be biologically based (e.g., Down syndrome) or caused by environmental factors (e.g., brain injury or fetal alcohol syndrome). Children with cognitive impairments often engage in more exploratory behaviors than true play behaviors. These children usually need many more opportunities to initiate and practice specific play skills before they are ready to apply these skills in spontaneous play situations. Typically, children with cognitive impairments find it difficult to engage in more advanced forms of play that entail abstraction, such as complex construction or sociodramatic play or play involving cooperative games with rules.

SOCIO-EMOTIONAL AND BEHAVIORAL DISABILITIES Emotional and behavioral disabilities often impede meaningful interactions that could further play skills. Constant withdrawal from others precludes social play. Some children's aggressiveness may limit the types of activities into which these children are invited to join and may lead to the children's misuse and destruction of materials. Emotionally disturbed children may have difficulty using play as a tool for generalizing skills because of their focus on repetitive or stereotypic use of materials. Other children may have difficulty concentrating on specific play activities long enough to become genuinely involved. Some children may be extremely fearful of new things and may be unwilling to risk exploration of materials with differing textures, sizes, or functions. Because the development of interactive play skills in children with disabilities moves from being adult oriented to object or toy oriented to peer oriented, these children may not be developmentally ready to focus on their peers. This lack of readiness may, in turn, inhibit the development of social interactions with peers and can delay the sequence of social play development.

HEALTH IMPAIRED Health problems may be serious enough to hinder the development of play skills or to inhibit the use of play in learning new skills. A child whose involvement is restricted by a health condition such as severe cardiac problems or asthma may tire easily and may engage in motor play in only very limited ways. Children who are frequently hospitalized may lack the ability to initiate social or play interaction with other children. Techniques in care and programming for hospitalized children, which focus on opportunities for learning, play, and interaction within the care setting, address the lack of stimulation in medical settings for young children; such programs and techniques are discussed later in this chapter, in the section, "Child-Life Programs."

INCLUSIVE EDUCATION

Since the late 1970s, early childhood programs and the primary grades have been moving away from segregated special-education settings for children with intellectual, behavioral, and physical challenges toward the creation of inclusive classrooms. By 1990, approximately 75% of programs that identified themselves as regular preschools enrolled one or more children with special needs in their classrooms (Wolery, Strain, & Bailey, 1992).

Inclusive classrooms are those designated to meet the needs of all children—normally developing children and those with special needs. One important result of this trend is an effort to unify special education and regular education, or at least to begin to remove barriers between these two allied professions. Children's play has proven to be a major actor in this unfolding professional drama, as teachers and other professionals in each camp rely on the power of play to restructure teacher roles, curriculum, and pedagogy to achieve effective inclusive education during the early years.

Whereas ineffective or bogus inclusion involve simply enrolling children with disabilities or delays into existing child care or early education programs designed for typical children without preparation and support, *effective inclusion* means developing programs for children with and without disabilities. This is different from providing the "least restrictive environment" or "mainstreaming" (integration) that is mandated by legislation (PL 94-142). Even in providing the least restrictive environment, a child with disabilities may end up having limited or even no opportunities for social commerce with normally developing children. Mainstreamed settings (10–20% disabled) and integrated settings (up to 50% disabled) are programs that have changed to accommodate children with special needs, but the original blueprints of these programs had typical children foremost in mind. In contrast, truly inclusive settings are ones that keep the needs of children with or without disabilities equally in mind from the start of program planning.

The goal of inclusive education is to develop curriculum, instruction, assessment, child management, and service-support systems that (a) facilitate children's learning, development, and well-being, and (b) are tailored to the individual needs and interests of each unique child. Inclusive settings or child-care programs are based on three fundamental assumptions: First, all children are entitled to learn and to play with their chronological-age peers. Children do not have to prove themselves to earn the right to be included. It is up to educators to redefine "regular setting" so that all children are accommodated and belong. Second, children should have multiple opportunities to engage in play behavior that matches their skills and interests. There is no such thing as "3-year-old play activities," lockstepped and rigidly preconceived. Rather, 3-year-old play is whatever type of play 3-year-olds choose to engage

"Hand over hand, vehicle over paint"—teacher and children working together in an inclusive classroom.

in, and this varies widely for different children. Third, all children need to be held responsible for helping each other play, learn, and grow. Teachers are responsible for helping all children to learn more about human interconnectedness, caring, and responsibility (Sapon-Shevin, 1992; Stainback & Stainback, 1990).

Play is an important element in inclusive education. Play contexts provide opportunities for social interactions to occur, relationships to form, and friendships to develop between children with and without disabilities. Playing can become an important means for teaching all children to understand, accept, and value human differences. However, play opportunities alone are usually not adequate. Appropriate teacher interventions are necessary to ensure the success of play involvement by all children. For instance, Odom and Brown (1993) found that young children with disabilities are less likely to participate in play groups and to be sought as play partners by normally developing youngsters unless specific social-interaction intervention is implemented.

Research shows the importance of adults in facilitating beginning or transitional stages of play activity in order to reach levels of cooperation and cross-ability interaction patterns congruent with the goals of inclusive education (Swadener, 1986). Adult involvement is crucial for reaching program ob-

Theory in Action

PLAY IN AN INCLUSIVE CENTER

At the child-care center, soon after two other children began to bring dolls to play with during "work" time, Jane started to bring her doll, as well. Jane is a 4-year-old who exhibits language problems, as well as other developmental delays and some behavior problems. At first, she needed several reminders that the doll could be brought out only at work time, as she was inclined to take it from her cubby during breakfast, bathroom, and outside times. After only a few weeks of verbal reminders, Jane now asks at the beginning of work time, "Get doll out now?" Jane takes the doll into the housekeeping center and cares for her baby with the other "mommies." Staff members intervene in this dramatic play by asking open-ended questions ("What are the mommies and babies going to do today?"), suggesting role expansion ("Jane, maybe your baby is hungry"), and modeling conversations with other mommies ("Let's give our babies baths").

Donald has cerebral palsy and significant motor impairments. During work time, he likes to go to the block area, where the staff members place him in a side-lying position so that his arms and hands are free to manipulate materials. To assist in his play, large cloth blocks and smaller magnetic blocks were added to the typical wooden blocks in the center.

Lynn, a child with a hearing impairment, communicates via a sign-language interpreter on the center's staff. Sometimes, while Lynn and other children engage in painting, making collages, or drawing in the art area, children with unimpaired hearing will approach the interpreter and ask how to sign something to Lynn.

Sandy, a 4-year-old, has spina bifida. During work time, she often chooses activities that require her hands to be free to manipulate objects and her body to be close to the equipment. The staff has arranged a standing block with hand rails to act as a stand for her. When Sandy is in her leg braces and uses the stand, she is able to paint at an easel, to participate at the texture and water table, and to play in the housekeeping area. Sandy chooses these play activities even though it takes 10 minutes to put her braces on and to situate her in the stand.

Dale has been diagnosed as autistic. He is fascinated with music but has limited verbal skills. The staff constructed song cards from observations of his favorites. Each card contains both a picture describing the song and the printed title of the song. Dale has access to these throughout the day and chooses one to be sung by an adult. Although he cannot sing along, Dale does complete many of the hand motions that go with each song.

"Hand over hand"—peer helping at the birdseed box.

jectives for spontaneous group play in particular (Swadener & Johnson, 1988), as well as for other program objectives, such as fostering understanding and responsiveness to the needs of others and greater acceptance of human diversity.

To illustrate, Swadener (1986) studied two child-care programs in a 9-month ethnographic case study involving extensive observations, document analysis, and interviews with teachers and children. One program used team or coteaching in which the regular teacher and the special-education teacher worked together, whereas the other program featured a resource teacher who *shadowed* (i.e., followed around) children with special needs. This study revealed increasing cooperation and homogeneity of the two groups of children over the school year, especially in the team-teaching program. Teachers in both programs encouraged friendships with diverse peers, employed activities tailored to individual differences, asked open-ended questions in discussions, provided shared activities, and assigned valued roles to children with disabilities (e.g., having them teach other children sign language or information about their braces).

The program that used team teaching had more success in fostering cross-ability friendships. Teachers in this program also encouraged parents to plan get-togethers involving children with special needs, and to keep their children with peers as much as possible. The teachers modeled their enjoyment of their interactions with children with disabilities, and they gave examples of varied forms of play to encourage children's acceptance of their differently abled peers. Another factor is that social stigma was reduced by not having children shadowed by a special educator in front of classmates.

Team teaching or coteaching is an important ingredient for effective play-based inclusion in early childhood education. Using this approach, a general practitioner in early or primary education works with a special-education specialist (i.e., teacher, language interventionist, physical therapist, or occupational therapist) as partners with equal classroom planning and teaching responsibilities, trying to make a professional marriage work (Friend & Cook, 1996, p. 50). This model is recommended over the more traditional models of *consultation* (where special-education teachers and related services personnel consult with and advise early childhood teachers on how to modify and adapt curriculum and procedures for students with disabilities) and *direct services* (where the early childhood special-education professional or inclusion specialist and the related services professionals provide direct services to the children with disabilities, either within the classroom or at another location).

Friend and Cook (1996) describe different types of coteaching approaches most common in elementary and intermediate classrooms, which have been extended downward to apply to early childhood education and a play-based inclusive setting:

- *One teaching, one supporting*—One teacher is responsible for and oversees the entire classroom (such as during free-play period or circle time), while another teacher circulates around the room, observing and assisting individuals or groups of children as needed.
- *Station teaching*—Teachers divide children into small groups for *rotated activities,* in which subgroups of children move about, following a predetermined but flexible schedule.
- *Parallel teaching*—Teachers plan together a play or project activity involving the same materials and procedures and divide children into heterogeneous or cross-abilities groupings for similar implementation.
- *Alternative teaching*—Teachers create a division of labor in which one teacher conducts the primary activity with children and the other teacher previews, reviews, or does related activities.
- *Team teaching*—Teachers plan and implement activities for the entire class together at the same time. They may alternate roles, such as one teacher involved in stage managing, another in parallel playing, another coplaying or play tutoring with the children, and so on.

The coteaching model of inclusive education requires transdisciplinary merging of responsibilities, which can be difficult in cases where turf issues or professional vanity cannot or will not be transcended. This problem arises frequently when coteachers come from different subdisciplines or disciplines with different theoretical backgrounds. Disagreements or confusion over basic terminology and concepts of play need to be overcome to prevent miscommunication. In addition, conflicts over curricular goals, teaching strategies, and the like need to be resolved in a collaborative fashion. When inclusive settings are created following the principle that "none of the teachers and the parents are as smart as all of the parents and teachers," better outcomes for children are likely. Teaming together helps everyone accomplish more.

At the preschool level, research has generally provided an impressive empirical base in support of inclusion. Higher levels of social play and more appropriate social interactions have been reported for children with disabilities in inclusion programs, compared with their counterparts enrolled in self-contained special-education preschool classes (Lamorey & Bricker, 1993).

There are benefits for normally developing children, as well. Children in inclusion programs have been found to be more sensitive and responsive to each other, more respectful of human diversity, and more likely to manifest cross-ability cooperative play and friendships in the peer group (e.g., Peck, Carlson, & Helmstetter, 1992). Inclusive settings also provide opportunities for children to learn to become sensitive to cues associated with disabilities (Diamonds & Hestenes, 1996).

These benefits in perspective taking, social competence, and play behavior are not associated with losses in other areas. An extensive review by Buysse and Bailey (1993) compared studies of mainstreamed and segregated programs for preschoolers with disabilities (70% of the programs were university affiliated) and found few differences between the two types of settings on standardized measures of development.

PEDAGOGY AND PLAY

When working with children with special needs in educational settings, play can be interwoven with all aspects of pedagogy. We begin by describing how play intersects with general teaching strategies and curriculum. This is followed by specific guidelines for customizing play for children with disabilities.

TEACHING STRATEGIES   Two major issues that have dominated discussions about teaching strategies with respect to play and children with special needs are (1) the extent to which teachers are directive or nondirective in their practices, and (2) the extent to which cognitive forms of play are targeted for intervention, over social play forms.

Recommendations for developmentally appropriate practice (DAP) include *scaffolding* or *contingency teaching,* in which the teacher considers the effects of an interaction on the child when taking the next step in an adult–child interaction (Bredekamp & Copple, 1997). When deciding whether or when and how to intervene in a particular case, the teacher needs to be sensitive to (a) the cognitive abilities of the child; (b) the child's motivational state, affect, and mood; and (c) the social and physical variables in the play or learning situation. Educators are trained to "teach up," or to stretch the child along to a higher level of functioning. Therefore, teacher directiveness can be expected to fluctuate a great deal over the course of any interaction, as the child displays varying levels of competence. Successful instructional scaffolding is teaching contingent on children's manifest behavior, which targets learning or play behaviors within each child's zone of proximal development (see Chapter 7, "Adult Involvement in Play").

Teachers can use a continuum of strategies for interacting with children at play or at work. Didactic-behavioral strategies and play-based, facilitative strategies have often been polarized in the past. Now, however, it is increasingly understood that play and work components in the curriculum can be blended activities, and a continuum of strategies ranging from directive to nondirective apply in any situation with any child, who may or may not have special needs.

In an interview study of early childhood teachers and special educators, McChesney-Johnson (1994) found that teachers' proposed actions during the play of typical children and of children with special needs could be said to fall along a low-directive (watching, being available, setting up the environment) to high-directive (intervening, enforcing rules, supervising) continuum. Teachers viewed a video of a play episode in which the target child was sometimes said to have special needs and sometimes not. Similar results were obtained for both the early childhood and the special education teachers. Although there was greater intensity expressed when teachers believed they were responding to a child with special needs, the strategies proposed for use with normal children and those with special needs were similar and could be placed along the continuum of directiveness. Rationales were congruent with proposed strategies and reflected an appreciation of subtleties associated with individual characteristics of behaviors expressed by the children in the video, as well as various unique features of the play context shown. These findings support the idea that teachers from the early childhood and special education traditions share a common ground of understanding and use the same teaching strategies. Philosophical differences between the disciplines are less apparent as one moves away from the ivy tower of academia and toward the concrete, practical realities of teaching children.

A second major concern is the extent to which teaching strategies focus on cognitive, as opposed to social, aspects of children's play. Researchers have reported findings suggesting that some teachers place undue emphasis on cognitive play, at the expense of social play. File (1994) and File and Kontos (1993) studied how teachers interacted with typical children and those with special needs during play. They coded teacher behavior as supporting *cognitive play* when the teacher interacted with the target child, focusing on the child's use of materials or toys; and they coded teacher behavior as supporting *social play* when the teacher interacted with the target child, focusing on children's interactions with peers. These studies found that teachers supported cognitive play six times more often than they supported social play.

These findings are disturbing because children with disabilities tend to score significantly lower in their levels of social play. These children are put at an unfair disadvantage when teachers seemingly operate on the implicit assumption that children acquire social skills on their own, without facilitation by the teachers. Inclusive educational settings may well consider adapting more structured means to help disabled children become more competent and integrated with their peers at the social level (Guralnick, 1990; Strain, 1990).

CURRICULUM   There is not a generally approved curriculum for inclusion or other programs serving young children with special needs. As in early childhood education, curricular models (i.e., brand-name programs) have fallen out of favor in the field of special education in recent years. No longer is there the same enthusiasm for prepackaged programs such as the Behavior Analysis Model Approach or the Engelmann/Becker Model for Direct Instruction. More prevalent are efforts to develop quality programs without preexisting allegiance to a certain philosophy or curricular model. An overriding preoccupation has been the pursuit of developmentally appropriate practice (DAP) for all children. In addition, DAP has been criticized as necessary but not sufficient for culturally diverse children, as well as children with special needs. Meeting various needs related to exceptionalities or cultural background requires individualized arrangements and supports over and beyond the usual DAP curriculum and instruction. However, the validity of this statement depends on how narrowly or broadly one defines DAP. A broad, inclusive definition of DAP covers the full range of human potential and manifestations.

An important issue in these debates over appropriate curriculum for children with special needs concerns the amount of structure that is needed. It is generally agreed that children with special needs are less likely to benefit from incidental learning opportunities inherent in play-based curriculum activities. Accordingly, teachers must modify and expand materials and activities to accommodate to individual differences—usually in the direction of more structure. However, the principles of providing the least restrictive environment and of normalization should always be kept in mind when adapting materials and play activities for children with disabilities. Children need to feel part of the normal flow of events and to be treated as such. Modifications should not be one iota more than what is absolutely necessary, so as not to call undue attention to the child or to promote dependency.

In choosing which strategies to use, the teaching team should (a) attend to the goals and learning outcomes of the children's individualized education plans (IEPs) and (b) consult with the related service staff, when available. Adaptations and modifications may be used alone or in combination to meet the needs of all the children. Remaining mindful of chronological age, in addition to developmental status and personality, is very important (see Chapters 3 and 4). An important benefit of being in an inclusive setting is the chance to learn to navigate around social and physical obstacles encountered in natural everyday life. Excessive interference undermines this goal.

CUSTOMIZING PLAY FOR CHILDREN WITH SPECIAL NEEDS   Procedures and techniques for modifying curriculum activities for children with special needs fall into the following categories (McCormick & Feeny, 1995): space, time, material, directions, special assistance, special positioning, or equipment.

Space   Entrances to play areas or activity centers (e.g., dramatic play, blocks, sand) need to be wide and unobstructed for children who are in wheelchairs or use walkers. Staff members should complete a walk-through to ensure that clutter is reduced. Tables need to be high enough for a wheelchair to fit underneath. Adjustable legs on large pieces of equipment, such as sand tables or easels, will make those activity areas accessible to all children. Play areas must not be so small that there is crowding, which can lead to aggressive behavior or withdrawal (see Chapter 9), but not so large as to reduce opportunities for social interaction and communication needed for collaborative play. Adults should consider providing a quiet place for children who may need either a less distracting environment or a place to calm themselves. Some children may need space cues, such as tape on the floor or distinctively colored carpet to help orient them to activity areas. Teachers need to experiment with the space available to determine whether space modifications are needed for a particular child with special needs.

Time   Time for play should be sufficient to allow for play episodes to develop and to take their course. Scheduling should be flexible and individualized for all children. Some children with special needs may need more time to process the information required to engage in a play sequence or to complete an activity. As children with disabilities learn new skills, they need opportunities to practice them over and over. As appropriate, available play time can be extended by permitting a child with disabilities to begin sooner. For example, pass out materials for constructive play first to a child with special needs, or help dress this child first when going outside to the playground. Do this in an inobtrusive manner so that peers are not aware of the extra time the child is afforded for play. In addition, time for play can be changed from the original schedule when children are deeply engrossed in a play episode or show evidence of losing interest.

Changes in activities are difficult for some children; they may need more time to clean up or to move from one activity to another. McCormick and Feeney (1995) suggest some ways for facilitating transitions for children with special needs:

1. Provide specific instructions and practice with transition behaviors, such as where and how to put away materials and how to move quietly to another activity.
2. Reiterate what the next activity will be.
3. Allow children who finish early to move independently to the next activity.
4. Give several notices that the activity will soon end before using an abrupt transition warning, such as a light or a bell.
5. Allocate sufficient time to end an activity and clean up before beginning preparation for the next activity.

Materials   Having an extensive array of toys and materials spanning across a wide band of age and developmental appropriateness is one key to creating an optimal play environment for a diverse group of children. Rich and varied options allow for meeting the needs and interests of all children. Gradations in what a child can do with different materials such as blocks or sand and water help bond the play groups and safeguard self-esteem. Most toys and materials that are suitable for young children are also appropriate for young children with disabilities. Consider the child's interests, disability, and developmental level, and provide toys and other materials that are appropriate and safe. When first meeting a child, the teaching team should observe closely and talk with the family to discover what toys and materials the child is interested in, what gets and maintains the child's attention, and how she or he manipulates the materials in play. To promote engagement with a variety of toys, adults should rotate the availability of materials, remembering to remove small objects if there are children who might swallow them. Adults should provide materials that can be used over and over again in a variety of ways. In an effort to promote peer interactions, the teaching team should select toys that require cooperation, such as sociodramatic play props, sand and water toys, or blocks and small people and cars, ensuring that there are sufficient materials available for the number of children. Peer-mediated strategies—such as social interaction training, peer initiation training, peer modeling, peer prompting, and reinforcement—are provided for children who are developing typically, to foster child–child interactions.

Ostrosky and Kaiser (1991) suggest the following presentations of materials to encourage language:

1. Provide interesting toys, materials, and activities, and show interest in them.
2. Place some toys out of reach but in sight, to promote the likelihood of the child requesting them.
3. Give the child inadequate portions, to stimulate opportunities for requesting or commenting.
4. Set up situations that will require the child to request assistance.
5. Create situations that are silly, to give the child opportunities to make comments.

Having multiples of children's favorite toys can reduce children's quarrels over toys, but this needs to be balanced with the need for environmental arrangements conducive to sharing and cooperating among the children, with or without direct teacher intervention. Generally, teachers should try to have the same expectations for all children with respect to appropriate versus inappropriate use of play materials.

Directions   Often, materials in and of themselves suggest appropriate play use, such as blocks or puzzles or finger paints. By setting out these materials, teachers provide clues as to what the children will be doing next. Some children with special educational needs lack either the knowledge or the ability to use their knowledge about materials and activities, especially if the materials or activities are embedded in a more complex context, such as that typically encountered in a center-based program. In the cases in which verbal and

Theory in Action

LEKOTEK

A *Lekotek* (*Lek* means "play" in Swedish and *tek* means "library") is a resource center for children with disabilities and their families. The first Lekotek was originated in Stockholm in 1963, by a small group of parents and teachers, who operated it from an apartment where parents and children began to meet to exchange toys among themselves and to offer each other socio-emotional support. From this grassroots beginning has developed a worldwide network of play libraries serving children with special needs. Sarah deVincentis opened the first Lekotek in the United States, in Evanston, Illinois, in 1980 (Sinker, 1985). Evanston still serves as the national Lekotek Center, with a current nationwide network of 46 Lekotek centers and 18 Compuplay sites (for computer instruction, in association with Lekotek).

Lekotek uses family-centered play as the primary way to facilitate the inclusion of children with special needs into the full range of family and community life. Currently, Lekotek's operations include monthly center-based play sessions and a toy-lending library for children from birth to 8 years old, as well as outreach services to families through inclusive play groups, home visits, toy-making workshops, and family literacy programs.

Lekotek play leaders facilitate family play sessions once a month, using specially adapted and off-the-shelf toys selected for the individual child. Emphasis is on creative use of materials and social interaction among family members and, most importantly, enjoyment. Positive and successful experiences are the most important goals of Lekotek. Monthly, each family borrows a number of toys for home enjoyment. Chosen toys are ones the parent had seen the play leader use and feels comfortable using to expand the child's play. Siblings, grandparents, and neighborhood children are encouraged to participate in play sessions to maximize transfer or carryover to the child's home and community environment.

During the 1-hour session, play leaders usually employ about seven or eight toys, preselected with the child's ability in mind, to stimulate the child's developmental progress. The relaxed, close atmosphere that prevails seems to foster the growth of familial bonds. The orientation is very child-centered. For instance, a game of catch that degenerates to simple throwing by the child can be salvaged by the play leader, who grabs a box as an open container to turn the activity into a simple form of basketball. By accommodating to the child in this sensitive and responsive way, the play leader is scaffolding the play episode and elevating the child's behavior to a more mature level through the energetic and clever use of attention recruitment and maintenance strategies. One parent remarked (McLane, 1984, emphasis in original),

(continued)

Theory in Action *(continued)*

> At Lekotek, I learned the joy of playing with my child. . . . The Lekotek leader looked at my child as though he had no handicap. She took all of the positive things about him, all the good things, and never said "you can't do this" or "you can't do that." "You *can* do this." The atmosphere was so relaxed and so tranquil. . . . The Lekotek leader is not judging you. And not judging your child. . . . They taught me how to play with my child again. . . . I had forgotten the more natural kinds of things to do with my child. . . . They taught me how to enjoy my child. It was like seeing my son for the first time.

In the United States, Lekotek libraries contain more than 50,000 toys. In addition to commercial and educational toys, the libraries include specially designed toys and ones adapted with special switches and motors to accommodate youngsters who are physically challenged. Lekotek also has a toy resource helpline to help family and friends choose toys to buy as gifts for children with disabilities. For individualized assistance in selecting appropriate toys and play materials, anyone can call toll-free the Lekotek Resource Helpline 800-366-PLAY (TTY 847-328-0001) Monday through Friday from 9:00 A.M. to 4:00 P.M. (central time).

Compuplay centers, which are run in conjunction with Lekotek centers or independently, have play sessions that allow children and their families to learn through play with computer programs and equipment. An extensive inventory of interactive software programs across diverse ability levels are available for preview and home loan. Compuplay's goal is to use technology to compensate for physical limitations and to help children have control over their environment.

physical guidance seem needed, the teacher can help the child understand the intent of the material and activity by following these suggestions: (1) orient and maintain the child's attention, to ensure that the child is attending to the task at hand; (2) use words the child can comprehend, and speak slowly and repetitively, as needed (one word per second); (3) position the child so that she or he can see the teacher and the other children; (4) break down any directions into smaller steps, and rephrase, as needed; (5) pair visual and verbal information, such as using objects, pictures, gestures, and facial expressions along with oral communication; (6) ask simple questions to see whether the child is understanding, such as "Now what?" or "Show me what happens next?" or "What can you do now?" (7) have the child repeat the directions; (8) physically guide the child to begin an activity bearing in mind that hand-over-hand assistance can be considered the most intrusive strategy.

Specially Designed Assistance Depending on the child's expressed competence in a particular situation, or lack thereof, the teacher or a more competent peer can draw on a number of techniques to help the child perform in a play or project activity situation. In order of increasing structure or intrusive-ness, specially designed assistance involves the following: (1) *modeling* (with the adult or peer providing a verbal or gestural or bodily demonstration of the behavior and expecting the child to imitate it); (2) *verbal guidance* (with the adult or peer providing information about what the child is to do), and (3) *physical assistance* (in which *partial* physical assistance involves touching a body part such as a leg or arm to indicate which one the child is to use, and *full* physical assistance involves physically supporting and guiding the in-tended behavioral process and outcome). Teachers may also offer *visual cues,* objects, pictures, or symbols designed to make it easier for a child to perform a particular activity. In general, the less intrusive the strategy, the more the teacher will prefer using it to help the child until the child shows that more help is needed.

Special Positioning   Positioning includes both *where* a child should be lo-cated in a play or activity setting and *how* a child should be positioned (standing, sitting, side lying) to achieve relaxation, focus, and control for maximum independent functioning. Adaptive equipment helps children with motor impairments in two ways: (1) by maintaining positioning for a short time, in order to perform the activity, and (2) by facilitating movement and mobility (e.g., modified chairs, stands). Children with multiple or intensive physical impairments may need several pieces of adaptive equipment (e.g., modified chair for trunk support to enable tabletop constructive play activity, wheelchair for outdoor play and transitions between daily routines, wedge and mat for lying on the side during free play, stand for support at sand and water table).

Assistive Technology   When used appropriately, assistive technology devices can enhance children's interactive skills so they can gain control and mastery over their environments. The National Council on Disability (1993) defined an *assistive technology device* as any item, piece of equipment, or other product that is used to increase, maintain, or improve the functional capabilities of in-dividuals with disabilities. Assistive technology devices include both low-tech and high-tech devices, such as adapted toys, computers, special seating sys-tems, powered mobility devices, augmentative communication systems, and contingency switches.

PLAY AND ASSESSMENT

Play assessment or play-based assessment can be used when working with children with special needs—both as a complement to other methods of ob-taining descriptive data about children and as a useful process that forms an increasingly seamless relation with instructional or therapeutic interventions. Compared to formal or standardized tests and structured tasks, play assess-ment is a relatively new and evolving approach to evaluation in early interven-tion and special education. A growing number of techniques and commer-

Theory in Action

STRATEGIES TO AID CHILDREN WITH SPECIAL NEEDS DURING PLAY

Below are suggestions for working with children with different kinds of special needs. Educators should determine strategies for individual children based on an examination of their particular strengths and needs.

Language and Communication Characteristics

The teaching team needs to be attuned to the developmental milestones in language acquisition and alert to the level of language development of individual children in order to make adaptations such as these:

- *Eye contact*—Use eye contact when addressing the child, and encourage the child to maintain eye contact while communicating.
- *Awareness of communicative intent*—Watch for nonverbal behavior exhibited by the child, and respond to the child's intent.
- *Careful listening*—It may be difficult to understand a child with special speech or language needs. Respond to what can be understood, thereby encouraging the child to use language.
- *Mirroring*—Imitate the child's actions, or make a restatement of the child's sounds or utterances.
- *Commenting*—Talk about what the child is doing or what is going on in the play situation. This draws attention to the actions and attaches language to them. There is no obligation for the child to respond.
- *Modeling*—Model gestures, sounds, and verbalizations, and expect the child to imitate some or all of what has been modeled. Prompts may be needed.
- *Wait time*—Allow the child enough time to respond; allow processing time.
- *Expansion*—Restate the child's vocalizations, and add new words or ideas. This confirms to the child that her or his message was received and understood, while providing a model of enriched language.
- *Requesting clarification or elaboration*—Ask that the child make clear his or her intent, or elaborate on the child's original request. ("What did you say?")

Pervasive Developmental Disorder Characteristics

Adults should intentionally:

- Create supportive environments for socialization and peer play.

(continued)

Theory in Action *(continued)*

- Help children with autistic behaviors to negotiate play routines, respond appropriately to peers, and initiate social activities (Wolfberg & Schuler, 1993).
- Increase the duration of eye gaze and creative toy play in children with autistic behaviors by modelling with identical toys (Dawson & Galpert, 1990).

Cognitive Characteristics

The team should be aware of the cognitive development of individual children in order to make adaptations:

- Allow time for extra demonstration and practice sessions.
- Use task analysis to break down activities into small steps.
- Start with small groups, shorter sessions, and fewer choices at the beginning, gradually increasing each over time.
- Reduce the amount of irrelevant cues within play materials to aid in successful completion of the task for children who are easily distracted.
- Provide toys and materials that promote understanding of cause–effect relationships, spatial understanding, representational thinking, and problem solving.
- Label storage spaces with real objects, as well as pictures.
- Provide frequent and positive feedback.

Socio-Emotional and Behavior Issues

The team needs to focus on the child's competence, behavioral tendencies, and emotional responses to make adaptations:

- Allow a shy child to observe group play activities until she or he is ready to participate.
- Help control aggressive behavior by providing additional structure (limiting toys, defining physical space, etc.), as well as consistently enforcing rules.
- Observe dramatic play for clues about the child's feelings and emotional concerns.
- Help the child express feelings in an appropriate way.
- Encourage independence and self-confidence by allowing the child to select play activities.

Hearing Impairment

The adult should:

- Seat the child close to voices and music.
- Use adaptive equipment (auditory trainer) when appropriate.

(continued)

Theory in Action *(continued)*

- Obtain the child's attention before speaking.
- Provide visual cues.
- Repeat or rephrase, as needed.
- Demonstrate new activities.
- Learn sign language, and teach signing to the entire group of children.

Vision Impairment

Teachers should:

- Introduce the child to the space, equipment, and materials verbally and through touch.
- Provide verbal and sound cues for play activities.
- Use toys that include auditory and tactile elements.
- Be attentive to lighting conditions.
- Enlarge symbols in the setting, use textured labels (sandpaper or felt), and use fluorescent colors.
- Provide visual and tactile cues to environmental boundaries (different surfaces, colored carpet, fluorescent tape).
- Pad the edges and backs of shelves and tables so the child will not get hurt.

Physical Characteristics

Teachers should:

- Provide adaptive equipment (bolsters or other supports for floor activities, stands).
- Establish motor patterns by moving the child into position or by modeling the position.
- Use adaptive materials (scissors, large crayons, pencil grips).
- Attach bells to wrists or ankles for added auditory stimulation.
- Stabilize materials to better enable manipulation (e.g., tape paper to table or easel).
- Put all items within reach (e.g., move blocks to a tabletop for a child in a wheelchair).
- Place the child in a position with good trunk control and with arms and hands available to manipulate toys. The child should be able to

cially available instruments are easing their way into practice, ranging from highly structured procedures to informal guidelines. Generally speaking, the more structured the approach, the less valid it is to call the child's behavior "play" during the assessment process.

BENEFITS AND LIMITATIONS   *Play assessment* has been defined as "the observation of one or more children for the purpose of understanding their developmental, sensorimotor, cognitive, communicative, social and emotional functioning" (Cohen & Spenciner, 1994, p. 300). Play assessment can give valuable information to use for program planning and monitoring. The information obtained during play assessment is called "process information." Often, this information is difficult or impossible to come by except through observational play assessment (e.g., how a child tries to join a group of other children). Process information can help the teacher plan activities to meet individual needs and interests. For instance, play assessment might reveal that Juan wanted to pour the milk in a dramatic-play scenario. However, when he attempted to open the milk carton and could not, he became frustrated and gave up. When planning opportunities for learning for Juan, the teacher may select activities in increasing order of difficulty to help him gain skill in the area of expressed interest.

Educators must conduct play assessment in a way that helps the child to feel as relaxed and safe as possible. The child is more likely to feel this way in a familiar and natural environment, with interesting playthings and with familiar adults or other children. Artificiality must be kept to a minimum to achieve this state of affairs. Benefits of play assessment include the range and the flexibility of procedures possible through play, with high potential for adaptations to be made for children with even severe disabilities. Parents can be part of the assessment, and any number of observations can be made. Toys and situations can vary because it is not necessary to follow the strict standardized procedures of other more formal assessments. The wealth of information usually generated through play assessments not only help in intervention, but also can be integrated with other sources of data about a particular child, yielding a more comprehensive assessment profile.

On the other hand, there are definite limitations to play assessments. One has already been mentioned—that the term *play* in the procedure is a misnomer. That is, the play assessment procedure is structured to such an extent that although the situation is natural and familiar, a valid play episode does not unfold according to the usual criteria of what constitutes play (i.e., positive affect, nonliterality, process over product, intrinsic motivation, etc.; see Chapter 1). Displayed behaviors can be anything but genuine play-state behaviors; what is exhibited are often various social and nonsocial behaviors that are clearly not playing types of behaviors (e.g., imitating, following directions, conversing, and gazing). This is a very loose interpretation of play, and what is displayed might not be anything close to the child's real potential, as observable in a genuine play state, as opposed to a bogus play state. As Vygotsky suggested, play can lead development (see Chapter 1).

Another limitation is the fairly primitive state of our ability to calibrate or measure play behavior for anything other than research purposes or informal teacher use. *Reliability* (consistency or stability of performance) and *validity* (really measuring what is claimed) of play measures are problematic. Children with disabilities, like all children, show great variability in performance.

What is observed during assessment is not necessarily what a child is capable of. How well (i.e., systematically and well-disciplined) the play assessment procedure is employed is a function of the skill level of the person using it. Partial, distorted, or misleading pictures of a child can result from play assessments. Additional forms of assessment are needed to evaluate and understand a child's strengths and challenges. Multiple norm-referenced assessment measures, including standardized tests, are required by federal laws and by some states to identify a disability and to determine eligibility for services. Further, play assessments do not provide information relating to many self-help skills (e.g., toileting, bathing, undressing, feeding) or to preacademic skills (or readiness skills). Other sources of information (e.g., from standardized tests, observations in other domains, and interviews) have to be completed along with play assessments to properly diagnose a child and to plan an individualized program of intervention.

MODELS AND METHODS   Three models of play assessment are multidisciplinary, interdisciplinary, and transdisciplinary. When professionals from different disciplines (e.g., educator, speech therapist, school psychologist, nurse) work together but independently in conducting and analyzing play assessment, each from her or his own discipline, they are implementing a *multidisciplinary* model. In an *interdisciplinary* approach, the diverse professionals conduct separate play assessments but share their plans, methods, and observations with each other. In the *transdisciplinary* model of play assessment, a facilitator engages in play with the child while team members and the parent observe, sharing expertise and true collaboration (Linder, 1990).

Many methods or instruments of play assessment have been proposed, but scant research on them necessitates a word of caution regarding their use. Practitioners are urged to combine other sources of information about the child with the results of employing these methods. Various instruments range considerably with respect to their degree of structure and intrusiveness (artificiality).

Representative play assessment instruments designed for evaluating the developmental level of general competence include *A Manual for Analyzing Free Play* (McCune-Nicolich, 1980), *Developmental Scale of Infant Play* (Belsky & Most, 1981), *Play Assessment Scale* (Fewell & Rich, 1987), and the *Transdisciplinary Play-Based Assessment* (Linder, 1990). Other observation instruments are described in detail in Chapter 8. Additional instruments have been devised especially for diagnosis (e.g., *ETHOS Play Session* [Siegel, 1991]) and for parent–child play interaction (*Parent–Child Interaction Play Assessment* [Smith, 1991]) and child–child play interaction (*Behavior Observation Record* [Segal, Montie, & Iverson, 1991]).

Currently, two very popular instruments in early childhood special education are the *Play Assessment Scale* (PAS) and the *Transdisciplinary Play-Based Assessment* (TPBA) procedures. Fewell and Rich (1987) developed PAS to estimate the level of cognitive, language, and social functioning in children between 2 and 36 months of age. As is typically done using these instruments, spontaneous behavior is observed, together with elicited imitative behavior. The PAS has 45 developmentally sequenced items. The examiner presents a set of toys appropriate for the developmental age of the child. Toys are re-arranged several times during the session to determine a play age score, based on how well the child engages playthings functionally or symbolically, either spontaneously or elicited. The examiner serves as a playmate, coplaying or parallel playing or engaging in play tutoring with the child.

Linder (1990), who advocates the transdisciplinary model for the assessment of play, invented the TPBA to estimate the level of cognitive, sociol-emotional, and sensorimotor development, as well as communication and language. A room sectioned into distinct areas (housekeeping, blocks, art, sand/water, woodworking, and gross motor) is recommended for use (either at home or in a center or clinic) to allow the child to select various objects and activities. TPBA is formatted in six phases, lasting from 60 to 90 minutes in total session time: Phase 1 is unstructured facilitation (20–25 minutes); Phase 2 is structured facilitation (10–15 minutes); Phase 3 is child–child interaction (5–10 minutes); Phase 4 is parent–child interaction subdivided into unstructured and structured play sessions, each 5 minutes in duration, with a brief break in between; Phase 5 is motor play, both unstructured (5–10 minutes) and structured (5–10 minutes); and Phase 6 is a snack time (5–10 minutes). After the play session, the team schedules a meeting to analyze the videotape, correlate observations, and complete some summary sheets. The team then develops preliminary recommendations and writes a formal report.

Despite the limitations and difficulties in gaining valid and reliable data, play assessments are becoming more widespread as instruments continue to develop and disseminate throughout the field of early intervention. Educators can evaluate the quality of play to infer developmental status, which can be used in interventions such as play tutoring or social-skill coaching, to elevate the child's level of play.

CONTEMPORARY CONCEPTIONS

Enthusiasm for play-based intervention, as well as assessment in early childhood special education and early intervention continues to grow. The power of play promises much for helping children and their families, as well as for serving the diverse needs and interests of groups of children in inclusive educational settings and in other environments (e.g., community parks, playgrounds, libraries, museums). Moreover, we hope that the fields of regular and special education can come closer together philosophically and in praxis, with continued collaboration in dealing with play theory and research, practice and policy. Our challenge now is to materialize the new visions of play assessment and intervention that have appeared on the horizon.

Meisels (in press) asserts that assessment and intervention stand in a reciprocal or bidirectional relationship. What Meisels says about this relation can be fruitfully applied to children's play and to the adult's role in it. First, we need to enlarge our lens to see not just the target child alone, to be evaluated or remediated, but the bigger social picture as well—the child must be viewed in relationship to his or her family, teacher, peers, and so on. Concomitantly, the range of situations in which play interventions and assessments take place must expand ever farther away from the gray-room model of formal testing with highly specialized procedures, and out into the rich colorful world of everyday reality where the context is familiar, the method is nonthreatening, and the stakeholders are transdisciplinary in composition, with the parent seen as the captain of the child's team. Meisels applauds both the demise of labeling as a reputable practice (although bureaucratically, it remains a necessary evil) and the rising endorsement of contemporary views, which fuse assessment and evaluation with teaching and learning. Current efforts replace static renditions of "developmental status," seeking instead to capture dynamic processes and their interdependence. Parents and others are much more empowered to take ownership of interventions when they are involved in assessment decisions and understand both the rationale and the scope and limits of the evaluation and intervention methods used.

A complement to Meisel's macrolevel analysis (of the child's network of family, school, and community support) is Joan Goodman's (1992) more microlevel analysis of the teacher and child. Specifically, Goodman's discussion of the problem of the "take" (responsive teacher–child engagement) in play offers a second example of contemporary thinking. Goodman intended to sharpen focus on what constitutes sensitive and responsive play strategies in early intervention. To illustrate, consider the following scenarios:

> *A child is removing animals and blocks from a shelf. The teacher suggests building a zoo with the blocks and animals. The child, interested in removing and lining up, cannot participate in the zoo construction. The teacher picks up an animal, pokes it in the child's stomach, and says: "Monkey is going to get you." The child giggles. The teacher then tries to retain the child's attention by constructing cages with the blocks and putting an animal in each.*

> *A child spontaneously moves a car back and forth without releasing it from his hands. The teacher, having successfully gotten the child to roll cars to her, asks, "Will you send me the big car or the little one?" No response. "The small car or the police car?"*

> *A child in a sandbox is filling a shovel with sand and watching it spill out. The teacher suggests building a roadway for cars. The teacher leaves and the child returns to former play.*

In each of these cases, there is a great psychological distance between the teacher and the child depicted in the play vignette. The teachers are trying to expand play on a symbolic level much higher than what the child initiated. Either they are not tuned in to the child's play (and mental) state or do not appreciate what the child is doing—perhaps finding the child's rather simplistic or repetitive behavior tedious. Moreover, in all these cases, the teacher could very well have been following familiar curricular guidelines advocating symbolic play, but, each time, the child loses interest, and the activity becomes the teacher's play or the episode terminates. Such intrusions can be seen as another kind of inappropriate "spokesperson-for-reality" adult play interventions (see Chapter 7) found all too often in early childhood education.

Careful observation of the child's play and the child's responses to teacher suggestions are needed for adult play intervention to be on the child's wavelength. For example, the child in the sandbox (the third example) filling the shovel with sand and watching it spill out could benefit from teacher suggestions closer to the child's behavioral level. The child's pleasure and interest in this episode probably derives from the simple in/out, up/down actions of filling the shovel with sand and releasing its contents, over and over again. Goodman (1992) notes that play shifts in response to teacher interventions are inconsequential to the child's learning and development unless there is "take."

Take is defined both in the sense of mutual engagement (i.e., both the teacher and the child are on the same wavelength) and in terms of the teacher's suggestions being permanently incorporated into the child's behavioral repertoire. On-the-spot imitation or forced compliance are not "take." Rather than trying to get the child to accommodate to the teacher's play idea about a road for cars, the teacher could attempt either *horizontal* or *vertical expansions* close to the meaning or intentions of the child's original play actions. Empathy for the child and respect for play is shown when the teacher accommodates to the child by showing or asking the child to perform the shovel play from different spatial locations or in conjunction with containers of different sizes or shapes or with different shovels or with different amounts of sand in a shovel—all following the in/out, up/down routine as an example of *horizontal* expansion. *Vertical* expansion extends play by going from the in/out, up/down schemata to other concepts known to be achieved at approximately the same developmental level, such as open/close, give/return, raising/dropping.

Teachers commonly misread a child's play intentions in cases when a child is 4 years old chronologically but mentally only 20 months old. It is easy to make the mistake of assuming an interest in and a capacity for symbolic play. Goodman urges, however, that teachers support the child's level of play and guard against hurting the child's self-esteem by making frustrating and unrealistic demands. Her position is an excellent example of contemporary conceptions about play and teaching in special education, involving a respectful orientation to play. Such an orientation is a 180-degree turn from older views, which saw play opportunities as rewards or as breaks from the serious business of nonplayful interventions aimed at remediating deficits and accelerating cognitive development in children with special needs.

An example of a current practice in early childhood special education not incompatible with Goodman's thinking is activity-based instruction or ABI (Bricker & Cripe, 1992). Here, children are not made to play or are not just left to play, but teachers flexibly and sensitively try to intervene into child-initiated play in order to further along intervention objectives woven into play episodes or other activities performed naturally by the child in familiar contexts. With program objectives increasingly becoming integrated constructs and processes (e.g., making a friend), rather than isolated behaviors and products (e.g., stringing beads), the child's affective state and the personal meaning that play has for a child is considered important in ABI (Novick, 1993).

CHILD-LIFE PROGRAMS

Child-life programs are a fairly recent response to the needs of hospitalized children. Play is the core of *child-life programs,* which exist to help maintain and support the child's development and well-being while in health-care settings. Current programs evolved from play programs for hospitalized children operating as early as 1917, although the movement only took hold in the 1950s and 1960s, with the pioneering efforts of such women as Mary Brooks and Emma Plank. These women considered it absolutely imperative for the medical profession to meet the need for play in children who experience the emotional upset of hospitalization (Thompson & Stanford, 1981). Now that child-life programs are becoming common, research is needed to evaluate their effectiveness (Thompson, 1995).

Child-life programs have been proliferating in recent years and, although varying in makeup (size of facility, number of staff members, patient population served, and availability of other services such as social work, psychological counseling, or occupational therapy), they have in common the mission to help children cope with the stress and anxiety of the hospital experience and to foster—to the extent possible—normal growth and development. People in the child-life profession, now usually called child-life specialists, hold bachelor and master degrees in psychology, human development and family studies, education, and recreation and leisure studies. First and foremost, young patients are helped to play freely, through the provision of play materials and guidance in play. In the past, those in the profession were often called "play leaders." Establishing consistent and trusting relations with children and learning firsthand about children's concerns and misconceptions, child-life workers share this information with parents and hospital staff to facilitate more sensitive and responsive treatment.

ROLES OF THE CHILD-LIFE SPECIALIST

In addition to providing for play, child-life duties include two important professional roles: (1) serving as an ally for the child and the family, and (2) being a case and class advocate for children who are hospitalized (Nelson, 1996). First, befriending the child and his or her family enables the child-life specialist to be emotionally supportive while the patient prepares for hospitalization, surgery, and other medical encounters. During preadmission visits and during the hospitalization period itself, children are given accurate and reassuring explanations about upcoming procedures, in order to prevent mistaken notions (e.g., beliefs that children go to the hospital because they have been bad or naughty or that injections are a form of punishment). Also, the child-life specialist can serve as a resource person, helping doctors and nurses take the child's point of view. For example, a child going to surgery may find the phrase "put to sleep" really scary, as a result of previous knowledge about sick pets who have been "put to sleep" permanently (Nelson, 1996, p. 3). Parents also need someone to talk to about their own feelings and uncertainties. Child-life specialists serve them, as well—from such simple matters as telling them where to stand in the room during a medical procedure to more involved exchanges of information or opportunities to express frustrations or conflicts. Child-life specialists help children and their parents and siblings know what to expect (e.g., what the child patient will smell, hear, see, touch, and taste in various circumstances) so that all parties are psychologically prepared.

In their second role, child-life specialists are case and class advocates. Both on an individual case-by-case basis and as an advocate for all families as a class, the child-life specialist serves as an intermediary within the hospital, communicating for patients and enabling their voices to be heard. Child-life staff, highly visible in hospitals and pediatric settings, are members of the hospital staff with unique roles. They are not involved in direct medical care of the child yet are frequently in contact with the patient and interact informally with parents. As the family begins to trust the child-life specialist, family members share complaints, major and minor, about the child's medical treatment and the child's stay in the hospital in general. Parents may be upset about a certain doctor or nurse, about a medical choice, or about something that made the child think a certain doctor or nurse is "mean" or "doesn't care." This information can be passed along in an appropriate way to improve practices at the hospital, making these practices more individually and culturally responsive.

PLAY IN THE HOSPITAL

Child-life specialists see play as something essential for children who are hospitalized and not as merely a diversion or a pleasant extra. Play empowers children, enabling them to become active participants in the hospital, rather than the passive recipients they often are. Play is valued because it offers a window on the patient's thoughts and feelings, providing useful information to adults caring for the child. Also, play can serve cathartic purposes, helping the patient psychologically to get used to having to encounter some unpleasantness in the future, or to get over past traumatic events. Play also provides opportunity for social interaction, allowing play life and social development to go on. Losing oneself in a play state can also provide important psychological relief from stress, a chance to forget and to hope for better days ahead.

Child-life specialists attempt to encourage play that is rich and varied, developmentally appropriate, and realistic and adapted to the child's medical condition. For most children, being in the hospital is a very frightening experience, which can easily impede play and development; for instance, some children fear that their condition makes them different from others. The child-life specialist works to overcome these psychological barriers to play, as well as the physical ones. Being confined to a wheelchair, bedridden because of traction, or encumbered with IV (intravenous) lines—all these limitations obviously interfere with various forms of physical and social play. Adaptations and opportunities for play are provided to the extent that they are medically permissible. For example, a young child with an IV line may visit the playroom under the watchful supervision of a child-life specialist or parent. Here, the patient can explore the play area and look on while other children play, or perhaps even play to some extent, either alone or with others.

Playrooms are a main feature of child-life programs. They need to be adequately furnished and equipped with toys to meet various developmental needs and individual interests and play preferences. There must be adequate space for children in the playroom to gather and to work on activities, and the room must be accessible to children in wheelchairs and to children who are rolled in on a bed. Colorful and physically attractive playrooms come to be valued as a haven by children in a hospital. Through the use of selected toys, theme prop boxes, and materials, and through adult facilitation, the targeted play forms are social (parallel or interactive), functional, constructive, or dramatic play. Arts and crafts and games with rules are also available for older children. Computers with assistive devices are also becoming more common in many hospitals with child-life programs. Computer technology as a sophisticated tool of play and learning can empower children to engage in many activities requiring mobility and dexterity otherwise denied them due to physical constraints brought on by their medical condition.

Encouragement of social play among patients need not be relegated to the playroom of a child-life program. Individual rooms and hallways and other areas of the hospital can also become play spaces. Child-life specialists can help patients visit each other's rooms to play, much like going over to a friend's house. Children can play catch, for instance, from their bed or wheelchair, even if a ball cannot be used to the patients' satisfaction unless a Velcro mitt is worn (Nelson, 1996, p. 7). In individual rooms, children can share art projects, game play, favorite stories, or puppet shows. "Busyboxes" (often seen in waiting rooms of doctor's offices and clinics but without adult facilitation) can be placed in hallways to encourage play and stimulate social commerce. Other worthwhile stimulating activities include orchestrating a treasure hunt, visiting and exploring different places in the hospital (e.g., laundry room, a laboratory, kitchen area), and setting up a children's hospital newspaper with a roving reporter. Some semblance of a normal social life is possible through the provision of rich play experiences.

Children are also encouraged to use materials conducive to self-expression, such as puppets, musical instruments, art supplies, dolls, and dramatic-play materials. Child-life specialists are open and nonjudgmental. They observe children playing and afford them ample opportunities to express feelings, such as not liking a certain child or wanting to kill a certain respiratory therapist or hating their doctor. Child-life specialists let the child patient know that it is all right to have these feelings, that they are normal and understandable. When the specialist summarizes and labels children's feelings, she or he helps children grow in self-understanding and move on to seeking to learn reasons for their affective states. For example, a child-life worker may suggest that a child seems to be feeling angry, upon displaying such nonverbal behaviors as growling, kicking toys, stomping around, and the like (Axline, 1947).

Finally, medical play is often seen exhibited by hospitalized children. Some children enjoy using real medical equipment, such as IV lines minus the needles, stethoscopes, cast-making materials, and the like. Other children find real material too threatening and prefer miniature replicas for enacting medical play themes. Either way, these opportunities for having children open up and vent their fears and anxieties should not be passed by. Often, it would be appropriate to ask a child questions in a nonthreatening way, to learn about the child's inner world (e.g., "How does your doll feel about having shots?"). Medical play allows a chance to master feelings about being in the hospital, and to overcome fear of medical equipment and procedures. Medical play can be very empowering, affording opportunities for the child to be the active agent using medical equipment, and not just always having the equipment used on them.

RECOMMENDATIONS FOR TEACHERS

Teachers of young children in preschool, child-care, Head Start, early intervention, or primary school programs should seek to help children who are chronically ill or scheduled for long-term hospitalization and their families better cope with this stressful and disruptive experience. This can be accomplished via anticipatory socialization and follow-up activities to lessen the disjointedness and discontinuities brought on by a child's leaving a program and later reentering a program, both for the hospitalized child and for his or her peers. In partnership with the child's family, this can become an excellent sharing time, benefiting children through the information exchange, as well as reducing the chances that the child who is hospitalized would risk a drop in peer status due to the medical condition, whether transient in nature or long-term.

While a child is hospitalized for an extended time, arrangements should be made to coordinate with the child-life program and to keep abreast of mutual activities. New technology is opening the path for various modes of two-way communication, which can be used to advantage by the enterprising teacher and child-life specialist for the benefit of the hospitalized child, as a normalizing and socially and intellectually stimulating activity. Last, it is recommended that early childhood educational programs look into the prospects of a field trip to a local hospital as an invaluable experiential base for thematically related dramatic play or other activities, and as an excellent anticipatory socialization experience for children who need to spend some time in a hospital. Certain children's books are also very helpful (e.g., *Curious George Goes to the Hospital*, by H. Rey).

PLAY THERAPY

Play therapy is the best-known type of adult intervention into the play of children, with a history going back to the early 1900s. The primary goal is to help socio-emotionally troubled youngsters resolve inner conflicts, integrate private scripts to gain cognitive control, and achieve a more realistic sense of their unique selves (Singer, 1994). Although play-therapy sessions have mainly occurred in clinics or offices, the basic principles and procedures may apply to classrooms or other settings, as well.

BACKGROUND AND BASIC TENETS

The earliest forms of play therapy were inspired by the psychoanalytic school of thought, where therapists such as Anna Freud and Melanie Klein used play expression with children as a substitute for the free-association techniques used with adults. Playing was a means by which the emotionally disturbed child could move from chaos to resolution of painful unconscious struggles and negative feelings. Play was seen as a way in which children could release blocked inner conflicts and emotions.

Elementary school counselors began to incorporate play into their work in the 1960s, influenced by private-practice child therapists. The therapeutic philosophy of Virginia Axline (1947), based on Carl Rogers's nondirective, client-based approach to treatment, was particularly influential as a source of ideas about the value of play in preventive counseling. Also in the 1960s, therapists commonly began to use puppets, music, and drama in applying play to foster social skills, as seen with the development of commercially available guidance materials (Campbell, 1993). The 1970s and 1980s saw the proliferation of a variety of approaches to the use of play and play media to foster beneficial interventions for emotionally troubled children (e.g., Gardner's therapeutic story-telling, Mitchell's work with sand play, Schaefer's play therapy techniques).

Practitioners of play therapy or play-related therapeutic or preventive interventions (whether used in private practice, in schools, or at home) all agree that freedom of expression within the context of limits is critical. The therapeutic value of play is seen in its many variations, which include bibliotherapy, horticultural therapy, dance therapy, art therapy, animal therapy, and game therapy. Axline's (1947) principles of child-centered therapy underscore the importance of the therapist developing a warm, caring relationship with the child, based on genuine interest and showing unqualified acceptance. Creating a feeling of safety and permissiveness (establishing only those behavioral limits that help the child accept appropriate personal responsibility in the relationship), the therapist respects the child's inner direction and allows the child to lead, empathizing with the inner state of the child and reflecting the child's feelings back to the child, to help develop self-understanding. The therapist realizes that therapy is a gradual process but that the child does have the ability to solve personal problems. In the therapeutic relationship, the therapist, counselor, teacher, or parent seeks to experience sensations along with the child and to respond and interact in such a manner so that the child feels that the adult is part of whatever the child is doing (Landreth, 1993).

PLAY SESSIONS

Play sessions following child-centered therapy are best used for children between the ages of 4 and 11 years. At the beginning, at least 30 minutes should be set aside for a play session, and later somewhat longer. The location typically should be an area set aside where it is quiet and free from interruptions, where spilling and messes are easily cleaned up, and where there is enough space to move around and play with toys. Schaefer's (1983) selection criteria for toys include (a) toys that can be used in many ways; (b) toys that encourage the most difficult feelings to deal with in life (e.g., aggression, dependency, jealousy); and (c) toys that can be used by one or two people.

Durability of playthings is important, but obviously some critical materials, such as drawing paper, colored markers, and bop bags, will need to be replenished. Axline (1947) recommends that play-session toys include a doll family with furniture, clay, crayons, paper, toy animals, soldiers, baby dolls, telephones, baby bottles, family hand puppets, building materials, and a sand table. Guerney (1983) adds water and water toys, rubber knives, wolf puppets, cards, play money, paints, easels, and masks. For older children, horseshoes, board games, miniature bowling, target games, basketball games, and so on can be used (Simmons, 1996).

At the beginning of the play session, children are told that the play area is a special place where children can generally do whatever they want to, but if there is something not allowed, they will be told (structuring). Basic limits are set on physical aggression, destruction of valuable objects, ignoring time limits, and leaving the area (Schaefer, 1983). The heart and soul of the art of therapy is deep empathic responding (i.e., acceptance and understanding of the child's feelings and activity), which requires careful wording of responses to the child to reflect back the child's inner state (silence and social conversations are discouraged). This skill requires practice and often extended training and supervision by an experienced registered play therapist. Careful wording of responses and nonverbal receptivity are required. In these sessions, therapists position themselves on the same plane as the child, this positioning helps to enhance nonverbal communication and to lessen the power differential. As a rule of thumb, the therapist should be distanced 3 feet from the child.

Generally, early sessions mostly deal with structuring and setting the tone of the relationship and the upper and lower limits of acceptable and unacceptable behavior. The child's exploration of the area and occasional need for adult encouragement or reassurances about play activity are also common during the early sessions. Aggressive behaviors are common as well, but they usually level off with the onset of regressive behavior, as the child deals with independence–dependence issues. As trust in the therapist builds, acceptance of self and personal well-being begins to occur. In the later stage, social behaviors occur much more frequently than antisocial ones; less aggression and a higher tolerance for frustration are evidenced. Play also becomes more reality oriented (Simmons, 1996).

APPLICATION TO EARLY CHILDHOOD SETTINGS

Play therapy is usually associated with a therapist or counselor office setting. However, the basic principles and procedures can be used in the classroom by teachers and paraprofessionals. Many areas of the early childhood education classrooms are conducive to therapeutic interaction (block area, art area, doll house), and toys of play therapy can be added to a play center. Guerney (1983) has suggested the use of play therapy on the playground, and Axline (1969) has used play therapy with a group of children in play. The storytelling and play techniques of Vivian Paley (1990) can be viewed as having therapeutic value. She has helped many kindergarten children cope with their feelings, fears, and concerns about friendship and fairness (the four "F" themes) in her play- and story-based therapeutic teaching practices. Teachers who are sensitive and empathic with children can help many children who are socially and emotionally hurt, through reflecting the children's feelings and social intentions while in the play episodes, thereby enhancing their perspective-taking skills and self-awareness.

Teachers and paraprofessionals most assuredly are not professional therapists. Unlike child psychologists and other individuals trained and educated as therapists, teachers must recognize a very clear distinction between their own appropriate roles (as described in the preceding paragraph) and those of certified or licensed play therapists who may legitimately engage in true play therapy. Accordingly, teachers must remain vigilant for when referrals to mental health professionals are in order and not hesitate in making them.

SUMMARY

Special education has different roots from early childhood education so it is not surprising that there has been divergent views on play. Early childhood educators view play as central to learning, development, and teaching practices, those in early childhood special education and early intervention have seen play as secondary to more structured learning intervention and remediation practices. In recent years, a better understanding of the importance of play has found its way into curriculum, teaching, and assessment of children with disabilities. Educators may target cognitive aspects of play over social aspects in special education practice. Modifying curriculum activities (e.g., space, time, materials, special assistance, positioning, and equipment) fosters social and cognitive play.

Child Life Programs and Play Therapy are germane to today's educator. Child Life Programs have come into prominence to meet the needs of hospitalized children. Play assumes a major role in these programs with the child life specialist performing essential duties: serving as an ally and being an advocate, and being a play leader. Play therapy is the oldest and best known intervention by adults into the world of child's play. Originally based on Freudian doctrine, elementary school counselors and psychologists, influenced by Carl Rogers and the work of Virginia Axline, began adapting clinical play therapy to other settings. Self-expression, self-understanding, acceptance, social perspective-taking skills are the goals of play therapy.

Chapter 7

ADULT INVOLVEMENT IN PLAY

Channing and several friends ask their teacher if they can play pizza parlor. The teacher agrees and brings out a prop box containing felt pizza pieces, pizza boxes, menus, tablecloths, and so on. The children spend about 10 minutes separating the pizza ingredients (olives, pepperoni slices, etc.) into bins. When they have finished, the teacher asks which pizza shop they would like to be today. They respond, "Pizza Hut." While the children watch, the teacher makes a sign with the Pizza Hut name and logo. Channing requests, "Make a 'closed' sign on the back." The teacher turns over the paper and writes, "CLOSED FOR BUSINESS." Channing then hangs the "closed" sign on the front of the play center. The children spend another 10 minutes rearranging furniture and setting up the eating and kitchen areas in their pretend restaurant. When the children have finished their preparations, Channing turns the "closed" sign over so that the Pizza Hut logo is showing. The teacher then pretends to be a customer, reads a menu, and orders a pizza with pepperoni, green peppers, onions, and lots of cheese. Several children then make the pizza and deliver it to the teacher. She pretends to eat it enthusiastically ("Best pizza I've ever eaten!"). ∎

Adult involvement in play has long been controversial. In the preceding episode, the teacher helps the children set the stage for play. She also takes on the role of customer and actually joins in the ongoing pizza-parlor play. Supporters argue that this type of adult involvement can enrich children's play experiences and maximize the impact of play on intellectual and social development (Jones & Reynolds, 1992; Kitson, 1994; Roskos & Neuman, 1993). Opponents, on the other hand, maintain that adult involvement can disrupt or inhibit children's play activities and can reduce their opportunities for learning during play (Miller, Fernie, & Kantor, 1992; Pellegrini & Galda, 1993).

Advocates cite many reasons for appropriate forms of adult involvement in play:

- *Approval*—When parents and teachers participate in play, they let children know that play is a valuable, worthwhile activity (Manning & Sharp, 1977).
- *Attachment*—Children who experience positive interaction with adults during play are likely to become more securely attached to those adults (Howes & Smith, 1995).
- *Cognitive complexity*—When interacting with adults, 4- and 5-year-olds tend to engage in more cognitively complex forms of play (Sylva, Roy, & Painter, 1980).

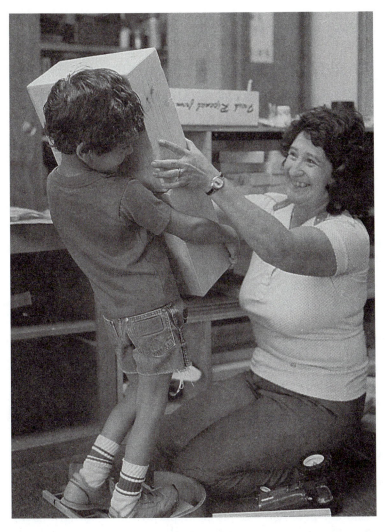

Adult participation can enrich children's play.

- *Attention span*—Children's (particularly girls') attention spans increase when an adult is present (Hutt, Tyler, Hutt, & Christopherson, 1989).
- *Peer interaction*—Adults can arrange contacts between peers during play and can coach children in successful techniques for getting along with others (Howes & Smith, 1995).
- *Enrichment*—Teachers can provide materials, ideas, and skills that can both expand the scope of children's play and enhance its impact on learning (Bennett, Wood, & Rogers, 1997).
- *Scaffolding*—Children's involvement with an adult can create a "zone of proximal development" (Vygotsky, 1978), allowing children to engage in activities that they could not do on their own, such as the sign making in the chapter-opening vignette.

Supporters of adult involvement maintain that adults can maximize the developmental potential of play by engaging in supportive and responsive interactions with children during play (Erwin, Carpenter, & Kontos, 1993).

Opponents counter these advantages by highlighting the potential dangers of adult participation in play. They cite examples of how an adult can overpower and overstructure play, limiting children's ability to play on their own terms and reducing their opportunities for discovery, problem solving, risk taking, and peer interaction during play (Miller et al., 1992). As Pellegrini and Galda (1993, p. 169) point out, "when children and adults interact, adults do most of the work." Some teachers also have a tendency to interrupt play to teach concepts or to redirect children toward academic activities. Such interruptions often have a disruptive effect on play episodes and can cause children to stop playing (Jones & Reynolds, 1992; Wood, McMahon, & Cranstoun, 1980). These types of abuses have caused Sutton-Smith (1990, p. 5) to comment, "It is better to encourage children to play amongst themselves than to infect them with our own didactic play bumblings."

We believe that there is merit to both positions. Adult involvement can have positive and negative effects on play. The crucial variable is *how* adults become involved in play. If adults interact with children in a sensitive, responsive, and supportive manner, play can be enhanced. On the other hand, if adults take over the control of play, provide too much structure, or interrupt play for academic purposes, play will usually suffer.

This chapter begins with a brief review of research on adult involvement in play, including play between parents and children, play training programs, and teacher–child play. The remainder of the chapter is devoted to strategies that adults can use to enrich children's play experiences: providing resources for play, play observation, and appropriate forms of involvement in play.

RESEARCH ON ADULT INVOLVEMENT IN PLAY

Given the controversy surrounding adult involvement in play, it is not surprising that this topic has been the focus of a considerable amount of research. Studies have focused on parent–child play, on play training programs in which adults attempt to teach children pretend-play skills, and on play between teachers and children.

PARENT–CHILD PLAY

Play is a natural part of childrearing, and most parents engage their infants and toddlers in a variety of simple games (see "Developmentally Appropriate Play Interactions with Infants and Toddlers"). These early parent–child games have been the subject of a considerable amount of research. While most of these studies have focused on mother–child play, researchers are also beginning to examine how fathers play with their children (e.g., MacDonald, 1987).

One strand of research has examined the outcomes of mother–child play. Results have indicated that many benefits accrue when mothers play with their infants and toddlers:

Theory in Action

DEVELOPMENTALLY APPROPRIATE PLAY INTERACTIONS WITH INFANTS AND TODDLERS

BILLIE ENZ

Age: Birth to Three Months

Physical Development

At this age, infants usually

- Lift head when placed on stomach
- Support weight on elbows
- Relax and grasp hands
- Visually track moving objects
- Push and kick feet
- Turn from side to back

Language and Cognitive Skills

At this age, infants usually

- Turn head toward familiar voice
- Coo and gurgle
- Respond to caregiver's facial expressions
- Observe caregiver's mouth and mirror movements

Developmentally Appropriate Play Interactions

Caregivers may

- Engage in "baby talk" or exaggerated speech while facing the baby. Likewise, it is also appropriate to imitate the baby's vocalization, as this will often cause the baby to smile and continue a cooing "conversation."
- Make all types of silly facial expressions, and the baby will watch intently and often respond with the entire body, as well as the voice.
- Provide a crib mobile to encourage visual tracking. Another visual-tracking game involves placing a bright sock on the baby's hand or foot. This visual stimulation fascinates the baby and encourages her or him to explore her or his feet and hands.
- Play "finger grab" and "hair grab" games. You can reinforce these games by describing the action; for example, "Carlos has Momma's finger."
- Label body parts when playing with the baby ("Look at your toes, aren't they sweet toes?")

(continued)

Theory in Action *(continued)*

Age: Three Months to Six Months

Physical Development

At this age, infants usually

- Slap at bath water
- Recognize their own reflections in a mirror
- Kick their feet when prone
- Play with toes
- Reach for, but miss, dangling objects
- Turn from side to back
- Rock on all fours, a precrawling action
- Sit up with help

Language and Cognitive Skills

At this age, infants usually

- Demonstrate appropriate facial responses: smile when happy; pout when fussy
- Laugh and chuckle
- Babble: babababa
- Vocalize: make sounds that approximate words
- Recognize familiar people

Developmentally Appropriate Play Interactions

Caregivers may

- Hold the baby in front of a mirror, expand the body-labeling game by asking questions such as, "Where's Tommy's nose?" The caregiver will then touch Tommy's nose and say "There's Tommy's nose."
- Provide crib gyms; these dangling objects give the baby an opportunity to practice grasping and improve hand–eye coordination.
- Play peekaboo.
- Begin to engage in fingerplays such as "patty-cake" or toe plays such as "This Little Piggy."
- Sing to the baby. The sound of singing is auditorially intriguing and emotionally comforting.

Age: Six to Twelve Months

Physical Development

At this age, babies usually

- Begin to crawl
- Sit alone steadily

(continued)

- Pull themselves to a standing position in a crib
- Successfully reach for and grab toys
- Transfer a toy from one hand to the other
- Walk around while holding onto furniture

Language and Cognitive Skills

At this age, babies usually

- Recognize some words
- Respond to tones/inflection
- Comprehend gestures such as waving "bye-bye"
- Follow simple directions, such as "Give Momma the toy"
- Imitate animal sounds
- Begin to use sounds, words, and gestures to express need

Developmentally Appropriate Play Interactions

Caregivers may

- Engage in a game of "crawling" chase. Babies also enjoy using adult hands to pull themselves to a standing position.
- Play ball by rolling a small, soft ball back and forth to the baby.
- Pretend to talk on a toy phone, then hand the phone to the baby, who will often begin to speak.
- Ask the child, "What sound does the doggie make?" "What sound does the kitty make?" Reading cardstock storybooks that show familiar animals is a way to reinforce this fun language game.
- Play cleanup games, as these reinforce simple routines and build vocabulary. "Let's put the blocks in the box."
- Encourage bathtub play. One way to help a baby enjoy bathtime play is to place a large plastic laundry basket (with wide slats) in the bathtub. Place both the child and tub toys in the laundry basket in the bathtub. You may also wish to place a large sponge in the bottom of the laundry basket for the baby to sit on. The sponge will help prevent the baby from slipping. This arrangement will also keep toys from floating away from the baby and will allow you more freedom to talk and play with the baby. *Caution: the caregiver must always stay with children whenever they are in the bathtub.*

Age: One to Two Years

Physical Development

At this age, toddlers usually

- Refine their walking skills

(continued)

Theory in Action *(continued)*

- Squat to pick up objects
- "Dance" in place to music
- Pull, push, and drag toys
- Walk up and down stairs, assisted
- Walk backward
- Mimic routines such as washing dishes or sweeping
- Use fingers to feed themselves

Language and Cognitive Skills

At this age, toddlers usually

- Jabber expressively
- Comprehend simple questions
- Know names of body parts
- Use 2-word sentences
- Have 20- to 25-word vocabulary by 18 months
- Have 270-word vocabulary by 24 months

Developmentally Appropriate Play Interactions

Caregivers may

- Play hide and seek and chase (running style) with toddlers. Children also like to play horsey on your back and be bounced on a knee. You can also dance with toddlers.
- Allow water play in the bathtub, and offer your child an opportunity to pour water from one container into other containers. Adults can support this play by asking questions, "Which has more water?"
- Play a "hunt for objects" game; for instance, "Where is the blue ball?"
- Show the photo book of family members. Toddlers are fascinated by seeing family members in a book. Ask, "Where is daddy? Can you find daddy in the picture?"
- Sing songs that have body involvement, such as "The Itsy Bitsy Spider," "One, Two, Buckle My Shoe," "BINGO," and the "Hokey Pokey."
- Show 2-year-old toddlers how to begin to blow bubbles and how to play with play dough and crayons.

Sources

Black, J., Puckett, M., & Bell, M. (1992). The young child: Development from prebirth through age eight. New York: Merrill,

Martin, E. (1988) Baby games: The joyful guide to child's play from birth to three years. Philadelphia: Running Press.

Silberg, J. (1993). Games to play with babies. Beltsville, Maryland: Gryphon House.

Sutton-Smith, B., & Sutton-Smith, S. (1974). How to play with your children (and when not to). New York: Hawthorn.

- Children engage in more pretend play with their mothers than when playing by themselves (Fiese, 1990; O'Connell & Bretherton, 1984).
- Children often shift to higher levels of pretend play while playing with their mothers (Beizer & Howes, 1992; Slade, 1987), although it is unclear whether this facilitation has a long-term effect on children's independent play (see Fein & Fryer, 1995).
- Playful mothers tend to have securely attached children (Blehar, Lieberman, & Ainsworth, 1977).
- While engaging in play with their mothers, young children learn important social skills such as turn taking and sharing (Bruner & Sherwood, 1976; Hay, Ross, & Goldman, 1979; Ross & Lollis, 1987).

A second group of studies have investigated the effectiveness of different maternal play styles (Beizer & Howes, 1992; Fiese, 1990; O'Connell & Bretherton, 1984; Slade, 1987). With respect to the amount of maternal involvement in play, findings indicate an inverted-U-shaped function. Fein and Fryer (1995, p. 378) explain:

> Mothers who are distant or indirect have little influence on their children; mothers who are intrusive and tutorial have a negative influence. Mothers who offer direct suggestions, solicit pretend behaviors from their children and participate in pretend exchanges have a positive influence on their children.

Thus, a moderate level of parental involvement in play appears to be most effective, a finding that is mirrored in the research on teacher–child play interactions.

Other studies have examined the degree to which mothers match their play scaffolding or other assistance with their children's developing play skills. Evidence suggests that many mothers are quite skillful play scaffolders. Hodapp, Goldfield, and Boyatzis (1984) found that as infants mature, mothers reduced the amount of structuring that they provided in peekaboo and roll-the-ball games. Damast, Tamis-LeMonda, and Bornstein (1996) found that mothers respond to children's play at levels equal to or slightly above the level of the child's preceding play, gradually nudging children toward higher levels of play.

A final group of investigations have researched parent–child play in different cultures. Findings have revealed both universals and differences. Fernald and O'Neill (1993) examined peekaboo in 15 diverse cultures and found striking similarities in the structural features and dynamics of the game. On the other hand, Farver's (1993) comparison of mother–child and sibling play in Mexico and the United States revealed cultural differences in family roles. Mothers provided play scaffolding in the United States, whereas siblings had this role in Mexico. More information on cultural influences on play can be found in Chapter 5.

PLAY TRAINING

Play training occurs when adults teach children how to engage in sociodramatic play. Interest in this type of training was initially sparked by a study conducted in Israel by Sara Smilansky (1968). She had observed that children from low-income North African and Middle-Eastern immigrant families engaged in less sociodramatic play than middle-class Israeli children. Because these immigrant children were also experiencing academic difficulties in school, Smilansky hypothesized that their school problems might be caused by their inability to engage in sociodramatic play. She reasoned that if sociodramatic play improves social skills, stimulates language development, and enhances the ability to use and interpret symbols, then children who do not engage in this type of play might be less able to cope with school tasks than those who do.

Smilansky conducted an experiment to discover the cause of the low-income children's lack of sociodramatic play. Large numbers of preschool and kindergarten students were assigned to four treatment groups: (a) *direct experiences,* such as field trips; (b) *play training;* (c) *combination* of play training and direct experiences; and (d) *control.* The play training, which was administered by the children's regular teachers, involved two types of intervention (see "Two Types of Sociodramatic Play Training"):

- *Outside intervention,* in which the adult remained outside of the play episode and used coaching to encourage play behaviors
- *Participation in the play* ("inside intervention"), in which the adult took part in the children's play and modeled desired play behaviors

Results showed that both the play training and the combination treatments were very effective in increasing the amount and quality of the children's sociodramatic play. Both treatments also appeared to improve some aspects of the children's cognitive performance. Simply providing extra direct experiences, on the other hand, had no effect on the children's play or their cognitive abilities. Smilansky concluded that it was lack of knowledge of specific play skills, rather than inadequate experiential backgrounds, that kept many low-income children from engaging in sociodramatic play.

Smilansky's study took on added significance as a result of a series of investigations on social-class differences in play behavior. Results of these studies indicated that low-SES children in the United States (Feitelson & Ross, 1973), England (Smith & Dodsworth, 1978), and Canada (Rubin, Maioni, & Hornung, 1976) all exhibited lower levels of sociodramatic play than their middle-class counterparts. These findings, combined with Smilansky's results, suggested that a lack of sociodramatic play may be inhibiting the cognitive development and educational progress of low-SES children in many countries. (See Chapter 5 for a discussion of problems associated with this deficit view of cultural differences in play behavior.)

Beginning in the 1970s, American, British, and Canadian researchers conducted a number of play-training experiments. The motivation behind these studies was twofold: (1) to gain evidence that play was a causal force in cognitive development, and (2) to determine whether play training was an effective means for stimulating low-SES children's cognitive growth. These studies used either of two types of training strategies:

Theory in Action

TWO TYPES OF SOCIODRAMATIC PLAY TRAINING

A preschool teacher observes that Bobby, a shy 4-year-old, frequently plays alone with blocks. He rarely engages in constructive or dramatic play with the blocks; instead, he merely stacks them up in piles and then knocks them down. Bobby has just gotten a new pair of shoes, which he is very proud of. Two types of sociodramatic play training can be used to encourage Bobby to engage in more challenging play: outside intervention or inside intervention.

Outside Intervention

In this type of tutoring, the teacher remains outside the play frame and makes comments and suggestions aimed at encouraging sociodramatic play.

TEACHER: Mr. Storekeeper, you certainly have a lot of shoes (pointing to the small blocks). Have you sold any yet?

BOBBY: No, I haven't.

TEACHER: Why don't you make some shelves out of the bigger blocks so people can see the shoes you have to sell. While you're doing that, I'll see if I can find some customers for your store.

The teacher might then approach some other children who are playing in the housekeeping corner and suggest that they make a trip to Bobby's "store" to buy some new shoes.

Inside Intervention

This type of tutoring requires that the teacher take on a role and join in the play. While engaging in the play, the teacher can model desired play behaviors and skills.

TEACHER: Mr. Storekeeper, I would like to buy a pair of your shoes (pointing to the small blocks).

BOBBY: Which ones?

TEACHER: How about these nice brown ones (picks up two small blocks and pretends to put them on her feet).

BOBBY: Do you like them?

TEACHER: No, they're too tight.

BOBBY: Here, why don't you try these on? (Hands the teacher two more blocks).

The teacher might then offer to become a salesperson and help Bobby try to sell his "shoes" to other children.

(continued)

Theory in Action *(continued)*

Phase Out

Regardless of whether outside or inside intervention is being used, it is recommended that adults phase out sociodramatic play training as soon as the children begin to exhibit the desired play behaviors. This can be done by either switching to the nondirective role of coplayer or withdrawing completely from the play situation. This stepping-back procedure returns control of the play to the children and helps promote independence and self-confidence. In addition, research suggests that phasing out enhances the impact of play training on children's subsequent play (Gershowitz, cited in Singer & Singer, 1977).

1. Sociodramatic play training—variations of Smilansky's "outside intervention" and "participation in the play" strategies described in "Two Types of Sociodramatic Play Training."
2. Thematic-fantasy play training—a more structured type of training in which an adult helps children to enact fairy tales (e.g., Three Billy Goats Gruff) or stories. The adult reads the story, assigns roles to the children, and helps them enact the story by prompting and at times by taking a role in the dramatization (see "Thematic-Fantasy Play Training").

The results of play-training research, on the whole, have been quite positive. Findings indicate that sociodramatic play training is very effective in increasing young children's group dramatic-play abilities and their participation in this advanced form of play (Christie, 1983; Dansky, 1980; Saltz, Dixon, & Johnson, 1977; Smith, Dalgleish, & Herzmark, 1981). In addition, sociodramatic play training has been found to lead to gains in some measures of intellectual and social development, including IQ scores (Hutt et al., 1989; Saltz et al., 1977), creativity (Christie, 1983; Dansky, 1980; Feitelson & Ross, 1973), language development (Levy, Wolfgang, & Koorland, 1992), and perspective taking (Burns & Brainerd, 1979).

Results also show that variations of thematic-fantasy play (TFP) training are effective in promoting sociodramatic play (Saltz & Johnson, 1974). TFP training has also been found to lead to gains in a variety of developmental outcomes, including IQ scores (Saltz & Johnson, 1974; Saltz et al., 1977) and various measures of story comprehension (Pellegrini, 1984; Saltz & Johnson, 1974; Silvern, Taylor, Williamson, Surbeck, & Kelley, 1986).

Unfortunately, these findings have been limited by a number of methodological weaknesses (Christie & Johnsen, 1985). One common problem has been the failure of experimenters to control for the effects of peer interaction and adult tutoring, which accompany play training (Rubin, 1980; Smith et al., 1981). The possibility exists that the social and cognitive benefits of play training were caused by social interaction, rather than by the play component of

Theory in Action

THEMATIC-FANTASY PLAY TRAINING

Thematic-fantasy play (TFP) training, originally developed by Saltz and Johnson (1974), involves having children act out familiar fairy tales such as "The Three Little Pigs," "Little Red Riding Hood," and "The Three Billy Goats Gruff." Any fairy tale or story with a simple, repetitive plot and a small number of characters can be used. The training involves four phases:

1. *Reading and discussion.* The story is read to the children and discussed. The teacher should ask questions to make sure the children fully understand the story plot. With *The Three Bears*, the following questions might be asked:

   Where did the three bears live?
   Why did the bears go for a walk?
   What did Goldilocks do first when she went into the house?
   Whose porridge did she try first? Did she like it? Why or why not?
   Whose porridge did she try second? Did she like it? Why or why not?
   Whose porridge did she try third? Did she like it? Why or why not?
   What happened to the porridge? [This sequence can be repeated for the chair and the bed]
   What happened when the bears returned?
   What might you have done if you were Goldilocks?

2. *Props.* Props are constructed to support the story enactment. In TFP, prop management is essential. Too many props can distract from make-believe play, drawing children into sensorimotor involvement with materials. Remember that props can be a means to an end in themselves. Two main questions need to be considered: Will the prop help children enact the story? Can children use it in the prescribed manner? As discussed in Chapter 10, children under $3\frac{1}{2}$ years of age require realistic, concrete props (e.g., a toy telephone) in order to engage in make-believe, whereas most older children can use props that are less physically similar to the reference object (e.g., a block of wood the same size as a phone).

3. *Preliminary enactment.* Children are assigned roles and attempt a preliminary enactment of the story. The teacher assists in this initial enactment, either by taking a major role in the story or by serving as narrator.

4. *Repeated enactments.* The story is acted out several more times, with children trading roles. During these later reenactments, the teacher phases out his or her assistance.

(continued)

Theory in Action *(continued)*

Table 7.1 lists several stories that can be used for TFP. Four components are listed for each story: roles, props, settings, and related activities. Of course, these elements can be adapted to fit specific situations. For example, if there are more children than roles, the teacher can suggest that several children play newly invented roles, such as forest creatures.

Table 7.1 STORIES FOR THEMATIC FANTASY PLAY

STORY	ROLES	PROPS	SETTING	RELATED ACTIVITIES
GOLDILOCKS AND THE THREE BEARS	Papa Bear Mama Bear Baby Bear Goldilocks	Table 3 chairs 3 beds 3 bowls	Arrange table, chairs, and beds	Trip to zoo to see bears Book versions of story Flannel-board story
LITTLE RED RIDING HOOD	Red Riding Hood Mother Wolf Grandmother Hunter	Cape Basket Cap and glasses Nose and teeth	Set up block area using tables and chairs to represent woods and grandma's house	Make food for the basket Trip to zoo to see wolf Book versions of story Draw pictures of story Flannel-board story
CINDERELLA	Cinderella Stepmother Two stepsisters Fairy godmother Prince Dancers Mice coachman	Broom Slippers Fancy dress Wand	Arrange table and chairs to represent house, carriage, and palace	Book versions of story Draw pictures of story Cut and paste carriages
THREE LITTLE PIGS	Three pigs Wolf	Straw Wood Bricks Pot for fireplace	Chairs for each house, with straw, wood, or bricks on chair to designate type of house	Explore sturdiness of the three materials Cut and paste houses Book versions of story Flannel-board story
JACK AND THE BEANSTALK	Jack Mother Seller Giant Giant's wife	Beans Money Chicken Beanstalk	Use platform play equipment outdoors to represent clouds	Grow lima beans in plastic bag, with wet napkins Color eggs Make beanstalk out of wrapping-paper rolls
HANSEL AND GRETEL	Hansel Gretel Father Stepmother Witch	Bread crumbs Box for cage Oven Rug for pond	Arrange tables and chairs to represent forest, witch's house	Bake gingerbread cake Book versions of story Draw pictures of story
THREE BILLY GOATS GRUFF	Three billy goats Troll	Large blocks and plank for bridge	Assemble bridge in block corner	Visit zoo or farm to see goats Flannel-board story

the training. From a theoretical perspective, this is a serious weakness because it prevents the findings of play-training research from being used as evidence that play has a causal role in child development. From an applied perspective, this limitation is less worrisome. Parents and educators are likely to be content with the finding that play training has been found to be a useful intervention strategy, fostering increased amounts of sociodramatic play and producing gains in various aspects of social and cognitive development.

TEACHER–CHILD PLAY

Beginning in the 1970s, British and American researchers began to investigate what teachers do while children are engaging in play. Initial findings indicated that teachers only spent between 2 and 6% of their time involved in children's play (Sylva et al., 1980; Tizard, Phelps, & Plewis, 1976; Wood et al., 1980) and tended to restrict their involvement to a very superficial level (Hutt et al., 1989). Researchers offered four possible explanations for this lack of teacher involvement in play.

1. The teachers may not have had enough time. Teachers are often so encumbered with administrative duties that they spend the entire play period checking worksheets, preparing for the next activity, handling discipline problems, and so on (Sylva et al., 1980).
2. They may have subscribed to the old psychoanalytic belief that play's main function is to enable children to work out their inner conflicts (Isaacs, 1930). According to this perspective, adults should never enter into or interfere in any way with children's play.
3. The teachers may have had a child-centered philosophy of education and believed that play is better if children are completely free to make their own choices and decisions (Bennett, Wood, & Rogers, 1997).
4. They may have been embarrassed about playing with children, particularly when other adults are present (Hutt et al., 1989).

Recently, attitudes have changed, due in part to the growing acceptance of developmentally appropriate practice (Bredekamp & Copple, 1997). The National Association for the Education of Young Children (NAEYC), in consultation with a wide range of educators and psychologists, has recommended a number of curriculum characteristics and teaching practices that match the developmental needs and characteristics of young children. One of the basic tenets of developmentally appropriate practice (DAP) is "the need for teachers to engage in supportive, responsive interactions with children during play" (Erwin et al., 1993, p. 2).

This positive endorsement of adult involvement in play is reflected in recent studies of teacher activity during play periods:

- File and Kontos (1993) found that preschool teachers spent an average of 15% of their time supporting play in classrooms with a mix of children with and without disabilities.

- Erwin et al. (1993) reported that preschool teachers were engaged in facilitating play 27% of the time.
- Grinder and Johnson (1994) discovered that child-care providers assisted in play 39% of the time.

While these findings indicate a sizable increase in teacher participation in play, compared with earlier studies, other results paint a less-favorable picture of the *qualitative* aspects of this teacher involvement. Both the File and Kontos (1993) and the Erwin et al. (1993) studies reported that teacher support focused almost exclusively on cognitive aspects of play (children's use of materials, toys, or ideas). Support for social aspects of play (e.g., facilitating peer interaction) was very rare, accounting for only 2% of play time in both studies. Howes and Clements (1994) also reported that child-care providers spent only 1–2% of free-play periods mediating peer interactions. File (1994, p. 237) conjectured that this lack of support of social play indicates

> a classroom environment in which children are generally left to their own devices to interact with their peers. It appears that children are implicitly expected to "pick up" social skills on their own. . . . The risk is that children with strong social skills will succeed in establishing mutual peer relations, leaving the children with weaker skills increasingly isolated from peer circles.

Grinder and Johnson (1994) also reported some negative findings. While the teachers in this study provided positive support for play 39% of the time, they spent another 27% of their time engaging in "play-interfering" behavior. These negative forms of interaction included distracting play, instructing, conversing, taking over play, inopportune questioning, and commanding.

In summary, the results of research on teacher activity during play periods have been mixed. Recent studies indicate that the amount of teacher involvement in play is increasing, but there are concerns about the quality of this involvement. Most of the recent reports recommend that teachers receive more training in play-facilitation strategies.

A second group of studies have examined the impact of teacher involvement on children's play patterns. Again, the findings are mixed. Positive findings include the following:

- *Duration and elaboration.* Observational studies of British preschools revealed that children's play episodes lasted twice as long and were more elaborate when a teacher was involved than when the children played only with their peers (Sylva et al., 1980).
- *Social interaction.* Farran, Silveri, and Culp's (1991) study of public preschools for low-income children reported that teacher involvement was associated with increased participation in social forms of play. Cooperative play, the highest category in Parten's (1932) social-play hierarchy, occurred *only* in the presence of a teacher.
- *Cognitive activity.* Howes and Smith's (1995) large-scale study of 150 child-care programs revealed that positive teacher interaction was associated with higher levels of cognitive activity during play.

- *Literacy activity.* A series of studies have investigated children's play in literacy-enriched play settings (see Chapter 11). Results have shown that teacher involvement results in increased amounts of reading and writing behavior during play in these settings (Christie & Enz, 1992; Morrow & Rand, 1991; Vukelich, 1991).

Other studies have reported negative effects of adult involvement on play. Zivin (1974) discovered that when adults asked children to state all the imaginable uses for an unpopular toy, the toy became even less popular with the children. As Zivin indicated in the title of her article, this type of intervention in play was a good way "to make a boring thing more boring" (p. 232). Tegano, Lookabaugh, May, and Burdette (1991) reported that when kindergarten teachers imposed a high amount of structure on construction activities by presenting models to copy or by giving instructions, the amount of constructive play decreased, and nonplay activity increased. File and Kontos (1993) found that teacher involvement that is heavily biased toward cognitive aspects of play can have a negative effect on the social quality of play. Finally, a number of other researchers have reported incidents in which overzealous teacher intervention disrupted children's ongoing play activities (Jones & Reynolds, 1992; Schrader, 1990; Wood et al., 1980).

The mixed results of the research reviewed in this section points out that *how* teachers interact with children during play is more important than *how much* they interact. The aforementioned positive findings show that when teachers get involved in play in appropriate ways, children's play experiences can be enriched, and other positive outcomes, such as increased social interaction and cognitive activity, can occur as well. On the other hand, if teachers intervene in a heavy-handed or insensitive manner, play can be seriously disrupted. Effective play involvement is a challenging skill, requiring teachers to walk a "fine line between responsive and intrusive interactions" (File & Kontos, 1993, p. 15). The ideal solution is for preservice and inservice teachers to receive additional training in play-interaction strategies, such as that offered in the *Linking Literacy and Play* program (Roskos, Vukelich, Christie, Enz, & Neuman, 1995).

A third strand of research provides valuable guidance for such teacher-training efforts. These studies have sought to identify the different roles that teachers can adopt during play and to determine which roles have positive and which have negative effects on play. The results of these studies are discussed in the next section, "Play-Enrichment Strategies."

PLAY-ENRICHMENT STRATEGIES

In order to maximize the positive impact of play on children's learning and development, adults need to take an active role in enriching children's home and classroom play experiences. As illustrated in Figure 7.1, play enrichment entails three basic steps:

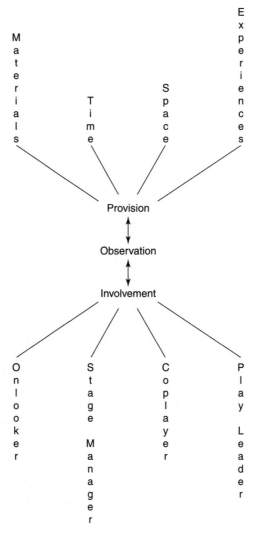

Figure 7.1

Enriching children's play: Provision, observation, and involvement

1. Providing resources for play
2. Observing play
3. Becoming supportively and responsively involved in play

We recommend that parents and teachers first set the stage by providing an environment that is conducive to high-quality play. Once the stage has been set for play, the next step is to carefully observe the play that ensues. This observation will reveal whether additional provision or direct involvement is needed to develop the play to its full potential. In addition, observation enables adults to tailor their involvement to fit with children's current play interests and activities.

PROVIDING RESOURCES FOR PLAY

Adults can help set the stage for play by providing four types of resources: (1) time, (2) space, (3) materials, and (4) preparatory experiences (Griffing, 1983). Each of these variables can have a powerful effect on the types of play in which children engage and on the content of their play.

TIME Cognitively complex forms of play, such as constructive play and sociodramatic play, require a considerable amount of time to plan and carry out. For example, in order to engage in sociodramatic play, children must recruit other players, negotiate the roles to be enacted, agree on the story line to be dramatized, designate the make-believe identities of objects, construct props, and determine the area of the room to be used. These preparations often take a considerable amount of time, sometimes far more than the time required to act out the story!

If play periods are short, children will often have to stop and clean up just after getting started acting out their stories. Sometimes, they will even have to quit before they have finished their preplay preparations. When this happens a number of times, children tend to give up on group dramatic play and settle for less advanced forms of play, which can be completed in short periods of time. Brief play periods are also not conducive to complex constructive play. Children just get involved in a construction when it is time to clean up and put the materials away. After a number of such experiences, children may abandon this type of play completely, or they may resort to building very simple structures. In this latter case, many important benefits of extended constructive play—planning, persistence, cooperation, and problem solving—are lost. The opportunity for the constructive play to evolve into dramatic play is also greatly reduced.

Research has shown that preschoolers are much more likely to engage in sociodramatic and constructive play during 30-minute play periods than during shorter, 15-minute sessions (Christie, Johnsen, & Peckover, 1988; Tegano & Burdette, 1991). Our own experience indicates that even longer periods are needed. One of the authors spent a semester observing a preschool classroom that had 40-minute play periods (Enz & Christie, 1997). Very often, the 4-year-olds had just finished preparing for a dramatization when it was time to clean up. Fortunately, the teachers were flexible and would let the children have an extra 10–15 minutes to act out their dramas. For this reason, we recommend that, at the preschool and kindergarten level, play periods last *at least 45* minutes. When it comes to time for play, in general the longer the period, the better.

Parents can foster creative, sustained play by allowing children to keep their constructions standing from one day to the next. During the week, children can add to or change their constructions and can use these creations as props in make-believe play. In addition, monitoring and limiting television viewing to several hours a day helps to free up time for play. Adult structured lessons (dance, tumbling, piano, etc.), club meetings, and team sports also need to be limited so that ample time remains for free play at home.

Finding time for play at school can be an even greater challenge. The "back-to-basics" movement, and the accompanying pressures to devote more time to structured academic activities, have made it difficult for many early childhood teachers to schedule adequate amounts of time for free play (Christie & Wardle, 1992). We are aware of some kindergarten classes that have play periods that are only 10–15 minutes long or that permit free play only during before-school transition periods.

The following guidelines, condensed from Christie and Wardle (1992), suggest some strategies to lessen these antiplay pressures and to provide all children with extended play periods:

- Work with parents so that they understand that play has educational value, that their children are not "just playing."
- Establish program expectations that value children's play as a critical curriculum component.
- Reevaluate the entire daily curriculum to create more play time. Perhaps naptime can be shortened, lunchtime curtailed, or other schedules adjusted to free up time for play.
- If several brief play periods are scattered throughout the schoolday, consider combining them into one longer period. Such a schedule would be more conducive to the occurrence of advanced forms of play.
- Avoid scheduling play *solely* as a before-school transition. Many children arrive just minutes before school starts, thus missing out on opportunities to engage in valuable forms of play.
- Make sure that support staff (therapists, psychologists, etc.) do not pull the same children out of play periods on a regular basis. All children—including those with special needs—benefit from sustained, enriched play experiences.

SPACE Children need spaces to play in. The space available for play and the way this space is arranged can have an important impact on both the type of play that children engage in and the quality of their play. At home, children's bedrooms are a primary play area. However, research has revealed that make-believe play frequently occurs in kitchens, family rooms, and other parts of the house:

> Pretending flourished in the thick of family life—while an older sibling watched TV nearby or did homework with a friend, while mother folded laundry or set the table. This is not to say that private space was unused: at times quiet solo pretending or intimate play with a close friend unfolded in seclusion. But for the most part, pretending occurred in public spaces, where play partners could be readily recruited and mundane activities appropriated.
>
> *(Haight & Miller, 1993, p. 119)*

This finding implies that parents can encourage make-believe by permitting children to bring their toys and play into communal areas of the home. Pretending can be further encouraged by placing a large cardboard box, especially reserved for make-believe, in a kitchen, family room, or other high activity area (Segal & Adcock, 1981). Many parents find that the added richness of children's play more than compensates for the mess and clutter that accompanies this arrangement.

Teachers can promote participation in constructive and sociodramatic play by providing spacious block and dramatic-play areas in their classrooms. Sociodramatic play can be further encouraged with the addition of a rotating theme center that is periodically changed to represent different settings, such as a restaurant, store, and doctor's office. Theme centers have been found to be effective in stimulating dramatic play, particularly in boys (Dodge & Frost, 1986; Woodard, 1984). Theme centers have the additional advantage of broadening the scope of the scripts that children enact during their dramatizations.

Teachers can also influence their students' play behavior by the way in which play centers are situated and arranged. For example, theme centers can be located near to the home or housekeeping center so that children can integrate the theme-center activities with their domestic play (Woodard, 1984). For example, children acting as "parents" for dolls, pets, or peers in the housekeeping area might take a sick baby to a doctor theme center for an examination, or they might take the family car to the classroom "garage" to get it serviced (Hall & Robinson, 1995). Chapter 9, "Play Environments," presents more information about arranging play spaces for children.

MATERIALS   Play materials are another ingredient needed for high-quality play. Research indicates that children's play is heavily influenced by the types of materials that are available (Rubin, Fein, & Vandenberg, 1983). For example, theme-related props such as costumes encourage sociodramatic play, whereas blocks, puzzles, and art materials stimulate constructive play. If adults wish to promote these two types of play, it is important that both types of materials are available.

Adults also need to pay attention to the realism and structure of play materials. Because of their limited representational abilities, 2- and 3-year-olds require highly realistic play materials, such as miniature replicas of household objects, in order to begin engaging in make-believe play. Older 4- and 5-year-olds can engage in dramatic play using low-realism materials and may actually play more creatively with these low-structure props. However, many older preschoolers *prefer* playing with highly realistic props. Dramatic play areas for this age group should include a combination of low-structure props— featureless dolls, clay, hollow blocks, and empty cardboard boxes—and realistic toys. Details on this research and additional guidelines for selecting play materials are presented in Chapter 10, "Play Materials."

PREPARATORY EXPERIENCES   Role playing requires that children draw on their prior knowledge and act out roles as they understand them. If children have had little experience with the roles they are attempting to portray, sociodramatic play can become difficult to sustain. Most children have had adequate experience with the roles of family members, but they may be unfamiliar with many work-related roles associated with theme centers. Woodard (1984), for example, relates how preschoolers became confused when attempting to act out the less-familiar roles of a chef and dishwasher in a restaurant theme center.

Teachers can help clarify children's understanding of themes and roles by providing relevant experiences such as field trips, classroom visitations by people in different occupations, books or videos about different jobs, and so forth. A field trip to a nearby restaurant to observe the kitchen, for example, would familiarize children with the roles of chef and dishwasher. Alternatively, people in these professions could visit the class and explain what they do in their jobs. Smilansky (1968) found that these types of preparatory experiences greatly increased the effectiveness of her sociodramatic play training procedures. Table 9.1 lists preparatory experiences ("Related Activities") that can be used with a variety of dramatic-play themes.

OBSERVATION

Successful adult involvement in play depends heavily on careful observation. Observation reveals what help, if any, children need to develop and extend their play. As illustrated in Figure 7.1, observation serves as a bridge linking provision with adult involvement, indicating when additional time, space, materials, or experiences should be provided and when direct adult involvement in play will be beneficial.

Observation lets adults know what already exists in play, enabling them to base their involvement on the children's current interests and needs. Manning and Sharp (1977) give an example of what happens when an adult intervenes without first carefully observing the ongoing play. A 6-year-old girl was playing with some seashells in a sand tray, making up a pretend story. The shells represented people and trees, and the girl's finger was a make-believe cat. A teacher aide intervened by trying to draw the girl into a conversation about the pattern she was making with the shells:

> Those shells are very pretty, aren't they? Doesn't the sand feel soft and smooth on your fingers—is it tickling? You have made a lovely pattern. Have you finished or are you going to put more shells or something in it? (p. 18)

This intervention disrupted the make-believe context or "frame" of the play, causing the girl to stop playing. It also failed to elicit the desired conversation. Unless adults carefully observe play prior to intervening, their involvement may do more harm than good.

Several systems for observing play are described in Chapter 8, "Observing Play." These systems specify exactly what to look for in children's play, making observation a much easier task.

INVOLVEMENT

As explained in the preceding section on teacher–child play, *how* adults interact with children during play is more important than the amount of this interaction. When teachers get involved in play in supportive and responsive ways, children's play experiences can be greatly enriched. On the other hand, when teachers take over control of play or intervene in insensitive ways, play can be seriously disrupted.

A series of recent descriptive research studies have shed valuable light on qualitative aspects of teacher involvement in play (Enz & Christie, 1997; Jones & Reynolds, 1992; Roskos & Neuman, 1993; Wood et al., 1980). These studies have sought to identify the different roles that teachers can adopt during play and to determine which roles have positive and which have negative effects on play. Different researchers have used different labels for similar roles, so we have attempted to consolidate these slightly discrepant categorical systems into a comprehensive list of adult roles in play:

- Uninvolved—The adult does not pay attention to play.
- Onlooker—The adult watches children as they play.
- Stage manager—The adult helps children prepare for play and gives assistance once play is underway.
- Coplayer—The adult joins in play and becomes a play partner.
- Play leader—The adult joins in play and actively attempts to enrich and extend it.
- Director/instructor—The adult takes control of the play and tells children what to do or redirects children's attention toward academic matters.

These adult roles form a continuum, ranging from no involvement to complete control of the children's play activities (see Figure 7.2). Research has shown that the *most productive* roles lie in the middle of this continuum: onlooker, stage manager, coplayer, and play leader. The roles on the extreme

Figure 7.2

Adult roles in play

```
                                 Supportive Roles
Minimal          ┌──────────────────────────────────────────────┐   Maximum
Involvement      │                                              │   Involvement

U                O              S              C              P                D
n                n              t              o              l                i
i                l              a              p              a                r
n                o              g              l              y                e
v                o              e              a                               c
o                k                             y              L                t
l                e              M              e              e                o
v                r              a              r              a                r
e                               n                             d                /
d                               a                             e                I
                                g                             r                n
                                e                                              s
                                r                                              t
                                                                               r
                                                                               u
                                                                               c
                                                                               t
                                                                               o
                                                                               r
```

ends—uninvolved and director/instructor—tend to have a negative effect on children's play experiences. As noted in the earlier section on parent–child play research, a similar inverted-U function was reported for parents. When mothers interact too indirectly or too intrusively in their children's play, play suffers. The most effective maternal play interaction strategies feature a moderate degree of involvement in play (Fein & Fryer, 1995).

The sections that follow describe the facilitative roles that adults can take in play, discuss some of the dangers associated with the precarious roles (uninvolved and director/instructor), and emphasize the need for flexibility in matching roles with children's current play activities.

FACILITATIVE ROLES   Several adult roles have been identified as having a positive impact on children's play. In this section, we briefly describe each of these roles and provide examples of the type of interaction that occurs when adults assume these roles in play.

Onlooker   Onlookers serve as an appreciative audience for children's play activities (Roskos & Neuman, 1993). Onlookers position themselves near the play space (but not actually in it), watch children as they play, nod or give other non-verbal signs of approval, and make verbal comments to the players. The adult also may occasionally ask children about what they are doing in their play. However, onlookers do not join in the play or do anything to disrupt it.

The following vignette, from the Roskos and Neuman (1993, p. 86) study, illustrates the onlooker role:

> *Several children are playing in the book corner, leafing through books and talking about the pictures in their books. Betty [the teacher] is sitting at a table nearby, watching the children with their books. She rests her chin in her hands, looking on with a smile. . . . She comments to the group, "You're having fun with your books. Aren't you having a good day?" The children look up at her momentarily, then continue to handle the books, pointing at the pictures.*

The onlooker role has several advantages. First, by paying attention to play, adults communicate approval and let children know that their play activities are important. Second, the observation that accompanies the onlooker role informs adults about what is going on in children's play. Armed with this information, adults can make sound decisions about when more direct forms of involvement—such as the stage manager, coplayer, and play leader roles—are needed. Observation also allows adults to tailor these more direct forms of involvement to match children's current play interests and activities.

Stage Manager   Stage managers also stay on the sidelines and do not enter into children's play. Unlike onlookers, however, stage managers take an active role in helping children prepare for play and offer assistance once play is underway. Stage managers respond to children's requests for materials, help the children construct costumes and props, and assist in organizing the play set. Stage managers also may make appropriate theme-related script suggestions to extend the children's ongoing play.

Enz and Christie (1997) provide an example of a teacher taking on the stage-manager role in order to assist several preschoolers playing "toy store." The children began their play by gathering toys that they wanted to sell. The teacher suggested making a list of things for sale in the store, and the children agreed that this was a good idea. The children then dictated the names of the toys, while the teacher wrote them down on a piece of chart paper. This inspired several children to make their own signs:

TEACHER: Okay. I'm going to put the toy list right here. Will you give me a piece of tape, Joey?

JOEY: Look what I signed.

TEACHER: Oh, you made a sign. Great!
[Joey puts his sign up next to the teacher's list. It says, "KZ FR."]

TEACHER: What's it say?

JOEY: It's closed forever.

TEACHER: Oh-oh! Well, maybe we should make one that says the store is open. Can you make one of those, too? So we'd have a closed forever sign and an open sign.

MONICA: [Leans in through the store window and addresses Joey] Mr. Storekeeper, I need a hat.

JOEY: Hey! Look at the sign. This store is closed forever!

Note how the teacher did not enter into the play itself. He remained outside the store play episode and provided suggestions and assistance. The children went along with the suggestion about making the list, but Joey ignored the idea of an "open" sign. This is typical of the stage-manager role. Teachers offer suggestions and help, but the children are free to accept or disregard this assistance. Also notice how the teacher provided a good example of Vygotsky's (1978) "zone of proximal development," helping the children make the toy list that they could not make on their own. This scaffolding, in turn, prompted Joey to make his own sign, using invented spelling.

Coplayer   In the coplayer role, adults join in and become active participants in children's play. Coplayers function as equal play partners with children. The adult usually takes on a minor role in the drama, such as a customer in a store or a passenger on a plane, leaving the prime roles (store clerk, pilot) for the children. While enacting this role, the adult follows the flow of the dramatic action, letting the children take the lead most of time. During the course of play, many opportunities arise for the adult to model sociodramatic play skills such as role-playing, make-believe transformations, and peer-interaction strategies (e.g., how to enter into an ongoing dramatization).

Roskos and Neuman (1993, p. 87) present a vignette, taken from a preschool teacher's journal, that recounts her experience in the coplayer role:

I ask Megan and Supraja if they want to play "making dinner." They say "Yes."... I sit at the table and I ask, "What's for dinner?" Megan begins looking for a bottle for the baby. Then she says she has to vacuum before dinner and begins propelling the toy vacuum around the area. Meanwhile, Supraja says she's making dinner. She points to the back of a box, points with her

In the coplayer role, teachers become children's play partners.

finger and pretends to read. She says, "We need a mixing spoon" and begins stirring some "food" in a pot. I say, "Is that a good recipe? I hope so. I'm really hungry." She looks at the back of the box again as if reading and wags her head back and forth. "Yup. It's good." She gives me a plate and says, "It's macaroni and cheese and eggs." I say, "Thank you," and start to eat. But they say, "Stop! Stop! You have to wait until everyone has their food." So I wait.

In this example, the teacher initiated the play episode by inviting the children to play "making dinner." However, once the play started, the locus of control shifted to the children. The children determined what was for dinner and when it should be eaten. While in her make-believe role, the teacher subtly influenced the course of the play by asking about dinner and stating that she was hungry. She also modeled make-believe with regard to objects and actions by pretending to eat the invisible food.

Play Leader   As in the coplayer role, play leaders join in and actively participate in the children's play. However, play leaders exert more influence and take deliberate steps to enrich and extend play episodes. They do this by suggesting new play themes and by introducing new props or plot elements to extend existing themes. Adults often adopt this role when children have difficulty getting play started on their own or when an ongoing play episode is beginning to falter.

Kitson (1994) recommends that when children lose interest in a drama, the teacher should refocus the children by adding "tension" to their story. He gives the following example of how he intervened with a group of nursery children who were acting out a story about building a house:

After sorting out what had to be done, the work started. It was not long before the children began to lose concentration in the 'building' as there was little to hold their interest. In dramatic terms, there was little or no tension. It was at this point that intervention was needed. I then pretended to receive a phone call from the boss who was going to come round and check up on our work. We would have to make sure that the house had been put together properly. Immediately, the children were drawn back into the fantasy play and found a renewed vigour and purpose, created by the injection of tension. (p. 97)

In the following example, from the Enz and Christie (1997) study, a group of preschoolers were making a pretend plane trip to Florida:

The drama got off to a good start as the children prepared for take-off and got their make-believe plane up into the air. After the meal had been served and naps were taken (it was a "sleeper" flight), the children began to lose interest. The teacher, who was in the role of passenger, reenergized and extended the drama by interjecting tension into the plot by mentioning rough weather and the possibility of a plane crash.

TEACHER:	The wind is blowing and the plane is bouncing up and down. Oh, the plane is bouncing.
CHANNING:	Don't worry. We have [air sickness] bags.
JOEY:	This airplane's going around and around.
CHANNING:	We had better get our stuff.
TEACHER:	Are we going to evacuate the plane? Okay, let's land. Maybe we'll have a crash landing. Let's land the plane. [Children start screaming.]
TEACHER:	Crash landing! Oh—crash landing!
JOEY:	Okay, guys, let's get off the plane now.
CHANNING:	Okay, let's abandon ship.

The play continued for many more minutes as the children got off the plane and discovered they had crashed in the swamps of Florida. The teacher enlivened the plot further by adding another crisis for the children to contend with: alligators!

PRECARIOUS ROLES When it comes to adult involvement in play, either too little or too much can have negative consequences. Problems can occur when adults are either totally uninvolved in play or when they get too involved and take over control of the play.

Research in preschool settings has revealed that some teachers ignore the play that is occurring in their classrooms (Enz & Christie, 1997; Sylva et al., 1980; Tizard et al., 1976; Wood et al., 1980). These teachers attempted to use play periods to prepare for upcoming activities, do paperwork, or chat with other adults. Enz and Christie (1997) found that when teachers adopted this uninvolved role, children tended to engage in large amounts of functional motor play and rough-and-tumble activity. When they did engage in sociodramatic play, the episodes were simplistic and often quite raucous, featuring themes such as monster, superhero, or dogs versus cats (the girls' favorite). The boisterous nature of this play had the unintended result of forcing the teachers to be "safety monitors," who attempted to curb undesirable or unsafe play behaviors. These teachers spent a considerable amount of time issuing verbal warnings ("Don't run," "Stop pushing"), intervening to settle disputes, and taking measures to ensure the safety of children (e.g., moving mats onto the loft stairs so that the children could slide down safely).

At the other end of the involvement continuum are the director/instructor roles in which the adult takes over total control of children's play. In both these roles, the adult remains on the sidelines, outside the children's play frame. *Directors* tell children what to do while playing, whereas *instructors* use questioning to redirect children's attention toward academic content.

Enz and Christie (1997) give the following example of a preschool teacher who used the director role to encourage the children to enact a birthday party.

TEACHER: Brittany, come here. Do you get to wear a party hat? Would you like to wear this? This is the special one for the birthday person. Could you put that on? It's like a crown.

BRITTANY: No. I already have this [referring to her hair ornament].

TEACHER: Can you make us a sign for November? We have to pretend it's your birthday.

TEACHER: Paco, Paco. Do you want to make the cake? Who wants to make the cake?

BRITTANY: Not me, I'm the birthday girl.

TEACHER: But see, lookit. She's gonna put candles on the cake, too. Real candles! How about if we make two cakes? Paco, you make one. You get one candle. Everyone gets a candle. And then, Joseph, you get one, too. You have to make the cake. Make one . . . make the cake. Take the candles out. Make the cake first, and then we'll put the candles on. Where's that "November" sign?

Some children responded to this excessive direction by engaging in simple, repetitive pretend behavior. Others quickly lost interest and left the play area.

A related role—the instructor—occurs when play is used as a medium for academic teaching. The adult remains outside the play and asks questions aimed at suspending make-believe and interjecting reality into the play episode. Wood and his associates (1980) reported that this role, which they referred to as "spokesman for reality," was used frequently by teachers but had mixed results. Sometimes the children's play was not seriously disturbed by the adult's reality-oriented comments and questions. The children would come up with thoughtful answers to the questions and continue on with their play. On other occasions, the adult's intervention would seriously disrupt the make-believe play "frame," causing the children to stop playing. The example cited earlier in this chapter, in which a teacher aide disrupted a girl's pretend play with seashells by trying to get her to discuss the shells' physical characteristics, illustrates the potential negative effects of being a spokesperson for reality.

Wood et al. (1980) also discovered that being a spokesperson for reality often had a restrictive effect on adult–child conversations. In the following example, an adult was coplaying with two children (C and C1), pretending to bake a cake using playdough:

ADULT: Did you put the cherry on the top of my cake?
C1: No. I thought, I'm going to make you a sandwich. I'm going to make you . . .
C: (breaks in) Cream in it this time.
ADULT: Oh, how delicious, I . . .
C: I'll make me one of with cream; 'cos I've I've sold out of jam.
ADULT: You've sold out of jam, have you? So you're having to use cream instead, are you?
C: Yes.
ADULT: Oh, I see.
C: Like ice-cream, ice-cream.
ADULT: Oh, how lovely . . .
C: I'm rolling it, making you a nice cake.
C1: I maked a bigger cake than you.

Later, the adult saw an opportunity to teach the children about fractions and switched to the instructor role:

ADULT: Look, can I cut it in half? That's a half, isn't it, I've cut there.
C: Yes.
ADULT: And then I cut it in half again. How many pieces have I cut now?
C: Two.
ADULT: No. How many pieces have I got altogether? Now I've cut that one piece in half?
C1: Ha ha! Look!
C: One, two, three.
ADULT: Three, right. Shall I cut this piece in half as well?
C: Yes.
ADULT: Now how many have I got?
C: Four.

Note how the children's comments shrank from phrases and sentences to one-word utterances when the adult switched from the coplayer to the instructor role. This is not an isolated instance. Wood et al. found the children's conversations were consistently richer when adults were coplaying than when they were acting as instructors.

The director and instructor roles are the types of adult involvement most likely to disrupt make-believe play. For this reason, caution and restraint should be exercised when using these roles. The director role is best reserved for use with children who are unable to engage in sociodramatic play on their own and should only be used briefly, to get play started. The instructor role should only be used with children who are securely involved in their pretend roles and when an opportunity exists for significant learning to take place. It should be quickly phased out so that children can focus their full attention on their play pursuits.

FLEXIBILITY OF ROLES   The key to successful play involvement is for adults to observe carefully and to choose an interaction style that fits with children's ongoing play interests, styles, and activities. Roskos and Neuman (1993) observed six experienced preschool teachers and found that they used a re pertoire of roles—onlooker, coplayer, and play leader—to enrich children's dramatizations and to encourage literacy-related play. These veteran teachers switched roles frequently, depending on the children who were playing and the nature of their play. The teachers' ability to switch roles to fit the children's play agenda appeared to be as important as the specific roles they used.

There are, of course, times when adult intervention is not advisable. The Sutton-Smiths have some good recommendations to parents about when not to join in children's play:

> There are times *not to play* with your children—not ever *if* you feel you are intruding (and you may be), or if you feel it is a duty (for their "own good"), or if you are too grumpy, preoccupied, or just plain exhausted to enjoy the fun you are supposed to be having together.
>
> *(Sutton-Smith & Sutton-Smith, 1974, p. 232, emphasis in original)*

These recommendations also hold for teachers, except for the one concerning duty. Best practice mandates that teachers help children engage in high-quality play so that play can have a maximum impact on their learning and development (Bredekamp & Copple, 1997). Therefore, teachers should participate in children's play because they have a duty to do so. Teachers should, however, trust their judgment and not intervene if they feel that they are intruding or if they are too tired or preoccupied to intervene effectively.

SUMMARY

Adult involvement in play is very controversial. Advocates of involvement maintain that adult participation can enrich children's play experiences and can maximize play's impact on intellectual and social development, whereas opponents maintain that adults often disrupt or inhibit play activities and reduce children's opportunities to learn during play.

Our position is that adult involvement can have both positive and negative effects on play. The crucial variable is *how* adults become involved in play. If adults interact with children in a sensitive, responsive, and supportive manner, they can enhance children's play. On the other hand, if adults take over control of play, provide too much structure, or interrupt play for academic purposes, children's play will probably suffer.

We recommend that parents and teachers first set the stage by providing resources that promote high-quality play:

- Time—play periods that last at least 45 minutes at the preschool and kindergarten levels.
- Space—spacious, well-arranged play settings.
- Materials—age-appropriate props and materials that encourage sociodramatic and constructive play.
- Experiences—field trips, classroom visitations, books, and videos that clarify children's understanding of themes and roles that they enact in play.

Once the stage has been set for play, the next step is to carefully observe the play that ensues. This observation will reveal whether additional provision or direct involvement is needed to develop the play to its full potential. In addition, observation enables adults to tailor their involvement to fit with children's current play interests and activities.

Finally, we recommend four roles for adults in play: onlooker, stage manager, coplayer, and play leader. When used in a sensitive, flexible manner, these roles enable adults to have a positive impact on children's play.

Chapter 8

OBSERVING PLAY

Megan is a 4-year-old student in Ms. Benson's Head Start class. Ms. Benson is concerned about Megan's behavior during the 45-minute play period that occurs right after circle time. Megan spends much of her time in dramatic-play areas but does not appear to be engaging in much group dramatic play. In order to gain more information about Megan's play patterns, Ms. Benson observes her on several different days, using the Sociodramatic Play Inventory. This checklist makes it easy to note which components of mature group dramatic play are present and which are missing in children's play. Examination of the completed checklist reveals that Megan is skilled at taking on roles and using make-believe transformations (e.g., pretending to eat "hamburgers" made out of playdough). She also regularly makes verbal comments that are appropriate for the roles she is enacting (usually monologues). However, the checklist also indicates that Megan rarely interacts with others or uses metacommunication with her peers to help plan and organize play. Megan appears to be lacking social and language skills needed to successfully engage in group dramatic play. On the basis of these data, Ms. Benson decides to pair Megan with a play partner who is very skilled in interactive play behavior. Within 6 weeks, Megan has learned quite a bit from her expert partner and is now regularly engaging in group dramatic play with other children in the class. ■

Observation is the key to understanding children's play behavior. By watching children at play, we can learn much about their play activities—the types of play they like to engage in, the toys and play equipment they prefer to use, the spaces in which they choose to play, the themes they enjoy enacting, and their interaction with peers and adults. We can also obtain valuable information about children's social and cognitive development.

Megan's example illustrates how observation can lead to effective interventions to enrich children's play. As was emphasized in Chapter 7, observation is the starting point for adult facilitation of play (see Figure 7.1). Observation can reveal when additional time, materials, space, or preparatory experiences should be provided to extend and enrich ongoing play episodes. Observation can also indicate when adult involvement or peer assistance in play is appropriate and can give clues as to which type of involvement will be most beneficial.

Not all forms of observation can serve these valuable functions. Parents and teachers frequently watch children at play, but this observation is often casual and unfocused. As a result, adults often "have very little idea of what children do during play time" (Frost, 1992, p. 77) and have only a vague understanding of children's play skills and interests.

Play is a very complex phenomenon, especially when groups of children are involved. In order to make sense out of what is occurring, observation must be systematic—the observer must know what to look for and must have a means to record the information that is gathered. Observation should also be objective, reflecting the true nature of children's play behavior.

This chapter begins with some general guidelines for making systematic, objective observations of children's play behaviors. Next, different observational methods are described, ranging from highly structured checklists and rating scales to unstructured anecdotal records and vignettes. We describe these procedures in detail, provide instructions for their use, and give examples of how the information they yield can be used to facilitate play. Finally, videotape recordings are discussed as another means of gathering information about children's play behavior.

GENERAL GUIDELINES FOR OBSERVING PLAY

Whichever method is used to observe play, several guidelines should be kept in mind in order to obtain an accurate picture of children's play behavior:

- Decide in advance what you wish to learn about children's play, and select a method that matches this purpose.
- Try to make the observations in a setting that will allow children to display the full range of their play abilities. Be sure that ample materials are available, which are conducive to a full range of play behavior, including *motor play* (e.g., climbing structures, balls, wheeled toys), *constructive play* (e.g., blocks, tinkertoys®, Legos®), and *dramatic play* (e.g., dolls, housekeeping props, costumes, theme-related prop boxes). There also needs to be enough time available for more complex forms of play to develop. If these resources are not available, the absence of these important types of play may be caused by lack of materials or time, rather than by lack of play skills.
- If possible, observe children in both indoor and outdoor settings. Research indicates that some children exhibit higher social and cognitive levels of play outdoors than when they are playing indoors (Henniger, 1985; Tizard, Philps, & Plewis, 1976).
- Delay observations until children have had a chance to get to know each other and get used to the school environment. Children tend to exhibit higher social and cognitive levels of play with familiar peers (Doyle, Connolly, & Rivest, 1980). Observations made at the beginning of the school year tend to underestimate children's true play abilities. Naturally, this also holds true for observations of children who have recently transferred into a classroom.
- Observe children's play behavior over time, to ensure that it is representative of their typical play behaviors. It is unwise to base decisions about play on a single day's observation. Children may happen to be paired

with playmates with whom they do not get along or with play materials that do not match their interests. Illness, problems at home, and other temporary conditions may also influence play on a particular day. Always try to spread observations over as long a period of time as possible in order to minimize the effects of any transient factors. Two or three observations spread over at least a week would be a bare minimum.

OBSERVATION METHODS

We have grouped play observation procedures into three broad categories: checklists, rating scales, and anecdotal records. Both checklists and rating scales are highly structured, specifying what to look for and how to record information. They are quick and easy to use, but they yield a restricted picture of children's play and limited information about the surrounding context. Anecdotal records, on the other hand, have very little structure. The observer writes a description of play on a blank card or piece of paper. Anecdotal records are more time-consuming than checklists, but they can yield richer descriptions of children's play activities and the contexts in which play occurs. Play observers, therefore, must choose between ease of use and richness of description when deciding which method to use.

CHECKLISTS

Checklists are observational instruments that (a) specify exactly which behaviors to look for, and (b) provide a convenient system for recording the presence or absence of these play behaviors. Checklists make play observation more systematic by focusing attention on specific aspects of play. Checklists also provide a quick way to record information, making them very time efficient.

Numerous observation checklists have emerged as an outgrowth of research on the development of play (see Chapter 3). Many of these instruments are lengthy and complicated, making them impractical for applications other than basic research. The 30-category "target child" system utilized by Sylva, Roy, and Painter (1980), in their study of British and American preschools, is an example of such a scale. It provides a wealth of data about children's play behavior, but most teachers do not have the time to learn or to use such an elaborate coding system.

We have chosen to focus on three scales designed for use with children between the ages of 2 and 8 years: (1) the *Social/Cognitive Scale*, which gives a broad view of the social and cognitive level of children's play; (2) the *Peer Play Scale*, which gives a fine-grained analysis of social play; and (3) the *Sociodramatic Play Inventory*, which provides a detailed look at group make-believe. All three scales are relatively easy to learn and use, and they provide information that adults will find very useful in enriching children's play experiences.

A teacher's choice of which scale to use should be based on her or his purposes for using it. The Social/Cognitive Scale gives an overall view of children's play patterns. It is a good screening device that will indicate when the other, more specific observation scales or procedures are needed. For example, if a preschooler's Social/Cognitive Scale sheet indicates a low level of social play, then the Peer Play Scale can provide more detailed information about this aspect of the child's play. If the check-off boxes for a 4- or 5-year-old's group dramatic play items contain few check marks, then the Sociodramatic Play Inventory could be used to identify which specific components are missing in the child's play repertoire.

THE SOCIAL/COGNITIVE SCALE   As was detailed in Chapter 3, children's play develops simultaneously along several dimensions. Infants' play is usually restricted to solitary motor activity. As children mature, their play tends to become more social in nature, and they begin to engage in more cognitively advanced forms of play, such as constructive play, make-believe, and games with rules.

Early play researchers who studied age trends in play behavior focused on one dimension at time: social or cognitive. In the mid-1970s, Kenneth Rubin and his associates combined Parten's (1932) social-participation scale with Smilansky's (1968) adaptation of Piaget's (1962) cognitive play categories, allowing both dimensions of play development to be assessed simultaneously (Rubin, Maioni, & Hornung, 1976). Rubin quickly modified the scale by collapsing several of Parten's social play categories—associative and cooperative—into one category: group play (Rubin, Watson, & Jambor, 1978). The resulting scale, which we refer to as the Social/Cognitive Scale, consists of 12 play categories (Table 8.1) plus several categories of nonplay behavior.

The Social/Cognitive Scale enabled researchers to obtain data that could not have been collected if either the social or the cognitive dimension of play development had been assessed in isolation. For example, it was generally accepted for many years that solitary play decreases with increasing age and is indicative of immaturity (Parten, 1932). However, research using the two-dimensional Social/Cognitive Scale has revealed that as children grow older,

Table 8.1   SOCIAL-COGNITIVE COMPONENTS OF PLAY: TWELVE CATEGORIES

	SOLITARY	PARALLEL	GROUP
FUNCTIONAL	Solitary–functional	Parallel–functional	Group–functional
CONSTRUCTIVE	Solitary–constructive	Parallel–constructive	Group–constructive
DRAMATIC	Solitary–dramatic	Parallel–dramatic	Group–dramatic
GAMES	Solitary–games	Parallel–games	Group–games

Note: There are also two nonplay categories: unoccupied and onlooking.

Source: Adapted from Rubin, Watson, and Jambor (1978).

Solitary-functional play is the first type of play exhibited by young infants

there is a shift from solitary–functional to solitary–constructive and solitary–dramatic play (e.g., Moore, Evertson, & Brophy, 1974; Rubin et al., 1978; Smith, 1978). Thus, only one form of solitary play—solitary–functional—appears to be associated with immaturity.

Teachers and parents will find that the Social/Cognitive Scale is a useful instrument for assessing children's overall level of play development. It is relatively easy to learn to use, and it provides useful information about children's overall patterns of play.

The first step in using the Social/Cognitive scale is to become familiar with the definitions of the various play and nonplay categories. These categories specify what to look for while observing play. The Theory in Action feature "Social/Cognitive Categories: Definitions" presents our interpretation and modification of these categories. Note that an additional category—nonplay activities—has been added. Our experience has shown that many children choose to do activities such as reading a book or feeding fish in an aquarium during play periods. The new category permits recording of these types of behavior.

Next, a recording sheet is needed to make a permanent record of the play that is observed. We suggest using a two-dimensional grid such as the one illustrated in Figure 8.1. This form has a separate box for each of the 12 play categories, allowing the occurrence of each form of solitary, parallel, and group play to be recorded, as well as boxes for the two categories of nonplay behavior. A separate form should be used for each child observed. The Theory

Theory in Action

SOCIAL/COGNITIVE CATEGORIES: DEFINITIONS

Cognitive Levels

1. *Functional play*—repetitive muscle movements with or without objects; examples include (a) running and jumping, (b) gathering and dumping, (c) manipulating objects or materials, and (d) informal games (e.g., parading)
2. *Constructive play*—using objects (blocks, Legos®, Tinkertoys®) or materials (sand, playdough, paint) to make something
3. *Dramatic play*—role playing or make-believe transformations; examples include (a) role playing (e.g., pretending to be a parent, baby, firefighter, shark, superhero, or monster) and (b) make-believe transformations (e.g., pretending to drive a car by moving an invisible steering wheel or giving a pretend injection with a pencil)
4. *Games with rules*—involving the recognition, acceptance, and conformity with preestablished rules, examples include tag, "Mother May I," marbles, checkers, and kickball

Social Levels

1. *Solitary play*—playing alone with materials different from those of children within speaking distance; no conversations with others
2. *Parallel play*—playing with toys or engaging in activities similar to those of other children who are in close proximity, but with no attempt to play with the other children
3. *Group play*—playing with other children, with or without assigned roles

Unoccupied/Onlooking/Transition

These include unoccupied behavior, onlooking behavior, and moving from one activity to another.

Nonplay Activities

These activities must conform to a preestablished pattern, as in academic activities and teacher-assigned tasks, such as activities involving coloring books, worksheets, computers, and educational toys (shoelace boards).

Source: Condensed from Christie and Johnsen's (1987) modification of the Rubin et al. (1978) scale.

Name: _____   Observation Dates: _____

COGNITIVE LEVEL

	Functional	Constructive	Dramatic	Games with Rules
Solitary				
Parallel				
Group				

SOCIAL LEVEL

	UNOCCUPIED/ONLOOKING/TRANSITION	ACTIVITIES
Nonplay		

Figure 8.1

Parten/Piaget recording sheet

Source: Adapted from Designing a Play Environment for Infants and Toddlers, by Doris Sponseller and Matthew Lowry, in D. Sponseller (Ed.) Play as a Learning Medium, *National Association for the Education of Young Children, p. 100.*

in Action feature "Coding Play with the Social/Cognitive Scale" illustrates how a variety of different types of play behaviors are coded on this recording form.

Finally, a sampling procedure must be selected so that observations can be made systematically. We have found that the "multiple-scan" sampling procedure developed by Roper and Hinde (1978) works very well with the Social/Cognitive Scale when used with 15-second observation periods. Fifteen seconds allows enough time for the observer to figure out what type of play is occurring but is also brief enough so that it is unlikely that two different types of play will occur during one observation period.

The sampling system works as follows. First, shuffle the recording sheets to establish a random order for the observations. Start your observations with the child whose sheet is on top of the pile. Observe this child for 15 seconds, and then place a tally mark in the cell corresponding to the category of play that was observed. For example, if the child was making a block structure with several other children, a mark would be placed in the group–constructive box. After coding the first child's play, place his or her recording sheet on the bottom of the pile, and shift your attention to the child whose recording sheet is

Theory in Action

CODING PLAY WITH THE SOCIAL/COGNITIVE SCALE

The following examples illustrate how different types of play behavior are coded with the Social/Cognitive Scale:

1. Two children are in the housekeeping corner. Each is pretending to cook and prepare a make-believe meal. The children are aware of each other's activities, but they do not interact. (parallel–dramatic)
2. Several children are chasing each other around the room. (group–functional)
3. A child builds a block structure. No other children are close by. (solitary–constructive)
4. Several children play London Bridge. (group–game)
5. Three children are on the floor building "transformer" robots out of interlocking plastic blocks. At the moment, they are not interacting. (parallel–constructive)
6. The three children from Item 5 pretend that their "transformer" robots are battling with ray guns. (group–dramatic)
7. A child, playing alone, pretends to make a phone call using a toy telephone. (solitary–dramatic)
8. A child is watching several other children playing in the housekeeping corner. (onlooking, nonplay)
9. Several children are in the library corner reading books. (nonplay activity)
10. Two children are rolling toy cars across the floor. There is no indication of make-believe, and the children are not interacting. (parallel–functional)
11. Three children are enacting a hospital scene. One child has taken the role of a doctor, one is a nurse, and the other is a sick patient. (group–dramatic)
12. One child is bouncing a ball on the floor. Several other children are nearby, but they are playing with blocks and are not interacting with the target child. (solitary–functional)
13. A child is wandering about, not doing anything in particular. (unoccupied, nonplay)
14. Several children are working together to build a highway out of blocks. (group–constructive)
15. Two children are feeding hamsters at a science interest center. (nonplay activity)

Figure 8.2 illustrates where these examples would be marked on the Social/Cognitive recording sheet. In actual practice, tally marks would be used, rather than numbered descriptions of the activities.

(continued)

Theory in Action *(continued)*

Name: _____   Observation Dates: _____

COGNITIVE LEVEL

		Functional	Constructive	Dramatic	Games with rules
SOCIAL LEVEL	Solitary	(12) ball bouncing	(3) block building	(7) telephone call	
	Parallel	(10) car rolling	(5) building robots	(1) meal preparation	
	Group	(2) chasing	(14) road building	(6) battling robots (11) hospital	(4) London Bridge

	UNOCCUPIED/ONLOOKING/TRANSITION	ACTIVITIES
Nonplay	(8) watching "house" play (13) wandering around	(9) reading book (15) feeding hamsters

Figure 8.2

Parten/Piaget coding examples

now on top of the pile. The second child is then observed for 15 seconds, the play coded, the recording sheet placed on the bottom, and so on. In this manner, children are observed in revolving order, each for 15 seconds. After all of the children have been observed once, begin the second round of observations. Approximately three observations can be made per minute (allowing 5 seconds between each observation for recording). At this rate, each child in a group of 12 children would be observed once every 4 minutes, or five times during a 20-minute play period. After 20–30 observations have been obtained on a particular child, the recording sheet grid will begin to reveal the child's play patterns.

To interpret the data, focus attention on two aspects of the Social/Cognitive Scale recording sheet, taking the child's age into consideration: First, is the social level of the child's play appropriate for his or her age? It would not be unusual for a 2- or 3-year-old's recording sheet to have a large number of tallies in the parallel play row, the solitary–functional box, or the unoccupied/onlooking/transition box. On the other hand, such a pattern for 4- and 5-year-old children would be indicative of socially immature play, raising the possibility that intervention might be needed to help them learn the skills necessary for engaging in group play. In such instances, we recommend that the Peer Play Scale, described in the next section, be used to take a more detailed look at the child's social-play skills.

Second, does the child regularly engage in cognitively mature forms of play? One would expect 4- and 5-year-olds to engage in a considerable amount of constructive and dramatic play. If the Social/Cognitive Scale record sheet reveals that most of an older preschooler's tallies fall in the functional-play column, this would indicate that intervention in the form of resource provision or adult involvement (see Chapters 7, 9, and 10) may be needed to encourage constructive and dramatic play. Also, pay particular attention to the group–dramatic play category. If 4- or 5-year-olds rarely engage in this developmentally significant form of play, play-training procedures such as those described in Chapter 7 may be beneficial. We recommend that Smilansky's Sociodramatic Play Inventory (described in a subsequent section) be used to learn more about the child's specific strengths and weaknesses in group–dramatic play before such training is attempted. The Penn Interactive Peer Play Scale, described in the following section on rating scales, can also be used to gain information about low-income African-American children's social-play skills.

PEER PLAY SCALE   Carollee Howes has developed an observation scale that examines children's social play behaviors in more detail than does the Social/Cognitive Scale (Howes, 1980; Howes & Matheson, 1992). The Peer Play Scale has two categories of parallel play: simple parallel play (Level 1) and parallel aware play (Level 2). In addition, there are four group-play categories: simple social play (Level 3), complementary and reciprocal play (Level 4), cooperative social pretend play (Level 5), and complex social pretend play (Level 6). See the Theory in Action feature "Peer Play Scale: Definitions" for our descriptions of these six levels.

The Peer Play Scale focuses on three dimensions of peer play: (1) the complexity of children's social interactions, (2) the degree to which children's interactions are complementary and reciprocal, and (3) the extent to which language is used to plan and maintain play. At Levels 1 and 2, play behavior is nonsocial, nonreciprocal, and nonverbal. At the intermediate levels, the children begin to engage in social (Level 3) and reciprocal activities (Level 4), many of which involve verbal exchanges. The highest two categories involve sociodramatic play in which children work together to act out make-believe scripts. In Level 5, their language is restricted to pretend communication, in which children speak from the roles they have adopted. At Level 6, children also temporarily suspend pretend play and engage in metacommunication exchanges, which are used to organize and plan the play. (See Chapter 2 for more information about these two types of play communication.)

Theory in Action

HOWES'S PEER PLAY SCALE: DEFINITIONS

Level 1: Parallel Play

Children are within 3 feet from one another and engage in the same activity but do not acknowledge each other through eye contact or language. For example, several children might be sitting near each other playing with blocks, each of them totally absorbed in their own play. It is as though they were not aware of each other's existence.

Level 2: Parallel Aware Play

This is parallel play (Level 1) with eye contact. For example, two children who are playing with blocks occasionally look at each other and at each other's block constructions. The children, though not socially interacting, are aware of each other's presence and activities. Children at this stage often imitate each other's play. One child might, for example, copy another child's block construction.

Level 3: Simple Social Play

Children engage in the same type of activity and interact socially. They talk, exchange objects, smile, or engage in other types of social interaction. For example, children playing with blocks might make comments on each other's constructions (e.g., "That's pretty").

Level 4: Complementary and Reciprocal Play

Children engage in social play or games that involve "action-based role reversals" (one child's behavior mirrors another child's actions). For example, one of the children playing blocks may offer a block to another child, who receives it and then offers another block back. Games such as hide-and-seek and run-and-chase also fall into this category.

Level 5: Cooperative Social Pretend Play

Children enact complementary roles while engaging in sociodramatic play. Roles do not have to be explicitly labeled, but they must be clearly identifiable from the children's actions. For example, children can take on the role of mother and father and pretend to give a doll a bath.

(continued)

Theory in Action *(continued)*

Level 6: Complex Social Pretend Play

Children demonstrate both social pretend play and metacommunication about the play. *Metacommunication* occurs when children temporarily leave their pretend roles to talk about the play. Examples include naming and assigning roles ("I'm the mom, and you're the dad"), proposing new play script ("Let's pretend we're lost in the jungle"), modifying current scripts ("I tired of cooking. Let's go to the library and get some books."), and prompting other children ("You don't buy books at the library. You borrow them").

Source: Based on Howes and Matheson (1992).

We have developed a recording sheet for use with the Peer Play Scale (Figure 8.3). In it, we have added Parten's solitary-play category, so that all levels of social play are included. We have also included a column to record instances in which a child interacts with an adult during play. A final column has been added, in which to note play areas and play materials that are being used by the child. As with the Social/Cognitive Scale, a separate recording sheet is needed for each child.

The Peer Play Scale lends itself to *focal-person sampling* (Pellegrini, 1996): First, decide on the child to observe. As explained previously, this will be a child who exhibits low levels of social interaction during play. Next, observe the child long enough to ascertain his or her peer play level. Code the level by placing a check in the appropriate column. If the child interacts with an adult, place a check in the "adult involved" column. Finally, jot down a brief description of the setting or materials that the child was using during the play.

Once several observations of a child have been made, the recording sheet can be examined for patterns in social-play behavior. Column totals for the six play levels will give a detailed picture of children's social-play skills. If children primarily engage in parallel play, are they unaware (Level 1) or aware (Level 2) of nearby peers? If children engage in group play, does this play typically involve just social interaction (Level 3) or also complementary and reciprocal behavior (Level 4)? If children engage in sociodramatic play, do they just use pretend verbal exchanges (Level 5), or do they also use metacommunication to plan and organize their play (Level 6)? This information can indicate which aspects of peer play specific children need help with: social awareness, reciprocal interaction, or metacommunication.

It is also informative to look across the record-sheet rows for patterns. A particular child might exhibit higher levels of social play when (a) adults are (or are not) involved, (b) the child is in a particular area of the classroom, or (c) the child is playing with particular play materials. This information can be

Date	Solitary Play Level 0	Parallel Play Level 1	Parallel Aware Play Level 2	Simple Social Play Level 3	Complem. & Reciprocal Play Level 4	Cooperative Social Pretend Play Level 5	Complex Social Pretend Play Level 6	Adults Involved	Settings and Materials

Figure 8.3

Peer play scale: Recording sheet
Source: Adapted from Howes & Matheson (1992).

very useful in attempting to enhance children's play. For example, if a child is observed engaging only occasionally in social play, and most of these instances occur in the home center, the teacher might encourage the child to spend more time in that area. Alternatively, if a child only exhibits social play in the few instances in which a teacher is present, then direct adult involvement in play might be an effective way to enhance the social level of the child's play (see Chapter 7).

SOCIODRAMATIC PLAY INVENTORY Sociodramatic play (also referred to as group–dramatic play) occurs when two or more children adopt roles and act out a story or situation. Although deceptively simple on the surface, this type of play places complex cognitive, linguistic, and social demands on children. In order to engage in sustained sociodramatic play episodes, children must be able to abstract out the critical features of their pretend roles, view things from the perspective of these roles, create and interpret make-believe transformations, use language precisely, engage in cooperative planning, share props with peers, inhibit aggression, and so on. As a result of these requirements, sociodramatic play is generally regarded as one of the most developmentally advanced and important forms of play.

Sociodramatic play places heavy cognitive, linguistic, and social demands on children.

The group–dramatic play box in the Social/Cognitive Scale indicates how frequently children engage in sociodramatic play. If the recording sheet for a child age 4 years or older contains few tally marks in the group–dramatic play box, then intervention in the form of provision or of adult involvement may be needed to encourage participation in this important form of play. First, however, it is useful to gather more information about the child's grasp of the skills needed for engaging in sociodramatic play.

Smilansky (1968), as part of her play-training study, developed an instrument that is ideal for this purpose. Her Sociodramatic Play Inventory consists of five components or attainments that characterize mature group–dramatic play: (a) role playing, (b) make-believe transformations, (c) social interaction, (d) verbal communication, and (e) persistence (see the Theory in Action feature "Sociodramatic Play Inventory: Definitions"). This system can reveal which of these components are present in a child's play and which are missing.

The Sociodramatic Play Inventory recording sheet is a checklist: Children's names are listed in rows, and the five play components are listed in columns. Note that this format allows one form to be used to observe a number of different children. We have modified Smilansky's scale slightly by adding separate columns for three types of make-believe transformations (object, action, and situation) and for the two major types of verbal

Theory in Action

SOCIODRAMATIC PLAY INVENTORY: DEFINITIONS

Role Playing

Children adopt roles (family member, firefighter, Count Dracula, etc.) and communicate these roles through verbal declarations (e.g., "I'm the mommy") and role-appropriate behavior (e.g., taking care of a pretend baby).

Make-believe Transformations

Symbols are used to stand for objects, actions, and situations.

1. *Objects* are used as substitutes for other objects (e.g., pretending that a block of wood is a drinking cup), or verbal declarations are used to create imaginary objects (e.g., staring at one's empty hand and declaring, "My glass is empty!").
2. Abbreviated *actions* are used as substitutes for real actions (e.g., raising one's hand up and down, pretending to be hammering), or verbal statements are used to create an imaginary action (e.g., "I'm hammering the nails in").
3. Verbal declarations are used to create imaginary *situations* (e.g., "Let's pretend that we're on a jet plane").

Social Interaction

At least two children are directly interacting with each other in connection with the play episode. (In terms of the Peer Play Scale, this requires at least Level 4 play, Complementary and Reciprocal Play, with mutual awareness.)

Verbal Communication

The children engage in verbal exchanges related to the play episode. These exchanges may take two forms:

1. *Metacommunication* statements are used to structure and organize the play episode. Children use these comments to
   a. Designate the make-believe identities of objects (e.g., "Let's pretend the rope is a snake")
   b. Assign roles (e.g., "I'll be the Daddy, and you be the baby")
   c. Plan story lines (e.g., "First, we'll go to the market, and then we'll go to the toy store")
   d. Rebuke players who act in an inappropriate manner (e.g., "Mommies don't talk like that!" or "That's not a hose, silly. It's a snake.").

(continued)

Theory in Action *(continued)*

2. *Pretend communication* statements are used to act out the roles children have adopted. A child enacting the role of a teacher might announce to other players, "You've been naughty children. You will all have to go see the principal."

Persistence

Children engage in sustained play episodes. Age should be a factor in determining the length of time required for crediting a child with persistence. Based on our own experience, we recommend that preschoolers be expected to sustain at least 5-minute episodes and that kindergartners be expected to keep their episodes going for at least 10 minutes. Play-period duration is another factor that needs to be taken into consideration. If play periods are very brief (10–15 minutes), these time requirements will need to be reduced.

Source: Adapted from Smilansky (1968).

communication in play (metacommunication and pretend communication). The resulting recording sheet, illustrated in Figure 8.4, allows a more detailed look at children's group–dramatic play skills than was possible with the original scale.

An observation procedure similar to that used by Smilansky (1968) in her play-training study should be used with the Sociodramatic Play Inventory. A single child is observed for a sustained period of time (at least 15 minutes), and then the elements that are present in the child's play are recorded on the checklist.

We recommend the following procedures when using this system:

1. Select two or three children to be the focus of your observations. These should be children who exhibited low frequencies of group–dramatic play when they were observed with the Social/Cognitive Scale.
2. Focus your attention on these children for the entire play period, shifting back and forth between them. Watch one child for about a minute, then shift to the next child.
3. At the end of the play period, place checks in the appropriate columns of the Sociodramatic Play Inventory recording sheet for the elements observed in each child's play.
4. If a child appears to be missing one or more of the play components, observe the child again on several other days. It is premature to conclude on the basis of only one observation that a child does not possess a particular play behavior.

| Name | Role Play | Make-Believe | | | Interaction | Verbal Communication | | Persistence |
		Objects	Actions	Situation		Metacomm.	Pretend	

Figure 8.4

Sociodramatic play inventory: Recording sheet
Source: Adapted from Smilansky (1968).

Once the observations have been completed, the recording sheet can be consulted to determine which elements are present or absent in specific children's play. If a child appears to be missing one or more of the components, the following interventions may help the child incorporate these behaviors into his or her play:

- Role playing—prop boxes (Chapter 10) and adult involvement (Chapter 7)
- Make-believe transformations—low-structure props (Chapter 10) and adult involvement (Chapter 7)
- Social interaction—toys with high social value (Chapter 10) and adult involvement (Chapter 7)
- Verbal communication—adult involvement (Chapter 7)
- Persistence—partitioned play areas (Chapter 9) and adult involvement (Chapter 7)

Be sure to take children's age into consideration when interpreting the Sociodramatic Play Inventory recording sheet. While group–dramatic play begins to appear by 2 years of age, most children do not engage in fully elaborated sociodramatic play until age 3 years or beyond (Rubin, Fein, & Vandenberg, 1983). Therefore, teachers and parents should not worry if 2- and 3-year-olds do not exhibit all five sociodramatic elements in their play. Evidence suggests that some children from low-socioeconomic status backgrounds tend to engage in more make-believe play outdoors than indoors (e.g., Tizard, Phelps, & Plewis, 1976). Therefore, be sure to observe low-income children's play across a variety of situations, in both indoor and outdoor settings before concluding that they are missing any group–dramatic play skills.

RATING SCALES

Rating scales are similar to checklists, in that they focus attention on specific behaviors and provide a convenient form for recording information. However, rating scales do more than simply indicate the presence or absence of behaviors. These scales allow observers to make decisions about the degree to which a behavior is present and judgments about the quality of the behavior (Irwin & Bushnell, 1980; Pellegrini, 1996).

Rating scales can be used to make judgments about a wide range of behaviors and attributes that are otherwise difficult to measure (Irwin & Bushnell, 1980). The playfulness scale described in this section is a good example of this versatility. Rating scales are also easy to learn to use and allow raters to draw on their long-term knowledge of individual children (Pellegrini, 1996).

On the negative side, the judgments required by these scales make them less reliable than checklists and more open to error. One example is the effect of "recency of memory". Raters tend to base their judgments on recent behavior, rather than on behaviors that are the most representative (Pellegrini, 1996). Other common problems include (Irwin & Bushnell, 1980):

- *Errors of leniency*—the tendency to rate familiar people higher than they deserve to be rated
- *Errors of central tendency*—the tendency to avoid extremely high or low ratings
- *Halo effects*—the tendency to let irrelevant information affect judgments

The best way to guard against these types of errors is to be aware that they exist. As Irwin and Bushnell (1980, p. 213) explain, "To be forewarned is to be forearmed!"

We have selected two numerical scales that rate different aspects of play. The first assesses playfulness as a personality trait and yields information about how playful children are. The second instrument is designed to rate the interactive peer play behaviors of African-American preschoolers.

PLAYFULNESS SCALE   As discussed in Chapter 4, playfulness appears to be a basic personality trait. Some children have personality characteristics that predispose them to engage in frequent play and that enable them to create their own play worlds out of the most sterile environments (Barnett, 1990). Other children rarely play at all, even in enriched play settings.

Barnett (1990) has developed a scale that enables researchers and teachers to rate each child's predisposition to approach the environment in a playful way. This scale utilizes versions of Lieberman's (1977) five dimensions of playfulness:

1. Physical spontaneity
2. Social spontaneity
3. Cognitive spontaneity
4. Manifest joy
5. Sense of humor

Based on her previous research, Barnett developed four to five behavioral descriptions that operationally define each of these dimensions. She also created a 5-point response scale to rate the degree to which each description characterizes the child's behavior (see Figure 8.5).

Teachers can use the playfulness scale to rate the playfulness of their students. Children who rate low on this trait may need extra help, in the form of adult involvement or assistance from a more playful peer, in order to benefit from play-oriented curriculum activities such as those discussed in Chapter 11.

PENN INTERACTIVE PEER PLAY SCALE   Most social competency measures and play scales have been derived from research on samples of white, middle-class children, casting doubt on the validity of their use with children who are neither white nor middle class (McLoyd, 1990). The Penn Interactive Peer Play Scale (PIPPS) is an exception. This teacher-administered rating scale was developed specifically to measure the interactive play behaviors of low-income African-American preschoolers.

Fantuzzo and Sutton-Smith (1994) began by selecting 25 children with the "highest" and 25 with "lowest" levels of interactive play from a sample of 800 Head Start children. The researchers then carefully analyzed videotaped play sequences to identify salient behaviors that distinguished the "high" from the "low" players. These behaviors were crafted into 36 rating-scale items that asked teachers to indicate the frequency with which each behavior had been observed over the most recent 2 months. In a later study, Fantuzzo, Sutton-Smith, Coolahan, Manz, Canning, and Debnam (1995) used factor analysis to identify three reliable underlying dimensions of Head Start children's interactive peer play:

1. Play Interaction—a positive dimension that is related to prosocial behavior, interpersonal skills, self-control, and verbal assertiveness
2. Play Disruption—a negative dimension that is related to aggressive behavior and lack of self-control
3. Play Disconnection—another negative dimension, related to withdrawn behavior

Figure 8.6 presents a 4-point numerical rating scale that contains items relating to these three dimensions.

	DEGREE TO WHICH ITEM SOUNDS LIKE THE CHILD				
	NOT AT ALL 1	A LITTLE 2	SOMEWHAT 3	A LOT 4	EXACTLY 5
Physical Spontaneity					
Child's movements are well-coordinated	1	2	3	4	5
Child is physically active during play	1	2	3	4	5
Child prefers being active rather than quiet	1	2	3	4	5
Child runs, skips, hops, and jumps a lot	1	2	3	4	5
Social Spontaneity					
Child responds easily to others' approaches	1	2	3	4	5
Child initiates play with others	1	2	3	4	5
Child plays cooperatively with other children	1	2	3	4	5
Child is willing to share playthings	1	2	3	4	5
Child assumes a leadership role when playing	1	2	3	4	5
Cognitive Spontaneity					
Child invents his/her own games	1	2	3	4	5
Child uses unconventional objects in play	1	2	3	4	5
Child assumes different character roles	1	2	3	4	5
Child changes activities during play	1	2	3	4	5
Manifest Joy					
Child expresses enjoyment during play	1	2	3	4	5
Child demonstrates exuberance during play	1	2	3	4	5
Child shows enthusiasm during play	1	2	3	4	5
Child expresses emotion during play	1	2	3	4	5
Child sings and talks while playing	1	2	3	4	5
Sense of Humor					
Child enjoys joking with other children	1	2	3	4	5
Child gently teases others	1	2	3	4	5
Child tells funny stories	1	2	3	4	5
Child laughs at humorous stories	1	2	3	4	5
Child likes to clown around	1	2	3	4	5

Figure 8.5

Barnett's Playfulness Scale

Source: Adapted by permission from Lynn A. Barnett, 1990, Playfulness: Definition, Design, and Measurement, Play and Culture, *3(4): 323–324.*

| | FREQUENCY OF BEHAVIOR DURING the PAST TWO MONTHS | | |
	NOT OBSERVED 1	INFREQUENT 2	FREQUENT 3	VERY FREQUENT 4
Play Interaction				
Shares ideas	1	2	3	4
Leads other children	1	2	3	4
Helps other children	1	2	3	4
Directs others' actions politely	1	2	3	4
Encourages others to join in play	1	2	3	4
Show creativity in making up play stories & activities	1	2	3	4
Play Disruption				
Starts fights and arguments	1	2	3	4
Is rejected by others	1	2	3	4
Doesn't take turns	1	2	3	4
Tattles	1	2	3	4
Destroys others' things	1	2	3	4
Verbally assaults	1	2	3	4
Cries, whines, shows temper	1	2	3	4
Grabs things belonging to others	1	2	3	4
Is physically aggressive	1	2	3	4
Play Disconnection				
Hovers outside play group	1	2	3	4
Withdraws	1	2	3	4
Wanders aimlessly	1	2	3	4
Is ignored by others	1	2	3	4
Is not invited into play groups	1	2	3	4
Refuses to play when invited	1	2	3	4
Confused in play	1	2	3	4
Needs teacher's direction	1	2	3	4
Seems unhappy	1	2	3	4
Has difficulty moving from one activity to another	1	2	3	4

Figure 8.6

Penn Interactive Peer Play Scale

Source: Adapted from Fantuzzo, J., Sutton-Smith, B., Coolahan, K., Manz, P., Canning, S. & Debnam, D., (1995). Assessment of preschool play interaction behaviors in young low-income children: Penn Interactive Peer Play Scale. Early Childhood Research Quarterly, 10, p.111.

Teachers working in Head Start programs or in other schools serving low-income African-American children can use the PIPPS scale to assess their students' social-play skills. Fantuzzo et al. (1995), (p. 117) explain how teachers can then use these ratings to plan instructional activities:

If the class as a whole is evidencing relatively low interactive behaviors and more disruptive and disconnected behaviors, the teacher could set up activities with more structure and adult supervision and support for positive interaction. On the other hand, if the class is showing high levels of social interaction, the teacher could build on these competencies and use peer interaction as a medium for instruction (e.g., employ cooperative learning methods).

PIPPS ratings can also help with the implementation of peer-mediated interventions—programs in which socially skilled preschool children help to raise the social competence of less socially skilled peers. Fantuzzo et al. (1995) point out that the success of such programs depends on the teachers' ability to identify children with nonadaptive play skills (the ones most in need of peer assistance) and children with adaptive play skills (the ones best suited to give assistance). The PIPPS is ideally suited for this purpose.

ANECDOTAL RECORDS: NOTES AND VIGNETTES

Anecdotal records are brief narrative descriptions of events or incidents that are written down either as they occur or shortly after they occur. These records can be used to document significant events that take place during play—events that shed light on children's play abilities and their overall social, cognitive, academic, and physical development.

ANECDOTAL NOTES Figure 8.7 illustrates an anecdotal note that was recorded while 4-year-old Noah was taking part in an airplane-trip dramatization. This description documents both Noah's sociodramatic play skills (role playing, make-believe transformations, and social interaction) and his developing literacy skills (use of personalized script and use of print for functional purposes).

The anecdotal note in Figure 8.7 is brief, but it contains a considerable amount of descriptive information: the child's name, date, play setting, and an exact description of the events and products that were observed. The following guidelines, adapted from Irwin and Bushnell (1980), offer useful suggestions for making anecdotal records:

- Include information about the date, time of day, setting, and basic activity.
- Record the key person's actions and comments.
- Preserve the sequence of the episode.
- Note the exact words spoken, to preserve the flavor of the conversation.
- Be objective and accurate.

When making anecdotal notes, the focus should be on accurate description of what was seen and heard in the play (Vukelich, 1995). Interpretation and evaluation can occur later, after the play period is over and the teacher has time to look over the notes that have been recorded.

Anecdotal notes can be written on a variety of materials. Rhodes and Nathenson-Mejia (1992) recommend that teachers use sticky notes (Post-it™ Notes), labeling each note with the date and name of the key student. These sticky notes can later be transferred to a notebook sectioned off by students'

Noah 4/17

Noah is in the store center pretending to be a ticket agent. He makes several plane tickets by scribbling on blank pieces of paper. He asks me, "Want a ticket?" I say "Yes" and pretend to pay with invisible money. He sells the rest of the tickets to other players in a similar fashion.

Figure 8.7

Anecdotal note on Noah's airplane play

names. Another system involves taping 3" × 5" index cards to a clipboard, in an overlapping manner (Christie, Enz, & Vukelich, 1997). Student names are written at the bottom of each card, and the cards are arranged so that the names are visible. When the teacher observes something significant happen during play, he or she can use this "flip chart" to locate the child's card and then write the anecdotal description, along with the date of occurrence. When a card is full, it is transferred to the teacher's folder on that child, and a new card is put in its place.

Observation guides are a valuable complement to anecdotal records (Rhodes & Nathenson-Mejia, 1992). These guides specify the aspects of play to be observed, making anecdotal recording more focused and systematic. Observation guides can easily be developed from the three checklists described earlier in this chapter. For example, one could take the categories from Smilansky's Sociodramatic Play Inventory and turn them into a brief guide. When observing sociodramatic play, be on the lookout for the following elements:

- Role play
- Make-believe with regard to action, objects, and situations
- Social interaction
- Verbal communication
- Persistence

Of course, guides can be prepared for any aspect of play in which one is interested: language used in play, social interaction skills, thematic content of play episodes, and so on.

ANECDOTAL VIGNETTES   If it is not possible to record anecdotal notes while play activities are taking place, teachers can write down what is recalled at a later time. These after-the-fact descriptions are called *vignettes*. Vignettes are recollections of significant events and look much like anecdotal notes, except that they are written in the past tense. Because vignettes are written when teachers are free of distractions, they tend to be more detailed than anecdotal notes. Teachers also have time to mention connections between play activities and other things that are known about the child. Unfortunately, this additional detail may come at a cost—important information can be forgotten during the interval between observation and writing the vignette.

Figure 8.8 illustrates a vignette of Noah's airplane play, which was also the source of the anecdotal note in Figure 8.7. Note how the vignette contains a more detailed description of the play and its setting. Also, note how the vignette connects this play with what is known about Noah's literacy development.

VIDEOTAPE RECORDINGS

Videotape equipment is now commonly available in homes and schools. The camcorder has replaced the 8mm movie camera as the primary means that parents use to record their children's early years. Video cameras are also becoming standard equipment in many classrooms, used for both assessment and instructional purposes. This equipment can be used in several ways to assist the observation of children's play.

First, video equipment provides a solution to a major problem associated with play observation: How can a teacher find the time to make systematic observations of play? A video camera can be aimed at play areas (e.g., the housekeeping center or block area) and can record ongoing play without requiring any attention or effort on the part of an adult. The tapes can be replayed and viewed later, when time permits.

Second, video recordings provide a much more detailed record of play behavior than is possible with observation. In addition to showing the type of play, videotapes can reveal (a) the materials that are played with, (b) the child–child and adult–child interaction that occurs, (c) the language that is used, and (d) the nonverbal gestures of children and adults.

Third, videotapes can be used to improve observation skills. For example, several teachers might view a play episode and code it with one of three checklists described earlier in this chapter, or they could make anecdotal records or vignettes to describe the play. They could then compare their codings or descriptions. This type of training can greatly increase the reliability and consistency of play observations.

Finally, teachers can use videotapes to evaluate and improve their play-involvement skills. In a study by Wood, McMahon, and Cranstoun (1980),

Noah 4/17

Several children had transformed the loft
into an airplane and were preparing to
make a trip to France. Noah was in
the store center pretending to be a
ticket agent. He made several tickets
by scribbling on blank pieces of paper.
Next, he sold the tickets to me and
the other players in exchange for
pretend money. He kept one ticket for
himself and joined the others on the
plane. However, before he left the store
center, he scribbled on a piece of paper
taped to the outside of the center.
Later when I asked him what it said, he
replied, "Closed for business." This was the
first time that I have seen Noah use the
regulatory function of print during play.

Figure 8.8

Vignette describing Noah's airplane play

preschool teachers taped their interactions with children during free-play periods
with audiocassette recorders. The recordings were then transcribed and examined by the teachers. As a result, many of the teachers changed their play-involvement strategies. Teachers who tended to be too directive and domineering became less so, and those who focused most of their attention on management
activities began to participate in their students' play. Teachers should be able to

accomplish this kind of self-evaluation more efficiently with video equipment. Video recordings provide a much more detailed record of the teacher's activities and children's reactions to those activities than Wood et al. obtained using audiotape. In addition, videotapes, unlike audiotapes, do not need to be transcribed.

Christie, Enz, and Vukelich (1997, pp. 116–117) give the following suggestions for making unmonitored videotapes:

- Place the camera on a tripod, and adjust the zoom lens so that it covers the main area where children will be interacting. Turn the camera on, and check it occasionally to make sure that the camera angle is capturing the significant action.
- Do a trial recording to make sure that the equipment is working correctly and that the children's language is being clearly recorded. This trial will also help desensitize the children to the equipment.
- View the final recordings as soon as possible so that your memory can help fill in the gaps in unintelligible parts of the recordings.

SUMMARY

Observation is the key to understanding children's play behavior and the starting point for adult facilitation of play. For these reasons, it is important that teachers know how to observe play accurately and systematically.

In this chapter, we described four different tools that teachers can use for systematic play observation:

- *Checklists* specify exactly what to look for when children are playing and provide a convenient record keeping system. They can be used to determine whether selected play behaviors are present or absent. We described three useful play checklists: (1) the Social/Cognitive scale, (2) the Peer Play scale, and (3) the Sociodramatic Play Inventory, which provides a close look at the components that constitute high quality group-dramatic play.
- *Rating scales* do more than simply indicate the presence or absence of play behaviors. These scales allow observers to make judgments about both the quantity and quality of play behaviors. We described two play rating scales: (1) the Playfulness Scale, and (2) the Penn Interactive Peer Play Scale.
- *Anecdotal records* are much less structured than checklists or rating scales. The observer writes a description of significant events that occur during play on a blank piece of paper (or a blank card). Anecdotal records and vignettes have the advantage of presenting a much richer description of play and its surrounding context than checklists do, but they are more time consuming.
- *Videotape recordings* of activity in play centers requires little effort or attention on the part of the teacher and provides a detailed record of all aspects of play behavior.

Chapter 9

PLAY ENVIRONMENTS

with Francis Wardle

The 40-minute "activity" period has just started in Ms. Johnson's kindergarten. The children are free to choose from a number of centers: library, science, math manipulatives, writing, art, blocks, dramatic play (home theme), and a rotating theme center that happens to be a grocery store this week. The only constraint on the children's freedom of choice is the hook-and-nametag system that Ms. Johnson uses to control the number of children who use each center (e.g., if a center has four hooks, only four children can be in the center at any one time).

The centers are clearly defined by partitions, signs, and the materials they contain. For example, the dramatic-play center is partitioned off from the rest of the classroom by screens and furniture, and it contains a variety of props (miniature kitchen appliances, dishes, an ironing board, dolls, telephone, television, tools, etc.) that identify the center as a place to engage in pretend play. Ms. Johnson has also placed the centers in good relationship to each other. The centers with high activity or noise levels—art, dramatic-play areas, blocks—are in one half of the room, and the more sedate activity areas—library, writing, science, math—are in the other half. This enables children to play actively in the noisier centers without distracting or interrupting children in the quieter areas. In addition, this grouping of complementary areas encourages positive interaction of children and activities between centers. For example, children in the library center go to the writing area to write about a story they have just read. Children in the housekeeping area visit the block area to get props for their dramatizations, and they make trips to a store center to buy food for an upcoming meal and hardware for an upcoming home-improvement project.

The clearly defined, well-arranged centers encourage children to engage in appropriate use of materials. For example, children are browsing through books in the library area, painting pictures and working with clay in the art area, and engaging in role play in the housekeeping and store theme centers. There is very little rough-and-tumble or aggressive behavior taking place. The children spend most of their time engaging in productive interactions with materials and/or peers. ■

Environmental factors—the space available for play, how space is arranged, and the toy and equipment selection—can have a considerable impact on children's play behavior. Settings can influence the type, amount, duration, and quality of children's play activities (Frost, Shin, & Jacobs, 1998; Petrakos & Howe, 1996; Smith & Connolly, 1980). The environment in Ms. Johnson's classroom, described in the preceding scenario, supports productive, high-quality play. Later in this chapter, we describe how another teacher, Ms. Walling, was experiencing the opposite type of environmental effect: Her classroom setting was interfering with the types of play that she wanted to promote.

It is very important for teachers to be aware of environmental influences on play so that they can provide children with settings that are conducive to high-quality play and that reinforce, rather than interfere with, curricular goals. McLean (1995) goes even further and argues that in child-centered early childhood programs, the environment is the basic building block of the curriculum. In such programs, children are viewed as active learners who construct their own knowledge as they explore and experiment with materials, solve problems, and interact with other people. The teacher's main role is to create a classroom environment that supports this active learning by encouraging active experimentation and risk taking on the part of children. She cautions that "in educational settings, the quality of physical and human environments cannot be left to chance. They should be purposefully created to provide the maximum support for children's development and learning" (McLean, 1995, p. 5).

Ecological psychologists use the term "environmental press" to refer to the forces at work in a setting, which shape the behavior of people in that setting (Garbarino, 1989). The principle of "progressive conformity" stipulates that as time passes, people's behavior tends to become congruent with the press of the environment (Garbarino, 1989). For example, if a play area is arranged in a manner that encourages solitary activity, children will tend to engage in solitary play while in that area (Petrakos & Howe, 1996). When play settings are stocked with books, writing materials, and other literacy artifacts, children will tend to incorporate literacy behaviors into their play (Neuman & Roskos, 1997). Children may initially attempt to engage in other types of behavior, but eventually they tend to give in to the influence of setting.

It is important to note that children's behavior is not totally controlled by the environment. Garbarino (1989, p. 21) explains:

> While environmental press is the environment's contribution to individual–environment transactions, the individual brings to the situation a unique arrangement of personal resources, a particular level of development, and other attributes. Different people thus may react differently to the same environment.

The study by Liddell and Kruger (1989), discussed in the subsequent section on indoor spatial density, is a good example of this principle. The investigators found that children responded to crowded classroom play centers differently, depending on their home experiences. Thus, it is important to remember that play–environment relationships reported in this chapter may not hold for all children.

Interacting with these individual differences, both physical characteristics of the setting and social factors can exert environmental press. In earlier chapters, we described how play can be affected by social factors such as adult involvement (Chapter 7), peer familiarity (Chapter 8), and surrounding cultural influences (Chapter 5).

This chapter and Chapter 10 deal with the influence of physical aspects of play environments. The current chapter discusses the effects of broad physical characteristics of play settings, such as the amount of space available for play, how that space is arranged, the amount of equipment available, the number of people in the setting, and so on. Chapter 10 focuses on play materials, describing how play is affected by the types of materials that are available in a setting and the characteristics of those materials.

This chapter is divided into two main sections. The first section deals with indoor play environments. Research is reviewed on a variety of features of classroom play areas, including spatial density, arrangement of space, amount of equipment, and activity centers. In addition, guidelines are presented for designing effective indoor play spaces. The second section focuses on outdoor play settings. Topics include differences between indoor and outdoor play, different types of playgrounds, and playground design features linked with high levels of play. Guidelines are given for designing safe and effective school playgrounds. Neighborhood play and natural play settings are also discussed.

INDOOR SETTINGS

A considerable amount of children's play—both at home and at school—occurs indoors. At school, indoor play is often an important component of the early childhood curriculum. By being aware of how specific features of indoor play settings affect play behavior, teachers can help maximize play's positive contributions to children's learning and development.

SPATIAL DENSITY

Spatial density refers to the amount of space per child in a play setting and is an index of crowding. Lower numbers (e.g., 20 square feet per child) indicate crowded settings, whereas higher numbers (e.g., 70 square feet per child) indicate less crowded conditions. Experiments with animals have established that social behavior tends to break down in very crowded conditions, raising the possibility that spatial density may have an impact on social aspects of children's play.

Early studies on the effects of spatial density on preschoolers' play yielded contradictory results. Some studies reported that increased crowding (less space per child) had negative effects on play, resulting in more aggression (Hutt & Vaizey, 1966). Other studies found that increased crowding resulted in less aggression (Loo, 1972) and more positive social interaction and group play (Fagot, 1977).

Smith and Connolly (1980) pointed out several problems that may account for these conflicting findings. In some of the investigations, the amount of space and the number of children were varied, while the amount of equipment remained constant, raising the possibility that differences in the amount of equipment per child may have affected the children's play. A second problem involves the definition of *aggression*. Some investigators distinguished between rough-and-tumble play and true aggression, while others lumped these two behaviors together (see the Theory in Action feature "Rough-and Tumble Play: Some Issues" in Chapter 3 for a discussion of the differences in these two types of behavior).

In order to solve these problems and to get a clearer picture of the effects of crowding, Smith and Connolly (1980) conducted an extensive study in which space, number of children, and amount of equipment were systematically varied. Spatial densities of 15, 25, 50, and 75 square feet per child were examined. Smith and Connolly found that reducing the space per child resulted in a reduction in the amount of gross-motor activity (i.e., running, chasing, and rough-and-tumble activity) during play. In other words, as crowding increased, gross-motor play decreased. Less space per child (i.e., increased crowding) had little effect on the children's social behavior until spatial density reached 25 square feet per child. When the density was changed from 25 to 15 square feet per child, there was a marked increase in aggression and a significant reduction in group play.

· A study by Liddell and Kruger (1989) in a South African township nursery school revealed that children's response to crowding is influenced by household density. The play of children who came from crowded homes was more negatively affected by crowding than was the play of children for whom crowding was a novel experience. The investigators hypothesized that children who face crowding and competition for resources at home are more vulnerable to the added stress that crowding causes at school. Interestingly, Kruger and Liddell note that opposite findings have been reported for adults. Adults tend to cope better with overcrowding when they live in crowded homes and communities.

The finding that reducing the space available per child also reduces gross-motor play has several educational implications. If teachers are concerned that there is too much chasing and rough-and-tumble play occurring in a classroom, perhaps there is too much space. Adding more furniture or rearranging existing furniture to break up large open areas might help alleviate this problem. Teachers wishing to increase gross-motor play should, of course, do the opposite.

Because spatial density can influence children's play behavior, teachers may wish to monitor this variable. The Theory in Action feature "Measuring Spatial Density" contains instructions for determining the spatial density of classrooms. If calculations reveal that less than 25 square feet of usable space is available per child, steps should be taken to reduce crowding or to alleviate its negative effects. The simplest solution is to obtain more classroom space, but often the amount of available space is beyond the teacher's control. If this is the case, teachers can still positively affect children's play interactions by manipulating how the available space is arranged and used (McLean, 1995). Classroom play areas and the arrangement of space are addressed in the sections that follow.

Theory in Action

MEASURING SPATIAL DENSITY

Spatial density refers to the amount of space available per child in a play setting. It can be easily determined by use of the following formula:

$$\text{Spatial density} = \frac{\text{room area} - \text{unusable space}}{\text{number of children}}$$

First, determine the total *room area* by measuring the length and width of the room and multiplying these two numbers together. Second, use the same procedure to determine the area (in square feet) of each piece of furniture and each space that cannot be used for play (e.g., narrow areas between furniture). Add all the unusable areas together to determine the total unusable space. Third, subtract the total unusable space from the room area to determine the total amount of space usable for play. Fourth, divide this last figure by the number of children in the class.

The following example, in which 12 children are in a classroom measuring 15×20 feet, will illustrate how these calculations are made:

		Sq. Ft.
Room area	15×20 feet	300
Unusable area		
Table 1	5×3 feet	15
Table 2	5×3 feet	15
Table 3	2×4 feet	8
Area between Tables 1 & 2	1×5 feet	5
Bookcase 1×9 feet		9
		Total 52

$$\text{Spatial density} = \frac{300 - 52 \text{ sq. ft.}}{12}$$

$$= \frac{248 \text{ sq. ft.}}{12}$$

$$= 21 \text{ sq. ft. per child}$$

Smith and Connolly (1980) found that reducing the amount of space per child from 75 square feet to 25 square feet had little effect other than reducing the amount of gross-motor play. However, reducing the space per child from 25 square feet to 15 square feet resulted in a large increase in aggressive behavior and a decrease in group play, both negative consequences. In the preceding example, there is only 21 square feet of play space available for each child. The setting may therefore be too crowded. Consult the text for suggestions on remedying this situation.

PLAY AREAS

Preschool and kindergarten classrooms are commonly divided into activity areas or learning centers, with each area having its own particular set of materials and activities. In center-based classrooms, children interact with focused sets of materials and help each other build their own knowledge and skills. The teacher's role is to set up the environment, observe as children interact with the materials, supply help and guidance when needed, and occasionally introduce new activities for each center. If centers are set up properly and if an effective management system is established, the classroom environment does much of the "teaching"!

Effective centers are stocked with materials that allow children to learn through exploration and experimentation. The following are examples of common classroom learning centers and some of their materials:

- Block center—unit blocks, large hollow blocks, and small replicas of vehicles, people, and animals
- Dramatic-play center—replicas of kitchen furniture and appliances, small table and chairs, dishes and eating utensils, used "adult" furniture, dress-up clothes, dolls, doll beds, baby strollers, telephone, television, computer, briefcase, and tools
- Rotating theme center—props and furniture that suggest specific settings familiar to children, such as a grocery store, restaurant, post office, or veterinary hospital
- Table-toy center—Legos®, puzzles, pegboards, dominoes, games, and math manipulatives
- Floor play center—large vehicles, bean bags, balls, tinkertoys and empty boxes
- Art center—paints, easels, brushes, scissors, glue, wallpaper books, small pieces of wood and styrofoam, paper, felt pens, crayons, clay, playdough, print pads and stencils, yarn and cloth samples, and old magazines
- Music center—phonograph, cassette player, rhythm instruments, autoharp, audiocassettes, and song books
- Library center—books, magazines, bookshelves, sofa or upholstered chair, rug, and book-related displays
- Writing center—pencils, markers, paper, blank books, alphabet chart, letter stencils, dictionaries, writing folders, individual journals, mailboxes, chalk and chalkboards, and computers
- Science center—animals in cages, aquarium, objects to sort and feel (e.g., shells, seeds, stones), magnifying glass, balance scale, seeds to grow, ant farm, water table, sandbox, and "found objects" display
- Math center—math manipulatives (Cuisenaire® rods, Unifix® cubes, beads), counting frames, math games and puzzles
- Woodworking center—tools, workbench, vise, nails, screws, bolts and nuts, brads, wood, styrofoam, yarn, glue, and paint

Few classrooms have enough space to contain all of these centers. Thus, teachers must decide which centers to include—a decision that will have an important impact on the activity and play that occurs in their classrooms. Many teachers set up six or seven permanent centers that focus on key areas of the curriculum (dramatic play, blocks, art, library, writing, math, etc.) and several temporary centers that change to coincide with thematic units (transportation, dinosaurs) and other areas of the curriculum (woodworking, music).

Research provides some guidance for selecting classroom play centers. Several studies have compared children's play patterns in different play areas. Results have generally favored dramatic-play and block centers, indicating that these areas encourage the highest social and cognitive levels of play. Shure (1963), for example, found that children tended to engage in solitary play in the game ("table toy") area, whereas group play was common in the block and dramatic-play areas. Art and book areas encouraged parallel play. Rubin and Seibel (1979) reported that blocks were associated with large amounts of constructive and dramatic play. Pellegrini (1984) discovered that children use more imaginative, explicit, and cohesive language in the dramatic-play center than in block, art, or water and sand areas.

One additional type of center is worthy of mention—the rotating theme center. Theme centers are settings that suggest specific themes for dramatic play. For example, a hardware-store center might have a table with a cash register, shelves, empty product boxes and cans, and shopping bags. Table 9.1 gives examples of props that can be used in a number of different theme centers. In addition, this table recommends related activities that can be used in connection with these centers.

Woodard (1984) describes how early childhood education students at her university set up a number of theme corners in the university's laboratory preschool. Some were extremely inventive. Entryways were made from refrigerator cartons to attract children's interest and to separate the centers from the rest of the room. The veterinarian's office included a waiting room with a table for a receptionist and chairs for patients, an examination room, and a kennel with cardboard cages with stuffed animals in them. The ice cream shop had yarn pom-pom balls that could be used as scoops of ice cream. One theme center was introduced at a time and left for several weeks. These centers were located near to the permanent housekeeping center so that children could integrate their domestic play themes with those of the theme corner. Woodard found that the children, particularly the boys, began engaging in more sociodramatic play when the theme centers were introduced. Other researchers have reported similar findings—boys prefer playing in theme centers more than in housekeeping areas (Dodge & Frost, 1986; Howe, Moller, Chambers, & Petrakos, 1994).

Which themes should be introduced first in a rotating theme center? A study by Howe, Moller, and Chambers (1994) sheds some light on this issue. Howe and her associates compared the play of preschoolers in familiar (dramatic play, bakery, pizzeria) and less familiar (pharmacy, hospital, pirate ship) theme centers. Results showed that the children engaged in more dramatic play in the familiar centers. The investigators recommended that teachers provide preparatory experiences (e.g., field trips, books, videos) when less familiar themes are introduced into theme centers. Of course, one must remember that what is familiar to one child may be unfamiliar to another, depending on their experiences. The "Related Activities" column in Table 9.1 lists preparatory experiences that can be used with a number of different play themes.

Table 9.1 THEME CENTERS

THEME	PROPS	SETTING	RELATED ACTIVITIES
POST OFFICE	Mail bag Mail boxes Pens, pencils Paper, postcards Envelopes Stamps Money Cash register Wall signs Posters Hats	Set up center near the home center or writing center	Trip to the post office Visitor: mail carrier Write letters and mail to parents Make stamps

GROCERY
STORE
	Cash register
	Empty product conainers
	Shopping bags
	Coupons
	Aprons
	Shelf labels
	Money
	Pad & pencil
	Signs
		Set up center
		near the home
		center; convert
		to hardware
		store to
		engage boys'
		interest
			Trip to greenhouse where
			  food is grown, trip to
			  store
			Visitor: store manager,
			  cashier
			Make papier-mâché fruits
			  and vegetables
			Make shelf labels, money
			Write shopping lists

RESTAURANT	Table
	Chairs
	Order pad & pencils
	Menus
	Dishes
	Silverware
	Placemats
	Tablecloth
	Money
	Cash register
	Telephone
	Cookbooks
	Baking pans
	Refrigerator
	Signs
		Set up near
		home center;
		have separate
		kitchen and
		eating areas
			Trip to ethnic restaurant to
			  observe kitchen, ordering
			  food
			Visitor: waiter, chef
			Prepare signs

DOCTOR'S
OFFICE
	Doctor kit
	Caps (doctor/nurse)
	Gowns
	Telephone
	Appointment
	  book
	Scale
	Eye chart
	Bandages, cotton pads
	Patient folders
	Magazines
	Wall signs
		Set up near
		home center;
		have separate
		waiting and
		examination
		areas. Make
		center into
		animal hospital
		with toy animals
		and cages
		(cubbies)
			Trip to doctor's office or
			  hospital
			Visitor: doctor, nurse
			  veterinarian
			Make emergency vehicle out of
			  large blocks or boxes

(continued)

Table 9.1 *(continued)*

THEME	PROPS	SETTING	RELATED ACTIVITIES

AIRPORT	Steering wheel
	Tickets
	Luggage
	Maps
	Serving trays
	Food containers
	Dress-up clothes
	  for travel
	Overalls
	Tools
	Travel brochures
	Dolls and blankets
	Telephone
		Construct
		  airplane with
		  large blocks
		  or row of chairs;
		  use table for
		  ticket counter
		  and a wagon
		  for loading
		  food and
		  luggage
			Trip to airport to inspect ticket
			  counter, gates, and planes
			Visitor: pilot, ticket agent,
			  flight attendant, mechanic
			Make tickets, luggage tags

LIBRARY	Books
	Shelves
	Shelf labels
	Rubber stamp
	Pad & pencil
	Library cards
	Check-out cards
	  in books
	Wall signs
		Convert regular
		  library center or
		  set up shelves
		  and table near
		  home center
			Trip to library
			Visitor: librarian
			Make check-out cards
			Make shelf labels

GAS STATION	Oil can
	Rubber-hose lengths
	Bucket & squeegee
	Plastic tools
	Cash register
	Play money
	Telephone
	Telephone books
	Maps
	Traffic signs
	Street signs
		Set up in block
		  area with large
		  trucks and cars
			Trip to gas station
			Visitor: gas station attendant
			Informational picture books
			  about vehicles
			Construct gas pump
			Make traffic & street signs

POLICE OFFICER	Hats
	Badges
	Flashlight
	Car licenses
	Driver licenses
	Pencil & ticket pad
	Telephone
	Radar gun
		Set up in block
		  area with large
		  trucks and cars
			Trip to police station
			Visitor: police officer
			Make traffic signs
			Make driver & car license
			Construct jail out of large
			  blocks

(continued)

Table 9.1   *(continued)*

THEME	PROPS	SETTING	RELATED ACTIVITIES
SPACE EXPLORATION	Helmets Rope Food containers Steering wheel Instrument panel	Make spaceship or space station out of large blocks	Trip to planetarium Visitor: astronomer Make helmets from ice cream cartons Make instrument panel Informational picture books about outer space
BAKER	Hats Pans Aprons Rolling pin Wooden spoons Plastic bowls Cookie cutters Playdough or raw baking materials Cash register Play money Signs Telephone Shelf labels	Set up near home center or snack tables	Trip to bakery Visitor: baker Make signs & shelf labels Write recipes Make play money Bake bread
FIREFIGHTER	Hats Boots Plastic raincoats Badges Ladder Wagon Telephone Rope (for hoses)	Make buildings out of large blocks, use table to represent fire station	Trip to fire station Visitor: firefighter Make hats, badges, ladders Informational books about firefighters

ARRANGEMENT OF SPACE

The amount of space in a play setting and the play areas that occupy that space are not the only spatial features related to play. How space is arranged can also have a major impact on children's play patterns. Key issues include whether space is open or partitioned into smaller areas, how well-defined the areas are, and the relationships among different areas.

Several studies have dealt with the issue of open versus partitioned space. *Open arrangements,* in which there are few barriers between areas in a classroom, have the potential advantage of making it easier for children to move from one activity to another. On the other hand, partitioning classrooms into smaller areas also has potential benefits. Screens and partitions can reduce noise and visual distractions, making it easier for children to concentrate and stay focused on activities. Partitions also tend to discourage gross-motor activity and rough-

and-tumble play. In addition, small areas have a more intimate atmosphere that may encourage social interaction and cooperation among children.

Research conducted in early childhood settings indicates that small, partitioned areas result in higher quality play than do large, open areas. Partitioned play settings have been linked with increases in verbal interaction, cooperation, pretend play, and activity with educational materials (Field, 1980; Moore, 1987; Neill, 1982; Sheehan & Day, 1975), whereas open areas have been associated with increased amounts of rowdy, withdrawn, and random behavior (Moore, 1987; Sheehan & Day, 1975). In addition, partitioning has been reported to have a positive impact on adult behavior, encouraging teachers to interact more with children and less with other staff members (Neill, 1982).

While partitioning large open spaces can be beneficial, teachers should be careful as to where partitions or barriers are placed. Openings should be left between areas in which activities can cross over and become integrated with each other. Kinsman and Berk (1979) found that removing a barrier between the dramatic play center and the block area had beneficial effects on preschool and kindergarten students' play. Removing the barrier resulted in more boy–girl play, particularly in the dramatic-play area. Play integrating materials from the two areas also increased (e.g., using blocks as props in the housekeeping center) among the older, kindergarten-age children.

The issue of open versus partitioned space is closely connected with the notion of spatial definition. Moore (1987) identifies *well-defined behavior settings* as "areas limited to one activity, with clear boundaries from circulation space and from other behavior settings, and with at least partial acoustic and visual separation" (p. 60). Neuman and Roskos (1993) point out that boundaries between areas can be established both with physical cues (semifixed partitions) and symbolic cues (print and pictures). For example, a post-office play center can be partitioned off from other areas by using a chart stand, bookshelves, and other furniture. A large wall sign ("Post Office"), U.S. Postal Service posters, and a mobile comprising objects found in post offices (stamps, envelopes, etc.) help to establish the fact this is an area for postal play. Neuman and Roskos (1993, p. 106) explain that "when teachers deliberately use concrete semi-fixed architectural features and highly visible symbolic cues to organize space, they are providing children with the locational detail they so often need to signal and guide their behaviors."

Moore (1986) compared the play of children in a variety of preschool classrooms, which were classified into three levels of spatial definition, ranging from poorly defined to well-defined. Results showed that children engaged in more exploratory behavior, social interaction, and cooperation in spatially well-defined settings than in moderately or poorly defined areas. The well-defined settings also had a positive effect on teachers' involvement with children. Teachers engaged in more "co-action" activities with children and gave more encouragement in classrooms with spatially well-defined activity areas.

A case study by Walling (1977) sheds light on some other important aspects of spatial arrangement. Walling was teaching a group of 3- and 4-year-old preschoolers and was disturbed by the amount of aggressive behavior and rough-and-tumble play that was occurring during free-play periods. She also was concerned that the children rarely used the dramatic-play center or engaged in dramatic play. She began to suspect that her room arrangement (see Figure 9.1) might be contributing to the low quality of the children's play. On close inspection, she discovered several problems:

Figure 9.1

Walling's original room arrangement
Source: Kritchevsky and Prescott (1977, p. 50).

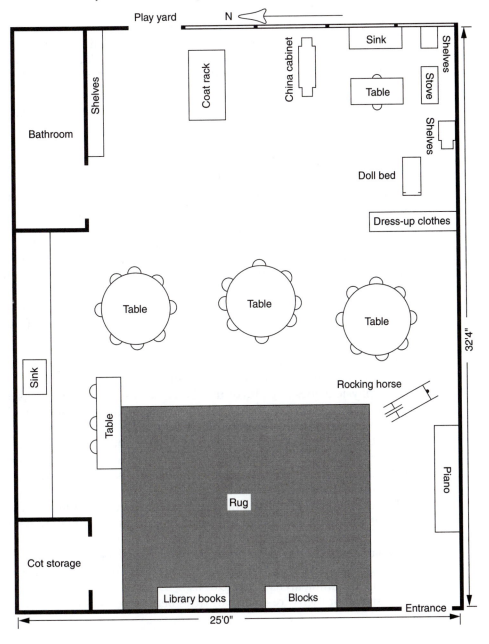

1. There was too much open space in the middle of the room. This may have contributed to the large amount of chasing and rough-and-tumble play.
2. The play areas—block, book, art, and housekeeping—were not well defined. For example, the housekeeping area was in an open corner of the room. As a result, it did not seem very "houselike," and the housekeeping equipment got strewn all over the room.
3. Some of the adjacent areas were in direct conflict with each other. For example, the block (noisy) and book (quiet) areas were next to each other.
4. There was no clear pathway through the room. To get from the entrance of the room to the other side, children had to go near the block area (often knocking down other children's block structures) and through a line of tables that were used for art projects. This led to many confrontations between children.

Walling rearranged her room in order to eliminate these problems. She moved the tables and added several partitions to break up the large open spaces and create a clear pathway through the classroom. The partitions also served to physically define the housekeeping and other play areas. Several areas were moved so that they would be in better relationship with each other. For example, the block area was moved away from the books and closer to the housekeeping corner. The resulting arrangement is illustrated in Figure 9.2.

After a week of becoming adjusted to the new arrangement, changes began appearing in the children's play. Play in the housekeeping center and block area increased substantially. There was also a marked decrease in rowdy and aggressive behavior. Walling found that she could spend less time settling disputes and disciplining children and more time interacting with children as they played.

The results of Walling's case study, combined with the findings of the experimental studies reviewed previously, suggest several guidelines for indoor room arrangements:

- Break up large open spaces with partitions and furniture, in order to discourage running and rough-and-tumble play.
- Use physical cues (e.g., furniture, bookshelves, chart stands, easels, aquariums) and symbolic cues (e.g., print, pictures, mobiles) to clearly define and delineate different play areas.
- Place complementary areas, such as the block and dramatic-play centers, close to each other to encourage overlapping of activity between the areas.
- Place areas that require water, such as art areas and water tables, near a sink or other water source.
- Place areas that tend to be messy (art, eating, etc.) on tile surfaces and areas that need warmth (e.g., place for circle time) or tend to be noisy (e.g., blocks) on carpet.
- Separate conflicting areas, such as noisy (e.g., block) and quiet (e.g., book) areas, so that activities in one area will not interfere with activities in adjoining areas (Day, 1983).
- Be sure that there are clear pathways between classroom areas.

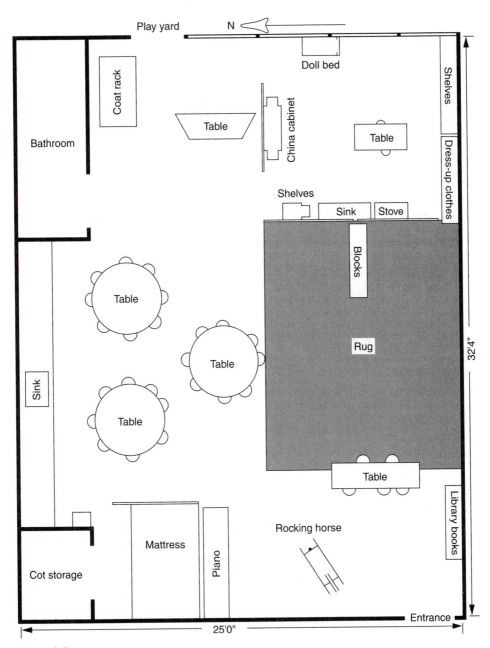

Figure 9.2

Walling's revised room arrangement
Source: Kritchevsky and Prescott (1977, p. 51).

Sandra Lawing's classroom, diagrammed in Figure 9.3, is a good illustration of these spatial features. Note how the activity centers are well-defined and placed in complementary relationships with each other. The quieter, aca-

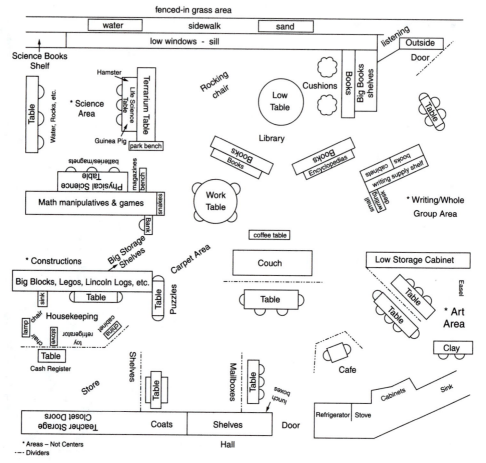

Figure 9.3

Sandra Lawing's classroom floor plan

Source: Reprinted from Building generative curriculum by Lester L. Laminack and Sandra Lawing, Primary Voices K–6, August 1994. Copyright 1994 by the National Council of Teachers of English. Reprinted with permission.

demically oriented math, science, library and writing centers are located in one half of the room, while the more noisy play and art areas are placed in the other half. Activity overlap is encouraged by placing complementary areas (e.g., block, housekeeping, and café theme centers; library and writing centers) adjacent to each other.

The preceding guidelines may need to be modified to accommodate some children with special needs. For example, the guidelines recommend that large, open spaces be partitioned into smaller, well-defined play areas. However, some children with physical disabilities require more open floor space in order to have freedom of movement (Winter, Bell, & Dempsey, 1994). Other possible adaptations include

- Providing wide entrances to play areas for children in wheelchairs or who use walkers
- Storing play materials both at table level and at floor level (Winter, Bell, & Dempsey, 1994)
- Using some tables that are high enough for wheelchairs to fit underneath
- Providing a quiet, non–visually stimulating place for children who need a less distracting environment (see Eddowes, 1993)
- Using spatial cues, such as tape on the floor or distinctively colored carpet, to help children with mental or visual disabilities find their way to different activity areas

The Theory in Action feature "Adapting Indoor Environments for Students with Specific Disabilities" provides further suggestions for adapting indoor play environments for children with special needs.

OUTDOOR SETTINGS

Research indicates that children tend to engage in different cognitive forms of play in indoor and outdoor settings. Predictably, gross-motor play—running, climbing, jumping—is more common in outdoor settings than indoor ones, whereas more constructive play occurs indoors (Henniger, 1985; Roper & Hinde, 1978; Smith & Connolly, 1972). It is less clear whether the social level of play differs between the two locations. Henniger (1985) reported that preschoolers engaged in more parallel play outdoors than in indoor environments. Two other studies, however, failed to find any differences in social play levels between the two settings (Smith & Connolly, 1972; Tizard, Philps, & Plewis, 1976).

Several age, gender, and social-class differences have been reported in connection with indoor and outdoor play locations. Boys and older children have been found to prefer playing outdoors more than girls and younger children do (Harper & Sanders, 1975; Sanders & Harper, 1976). Preschool-age boys have been found to engage in more make-believe play outdoors than girls do, whereas girls exhibit more pretend play indoors than boys do (Sanders & Harper, 1976). Tizard et al. (1976) reported that low-income preschoolers, unlike their middle-class counterparts, engaged in more dramatic play and longer play episodes in outdoor settings than in classrooms.

Taken together, these findings highlight the importance of providing ample amounts of *both* indoor and outdoor play. Outdoor play provides opportunities for children to engage in the gross-motor activities needed for proper physical development. In addition, outdoor play appears to facilitate pretend play in middle-class boys and in low-income children of both genders. Indoor settings, on the other hand, tend to facilitate constructive play among both sexes and dramatic play in girls. For children to have a balanced diet of play activities, lengthy periods of both indoor and outdoor play are necessary.

Theory in Action

ADAPTING INDOOR ENVIRONMENTS FOR STUDENTS WITH SPECIFIC DISABILITIES

FRANCIS WARDLE

Classroom furniture, equipment, and instructional materials are designed and made for children who approximate the norm in physical development, abilities, and behavior. As children differ from the norm in terms of physical size and abilities, giftedness, specific learning challenges, and so on, these materials and equipment are less likely to meet their needs. Teachers of young children can respond to this problem in one or more of four specific ways: adapt the way they respond to the child, adapt the lesson or activity, use adaptive materials and equipment, and restructure the environment. This feature examines both using adapted equipment and materials and restructuring the environment. It should be remembered, however, that working with children who have special needs requires an interaction of all four approaches.

Changes made to materials and the environment depend, obviously, on the specific disability or disabilities a child may have. In this feature, we discuss a few of these disabilities, to give the reader an idea of how to adjust the classroom environment to meet children's needs.

Attention Deficit Disorder/Attention Deficit Hyperactivity Disorder (ADD/ADHD)

ADD/ADHD children often are easily distracted, like to debate rules and expectations, and can become easily bored. Provide these children an environment that minimizes distractions—a setting that is well-defined, partitioned, and located away from windows and the phone. Provide many opportunities for hands-on, project-related activities. Make sure that when a task is completed, there are other activities the child can immediately select. Try to make movement from one activity to another simple and clear, placing areas of sequential activity next to each other. Post rules clearly, and keep them short. Make sure instructions are simple, sequential, and very easy to follow. Provide several modes of communication, such as oral, written, and visual symbols.

Children with Visual Challenges

Any sorting activities should allow children to sort and classify by touch. All visual cues, pictures of where materials are stored, alphabet cards, instructions, and so on, should have tactile cues, as well. Make magnifiers

(continued)

Theory in Action *(continued)*

available for when a child might need them. Frequently provide painting activities using big paintbrushes. Use big books for prereading and reading activities. Always offer children the opportunity to feel objects that are being discussed. Adapt all written materials to large letters with lots of white space. Provide felt boards and other ways to give tactile information.

When any changes are made in the environment, such as an addition of a new piece of equipment, rearrangement of the environment, and so on, show the changes to the child and let her or him feel the changes made.

Children with Hearing Challenges

Use picture charts for directions and rules when needed. Limit noise that can interfere with a child's learning, such as traffic, other children, noisy activities, and so on. Send written notes home to reinforce verbal instructions given to children. Provide sign-language materials, and give rules and instructions in sign language.

Children with Physical Challenges

Provide specialized seating that gives the child needed support when engaging in all activities, such as water play, art, blocks, and so on. This may require specially designed equipment or adaptation of equipment—for example, altering the height of the surface to match the correct height for the child. Provide large brushes and mural paper for art projects, and offer unit- and hollow-block construction activities for children with fine-motor challenges. Individual sand and water tubs can be provided for children who cannot comfortably gain access to the larger water table. Provide bigger tools, such as large paintbrushes and pencils, for children who need them. Adjust the environment so that children with physical challenges can work cooperatively with other children.

The amount of outdoor play in which children engage varies greatly and depends on a number of factors, including geographic location, season of the year, time of day, and weather (Naylor, 1985). Part of this play occurs in organized areas known as playgrounds, and the rest takes place in undesignated neighborhood and outdoor settings.

Prior to the beginning of this century, most outdoor play occurred in unstructured neighborhood or rural settings. However, between 1880 and 1920, there was a concerted effort to establish a network of *playgrounds,* special play spaces containing an array of organized play experiences. This movement was motivated by concern over the effects the Industrial Revolution and growing numbers of impoverished immigrant children who had no place to play except in city streets (Brett, Moore, & Provenzo, 1993; Mergen, 1982).

Proponents of the playground movement believed that poor children would be much better off playing in organized settings. The resulting playgrounds—with their swings, jungle gyms, slides, and other immovable equipment set in concrete or asphalt—are still with us today in many communities.

Fortunately, there have been exciting new developments in the playground field, leading to the development of better, more stimulating play environments. Instead of cold iron and steel, modern playground equipment is made out of wood, powdered-coated metal, and plastic (Hartle & Johnson, 1993). Resilient surfaces such as sand, wood chips, and rubber or plastic mats have replaced the hard asphalt and concrete surfaces that have caused countless injuries. Isolated pieces of equipment have been replaced with linked decks of varying heights, with attached features such as swinging bridges, ramps, pulleys, and wide slides. Many modern playgrounds also feature loose items such as trikes, wooden and plastic blocks, sand toys, and lumber.

We begin by describing the different types of playgrounds that are now available, and then we focus more narrowly on the specific features of playgrounds that lead to richer play. Next, guidelines are presented for designing and building high-quality playgrounds. Because not all outdoor play occurs on organized areas, the chapter concludes with an examination of children's play in undesignated neighborhood and natural settings.

PLAYGROUND TYPES

Until recently, only one type of playground was available in this country: the traditional steel-and-asphalt kind. Growing awareness of deficiencies in these traditional playgrounds, coupled with the influence of European play environments, has led to the development of new, more effective types of outdoor play environments.

TRADITIONAL PLAYGROUNDS   Traditional playgrounds consist of large, open areas covered with packed dirt, concrete, or asphalt. Positioned around this hard surface are isolated, widely spaced pieces of steel equipment: monkey bars, swings, slides, seesaws, and merry-go-rounds. The site is usually surrounded with a chain-link fence. This design, which stems back to the early 1900s, is still the most common type of playground in America (Brett, Moore, & Provenzo, 1993).

The main advantage of the traditional steel-and-asphalt design is that it requires very little maintenance. This perhaps explains the traditional playground's popularity with some city and school officials. Such playgrounds also provide lots of room and equipment for gross-motor exercise, which many people believe is the only type of play that playgrounds should encourage. Finally, many people view traditional playgrounds as aesthetically pleasing and perceive that such playgrounds fit in well with the architecture of local schools and neighborhoods (Brett et al., 1993).

From the child's perspective, however, traditional playgrounds have many disadvantages. The static pieces of equipment, which can be used only in limited ways, make these playgrounds boring. As a result, children rarely use them, and when they do, it is only for brief periods. A study conducted in New

York City found that during peak play hours, traditional playgrounds were empty more than 88% of the time. The average length of stay was only 21 minutes (Hayward, Rothenberg, & Beasley, 1974). Naylor (1985) cites a number of studies indicating that when children are given a choice, they prefer playing in the street to playing on traditional playgrounds.

A second disadvantage is that these playgrounds encourage only gross-motor play. Campbell and Frost (1985) found that more than 77% of the play occurring on a traditional playground was of the gross-motor variety, compared to less than 3% dramatic play. The social level of the play on such playgrounds also tends to be very low. Boyatzis (1985) reported that almost 60% of the play on traditional playground equipment was of the nonsocial, solitary, or parallel variety.

Finally, there is the matter of safety. It is estimated that 200,000 playground injuries are treated by doctors and hospitals every year. The most common cause of these injuries (70–80%) is falling onto the hard surfaces that cover traditional playgrounds (U.S. Consumer Product Safety Commission, 1991). The metal equipment found on these playgrounds is also responsible for many serious injuries: the revolving mechanism on merry-go-rounds and the rocking apparatus on seesaws can break, crush, or even amputate limbs; heavy cast-iron swing seats can cause severe head injuries; and metal slides can cause burns in hot weather and frozen-stuck tongues in winter (Frost, 1992).

These three serious disadvantages—low usage, restricted play, and high injury rates—have led to growing dissatisfaction with the traditional playground and have spurred the development of creative/contemporary playgrounds and adventure playgrounds.

CREATIVE/CONTEMPORARY PLAYGROUNDS Creative playgrounds, sometimes referred to as contemporary playgrounds, were developed to provide children with a more varied, stimulating environment for play. They are made primarily of wood or plastic, with selected metal fixtures. Equipment commonly found in these playgrounds include climbing platforms, ladders, tire nets, suspension bridges, pulley cables, tire swings, monkey bars, rings, enclosures for dramatic play, and balance beams, tunnels, slides, and traditional swings. Equipment is not spread out and isolated, as it is on traditional playgrounds. Rather, it is centrally located and linked together. There are usually three types of surfaces: (1) hardtop surfaces of concrete or asphalt for tricycles, wagons, and other wheeled vehicles; (2) soft surfaces of sand, wood chips, pea gravel, rubber, or plastic under and around all of the equipment; and (3) grass for children to sit and play on (Wardle, 1997a). Sandboxes, water ponds, and gardens are often also included, thereby exposing children to a variety of natural materials. Figure 9.4 illustrates a creative/contemporary playground incorporating all of these features. It should be noted that creative/contemporary playgrounds vary considerably, and many do not include all of the aforementioned features (sometimes dictated by licensing regulations). Even with some features missing, however, these playgrounds still provide a much greater variety of play experiences than their traditional counterparts have done.

Contemporary playgrounds are designed to provide children with a varied, stimulating environment for play.

Creative/contemporary playgrounds can be divided into two subgroups: commercial play environments and community-built playgrounds. Commercial equipment manufacturers produce very attractive modular structures made of wood, plastic, and steel, which place heavy emphasis on physical play and safety. Community-built playgrounds, on the other hand, are made from lumber and salvaged materials such as tires, railroad ties, cable spools, and pipe (Frost & Klein, 1979).

As summarized in Table 9.2, both types of playgrounds have advantages and disadvantages. The commercial structures offer the convenience of being ready-made, visually attractive, more highly durable, and less susceptible to splinters and other protrusions. However, they are also very expensive. Community-built playgrounds are much more economical and can offer a wider variety of play experiences than most commercial models. Because they are constructed by parents and teachers for the children who will use them, these playgrounds become ventures in which the community can take pride (see the Theory in Action feature "Building a Community Playground in Brazil"). This sense of community pride tends to discourage vandalism, which is often a problem with playgrounds these days. In addition, the playground design can take into account unique characteristics of the setting, such as available space, climatic conditions, and the unique play needs of the children. A major

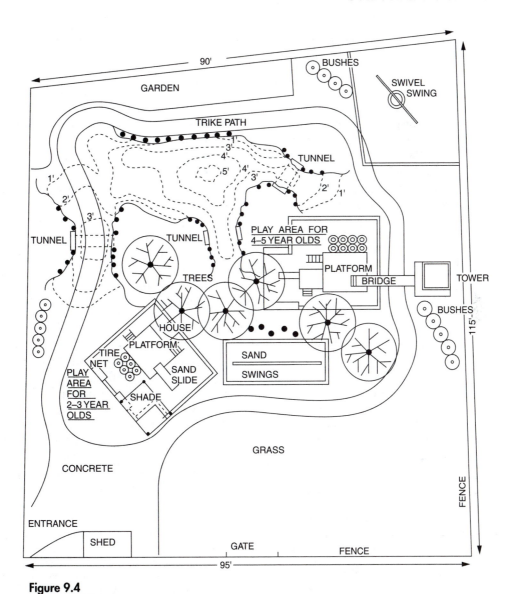

Figure 9.4

Creative/contemporary playground with separate sections for 2- to 3-year-olds and 4- to 5-year-olds

disadvantage is that some insurance carriers will not cover them. The safety of this type of playground varies considerably, depending on design, construction features, and safety knowledge of the designer/consultant.

Research comparing the effects of creative/contemporary and traditional playgrounds has been quite limited, and the few findings have been mixed. Campbell and Frost (1985) found that children engaged in more dramatic play and more group play on creative/contemporary playgrounds, while functional play was more common on traditional ones. Hart and Sheehan (1986)

**Table 9.2   ADVANTAGES AND DISADVANTAGES OF COMMUNITY-BUILT AND COMMERCIAL
PLAYGROUND EQUIPMENT**

ADVANTAGES	DISADVANTAGES
PLAYGROUNDS BUILT BY A PROGRAM WITH VOLUNTEERS AND A PLAYGROUND EXPERT	
• Involve staff, families, and volunteers • Build to the children's, program's, and location's unique needs • Change and upgrade as needed • Use community resources • Inexpensive • Good for programs that are not permanently located • Tend to be more child oriented	• Surfaces may splinter • May not last very long • Soon looks weathered • Needs constant maintenance • Only as safe as the knowledge of the consultant and the skills of the builders • Easy to vandalize • May not be highly attractive to new families • Viewed more critically by licensing officials
PLAYGROUNDS BUILT BY A COMPANY	
• Installation and design handled by builder • Looks upscale • Lasts a long time • Withstands abuse • Sometimes meets guidelines (ASTM/CPSC and ADA) • Has smooth surfaces • Requires limited maintenance • Meets liability requirements	• Equipment is static and predictable • Tends to satisfy adult rather than children's needs • Looks similar to park playgrounds • Very expensive • Limited choices • Little available for children younger than age 3 years • Surfaces may be slippery • Usually only meets physical needs

Note: Some commercial playground companies provide an option for volunteer installation.

Source: Reprinted from Playgrounds: Questions to consider when selecting equipment, by Francis Wardle. Dimensions of Early Childhood, *Winter 1997.*

observed the behavior of children on a preschool playground divided into a contemporary and a traditional side. They observed very little constructive or dramatic play on either playground. Significantly greater incidents of unoccupied behavior, solitary play, and sitting and walking behavior were observed on the contemporary side, whereas more motor play and climbing activity occurred on the traditional side. Hart and Sheehan expressed concern that efforts to make contemporary playgrounds attractive to adults mask "an influence toward passivity and inactivity" (p. 668).

These mixed findings may be due, in part, to the fact that the traditional and creative/contemporary playgrounds vary considerably from study to study. For example, the traditional playground in the Hart and Sheehan study contained a number of loose items, whereas the traditional site in the Campbell and Frost (1985) investigation did not contain any loose materials. Camp-

Theory in Action

BUILDING A COMMUNITY PLAYGROUND IN BRAZIL

FRANCIS WARDLE

It felt like old times when I consulted with local Head Start programs on building and designing playgrounds. The challenge was always the same: not enough space, not enough money, but lots of volunteer help, community resources, and enthusiasm. The only difference this time—as I gaze at a sun-drenched slab of concrete surrounded by an 8-foot wall, site of the proposed playground—is the location. I'm in the middle of Brazil! Actually, I'm 350 miles north and inland from Rio de Janeiro.

My first task in designing and building any playground is to examine the available space, discuss with school officials their ideas and needs, and inventory the fiscal resources and volunteers. This playground is for 60 3- to 6-year-olds who have no play equipment and few learning materials of any kind.

After drawing out the playground area, volunteers from Sete Lagoas drive me to Belo Horizonte, the capitol of Minas Gerais, to purchase equipment. I had hoped to find equipment that we could transport to the school and install. I assumed the same kind of metal and plastic equipment available in the United States existed in Brazil. No such luck! We could not even find safe swing seats or a slide that was not metal or wood.

So we decided to construct our own equipment, using available materials and volunteer skills and labor (Wardle, 1997a, 1997b). The next few days, we toured the town to check out materials and determine what could be made by local craftspeople and what we could build ourselves. For construction methods and community-based solutions, I relied on experiences I had building playgrounds for child-care centers and directing the construction of a model Head Start playground (Wardle, 1987).

In Brazil, playground safety and litigation are not the big issues that they are in the United States. However, I decided to design as safe an environment as possible, relying on the U.S. Consumer Products Safety Commission's (1991) *Handbook for Public Playground Safety* (see the Theory in Action feature "Playground Safety Guidelines"). I was particularly careful with fall zones, entrapment, and protrusions.

Equipment dimensions needed to be adjusted to the smaller physical size of the Brazilian children. We decided to build a swivel swing, a traditional swing with two seats, a platform with two ladders and a slide, and a tunnel made from a drainage culvert. Because of limited space and the configuration of the playground, we created a single fall zone of sand under all the equipment. The sand also provided a great material for constructive play for the children.

(continued)

Theory in Action *(continued)*

The frame of both swings is made from eucalyptus posts, plentiful in this part of Brazil. Hardware for the swings came from hardware stores, chain from a local car shop, attachments were made by a welder, and swing seats cut from car tires were made by an auto mechanic. The framework for the platform was made using a common Brazilian construction lumber. This finished wood is very hard and splits easily. It also does not come in standard U.S. sizes (partly because Brazil is a metric country). We found no dowels for the ladder rungs, so a local carpenter milled us some from standard pieces of wood.

One of the local volunteers, Luis Viera, owned a slate factory, so he provided the sand, culvert, and trucks. He also supplied slate for the sand retainer. I stayed with Luis and his young family in a typical two-story house, where I enjoyed meals of fresh fruit and fruit juices, meats and fish, and lots of pastries.

The playground construction proceeded slowly. I enjoyed working with the volunteers in the hot sun, even though we could not understand each other, and I was frustrated by strange wood sizes and properties. On my last day building the playground, it rained all day. I didn't get to finish the playground, but I know the volunteers completed it, with the exception of the plastic slide. We could never find one in Brazil, so I am sending one from the United States.

My visit to Stete Lagoas, Brazil, was a once-in-a-lifetime experience. The children at the Andre Luiz School will enjoy the playground, the volunteers are proud of our accomplishment, and I will always remember the new friends I met.

bell and Frost's contemporary playground had a boat, a houselike enclosure for dramatic play, and loose parts for construction activity, whereas the contemporary playground in the Hart and Sheehan study contained none of these features. The reader will note that loose parts are a feature of the traditional playground in one study (Hart & Sheehan, 1986) and a feature of the contemporary playground in the other study (Campbell & Frost, 1985). Because of the diversity within playground categories, it may be more profitable to focus on specific playground features—types of equipment and how that equipment is arranged—rather than to compare broad types of playgrounds (Wardle, 1983). Specific playground design features are discussed later in this chapter.

ADVENTURE PLAYGROUNDS *Adventure playgrounds* are play spaces that use the natural environment and an assortment of discarded materials as their equipment. They differ from the previously described types of playgrounds in several important respects. The structures, except for storage sheds and perhaps a clubhouse, are temporary. The children build, tear down, and rebuild their own play structures. More natural materials are available, such as mud, ponds, gardens, fire pits; animals often inhabit the area. There are many more loose parts for children to manipulate: lumber, crates, rope, cable reels, tires, hammers, nails, and saws and other old tools. A much wider variety of activities are permitted, including building, tearing down, fires, cooking, digging, and mud sliding. Finally, there is always at least one adult, called a play leader, who supervises and facilitates the play.

Adventure playgrounds originated in Denmark in 1943 and became very popular in England after World War II. Bombed-out city blocks provided an ideal setting for these junk playgrounds (Frost, 1992). This type of playground has slowly gained a foothold in the United States. The American Adventure Playground Association was founded in 1974, and by 1982, adventure playgrounds were located in at least 25 American cities (Vance, 1982).

Advantages of adventure playgrounds include the tremendous diversity of activities that are available, the flexibility created by all the loose parts in the environment, the sense of competence and responsibility instilled in children as a result of being able to build and shape their own environment, the skills that are learned in the process of building structures, and the sustained interest generated by children being constantly challenged. Not surprisingly, research has shown that children engage in a far greater variety of activities on adventure playgrounds and that this type of playground is much more popular with children than either traditional or creative/contemporary designs (e.g., Hayward, Rothenberg, & Beasley, 1974).

Unfortunately, several disadvantages also exist. First of all, adventure playgrounds tend to be unsightly, causing some neighbors to object to their presence. This problem can sometimes be alleviated by building high fences around the area. Adventure playgrounds are also relatively expensive, at least in the long run. Start-up costs are not high, but the salaries of play leaders are a continuing expense. Finally, the worst drawback concerns liability. On the surface, adventure playgrounds appear to be very dangerous, with their open fires, ponds, loose nails, and sharp tools. Fears of injury and resulting litigation, coupled with the high cost of liability insurance, have caused many a city official to have second thoughts about establishing adventure playgrounds. It is somewhat ironic that an impressive array of evidence from the United States, England, and Europe indicates that adventure playgrounds are no more dangerous than traditional playgrounds (Frost, 1992; Vance, 1982), due no doubt to the constant supervision of play leaders. As long as adventure playgrounds are perceived as dangerous, they are going to be very difficult to establish in this country, but the important advantages offered by this type of play setting make such an undertaking well worth the effort.

PLAYGROUND DESIGN FEATURES

Attempts have recently been made to identify the specific properties of playgrounds that hold children's interest and lead to a wide range of play. While this area of research is still in its infancy, several design features appear to be associated with high levels of play: linkages, flexible materials, graduated challenge, a wide variety of experiences, and promotion of different types of play (Dattner, 1974). These five features are related to the amount of diversity and complexity that a playground has to offer. *Diversity* concerns the different types of experiences that a setting offers and is related to getting children initially started in play. The more play options that are available, the more likely children are to engage in play. *Complexity* refers to the number and variety of responses that a particular piece of play equipment elicits (Ellis, 1984). The more complex a piece of equipment is, the more children can do with it. Complexity determines how long objects can keep children's attention once they start playing with them.

LINKAGES One of the best ways to increase the complexity of individual pieces of playground equipment is to link them. A lot more can be done with a platform, slide, and tire net when they are connected together than when they stand in isolation. Linkage has the additional advantage of promoting a continuous movement from one activity to another. It also gets children together in a central location, promoting social interaction. These advantages of linkage are supported by research. Bruya (1985), for example, found that preschoolers spent more time playing on wooden platforms when the structures were linked together rather than separated. The linked arrangement also resulted in more social contacts among the children.

Most creative/contemporary playgrounds rate highly on this feature. In Figure 9.4, note how the structures are linked together in several clusters and how the separate play areas are connected by the concrete pathway. Traditional playgrounds, on the other hand, are characterized by widely scattered, isolated pieces of equipment. Linkages are not inherent in adventure playgrounds because the structures are built by the children themselves. However, experience has shown that children often link together the structures they build on these playgrounds (e.g., see the photos in Frost & Klein, 1979, pp. 209–214).

FLEXIBLE MATERIALS *Flexibility* refers to the extent to which materials can be manipulated, combined, and changed. The more flexible the material, the more children can do with it. Flexibility is therefore directly related to complexity and play materials' ability to hold children's interest.

The static, single-use pieces of equipment found on traditional playgrounds are very low in flexibility. Sand and water, found in many creative/contemporary and adventure playgrounds, represent the other extreme. These materials are infinitely manipulable. Adventure playgrounds have the additional advantage of having a number of loose parts (e.g., pieces of wood, tires, ropes, tools, pieces of pipe) which children can use in a multitude of different ways. According to the "theory of loose parts" espoused by Nicholson (1974, p. 223), "In any environment, both the degree of inventiveness and creativity, and the possibility of discovery, are directly proportional to the number of and kind of variables in it." Loose parts allow children to impose their own meaning and structure on the environment, making the environment more responsive to children. Because adventure playgrounds have more loose parts, they are the definite leader with respect to flexible materials. Creative/contemporary playgrounds that feature sand, water, and a number of loose parts also rate highly in terms of flexibility.

A study by Weilbacher (1981) sheds additional light on the flexibility issue. She examined differences in how children played when the same equipment was either movable or immovable. Although the study was set on an indoor stage, the gross-motor equipment was the type commonly found on playgrounds. The nonmovable equipment was called "static" because the children could not manipulate or change the pieces of the apparatus, while movable equipment was termed "dynamic" because youngsters could disassemble the pieces and use them in many different ways throughout the play area. Analysis of videotapes revealed that children in the static environment often used the equipment in unique ways (e.g., climbing up a ladder backward) but then eventually abandoned the equipment altogether and played social games such as "ring-around-the-rosie." In contrast, children in the dynamic environment discovered that the movable equipment suggested alternative uses in pretend play (e.g., turning the ladder over and using it as if it were a car), which led to more cooperative behavior. Weilbacher concluded that the loose parts of the dynamic environment fostered a variety of sociodramatic play episodes dependent on the equipment, whereas the social games occurring in the static environment were independent of the equipment. She noted that both types of environments provide valuable play opportunities.

GRADUATED CHALLENGE *Graduated challenge* involves presenting several levels of difficulty for each activity. It ensures that developmentally appropriate activities are available for children of varying ages and abilities. A playground should have simple challenges for very young children, such as low things to climb and short slides with gentle inclines. There should also be bigger challenges for older children, such as higher platforms, rope ladders, and longer, steeper slides. Graduated challenge enables each child to find an optimal level of challenge—not too easy or too difficult—that leads to mastery of new skills and calls forth new learning (Wardle, 1990).

Lack of graduated challenge is one of the major problems with traditional playgrounds. Such playgrounds usually have only one size of each type of equipment and therefore offer only one level of challenge. This level is too difficult for some children, causing them either to avoid playing on the equipment or to risk accidents. It is too easy for others, resulting in boredom or inappropriate use. If playground equipment does not provide a range of challenges, older children are tempted to increase the challenge level of the equipment by using it in an unsafe manner (e.g., swinging crookedly, climbing up slides backward, walking on top of the monkey bars). This can lead to serious injury.

Most creative/contemporary playgrounds rate highly on graduated challenge. The linked structures on these playgrounds usually provide at least two levels of challenge. In Figure 9.4, for example, note that there are actually two separate playgrounds, each with its own level of challenge. The main structure for 2- and 3-year-olds has a low platform, a gently inclined ramp, and short stairs, whereas the main structure for the 4- and 5-year-olds has much higher platforms, taller ladders, a slide, and a tire net. The latter structure also has a ramp and stairs for less experienced players.

Adventure playgrounds also rate highly on graduated challenge. Because children construct their own structures, they can adjust the structures to fit their needs and abilities.

VARIETY OF EXPERIENCES   *Variety* refers to the number of different types of activities available in the playground. As mentioned earlier, diversity is needed to initially catch children's attention and get play started. A large number of different activities ensures that children will find activities that suit their momentary interests. In addition, variety enhances the learning potential of the environment. Richard Dattner (as cited by Frost & Klein, 1979, p. 196) explains:

> A playground should be like a small-scale replica of the world, with as many as possible of the sensory experiences to be found in the world included in it. Experiences for every sense are needed, for instance: rough and smooth objects to look at and feel; light and heavy things to pick up; water and wet materials as well as dry things . . . things that make sounds (running water) or that can be struck, plucked, plinked, etc.; smells of all varieties (flowers, bark, mud). . . . The list is inexhaustible, and the larger the number of items on it that are included, the richer and more varied the environment will be for the child.

Adventure playgrounds obviously offer the greatest variety of experiences, but creative/contemporary playgrounds with running water, sandboxes, hills, and gardens can come in a close second (see Figure 9.4). Traditional playgrounds, with their single-use equipment, are extremely deficient with regard to this feature.

PROMOTING DIFFERENT TYPES OF PLAY   Ideally, playgrounds should provide opportunities for all types of play. A variety of exercise equipment is needed to promote gross-motor play and to develop strength, balance, and coordination (Wardle, 1988). Loose parts and natural materials—sand, pieces of wood, small rocks—are needed to encourage constructive play. Enclosed, houselike structures and elevated forts encourage dramatic play (Wardle, 1990). Finally, some equipment should foster social interaction and group play. Three types of equipment are ideal for this purpose: (1) linked platforms, which allow children to congregate and watch others play; (2) equipment such as wide slides and tire swivel swings, which can be used by several children at a time; and (3) equipment that requires more than one child to work effectively, such as seesaws and swings.

Traditional playgrounds rate very low on this feature, providing only for gross-motor play, whereas adventure playgrounds rate the highest, providing for all types of play. Not only do adventure playgrounds offer many opportunities for exercise and dramatic play, but also the loose parts and tools encourage lots of constructive play activity. Creative/contemporary playgrounds are in the middle, having structures that encourage both

Table 9.3   PLAYGROUND DESIGN FEATURES

	TRADITIONAL	CREATIVE/ CONTEMPORARY*	ADVENTURE
LINKAGES	−	++	+
FLEXIBLE MATERIALS	−	+	++
GRADUATED CHALLENGE	−	+	+
VARIETY OF EXPERIENCES	−	+	++
TYPES OF PLAY PROMOTED			
FUNCTIONAL PLAY	++	+	+
CONSTRUCTIVE PLAY	−	+	++
DRAMATIC PLAY	−	+	++
GROUP PLAY	−	+	+

− = weakness. + = strength. ++ = major strength.

Assumes that the playground contains all of the positive features discussed in the text (e.g., sand, a variety of exercise equipment, a dramatic-play enclosure, wide slides, and platforms). Without these features, some of the "pluses" would change to "minuses."

gross-motor exercise and dramatic play (and constructive play if they contain loose parts). The playground illustrated in Figure 9.4 has three enclosed structures to encourage make-believe play: a house structure for the younger children and a house plus a tower for the older ones. A variety of exercise equipment is also available, including swings, ladders, tire nets, and tricycles (stored in the shed). It is important to note that playgrounds in this category vary widely and that some do not provide for diverse play experiences. Beckwith (1982) cautions, for example, that some commercial play structures consist primarily of linked decks, with few exercise apparatuses. Such structures do not provide for the exercise needs of growing children.

Table 9.3 summarizes how each playground type rates on the design features discussed here. Adventure playgrounds are clearly superior with respect to these criteria, with creative/contemporary playgrounds a close second. Given the difficulties associated with establishing and maintaining adventure playgrounds in this country, creative/contemporary playgrounds are probably best suited for most schools and communities. These playgrounds can be made more effective by incorporating some of the key features of adventure playgrounds. For example, adding loose parts will greatly increase the complexity of the setting and will provide a stimulus for constructive play. Another desirable feature is the constant presence and supervision of a play leader needed with all types of playgrounds if they are to be truly safe. An adult should always be available to assist and encourage children in their play endeavors and to prevent equipment from being used inappropriately and unsafely.

CRITERIA FOR PLANNING OPTIMAL OUTDOOR PLAY ENVIRONMENTS

Good playgrounds increase the intensity of children's play and encourage a wide range of play behaviors—physical play, social play, constructive play, and games with rules (Wardle, 1997b). Adventure playgrounds are ideally suited for achieving these goals, but well-designed creative/contemporary playgrounds can also provide children with enriched, diverse play experiences. The following criteria, drawn from a series of articles by Wardle (1988, 1990, 1997a, 1997b), specify the components of an optimal outdoor play environment.

SURFACES Playgrounds should feature different surfaces to promote safety and different types of play:

- Flat, grassy, or dirt areas—Quick-moving activities, such as running, chasing, and follow-the-leader games, require a great deal of open space and a relatively soft surface to cushion falls. Large, open spaces of grass are ideal. Open dirt areas provide the space for these physical forms of play but are more apt to cause injuries when children trip or fall. If grass is not available, gym mats can be placed on selected areas to provide a soft surface for rolling, crawling, and hopping.
- Hard surfaces—Bikes, wagons, and scooters move best on concrete or asphalt surfaces. Children can learn about stop signs, pedestrian walkways, and parking areas when they use these "roads." Hard surfaces can also serve as walkways that lead to different play areas, as surfaces for art activities and ball games, and as access to the playground for children with wheelchairs.
- Fall zones—A soft, absorbent surface (sand, pea gravel, wood chips, wood fiber, rubber mats and tiles, or continuous poured rubber) should be placed under all equipment and should extend 6 feet beyond the edge of the equipment (see the Theory in Action feature "Playground Safety Guidelines").

AREAS AND EQUIPMENT Playgrounds should contain a variety of equipment and areas to promote a wide range of play behavior:

1. Physical play

   - Structures for climbing, such as rope and tire nets, ladders, steps, monkey bars, and horizontal tire swings
   - Areas for balancing, such as balance beams and short posts or car tires set into the ground
   - Equipment for grabbing and grasping, such as swing chains, railings, ladder rings, and tools for playing in the sand
   - Areas for crawling, such as tunnels or highway culverts
   - Things to push and carry, such as swings, trikes, wagons, large trucks, and wheeled sand toys
   - Areas for digging, such as sandboxes
   - Equipment for jumping, such as balance beams surrounded by sand or low platforms and steps with an absorbent material underneath

Theory in Action

PLAYGROUND SAFETY GUIDELINES

FRANCIS WARDLE

Playground safety has become a very important issue in this country. There are two basic reasons for this development: real safety concerns, and liability costs. Currently, more than 200,000 playground-related injuries are reported on U.S. playgrounds every year. A study of playground-equipment-related injuries treated in U.S. hospital emergency rooms documented that most of these accidents were caused by children falling off equipment onto hard surfaces (Tinsworth & Kramer, 1990). Other accidents were caused by entanglement of clothing and rope, head entrapments, swings hitting children, protrusions, pinch points, sharp edges, hot surfaces, and trash on playgrounds (U.S. Consumer Product Safety Commission, 1991). These accidents are a concern for all people involved with children. They also cost child-care providers, schools, and playground manufacturers a great deal of money. Litigation tends to follow the "deep-pocket rule": The higher the company's or agency's insurance coverage, the more likely it is to be sued.

To address hazards that result in injury, death, and expensive legal settlements, safety guidelines for U.S. playgrounds have been developed:

1. *U.S. Consumer Products Safety Commission Handbook.* This is the most popular and user-friendly set of safety guidelines. The handbook covers the ages of 2 to 12 years, broken down as 2- to 5-year-olds and 5- to 12-year-olds. Equipment covered includes swings, climbing structures, ladders, slides, upper-body equipment, merry-go-rounds, and spring animals. Installation and maintenance are addressed, as are overall design and fall zones (areas under equipment that provide a safe fall). While the U.S. Consumer Products Safety Commission (CPSC) insists that these are guidelines, they are, in reality, being adopted by most licensing agencies and have become the legal standard for lawsuits. To get a copy of the CPSC guidelines, request them from any major playground equipment company, or phone 800-638-2772.

2. *ASTM Guidelines.* The American Society for Testing and Materials (1995) has developed the *Standard Consumer Safety Performance Specifications for Playground Equipment for Public Use.* To a large extent, this is a technical, and more detailed, version of the aforementioned CPSC handbook. Like the handbook, the ASTM guidelines also cover children 2 to 12 years old. It differs in that it is

(continued)

Theory in Action *(continued)*

industry driven, rather than government developed, and is preferred by playground manufacturers. Standards are currently being developed for indoor play equipment and for play settings for children under age 2 years.

3. *National Program of Playground Safety.* The National Program of Playground Safety (1995) was established to help communities address issues of playground safety. A national action plan was developed, which utilizes existing national, state, and local organizations to implement these goals: (a) to design age-appropriate playgrounds, (b) to provide proper surfacing under and around equipment, (c) to provide proper supervision of playgrounds, and (d) to properly maintain playgrounds.

In addition, many organizations concerned with children's safety, such as the American Academy of Pediatrics (1994) and the Association for Childhood Education International (Frost & Drescher, 1995), have created playground safety brochures for parents and teachers.

2. Social play

- Equipment that requires or encourages the participation of two or more children, such as trikes, wagons, balls, jumpropes, large wooden crates, sandboxes, swivel swings, and traditional swings
- Spacious decks and secluded areas that encourage children to congregate and chat

3. Constructive play

- Sandbox and sand equipment, such as shovels and rakes
- Woodworking bench, tools, pieces of wood, and fasteners such as nails, bolts, and nuts
- Loose parts, such as tires, cable spools, wooden or plastic crates, large wooden or plastic blocks, and odd lengths of wooden boards
- Art activities, including painting, clay, crafts, and large colored chalk for sidewalks
- Garden plot, gardening tools, and seeds

4. Dramatic play

- Generic-shape buildings and enclosures that can be used as houses, forts, ships, airplanes, schools, and doctor offices
- Dramatic props that can be brought from the classroom (see Chapter 10), along with materials that are better kept outside (carpentry tools, etc.)

5. Games with rules

- Balls, jump ropes, and other game equipment
- Hard surfaces to play games on
- Chalk for drawing boundaries and configurations

MATERIALS Modern playgrounds are made of pressure-treated pine, redwood, laminated plywood, polyethylene plastic, painted or coated metal, recycled plastic, fiberglass, or a combination of these materials. Table 9.4 presents the advantages and disadvantages of each of these materials.

Does color matter? Research suggests that children are chiefly attracted by what they can do with a piece of equipment (Campbell & Frost, 1985). Even if children are attracted by bright colors, this initial interest will quickly fade if the equipment fails to challenge and excite them, so the question of color is really a question of adult, rather than child, preference (Wardle, 1997b).

SAFETY Because of the high rate of playground injuries and the growing threat of litigation, safety is an issue that needs to be given high priority when designing and building outdoor play environments. Except for state licensing requirements (which differ from state to state), there are not overall federal safety regulations for playgrounds. The Consumer Product Safety Commission (CPSC) and the American Society for Testing Materials (ASTM) guidelines are used by many programs and licensing departments and are followed by most manufacturers (see the Theory in Action feature "Playground Safety Guidelines," cited previously).

The following playground safety guidelines, drawn from the CPSC (U.S. CPSC, 1991) and ASTM (1995) documents, apply to playgrounds designed for children ages 18 months to 12 years:

- Provide absorbent surfaces under all equipment. This fall zone should extend 6 feet beyond all equipment (farther for slide exits and swings).
- Avoid parts that can pinch or crush fingers.
- Avoid openings (rings, nets, windows, railings, steps, etc.) between 3 1/2" and 9" so that children's heads cannot be entrapped.
- Avoid sharp edges and angles less than 55 degrees, which can entrap parts of children's bodies.
- All "S" hooks must be closed.
- Avoid heavy metal, wood, or hard plastic swings.
- Include no more than two swings in any swing structure.
- All slides must have at least 4" sides and an exit parallel to the ground.
- Prevent having any exposed screws, nails, bolts, pieces of metal, or protruding pipes, especially on slide entrances.
- All concrete footings must be below ground level.
- Except for entrances and exits, all surfaces 2' or more above the ground must have railings.
- Avoid using cables, wires, and rope between equipment or to hold up trees. If rope is used, it must be attached at both ends, to avoid strangulation.

Table 9.4   ADVANTAGES AND DISADVANTAGES OF VARIOUS PLAYGROUND MATERIALS

ADVANTAGES	DISADVANTAGES
WOOD (CCA PINE, REDWOOD)	
• Easy to use	• Splinters, cracks, and splits
• Well-suited for volunteer construction	• Burns
• Looks natural	• Soon looks weathered
• Easy to repair	• Requires a lot of maintenance
• Easy to attach elements (slides, handles, climbers)	• Does not last as long as other materials
• Relatively inexpensive	• Does not look upscale
• Lends itself well to creative designs	
• Often can get donated materials	
LAMINATED PLYWOOD (PAINTED COMMERCIALLY)	
• Very colorful paint choices	• Can chip and deteriorate more quickly than plastic and metal
• Good for flat surfaces	• Restricted to flat designs
• Easier to use for infant/toddler pieces	• Expensive
• Can be repaired	• Only available in bright colors
• A natural material that lasts	
POLYETHYLENE PLASTIC	
• Does not get hot	• Colors fade with time
• Has no splinters	• Overuse makes the playground look like a new-car salesroom
• Initially bright	• Limited number of uses and possibilities
• Shapes are safe (e.g., a curved slide)	• Expensive
• Structurally strong if used with metal	• Unitized manufacturing method limits challenge and variety
• Smooth and friendly to hold	
• Lasts a long time	
STEEL OR ALUMINUM (COATED, PAINTED, OR UNTREATED)	
• Strong	• Slides become very hot and should not be used
• Lasts a long time	• Posts and railings get hot
• Large choice of paint colors	• Has no resiliency, so children are more likely to be hurt when they fall against metal
• Offers a variety of options	• Difficult to repair or add
• Resists vandalism	• Expensive

Source: Reprinted from Playgrounds: Questions to consider when selecting equipment, by Francis Wardle. Dimensions of Early Childhood, Winter 1997.

- Avoid metal slides in hot climates.
- Provide ample safety zones for traffic areas where children will travel.
- Swings should not be attached to other pieces of equipment, such as platforms.
- A playground should only be used by children for whom it is designed. Children who are too young can have serious accidents; those who are too old tend to use equipment inappropriately and get hurt.
- Provide regular repair and maintenance.

As our knowledge about the dangers of ultraviolet radiation exposure grows and children spend more time in organized care, shade on playgrounds is becoming a critical safety issue (Rivkin, 1995). We recommend that playgrounds be equipped with shade structures, awnings, or trees to reduce exposure to the sun and the resulting risk of skin cancer. All children should avoid excessive exposure to the sun between 11 a.m. and 2 p.m. Children with sensitive skin should avoid the sun between 10 a.m. and 3 p.m.

SUPERVISION   Adult supervision is a key to playground safety. The Consumer Product Safety Commission's in-depth study of 54 playground injuries revealed that an adult was present in only 4 instances (Frost, 1992). In the 1996 brochure "Playgrounds: Keeping Outdoor Learning Safe," the National Association for the Education of Young Children emphasizes the need for adult supervision of playgrounds:

> The play area should be monitored by adults with a knowledge of injury prevention and first aid. Their responsibilities include scanning equipment, gates, and surfaces before children enter to check for stray animals, broken objects, or other hazards. Adults should set reasonable, appropriate rules for what children may do, such as sit down on the slide or wear sneakers to climb on the monkey bars.

In addition to scanning for hazards and setting basic rules, adult supervisors also need to help keep the peace on playgrounds, taking steps to minimize fighting and bullying (Rivkin, 1995). One important step is to learn to distinguish rough-and-tumble play, which is usually harmless, from true aggression, in which children can get hurt. Research indicates that teachers have difficulty distinguishing the two behaviors and have a tendency to overestimate the amount of aggression that occurs on school playgrounds (Schaefer & Smith, 1996). As a result, some teachers waste a lot of time and effort trying to stop relatively harmless rough-and-tumble play—an activity that appears to be beneficial for younger boys' social development (Pellegrini, 1995). For more information about play fighting, see the Theory in Action feature "Rough-and Tumble Play: Some Issues" in Chapter 3.

Increasing attention is being focused on the problem of bullies and their victims (Smith & Thompson, 1991). There appear to be two sets of causes for these unfortunate relationships: (1) the bullies' aggressive tendencies and lack of social skills, and (2) the victims' nonassertive behavior. Playground supervision can help reduce bully/victim problems. A study in Bergen, Norway, found a strong negative correlation (−.45) between teacher density during recess and bullying incidents (Olweus, 1993). With help from Olweus (1993), teachers in the Norwegian schools developed a comprehensive plan to combat bullying. Steps included these:

- Developing clear rules against bullying behavior
- Teacher conferences with bullies, victims, and their parents
- Using group-process strategies, including class discussions, role playing, and conflict-resolution programs, to get the whole school involved in the effort to end bullying
- Assigning a neutral, well-adjusted student to provide support for victims
- Teaching victims how to assert themselves in class

The program has been very successful, resulting in a marked decrease in bully/victim problems.

Playground supervisors also need to know when not to intervene in play. Frost (1992) points out that there is a fine line between positive teacher supervision of play and overzealous supervision that stifles children's play. Too many rules and too much teacher intervention can inhibit risk taking that leads to discovery and growth. Teachers need to take active steps to remove hazards, prohibit overtly dangerous activities, and stop bullying, but the rest of the time, they should step back and let children play on their own. A well-designed playground minimizes the need for rules and overzealous supervision.

Wardle (1990) recommends that playgrounds include such features as hills and tunnels, which can provide temporary separation of children from adults. He explains:

> While all playgrounds must provide easy access for adults to respond to children in trouble, or to children who genuinely want adult assistance, children need to be sufficiently removed from adults to make mistakes, risk, fall, be clumsy, be silly, engage in trial and error, and try something very new without the interference of adults. Children delight in the freedom and power to act independently, while keeping security—adults—safely in sight. (p. 33)

ADAPTATIONS FOR CHILDREN WITH SPECIAL NEEDS The intent of the Americans with Disabilities Act (ADA) is that children with physical disabilities have access to playgrounds and equipment. Whenever possible, these children should have play opportunities similar to those of children without disabilities. With a few alterations, playgrounds can offer a variety of play options and physical challenges for children with specials needs, without reducing their use or safety for children without disabilities:

- Provide wide gates and pathways (44 inches) and cuts in curbs to provide access to various parts of the playground for children in wheelchairs and those with impaired walking ability (Goltsman, Gilbert, & Wohlford, 1993).
- Line pathways with Braille markers for visually impaired children.
- Adapt basic equipment, such as decks and bridges, with additional railings for support.

- Use solid fall-zone materials, or place mats over fall zones to provide access to children in wheelchairs.
- Construct transition points (a 15″ to 17″ high step) so that children can safely move from a wheelchair to pieces of playground equipment (Goltsman et al., 1993).
- Place equipment for dramatic play, such as dramatic-play panels and steering wheels, at ground level.
- Install special swing seats to swing a child in a wheelchair.
- Construct monkey bars, a rope, or a metal bar over a smooth surface to provide a pulling activity for a child in a wheelchair.
- Raise sand tables 30″, with adequate knee space to allow a child in a wheelchair to pull under the tables (Goltsman et al., 1993).
- Make sure that adaptations for handicapped children do not pose safety hazards for their nonhandicapped peers.

NEIGHBORHOOD AND NATURAL PLAY HABITATS

The basic environment for many young children has changed dramatically in recent years, shifting from the freedom to explore neighborhoods and natural areas such as woods and rivers to an environment dominated by fear (of kidnapping, gang violence, and automobile accidents), parent fatigue, organized sports, and passive watching of TV (Rivkin, 1995; Wardle, 1995). As a result, children's access to outdoor play and nature has been severely reduced.

As a result of this loss of access to natural areas, children today know less about nature and have more difficulty developing empathy for the environment (Rivkin, 1995). Limitations on neighborhood play in urban areas also exact a price:

> The outdoor world is where things happen. In addition to natural events, outdoors is where fire trucks scream and race, where cranes dig deep holes, where doors open to new kind of buildings, where gas is put in cars and bike tires are pumped. It is where one learns to cross streets and go into stores and spend an allowance or to poke through neighbors' intriguing curbside castoffs. . . . All of these important learnings and more are in the outdoors. When children are inside or in cars, they miss out on such experiences. (p. 14)

Efforts are currently underway to restore safe outdoor play opportunities for children. Rivkin (1995) describes some of the most promising of these undertakings:

- Greenways—"corridors of protected open space" that connect parks, playgrounds, nature reserves, rivers, and historic sites with each other and with people's homes
- Urban initiatives—projects, such as the "Revitalizing Baltimore Program," that attempt to make cities safer and better places to live and play
- "Child-aware" land development—planned communities that set aside undeveloped "wild areas" for children to play

- "Calming traffic"—altering roads (narrowing, adding trees and other plantings, lowering speed limits) to reduce traffic speed and to make streets safer for play.

In addition, Wardle (1995) stresses the need for urban schools to provide children with regular trips to outdoor environments that allow children to explore nature and to learn basic information about the natural world. Some of these places, such as botanical gardens and river embankments, may be within walking distance from school. Others—forests, wetlands, working farms, old quarries—often require bus transportation.

SUMMARY

Research indicates that several features of indoor play settings have an impact on play patterns. Spatial density affects the social level of children's play, particularly when there is less than 25 square feet of space available per child. Such crowded conditions should be avoided. The arrangement of space is another important variable. Partitioning large, open areas into smaller areas is usually beneficial. However, it appears that openings should be kept between complementary centers such as the block and housekeeping areas. Other recommendations for room arrangement include separating conflicting activity centers, clearly delineating different play areas, and maintaining clear pathways through the classroom.

Several design features of playgrounds have been found to encourage rich, diverse play. These features include linkages, flexible materials, graduated challenge, a wide variety of experiences, and provisions for all types of play. Adventure playgrounds rate highest in terms of these criteria, and creative/contemporary playgrounds come in a close second. Traditional steel-and-asphalt playgrounds, on the other hand, rate poorly on all of these features. We hope that as the shortcomings of the traditional design become increasingly apparent, these playgrounds will be replaced with creative/contemporary or adventure playgrounds.

The chapter ended with a discussion of children's reduced access to outdoor play in neighborhoods and natural areas. Promising efforts are currently underway to reverse this trend, including greenways, urban initiatives, "child-aware" land development, calming traffic, and field trips to natural areas.

Chapter 10

PLAY MATERIALS

Cassie, at two years and two months of age, takes her puzzle making seriously. She selects a six-piece shape puzzle and commences working on it by lining up all six pieces in sequence. She then inserts them into the corresponding spaces. She chatters away in mumbled speech with an occasional intelligible word ("circle"). She completes the puzzle three times before she applauds her success and puts the puzzle away on the puzzle shelf.

(Maldonado, 1996, p. 4) ■

When one thinks of play, toys inevitably come to mind. This is because most forms of play are closely linked with toys and other types of play materials:

- In functional play, children pound, push, roll, bounce, and otherwise manipulate a variety of toys and playthings.
- Constructive play involves using blocks, building sets, or other materials to build things.
- In dramatic play, objects become props to support make-believe stories, or in the case of action figures, toys become the actors.
- Many games involve materials such as cards, dice, or balls.

This toy-related activity accounts for much of children's play time. Research has shown that at home, children spend an average of 4 hours a day playing with manufactured toys, household objects, and natural materials such as mud and sticks (Giddings & Halverson, 1981). At school, the proportion of time spent interacting with playthings may be even higher. One study of British preschools found that 97% of children's free-play activity involved some kind of play material (Tizard, Philps, & Plewis, 1976).

Parents and educators recognize the toy–play relationship and spend billions of dollars per year keeping children well supplied with play materials. In the United States, more than 800 companies sell 150,000 different kinds of toys, with total retail sales of more than $20 billion in 1996 (Sutton-Smith, 1986; Toy Manufacturers of America, 1996). These firms employ 60,000 people and consume about 250,000 tons of plastic and 200,000 tons of metal (Sutton-Smith, 1986). Toys are important not only for children's play, but also for the American economy!

This chapter begins with a brief discussion of the two-way relationship between playthings and child development. We then describe the different types of play materials that are available. Research on the effects of materials on play is then briefly reviewed, followed by a discussion of factors to be considered when selecting toys and play materials for children. The chapter concludes with an examination of electronic media such as computer toys and video games.

PLAY MATERIALS AND CHILD DEVELOPMENT

A two-way relationship exists between play materials and children's development. Play materials indirectly influence development by affecting the type of play in which children engage and the content of their play. Play materials may also directly affect development by providing opportunities for learning. At the same time, children's individual characteristics, such as age, developmental level, and play styles, have an effect on how particular materials are used in play.

While there is scant evidence that toys and play materials have a direct effect on development (Almqvist, 1994; Sutton-Smith, 1985), we do know that certain types of materials tend to elicit specific forms of play. Materials such as blocks, tinkertoys, and Legos® inspire constructive play, whereas dolls, dress-up clothes, and housekeeping props encourage make-believe. Materials can also affect the social quality of play, with some encouraging solitary play and others group play. Play materials can therefore *indirectly* affect children's growth by stimulating developmentally important types of play. Later in this chapter, we examine research data on how materials influence play patterns and suggest how adults can use this information to encourage specific forms of play.

It is also quite likely that children learn important concepts while playing with toys and other play materials. For example, when a toddler engages in repetitive functional play with a rubber ball, the child assimilates the ball to action schemes that he or she already possesses (e.g., rolling). At the same time, the child must also change or accommodate those actions to fit the characteristics of the object. In our example, the child's movements are adjusted to the size and weight of the ball. As specified by Piagetian theory, intelligent adaptation takes place, and intellectual growth occurs.

Such causal relationships have been very difficult to prove, in part because so many factors affect children's learning. For example, Bradley (1985) found a moderate correlation between children's IQ scores and the availability and use of toys. However, part of this correlation appeared to reflect the influence of family social status and parental encouragement of development. In spite of these difficulties, common sense dictates that if children spend time interacting with various play materials, some learning is bound to occur (Sutton-Smith, 1986).

Belief in the developmental significance of toys has led to the establishment of toy libraries to assist children with special needs (see the Theory in Action feature Chapter 6, "Lekotek") and those at risk of academic and/or social difficulties. The Theory in Action feature "Damaia Toy Library" describes an exemplary program that has been established to assist children in one of the poorest neighborhoods in Lisbon, Portugal.

Children's development also influences how specific play materials are used by children. Because 1- and 2-year-old children are in the sensorimotor stage of development (see Table 1.3), their play with materials tends to be limited to practice or functional play (repeated physical movements). For example, a toddler would play with a toy car by rolling it around the room. As children reach preschool age and enter the preoperational stage of development, their play shifts from functional to constructive and dramatic. In the process,

Theory in Action

DAMAIA TOY LIBRARY

ANA MARIA ARAÚJO PESSANHA

In Damaia (Amadora), a suburban area near Lisbon, tall apartment buildings stand alongside very poor wooden huts. This area does not have a single playground or any green space, and pedestrian areas are nonexistent. Two groups of people live in this area: (1) low-middle-class white Portuguese people, normally living in small flats; and (2) very poor, mostly black, Cape Verde Island natives who live in wooden huts made of refuse materials and old tires.

With a grant from the Gulbenkian Foundation, Damaia's Local Community Administrative Council created a toy library in 1987, to serve the play needs of the Damaia children. The main objective of this playroom was to promote children's mental, social, and cognitive development by providing them with opportunities to play together freely in safe, enriched environment.

The toy library was originally housed in a room in the community's administrative building, but now it occupies the basement of a new building in a space not shared with any other activity. The playroom contains a wide variety of play materials, organized into separate play areas:

- *Doll house corner* with dolls, doll-size furniture, and accessories
- *Doctor's kit* with scissors, stethoscope, tape, gauze, tubes, and so on
- *Dress-up corner* with large mirror, dress chest, old fashioned dresses, costumes, handbags, photo camera, and so on
- *Game area* with cards, dominoes, puzzles, magnetic fishpond, matching cubes, tops, lotto, marbles, and so on
- *Garage corner* with petrol pump, filling station, miniature cars, trucks, taxis, sport cars, buses, police cars, fire engines, trains, rails, railway tracks, and so on
- *Construction toys*—blocks of different sizes, Legos®, wooden colored blocks, rectangular and cylindrical blocks, trucks with blocks, cubes, human figures, and so on
- *Post-office theme area* with letters, stamps, envelopes, stickers, small labels, small mailbox, telephone, pen, pencil, rubber stamps, mail canceller, and so on
- *Miniature farm* with farm house, stall, fences, corral, farm truck, trees, human figures, animals, and so on
- *Miniature zoo* with trees, hills, and animal and human figures
- *Grocery store* with cash register, money, scales, small market cart, blackboard, fruit, vegetables (e.g., potatoes), bread, cheese, eggs, empty food boxes and containers, and so on
- *Puppet* collection

(continued)

Theory in Action *(continued)*

The toy library provides the opportunity for children's free play in its main playroom and also gives the possibility to all schools of the area to use this facility and to borrow toys from it. Taking into account public demand, the toy library has a very flexible schedule. The timetable is published as early as possible, and it is known by the community and in all the schools. Every 3 months, all the interested teachers have the opportunity to request and make a reservation. Normally, teachers visit the playroom once a month with their students. The toy library is also open for free visits twice a week, and children are always welcome.

Ten years after its creation, we have reached the conclusion that children's play behavior in the toy library is different from that shown in schools. Their play is more elaborate, more imaginative, and more social. Thus, the toy library provides children with enriched play experiences that are beneficial for their development. In addition, teachers have the opportunity of discovering new positive aspects about their students.

the role of play materials changes. Children begin to use objects to stand for other things, gaining valuable experience with symbolic representation. While still cognizant of the physical properties of the materials with which they play, children are increasingly able to ignore these properties and to use the materials in any way they see fit. For example, 3-year-olds will tend to use a toy car as if it were a real car and to use it in car-related dramatic-play episodes. Four- and 5-year-olds are apt to use the same toy car as a "space ship" in conjunction with a Star Wars theme. As children grow older, play materials become increasingly subject to the requirements of their play (Sutton-Smith, 1986).

TYPES OF PLAY MATERIALS

In the sections that follow, we describe some of the many types of play materials that are currently available. Our list is not exhaustive by any means, but we have tried to include the types of materials most often found at home and at school. Electronic toys and video games are not included because they are discussed in a separate section at the end of this chapter. Several of our categories—educational toys, construction materials, gross-motor play materials—denote probable or intended uses of materials. As discussed in the previous section, however, children often ignore these intended uses and transform the toys to fit their play purposes. Sutton-Smith (1986, p. 251) warns that "whatever toys may have originally signified to their makers . . . when children play with them this signification is often destined to be betrayed."

REPLICA TOYS

Replica toys are miniature versions of larger objects in the child's physical and social environment. Some toys are replicas of real objects, such as houses, cars, and animals, while others are replicas of fantasy objects, such as space-ships and superheroes (X-Men, Ninja Turtles), which often have ties to television shows or movies. Because these play materials are miniatures, children can easily manipulate them and use them anywhere. In addition, these toys are very effective in encouraging dramatic play.

ANIMATE TOYS This group of toys represent animals, people, and creatures of all types and varieties. Usually, animate toys are made of plastic and are ideal as a base for both solitary and group make-believe play. Others, such as the perennially popular teddy bear, are made of plush material and designed for snuggling. Replicas of television, movie, and cartoon characters are extremely popular with children of all ages. Children usually endow these toys with life-like properties and use them as characters in dramatic play. This miniaturized type of dramatic play often remains popular with school-age children long after they have abandoned life-size dramatic play with child actors.

TRANSPORTATION TOYS *Transportation toys* include miniature trains, cars, trucks, wagons, ships, and trains. They appeal to children of all ages and come with many accessories (e.g., garages). As with animate toys, transportation toys are often used by children in "miniature" dramatic play, frequently in conjunction with structures and roadways made out of blocks.

DRAMATIC-PLAY PROPS This group of toys consists of miniature versions of objects that can be used in life-size dramatic play (i.e., play in which *children take on roles and act out stories*). Many of these toys are related to domestic, home-related themes and are commonly found in the housekeeping or home center of preschools and kindergartens. Toys in this group include

- Dolls and doll accessories
- Kitchen utensils—silverware, pots, pans, dishes
- Miniature tables, stoves, and refrigerators
- Toy irons, ironing boards, and brooms
- Baby carriages and cradles
- Toy phones
- Dress-up clothes

Commercial props and dress-up clothes are also available for a number of other themes, including medical, police, firefighting, post office, and grocery store. As mentioned in Chapter 9, these community helper and occupational themes expand children's play possibilities and often get more children, especially boys, involved in dramatic play.

It should be noted that many real-life objects can also be used as dramatic-play props. For example, a nonfunctional real phone can be as effective as, if not more so than, a toy phone in stimulating children to incorporate make-believe phone calls into their dramatizations. Utilization of nonfunctional real-life materials can greatly reduce the cost of equipping dramatic-play centers.

EDUCATIONAL TOYS

Educational play materials are manufactured by commercial toy companies to promote learning and development. Because these materials are designed to teach specific skills and concepts, they are more didactic, structured, and outcome oriented than other types of play materials. All areas of the curriculum, including reading, mathematics, science, and social studies are sources for skills taught by these materials. Examples of skills and concepts embedded in these materials include:

- Building part-to-whole relations
- Self-help skills such as tying shoelaces
- Recognizing colors and learning color names
- Arranging items by size
- Understanding one-to-one correspondence

Materials in this category include puzzles, stacking toys, stringing toys, nesting objects, and pegboards.

PUZZLES   Puzzles are usually designed to practice matching various shapes and sizes, developing one-to-one correspondence, and ultimately constructing part-to-whole relations. The most common type of puzzle for very young children is a formboard with removable inserts. Formboard puzzles are easily manipulated by toddlers because of the small number (from four to six pieces) and large size of the inserts. Knobs are often attached to the inserts to assist in manipulation. Maldonado (1996) provides the following general guidelines for formboard puzzles for different ages:

- 2-year-olds—knobbed puzzles with a complete figure (no pieces)
- 3-year-olds—knobbed puzzles with 5 to 8 pieces
- 4-year-olds—puzzles (knobless) with 12 to 18 pieces
- 5-year-olds—puzzles with 18 to 35 pieces
- 6-year-olds—puzzles with 35 to 62 pieces

Jigsaw puzzles are designed for older children. The pieces of a jigsaw are smaller than those used in formboard puzzles, and there are many more of them. For these reasons, jigsaws require more advanced small-motor skills and a higher level of conceptual development than formboard puzzles. Of course, jigsaws do vary in difficulty. Those intended for 5-year-old beginners may have as few as three to eight pieces and contain very simple pictures.

STACKING TOYS   These toys are designed to provide children with practice in ordering objects by size, from smallest to largest, or by color. Stacking toys help to teach children the concept of seriation and promote hand–eye coordination, as well.

STRINGING TOYS   There are many kinds of stringing sets, including objects made of wood, plastic, and metal. Stringing sets usually consist of a waxed cord and small pieces with their centers drilled out. Children put the cord through the centers of each of the pieces, thereby gaining practice in hand–eye coordination and in sequencing.

NESTING MATERIALS   These materials are designed to develop sequencing skills and an understanding of size relationships. The child's task is to order the pieces by size, one inside the other, in successive fashion. These toys provide a version of the game peekaboo. The child sees an object, inserts it in a larger one, and then watches it disappear from view. Nesting toys come with four or more pieces, in numerous shapes (eggs, matrushka dolls, kangaroos, etc.).

PEGBOARD SETS   This popular type of toy promotes recognition of shapes (e.g., square, circle), as well as hand–eye coordination. Children insert pegs into holes in the pegboard to copy patterns or to make original patterns of their own.

OTHER EXAMPLES   Other instructional materials include sorting games (arranging objects by one or more dimensions), templates (drawing around the outlines of various objects), locking games (opening and closing various items), button boards (matching buttons to button holes), shoelace boards (lacing and tying), and zippering boards (opening and closing).

CONSTRUCTION TOYS

Construction toys are open ended and can be used by children in numerous ways. Unlike educational toys, which have rather specific uses, construction materials have many possible uses. Legos®, for example, can be built, torn down, and rebuilt again hundreds of times in hundreds of different ways. In addition, children can complete the building process at any point in the construction. Puzzles, on the other hand, are not complete until the last piece is inserted to finish the picture or design.

BLOCKS   Blocks come in many different varieties, shapes, sizes, and colors. It is traditional to divide blocks into two subcategories: small building blocks and large hollow blocks. Small building blocks are further divided into unit blocks and table blocks. The unit blocks come in a standard unit, and all other sizes and shapes in the set are multiples of the unit. Although the standard unit varies among several manufacturers, the size of $1\,\frac{3}{8} \times 2\,\frac{3}{4} \times 5\frac{1}{2}$ inches is used by most toy companies. This standardization permits mixing of blocks from different manufacturers without destroying the size relationships or the building quality of the blocks. The blocks are usually made of kiln-dried maple or birch. The edges are beveled, and the surfaces are sanded—which reduces splintering. These features make unit blocks very safe and durable but

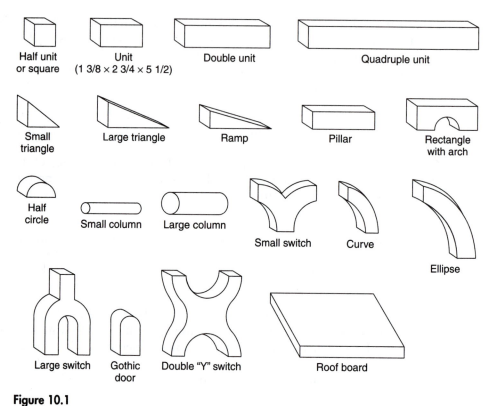

Figure 10.1

Nineteen types of unit blocks

also quite expensive. Figure 10.1 illustrates the different shapes and sizes in a typical set of unit blocks. Readers wishing to learn more about unit blocks should read *The Block Book* by Hirsch (1996).

Table blocks, the other type of small building blocks, are smaller in size and less expensive than unit blocks. These blocks vary considerably in size and shape from manufacturer to manufacturer. Several companies add other wooden objects, such as toy houses, to their table-block sets to encourage dramatic play.

The second major subgroup of blocks consists of the large hollow wooden, plastic, and cardboard blocks. These blocks, which are so large that children must use both hands to carry them, are among the most versatile construction materials. Their large size encourages collaborative building and permits children to construct life-size structures (houses, boats, spaceships) for use in dramatic play. Wooden hollow blocks, which are our favorites, come in six shapes: unit, half unit, double unit, half-double unit, diagonal, and plank. The unit size varies across toy companies. They are usually made from pine or maple or a combination of the two woods. The edges are beveled, sides sanded, and surfaces waterproofed. If maintained properly, these blocks can last for decades.

Large cardboard blocks and plastic blocks tend to be less durable and lack the feel and precise fit of wood. However, these other types are considerably

Large hollow blocks encourage both construction activity and dramatic play.

less expensive and have other advantages. The cardboard blocks are surprisingly strong, with several brands being able to support as much as 200 pounds. Several brands of large plastic blocks are filled with foam, making them safer for use with very young children and children with special needs.

BUILDING SETS   These sets have many pieces, which children are required to put together. As is characteristic of all construction materials, the pieces can be put together in many different ways. They are exceptional playthings for almost any age because they are so flexible and versatile. Examples include tinkertoys, Lincoln Logs®, and Legos®.

GROSS-MOTOR TOYS

Gross-motor toys are designed to foster large-muscle development and coordination. In her book *The Right Stuff for Children Birth to 8*, Bronson (1995) makes the following age recommendations for gross-motor toys:

- infants
  clutch and texture balls, chime balls, flutter balls
  push toys without rods (simple cars, animals on wheels)
  low climbing platforms

- 1-year-olds

  push toys with rods
  pull toys on short strings
  soft lightweight balls and larger balls (including beach-ball size)
  stable ride-on equipment
  swings (pushed and monitored by adult)
  tunnels

- 2-year-olds

  simple doll carriages and wagons
  push toys that look like adult equipment (e.g., a lawn mower)
  balls of all shapes and sizes, especially 10- to 12-inch balls for kicking
    and throwing
  stable ride-ons propelled by pushing with feet (no pedals)
  low climbing structures and slides

- 3-year-olds

  small wagons and wheelbarrows
  tricycles sized to child
  full-size rocking/bouncing horse
  stationary outdoor climbing equipment

- 4-year-olds

  hollow plastic softball and lightweight bat (with constant supervision)
  slides with side rails and ladders
  ropes, hanging bars, and rings on swing
  climbing equipment
  outdoor building equipment

- 5-year-olds

  full-size wagons, scooters
  jump rope

GAMES

Between the ages of 3 and 5 years, children develop longer attention spans, learn to take turns, and become able to follow simple rules. These attainments pave the way for playing simple sit-down games (Bronson, 1995). Games for preschool-age children should have few rules, simple scoring systems, and depend more on chance than on strategy (Bronson, 1995). Appropriate games for this age group include bingo and simple card games that involve matching. By age 5 or 6, many children are ready for simple board games (Candyland®, Chutes and Ladders®), memory games (I-Spy®, concentration), and counting games (dominoes). By age 8, they are ready for beginning strategy games, such as checkers.

Isenberg and Jalongo (1997) recommend that teachers encourage children to modify the rules of commercial games and create new variations. Children should also be encouraged to invent their own child-constructed games. The process of inventing or modifying games helps to promote both intellectual autonomy and the development of social skills such as negotiating and reaching consensus with peers.

REAL MATERIALS

Real materials are objects that have specific, nonplay uses in the adult world. These materials make excellent playthings because they tend to be versatile and self-motivating (adults use them, and children want to be like adults). Example of playthings in the real-material category include sand, mud, water, art materials, literacy materials, and wood and woodworking tools.

SAND, WATER, AND MUD These materials have no defined form and are shaped by the containers in which they are placed. These inexpensive play materials are extremely versatile. While using sand and water with containers and other play objects such as funnels and tubes, children spend large amounts of time filling, pouring, and immersing objects. Through such activities, children come to understand how these materials act and react. Although a bit messy, these materials can be easily used indoors by putting them in commercially manufactured water and sand tables. Sand can, of course, also be housed in sandboxes in both indoor and outdoor settings.

Sand and water play can be enriched by adding simple accessories. Hill (1977) and Crosser (1994) recommend the following play enhancers:

- Sand play—shovels and pails; funnels and sifters; bulldozers, dump trucks, road graders; molds and cookie cutters; magnifying lenses; and magnets
- Water play—funnels; plastic tubing; squeeze bottles; soup ladles and large spoons; jars, margarine tubs, and other containers; sponges; egg beaters and kitchen whisks; corks, popsicle sticks, and fishing bobbers; and food coloring

Coarse sand, commonly called "builder's sand," is preferable to fine sand for indoor play. Fine sand of the type found on beaches is more expensive, has a tendency to cling to children's clothing, and is more difficult to clean up from floors.

Mud is another versatile natural play material. It can be smooth or gritty, runny or dry, and it is easy to mold. Of course, it is also quite messy. For practical suggestions on how to use mud in preschool settings, see Hill (1977).

ART MATERIALS During the early years, art and play are closely intertwined. When children play with art materials, they are also beginning to learn to use art as a form of self-expression. Frank and Theresa Caplan (1974, p. 165) explain:

> There is something special about raw art materials that free a child to create spontaneously. The forms the child makes may have meaning only to himself. In fact, very young children never regard their "finished" art work as adults do. Yet a deep impression is made on the child as he works with the material. . . . A child can paint with great blobs of color and feel that he has created something wonderful. He finds that he can invent colors, and mixing them is an adventure to him. He can draw or paint a shape and appreciate it as something he knows.

Play with water, sand, and other natural substances provides many opportunities for learning.

If he wishes, he can even give it a name. As he continues to form other objects, his mental images grow stronger. This is the beginning of the creative process at work.

According to the Caplans, poster paint is the best type of paint for children because it is water-based and cleans up easily. It also flows easily from brush onto paper. Powder paint is almost as good as poster paint, provided that it is mixed with water to the consistency of heavy cream. Long handled brushes with short, flat bristles are ideal for young painters.

Clay is another natural material that is ideally suited for play. It is a workable substance that can be rolled, torn, meshed, pounded, or used with many other items such as popsicle sticks and cookie cutters. Caplan and Caplan (1974, p. 168) discuss the advantages of "real" clay:

> Among the three-dimensional art materials, an inexpensive, nonfirming moist clay is the best plastic medium for children of all ages. It hardens when it dries and can be painted. . . . Because it is easy to mold and responds readily even to tiny fingers, moist clay can be used by the youngest of children, who enjoy squeezing it, pounding it, and even smelling it . . . as they explore its properties.

Unlike real clay, plastic modeling clay and playdough do not harden. Goldhaber (1992) points out that playdough and other modeling materials are "the perfect medium for creating, observing, and thinking about change" (p. 26).

When children play with playdough, they are constantly transforming the material's consistency (from dry to sticky), color (blue + yellow = green), and identity (from round ball to flat pancake). This can broaden children's knowledge about the relationship between actions and events.

LITERACY MATERIALS   As is explained in detail in Chapter 11, children's play can be greatly extended by the addition of theme-related reading and writing materials. For example, the kitchen area of a home center might contain empty product containers (cereal boxes, soft-drink cans, catsup bottles), cookbooks, telephone directory, food coupons, message pads, and pencils. A restaurant center could be equipped with menus, wall signs, pencils, and notepads (for taking food orders). Research has shown that the addition of these types of materials to play settings results in large increases in emergent reading and writing activity (Christie, 1994b; Neuman & Roskos, 1997). In addition, literacy props expand children's play possibilities and can result in longer, more complex dramatic-play episodes (Neuman & Roskos, 1992).

WOOD AND WOODWORKING TOOLS   Wood in many varied and different sizes can usually be obtained free of charge from local lumberyards. White pine, rather than plywood or any of the hardwoods, is best suited for play because it is soft, pliable, light in weight, and relatively free of splinters.

Children need tools to construct things out of wood. Basic woodworking tools include

- hammer and nails
- screwdrivers and screws
- workbench and vise
- saws
- nuts, bolts, and wrenches

To protect against injuries, children using woodworking tools must be *closely* supervised. We also recommend that they wear safety goggles.

PLAY-MATERIAL RESEARCH

Early childhood educators have long been aware that children's play is affected by the available play materials. That realization has sparked a number of studies, beginning in the 1930s. Results of this research have important implications about which types of play materials to provide to children.

TYPE OF MATERIAL

Early researchers investigated the effects of different types of play materials on the social quality of preschoolers' play (Parten, 1933; Van Alstyne, 1932). They found that certain materials elicited group play, whereas others tended to encourage solitary or parallel activity. These early findings have been replicated by more recent researchers (e.g., Hendrickson, Strain, Tremblay, & Shores, 1981; Rubin, 1977). Taken together, the results of this research indicate that housekeeping props, dress-up clothes, dolls, cars, and other toy vehicles are associated with large amounts of group play. Art construction materials (scissors, paints, crayons), educational toys (beads, puzzles), and clay tend to be used in solitary and parallel play. Play with blocks appears to be equally divided between the social and the nonsocial categories.

Researchers have also found that certain materials tend to encourage different cognitive categories of play. The same materials that promote group play (housekeeping props, dress-up clothes, dolls, action figures, and toy vehicles) also tend to be associated with dramatic play (Bagley & Chaille, 1996; Rubin, 1977). "Transformer" toys, which change from vehicles into robots, tend to encourage functional, manipulative play (Bagley & Chaille, 1996). Playdough, clay, sand, and water also tend to be used in functional play, whereas paints, crayons, and scissors encourage constructive play (Rubin, 1977). Blocks are associated with both constructive and dramatic play (Rubin & Seibel, 1979).

The social and cognitive forms of play encouraged by these different play materials are summarized in Table 10.1. Adults wishing to facilitate a particular form of play can do so by providing ample supplies of the materials with a "+" in the play form's column. For example, if a teacher wishes to promote group play, then housekeeping toys, dolls, dress-up clothes, vehicles, and blocks would be the materials of choice.

Table 10.1 TYPES OF PLAY ENCOURAGED BY SELECTED PLAY MATERIALS

| | SOCIAL LEVEL | | COGNITIVE LEVEL | | |
	NONSOCIAL*	GROUP	FUNCTIONAL	CONSTRUCTIVE	DRAMATIC
DRAMATIC-PLAY PROPS		+			+
DOLLS		+			+
DRESS-UP CLOTHES		+			+
VEHICLES		+			+
BLOCKS	+	+		+	+
PUZZLES	+			+	
BEADS	+				
ART CONSTRUCTION (SCISSORS, PAINTS)	+			+	
CLAY, PLAYDOUGH	+		+		
SAND, WATER	+		+		

*Nonsocial = solitary and parallel play.

TOY REALISM AND STRUCTURE

Realism and structure are related features of toys. *Realism* (and related terms *detail* and *verisimilitude*) refers to the degree to which a toy resembles its real-life counterpart. Barbie dolls, with their detailed features and lifelike accessories, are much more realistic than rag dolls. *Structure* refers to the extent to which toys have specific uses. High-realism toys are considered to be highly structured because they have very specific uses. For example, a realistic replica of a police car lends itself to only one use—being a police car. Less realistic wooden cars, which look like blocks of wood with wheels attached, are less structured and can be easily used to represent many kinds of vehicles. Figure 10.2 illustrates how play materials form a continuum from completely unstructured materials such as mud, sand, and water to highly structured educational toys such as shoe-lacing boards, which are intended to be used in one, adult-specified way.

During the 1970s and 1980s, a number of researchers investigated the effects of toy realism and structure on children's dramatic play (e.g., Jeffree & McConkey, 1976; Johnson, 1983; McLoyd, 1983; Olszewski & Fuson, 1982; Pulaski, 1973). In general, the findings of these early studies suggest that realistic, highly structured props facilitate make-believe in younger (2- and 3-year-old) preschoolers but not in older children. Very young children, due to a lack of representational skills, appear to need realistic replicas of theme-related objects in order to get started in dramatic play. With increasing age, children's representational skills grow to the point where realistic toys are no longer required for engaging in make-believe. Results of Pulaski's (1973) study indicated that realistic toys may actually interfere with the imaginativeness of kindergarten and primary-grade students' pretend play.

The assumption that highly realistic toys inhibit make-believe in older, 4- to 6-year-old children has come under attack in recent years. Trawick-Smith (1990) pointed out that earlier researchers had restricted make-believe play to "Level 2" transformations in which objects are used in ways that are different from that suggested by their form and function (e.g., using a toy telephone as if it were a fire extinguisher). Trawick-Smith expanded the definition of make-believe to include "Level 1" transformations in which objects are used in prototypical ways but within a make-believe context (using a toy telephone as if it were a real telephone to make pretend calls). He found that boys, ages 3 to 6 years, and girls, up to age 5, exhibited more make-believe with realistic play props than with less realistic toys. Similarly, Robinson and Jackson (1987) found that highly detailed toy cars elicited more make-believe play in

Figure 10.2

The structural quality of play materials

Mud Sand Water	Blocks	Featureless dolls Vehicles, etc.	Replica toys	Educational toys
UNSTRUCTURED				STRUCTURED

4- and 5-year-olds than less detailed toy cars. Results of these two studies, combined with those of earlier studies, indicate that high-realism toys result in more make-believe play than less realistic toys across the entire 2- to 6-year-old age range.

On the other hand, less realistic toys do appear to encourage 4- to 6-year-olds to engage in more creative make-believe transformations. Trawick-Smith (1990) and Robinson and Jackson (1987) both found that less realistic toys, while not generating as much total make-believe, did result in more "nonprototypical," Level 2 transformations (e.g., using a toy car as if it were an airplane).

There also is a philosophical reason for using less structured, low-realism toys. Instead of shaping children's play behavior, these materials are controlled by the child and molded to his or her play purposes. Wardle (1997, p. 9) explains why this feature is very important in today's society:

> Young children need a variety of opportunities to create, imagine and construct their reality—to control their world. This activity of imposing their individual meaning on the play experience is critical for the development of a healthy self-esteem, and to develop a belief that learning can be a meaningful experience. As we control more and more of a child's experience—schedules, TV and video programs, structured academic experiences—we need more than ever to provide simple, unstructured materials for children to play with.

We recommend that preschools serving 2- and 3-year-olds have a large supply of realistic toys available in order to stimulate make-believe play. These materials fit the representational skills of this age group. Schools serving older, 4- to 6-year-olds, should also be well stocked with realistic toys because these are the types of props that encourage the largest amounts of make-believe play. At the same time, classrooms for these older children should also have ample supplies of less-realistic props to encourage creative, nonprototypical make-believe transformations.

AMOUNT OF MATERIALS AND EQUIPMENT

The amount of toys and equipment available in a setting can influence children's play patterns. In an early study, Maguerite Johnson (1935) varied the amount of equipment on three preschool playgrounds. Equipment was added to one playground and taken away from two others. Results showed that when the amount of equipment was *increased,* children engaged in fewer social games but also less aggressive behavior. When the amount of equipment was *reduced,* there were more positive social contacts among children but also more aggression. Smith and Connolly (1980), as part of their study of indoor play settings, reported similar findings. They found that fewer playthings per child resulted in less solitary play, more parallel play, and more sharing, as well as more aggression. The overall amount of group play was not affected. However, as the number of playthings per child decreased, the mean size of play groups increased.

These findings indicate that in both indoor and outdoor settings, there is an inverse relationship between the amount of play materials available and the level of social interaction in children's play. A *decrease* in the amount of materials in a setting brings about an *increase* in social interaction of both a positive (sharing and positive contacts) and negative (aggression) nature. Increasing the amount of materials has the opposite effect, reducing both aggression and prosocial contact.

The type of materials available in the setting is also relevant, according to two studies by Patrick Doyle. The first study investigated the effects of single- and multiple-niche equipment on preschoolers' play (Doyle, 1977). The concept "niche" was borrowed from ecology, where it refers to the part of the environment that is necessary for a species' or organism's survival. If there are too many occupants for the same niche, the result is antagonistic relations and possible extinction. As applied to play equipment, *single-niche items* are materials that provide activities for just one child (e.g., rocking horses, tricycles, toy brooms, and short jump ropes), whereas multiple-niche items provide activities for several children (e.g., teeter-totters, large jump ropes, and jungle gyms). Doyle found that multiple-niche materials were associated with children's getting along and exhibiting prosocial behaviors. Single-niche equipment, on the other hand, frequently led to interpersonal conflicts and aggression.

In a follow-up study, Doyle (1978) found that materials with interchangeable parts (e.g., blocks, Lincoln Logs®, and tinkertoys®) resulted in more antisocial behavior than materials with noninterchangeable parts (e.g., puzzles). He interpreted this finding to indicate that the former materials lead to struggles over their use because they have utility for children engaged in a number of different activities, whereas the latter have parts that no one else would want except the child currently using the material. Children were therefore more likely to struggle over interchangeable materials such as blocks than over puzzles with noninterchangeable pieces.

Several applications are suggested by these findings. If parents or teachers wish to increase social interaction in children's play, one way to accomplish this goal is to reduce the amount of equipment and play materials in the setting. They should be cautious, however, not to remove too much, or high levels of aggression may result. On the other hand, if educators or parents are concerned that there is too much aggression going on in play, additional equipment will reduce the competition for materials and should lead to lower levels of aggressive behavior. Aggressive behavior can also be reduced by using multiple-niche play equipment and toys with noninterchangeable pieces.

SELECTING APPROPRIATE PLAY MATERIALS

With so many different types of play materials available, parents and teachers have an important role in selecting and purchasing play materials. Adults should attempt to provide play materials that are well made, safe, and suited to children's abilities and play interests.

Research on play materials, reviewed in the previous section, provides some guidance in selecting appropriate play materials. In addition, several excellent resources are available to help with this daunting task:

- *The Right Stuff for Children Birth to 8* by Martha Bronson (National Association for the Education of Young Children, 1995). This book contains detailed lists of materials that are developmentally appropriate for children at different ages. Materials are organized by the types of play they encourage: social and fantasy play; exploration and mastery play; music, art, & movement play; and gross-motor play.
- *Selecting Educational Equipment and Materials for School and Home*, edited by Joan Moyer (Association for Childhood Education International, 1995). This extensive resource contains lists of all types of educational equipment needed in classrooms designed for children from infancy through age 10 years. In addition to general types of equipment (e.g., chairs, wastebaskets, mops, bandages) and academic materials (mathematics, science, language arts, etc.), this book contains lists of developmentally appropriate play materials for promoting functional, constructive, and dramatic forms of play.
- *Which Toy for Which Child: A Consumer's Guide for Selecting Suitable Toys: Ages Birth Through Five* and *Which Toy for Which Child: A Consumer's Guide for Selecting Suitable Toys: Ages Six Through Twelve* (U.S. Consumer Product Safety Commission, 1993, 1994). These valuable resources contain basic toy safety guidelines, along with lists of toys that are safe and suitable for children at different ages. They also contain succinct overviews of children's physical, mental, and social abilities for each age range. For more information about toy safety, see the Theory in Action feature "Toy Safety."

ELECTRONIC MEDIA AND PLAY

Many types of contemporary play materials derive from the electronic media—computers, television, movies and videocassettes, video and virtual reality games, and electronic or computerized toys. These electronic media can serve as vehicles or as objects of play. In addition, these media can directly influence the content of more traditional forms of play, particularly dramatic and constructive play.

Technological advances continue to bring important opportunities and challenges to early childhood education. Parents and teachers need to know how to use technology to enrich children's play and to guard against possible negative influences. For example, virtual-reality software can provide incredibly rich make-believe experiences, taking young children exploring in an air balloon over a battlefield or sending them traveling down a forest river in a canoe. Children wearing special gloves and goggles can have altered perceptions and sensations to make them feel as if they are actually on these expeditions (Shade & Davis, 1997).

Theory in Action

TOY SAFETY

Toy safety is a serious issue. In 1995, the U.S. Consumer Product Safety Commission received reports of 21 deaths and more than 150,000 serious injuries attributed to toys (Health Resources and Services Administration, 1996). Sixty percent of these injuries occurred among children under age 5 years. The SAFE KIDS Coalition estimates that among children ages 4 years and under, the annual cost of toy-related injuries treated in hospital emergency rooms is $385 million (MCHD Online, 1996). Leading causes of toy-related injuries include falls from riding toys and choking on small toys or toy parts. Other serious toys hazards include sharp points, flammable material, and long strings that can cause strangulation.

The Consumer Product Safety Commission (1996) and the Toy Manufacturers of America (1997) offer guidelines that can help reduce the risk of toy-related injuries:

- Select toys that are suited to children's age, ability, skill, and interest levels.
- Be sure to read toy labels and follow the age and safety recommendations on labels.
- For infants and toddlers (and all children who "mouth" objects), avoid toys with small parts, which could cause choking.
- For all children under age 8 years, avoid toys with sharp points or rough edges.
- Avoid electric toys with heating elements for all children under age 8 years.
- Do not purchase toys with long strings or cords for very young children; such toys may cause strangulation.
- Throw away plastic wrappings so that they do not pose a safety hazard.
- Check toys periodically for wear and damage. If a toy cannot be repaired, it should be replaced or discarded.
- Supervise children's play to make sure that toys are being used properly.
- Store toys intended for older children in locked enclosures or on high shelves so that young children do not have access to these toys.
- In order to prevent falls, teach children to put their toys away on shelves or in toy chests. Storage chests should have removable lids or safety latches to keep the lid securely open

More information on toy safety can be obtained by writing to the U.S. Product Safety Commission, Washington, D.C. 20207. To report a toy-related safety complaint, call their toll-free hotline: 1-800-638-CPSC.

On the flip side, we must prevent "technological child abuse" through inappropriate use of electronic media. For example, the electronic media may tempt unwary or insensitive educators with sophisticated but stifling tools for play and learning. For example, "work-disguised-as-play" computer games and other rote-learning kinds of software can stifle children's imaginations if overused. In addition, television can threaten children through the seductive appeal of mindless, passive entertainment. Excessive viewing of cartoons and sitcoms can rob children of precious time for more productive play experiences. Unwholesome cumulative exposure to violence in television, videos, and movies poses another potential negative influence on play behavior.

TELEVISION

Of the several important forms of the electronic media that affect the play and development of young children, the most influential is television. More American households have televisions than have indoor plumbing, and *TV Guide* is the best-selling periodical in the United States, selling more than 20 million copies weekly. At least one television set is available in well over 97% of homes in the United States, and VCRs are in at least two thirds of American households (Levin & Carlsson-Paige, 1994). Estimates are that young children watch 4 hours of television per day, on average, and up to 6 hours per day if they live in low-income homes. Children as young as 9 months have been reported to watch as much as 90 minutes of television a day (Spring, 1993). The concerns here are that television can diminish creative, imaginative play tendencies in general, stimulating instead low-level, imitation-like play that tends to be highly aggressive in nature (Carlsson-Paige & Levin, 1990).

NEGATIVE EFFECTS ON PLAY   In their books, *The War Play Dilemma* (1987) and *Who's Calling the Shots?* (1990), Nancy Carlsson-Paige and Diane Levin discuss the diminution of children's play due to TV. As these authors see it, the problem stems from the Federal Communications Commission's deregulation of children's television under the Reagan Administration. Since 1984, it is no longer illegal to market television programs and products together. This deregulation led to TV programs produced by toy companies, with top-selling toys yoked to aggressive television characters. The media and toy industries were allowed to cross-feed each other, flooding the toy market with media-related products. For example, 1,000 items bore the Teenage Mutant Ninja Turtle logo when the cartoon show first came out in the 1980s. Sadly, these marketing practices have been left virtually unaffected by the Children's Television Act of 1990. Currently, there are many cases similar to the Ninja Turtle example (e.g., *Mighty Morphine Rangers, X-Men, Mighty Ducks*).

Adverse effects on children's play were reported by hundreds of parents and teachers almost immediately after deregulation (Carlsson-Paige & Levin, 1990). According to many adults interviewed, children imitated aggressive scripts from television, showing little evidence of original or creative play. Other researchers have noted similar findings. In a naturalistic study of 4-year-olds on a preschool playground, Shin (1994) found that boys identified strongly with aggressive Saturday-morning cartoon superheroes. They knew all the characters' names and what weapons they possessed, and they imitated the characters' aggressive behaviors.

This kind of behavior can pose psychological and physical safety hazards. It can also interfere with the generative or healing powers of genuine play expression. In fact, Levin and Carlsson-Paige (1994) have taken a strong position that this kind of behavior is not play behavior at all, but merely imitation. They urge parents and teachers to distinguish what "looks like play" from what is really play. They remind us that play is assimilatory and transformative for the child, allowing for creative self-expression or working through of past experiences. Imitative "playlike" behavior, in contrast, involves accommodation and is limited to copying behaviors seen on scripted television shows.

Levin and Carlsson-Paige (1994) do not recommend that adults ignore or forbid this low-level, highly stereotyped and thematically aggressive behavior. Instead, adults should seek to convert it into more constructive play forms. For instance, teachers can suggest that superheroes with family members go to the annual superhero picnic at the beach! Other suggestions for managing superhero and aggressive play can be found in Boyatzis (1997), Boyd (1997), Greenberg (1995), and Kostelnick, Whiren, and Stein (1986).

It should be noted that other researchers have voiced assertions strongly at odds with the views of Levin and Carlsson-Paige. Has the play of children really become less creative and more aggressive in recent years—in particular since the deregulation of the television industry in 1984? Sutton-Smith (1986, 1988) answers this question by giving a historical view of the matter. He notes that each new cohort of children receives new toys, scripts, and characters from their generation's popular culture, which they can incorporate into their play episodes. Children only imitate whatever serves their overarching play purposes. According to Sutton-Smith, this is not mindless imitation, as Levin and Carlsson-Paige (1994) have claimed. In the case of play fighting and superhero play, children (especially boys) are acting out and expressing universal historical phenomena—"age-old play habits of chase and escape, attack and defense, and acceptance and rejection between good and bad characters which have dominated the play of people (and animals) throughout history" (Sutton-Smith, 1988, pp. 66–67). He grants that today's mass media entertainment industry exposes a wider audience of young children to aggressive fantasy scripts than ever before. However, these are variants of "cops and robbers" and "cowboys and Indians," so popular with earlier generations of children. These earlier forms of "good guy versus bad guy" play were also based on media—villains from the national news (e.g., Al Capone) and heroes from movie or television Westerns (e.g., Roy Rogers).

Goldstein (1995) also disagrees with Levin and Carlsson-Paige. He argues that (a) adults often confuse *play* fighting with *real* aggression, and (b) there is little evidence that children play in a worse or less imaginative fashion today than they did in 1984. Recall that the data in Carlsson-Paige and Levin (1990) are based on interviews with adults, rather than on direct observations and interviews with children. Research is needed to learn more about this topic from the child's point of view, in addition to the points of view of parents and teachers.

USE OF TV TO FOSTER PLAY   The bulk of research conducted on television viewing and the play of young children suggests that television is a negative influence, preempting playtime and possibly impeding creativity. Some researchers, however, believe that television can be used to build play competence in children. These researchers have reasoned that, after all, there are some common elements that the medium shares with make-believe play—visual fluidity, time and space flexibility, and blurry fantasy–reality distinctions.

The content of specific programs, furthermore, may stimulate fantasy play by giving children ideas for certain play episodes. However, the shows must be comprehensible to children. Singer and Singer (1990) recommend that parents be present as much as possible when their young children watch television. Family mediation of television viewing during the early years can help children view programs more actively and also gain social understanding. For example, Singer, Singer, Desmond, Hirsch, and Nichol (1988) found that parental discussion with young children about TV shows fostered in children a better appreciation of the difference between fantasy and reality. This discrimination can help inhibit inappropriate play aggression—such as when the urge strikes to act like King Kong and go on a rampage knocking down other children's buildings in the block center. Teachers can be thankful in such cases for prior family mediation and monitoring of TV viewing—as a factor contributing to children's receptivity to admonitions for proper behavior!

Certain children's shows have been reported to aid in the development of prosocial behavior and imaginative play. *Mister Rogers' Neighborhood* is a standout example in this genre. This show has been on the air for more than 25 years, reaching millions of children each year, with the express intent of meeting the triumvirate needs of every child—hope, trust, and imagination (Collins & Kimmel, 1996). As host, the avuncular Fred Rogers helps children make sense of the world through the use of emotionally warm eye contact and his slow-paced and soft-spoken manner of communication. About half the show is in the "reality mode," in which Mr. Rogers personally deals with factual information conveyed with visitors, field trips, explanations, music, and the like. The remaining part of the show is in the "fantasy mode," when the red trolley takes the audience to the Neighborhood of Make-Believe, inhabited by puppets ruled by King Friday. Socio-emotional content and learning regarding various relevant developmental and human issues are explored in this segment of the show. The value of pretending is explicit.

Early play-intervention studies using *Mister Rogers' Neighborhood* revealed that the television show, by itself, had little holding power over children in a group setting. Singer and Singer (1976) reported that children found peer interaction more appealing than watching *Mister Rogers' Neighborhood*.

However, the Singers found that adult-mediated television viewing (an adult helping children to pay attention to certain aspects of the program) increased viewers' imaginative free play. Friedrich and Stein (1975) also reported that the most reliable positive effects on preschool play occurred when television is combined with having a teacher actively tutor children at play.

Recent research by the Singers and their associates at Yale University corroborates a correlation between home viewing of *Mister Rogers' Neighborhood* and children's tendencies to play imaginatively, as well as to share and to cooperate. Current work is also examining *Barney and Friends,* another very popular show for younger preschoolers that also puts the accent on the importance of make-believe (Singer, 1995). These TV shows affirm the value of pretending in early childhood and cast a positive light on what the electronic media can accomplish for children at play.

COMPUTERS

Computers represent another major form of the electronic media, which reach more and more young children every year. At present, computers are in schools and libraries and in many early childhood programs; moreover, about 50% of American households include personal computers (Edwards, 1993).

Tremendous strides have been made in hardware since the decades of the 1970s and 1980s, when monochromatic monitors and 5.25″ floppy disks were state-of-the-art equipment. Software programs for young children back then were correspondingly feeble and hardly recognizable by today's standards. They were very limited in graphics, heavily textual, and mainly of the drill-and-practice variety.

Today, computers are, by comparison, much more powerful and faster. We have high-speed CD-ROM drives, monitors and printers capable of generating tens of thousands of colors, and computers with internal sound sources, including voice activation. Hard-drive memory storage is now measured in gigabytes, where 1 gigabyte equals 1.2 million times the storage capacity of the 800K floppy disk. Current software is graphics intensive and capable of showing realistic scenes and colorful animations with much less reliance on text. Accordingly, a great deal of current computer software is developmentally appropriate and capable of independent use by children during the early childhood years—especially when a "child-proof" interface program is available, which can serve as a protective buffer between the young child and the hard drive's filing systems (Shade & Davis, 1997).

A quantum leap has also occurred in our understanding of young children's ability to use computers in early childhood education. Previously, there was concern over the developmental appropriateness of computers, given that computer-based activities were considered to be symbolic and not concrete. However, as Clements and Nastasi (1993) note, "what is 'concrete' to the child may have more to do with what is meaningful and manipulable than with its physical nature" (p. 259). Familiarity is also important. Today's children grow up in a computer age. Children's manipulation of symbolic content on a monitor with a mouse-driven cursor has become an everyday experience comparable to actions on any other real physical object. The *appropriateness* question, then, has been replaced with questions about *how, when, and why* computers can be used to support play, creativity, and learning.

Still, Elkind (1996) cautions that how children use computers should not be taken as an estimate of cognitive maturity. With computers, children may appear more competent than they really are. Clicking a mouse and manipulating computer icons is not the same thing as concrete operational thinking (e.g., the ability to conserve or to solve class-inclusion problems). Elkind believes that computers should not displace traditional play activities such as painting, pretending, and gross-motor movement and that they should not be viewed as a substitute for teacher interaction. Computers and software are an accompaniment to other activities and materials. Teachers must seek ways to integrate computers into the curriculum to serve overall educational goals within a program.

SOFTWARE QUALITY How should young children experience computers to optimize play and development? This immediately leads to the question, "What is quality software for young children?" There are a number of important factors to consider. First, programs should provide "microworlds," where children have options to explore and opportunities to follow their curiosity and make things happen. Programs should not be expensive drill-and-practice "electronic worksheets" that are closed-ended and limit children's initiative and decision making.

Second, according to the NAEYC's Position Statement on Technology and Young Children (National Association for the Education of Young Children, 1996), software should have content reflective of real-world models and diverse cultures (multiple languages, mixed gender, role equity, people of color, differing ages and abilities, and diverse family styles) and be devoid of violent themes. Positive benefits to children are deemed more likely when the child is in control, with expanding complexity or graduated challenges inherent in the program. Clear instructions for software use are also important, as are guidelines for linking software programs to other curricular activities, such as puppets, picture books and the like (Haugland & Wright, 1997; Wright, Shade, Thouvenelle, & Davidson, 1989).

Next, high technical quality is essential, together with the capacity to depict visible transformations. The former includes colorful, uncluttered, realistic animated graphics, with sound effects and music corresponding to objects on the screen. The latter include changes in objects and situations occurring in response to child input. These visible transformations give children the opportunity to see hidden processes normally not witnessed in everyday life, as well as to learn the nature of cause-and-effect relationships. A *Developmental Software Evaluation Scale* is available, which discusses these and various other criteria (Haugland & Shade, 1994).

PLAYING WITH COMPUTERS   Certain software-design features are more conducive to the play state than are others. Also, certain teacher behaviors can turn children's use of computers into a playful experience. For example, Henniger (1994) proposes that software programs can stimulate children's imaginations and creative play when they are simple in design but complex in their potential use. Instructions must be clear enough and simple enough that children can use the program with minimum adult involvement, and children must be able to manipulate the program and be able to enter, exit, and save work independently.

Some but not all behavior with the computer can be called play. Play does not involve having children do computer activities that are obligatory and that have extrinsic rewards (such as when using drill-and-practice software controlled by adults). On the other hand, consider children using drawing programs such as LOGO. Often, such activity transcends exploration and learning and can become a form of constructive play. As a second example, consider simulation software programs in which the program casts learning and use in terms of hypothetical situations, such as going on a whale hunt (*Voyage of the Mimi*) or conducting a small business (*Lemonade Stand*).

These creative programs possess the three characteristics that Malone (1984) believes are required to make a computer activity appealing and interesting to children: challenge, fantasy, and curiosity. *Challenge* means that the program is developmentally appropriate and stimulates the child with a problem at or slightly ahead of the child's existing ability level. Papert (1996) calls this "hard fun." *Fantasy* means that the program depicts some make-believe adventure or event. *Curiosity* means that the software captivates the child. Malone was first to note that programs with internal fantasy have more appeal than ones with external fantasy. In programs with *external fantasy*, the fantasy is artificial and imposed externally, as in a drill-and-practice game in which children pretend to kill off monsters by solving math problems. *Internal fantasy*, in contrast, unites the activity with the goal, such as in *Lemonade Stand*, in which children try to reach their sales projections through problem solving, estimation, and the use of other thinking strategies. The former type of program is more blatantly work-disguised-as-play; the latter type of program can be more genuinely enjoyed as play.

According to Papert (1996), as computers pervade the world of children, parents and teachers must try to retain the play potential in this new toy. He contrasts "real" toys made of atoms with new computational toys made of bits. For example, a "real" cuddly teddy bear may have less built-in personality than a screen bear made of bits. Even though a child can and often does impose personality on the "real" teddy, computational toys (such as Nicky the Dragon in *My Make Believe Castle*) have advantages. Microworld characters can be inviting and open-ended enough to invite fantasy projections and elaborations by the imaginative child. Technology allows children to use and change characters such as Nicky the Dragon, and even carry them over to a different software program. For Papert, computers can provide extremely valuable "building" toys and "social" toys conducive to high-level constructive and fantasy play.

Clearly, the play potential of computers is growing. The early childhood literature contains numerous anecdotes or informal discussions about young children playing with computers. For example, Beaty and Tucker (1987) discuss the computer as a "playmate," a friend that youngsters come to know through exploratory manipulation, leading to mastery and then on to meaningful play or related behaviors. Children can make up stories and practice language and emergent literacy skills using a program such as *Facemaker* or *Picture Programming,* or they can play in a functional or constructive manner at painting, drawing, or coloring activities, using any number of available computer programs designed for these purposes. However, rigorous empirical research on computer-related play remains limited.

Davidson (1989) found that young children used the *Explore a Story* software to create imaginative stories and to get into a form of dramatic play. Wright and Samaras (1986) reported computer play behaviors to occur in a sequence from functional play to constructive play to dramatic play. Silvern, Williamson, and Countermine (1988) reported a high level of functional play when children are first introduced to the computer. These sequences are consistent with what is known about how children play microgenetically with other material playthings, as we noted in Chapter 3, on the development of play. As proposed by Sutton-Smith, children go through phases in any situated play: "First children examine, re-examine, then combine and transform."

CLASSROOM APPLICATIONS Computer use in a curriculum should be subsumed under larger educational goals serving broader philosophical purposes. Computers need to be coordinated with other forms of instructional delivery in an integrated curriculum promoting educational play.

There are three kinds of software: *tutor, tutee,* and *tool* (Taylor, 1980). *Tutor* software is a computerized worksheet in which the computer is teacher, providing children with drill and practice on various skills (e.g., *Reader Rabbit 2*). *Tutee* programs, on the other hand, allow the children to teach the computer. For example, the *LOGO* turtle permits the child to send instructions to the computer, resulting in movement or drawing on the screen. With this type of program, the child learns about the computer. *Tool* software allows the child to do different things with the computer. Examples include word processors, paint programs, databases, and various authoring programs such as *HyperStudio, Creative Writer, Kid Pix,* and *Imagination Express Neighbor.* With this software, the child learns (and plays) with the computer (Papert, 1993). In general, the potential for play is limited in *tutor*-type programs (although in principle, play is not impossible). *Tutee-* and *tool*-type software have much higher play potential. Not coincidentally, these two types of software are considered developmentally appropriate by the National Association for the Education of Young Children (1996).

Multimedia and multimodal computer learning centers are advised whenever possible. Children's play can be stimulated and enriched in new ways, associated with the scanned images, colors, sound files, graphical images, text, and motion made available by computer multimedia centers.

Electronic media can benefit the teacher seeking to integrate computers with free play, structured free play, and play tutoring sessions. For example, Haugland (1995) urges teachers to help children get the most benefits from computer use by always providing related activities with concrete materials near the computer. For instance, if the children are using *Gyphon Bricks* (software in which children construct objects on the screen with what looks like Lego® blocks), actual Lego® blocks could be placed on a table near the computer during a free-play period.

Computer activities should be blended with other educational play and learning activities and not used in isolation or merely for "playing games." Computers need to serve children's investigations and explorations around projects or themes. For example, Scali (1993) described an integrated unit involving *Goldilocks and the Three Bears*, which she used with her kindergarten class. Children discussed the story and enacted it in the dramatic-play center, and they painted pictures of bears in the art center. They also drew pictures about the story on a computer, using a painting program, and they videotaped one another telling parts of the story. Computer drawings and video clips were put side by side on a page of a *HyperStudio* book. The end result was a pop-up multimedia storybook produced by the kindergarten class, which was placed in the class library for second-language students. The multimedia book also preserved memories of the children's playful collaboration.

Above all, adults should help children see computers as fun and valuable, in the same way that a good swimming instructor makes beginners feel about water. First impressions are so important. Both *thinking with* computers and *thinking about* computers are important early childhood educational goals. The latter is particularly important; children need to be taught how to put computers into the scheme of things.

Finally, we need to continue to design better programs and to learn more about sequencing computer experiences for children. Related activity planning is very important. Eventually, we will obtain a better understanding of the consequences of computer use and what, if any, are the unique contributions of computer use to children's development and well-being. Important goals of teaching with computers are to enhance development in general and play skills in particular, and to delineate the different ways children play with computers.

OTHER FORMS OF ELECTRONIC MEDIA

MOVIES AND VIDEOS As with television, movies and videos can influence the play and development of children. Time spent watching movies and videos, however, is a much smaller percentage of most children's weekly activities.

Movies and videos often are made especially for young children. Characters such as Winnie-the Pooh, the Care-Bears, and the Smurfs reflect a concern for fostering positive social behavior in children. Plots or story lines are usually simple and provide good material for later make-believe play. As noted earlier, there are action–adventure movies and videos, as well as television programs. These have a powerful influence on the child's imagination and play. Superheroes and supervillains are very popular in children's role enactments. Adults should shape and redirect content from such movies to match more acceptable play patterns and cultural norms.

Watching movies and videos or television is essentially a passive activity that may affect play at a later time by triggering the imagination in some way. We must recognize, however, that the acts of watching these media are themselves forms of play. When children participate in these activities, they not only escape from reality in some sense, but also enjoy what they are doing. As Mergen (1982) notes, "Roller coaster rides, car chases, aerial combat all become almost as exciting on the screen as they are in life." The enjoyment of motion in the playground or on the screen is an aspect of physical play sometimes referred to as *vertigo play* (Caillois, 1961).

VIDEO GAMES AND VIRTUAL REALITY There has been a meteoric rise of video games and virtual reality since the late 1980s. Video games are made possible by the marriage of television and the computer. CD-ROM disks also allow participants to interact with video footage photographed in the real world. Both real-world images and bodily sensations are incorporated into the play in virtual reality games. *Virtual reality* is a three-dimensional computer-simulated scenario in which the child or adult can look in, move around, and experience an artificial world by wearing virtual-reality goggles and other special gear. Although educational virtual reality and video games exist, most items found under this genre of the electronic media are primarily for entertainment. Very popular with adults and adolescents and older children (Greenfield, 1994), they are finding their way into the lives of younger children, as well.

Video games and virtual reality are forms of electronic media that are interactive, like computers, in contrast to television, radio, and movies, which are all essentially one-way communications. One of the major attractions of video games and virtual reality is that they allow the child to be in control (Greenfield, 1984). The combination of visual attractiveness and interactivity is very appealing.

Few adults would recommend the use of video games as a lead-in to computer use or to foster learning in children during the preschool years. Hypotheses advanced over the years by researchers such as Greenfield (1994)— that video games promote hand–eye coordination, visual scanning, auditory discrimination, and spatial skills—lack convincing empirical support. Studies are needed to buttress theoretical claims that playing computer, video, and virtual-reality games rehearse children on skills and mind-sets needed for their futures in our postmodern world of computers and images. On the negative side, there is evidence that violent video games may desensitize young children to violent behavior and may make them feel more comfortable with violence, much as violent television shows do. Silvern, Williamson, and Countermine (1983), for example, found that the video games *Space Invaders* and *Roadrunner* raised the level of aggressive play and lowered the level of prosocial behaviors in 5-year-old children. Preschool children are on record for saying they prefer video games to academically oriented computer software (Johnson & Hoffman, 1984). For this reason, a need remains to develop appealing educational and nonviolent, nonsexist entertainment video and virtual reality games. The potential here is great for enriching play and learning. Resources within this category of electronic media have yet to be tapped and factored into curricular development in early childhood education. Rich possibilities may be looming on the horizon (Shade & Davis, 1997).

ELECTRONIC TOYS Electronic toys, such as battery-operated toys and electric trains, are rarely found in child-care centers, preschool classrooms, or children's bedrooms or toy boxes. Safety reasons preclude their use by young children without careful supervision. However, there is a subcategory of electrical toys that pose fewer risks and that are becoming a more prevalent part of the early childhood environment. These are computerized toys.

Smith (1981) divides computerized toys into several categories, including toys that make music and game toys. These kinds of toys have flooded the market in recent years. *Toys that make music* have preprogrammed tunes that can be brought up by pressing the right buttons or keys. Sometimes there is a delay in tone after the switch is pushed, which might be confusing to a child, but in general, these musical activities offer the child a way to discover a sense of rhythm, not likely to be discovered with simple band instruments. Computer-toy versions of musical instruments sometimes lure children into musical appreciation and interest. These toys can also promote cognitive development by demonstrating cause-and-effect relationships. For other children, they are just noisemakers.

Computerized *game toys* include hand-held, lap, and table toys of speed, sport, and wit. *Simon Says®* requires the child to remember a numbered sequence of musical notes, with brightly colored flashing lights. Sport games, which include baseball, football, hockey, and soccer, are hand-held versions of arcade or video games. Some of these games involve different levels of built-in difficulty, which can be selected by the player. These games are usually not intended for younger children, however, and may become frustrating for them. For the skilled player, these games often become boring because the player can win at will.

PROGRAMMABLE TOYS The computer age has resulted in an overwhelming number of programmable computer toys. Unlike video games or electronic toys, which are "prescripted," programmable toys involve a computerized activity that must be performed by the child or adult in order for the toy to work. Toys such as *Big Track,®* for example, are programmed by the child. The child learns basic concepts of programming by directing the robot or army tank to move in certain directions for certain distances, taking a specified number of turns and steps. Programmable toys can be used in make-believe play and are considered by many educators to be an excellent prerequisite or alternative activity to computers.

SUMMARY

Toys and other playthings are important aspects of children's world of play. Research has shown that the types of materials available in a setting have a considerable effect on children's play behavior. In addition, studies have shown that the dimensions of toy realism and structure and the amount of play material available in a setting can influence play. Parents and teachers can use this research data, along with resources such as *The Right Stuff for Children Birth to 8* (Bronson, 1995) and *Selecting Educational Equipment and Materials for School and Home* (Moyer, 1995), to select the types of materials that will stimulate developmentally appropriate, challenging forms play.

Television, computers, and other forms of electronic media are becoming increasing powerful influences on children's play. These media are like double-edged swords, having the potential both to enrich and to inhibit the richness and creativity of children's play. It is essential that parents and teachers take steps to accentuate the positive influence of electronic media on play, such as by controlling the amount of television viewing, watching prosocial television shows *with* children, and providing developmentally appropriate computer software programs and computer games for children to play with.

Chapter 11

PLAY AND EDUCATION

According to her district's kindergarten math curriculum, Marilyn is expected to teach rote counting and recognition of numerals from 1 to 20. She decides to experiment with turning the dramatic-play center into a store. In addition to a balance scale, she is lucky enough to obtain an old hanging scale. She includes a stamp with numbers that the children can rotate and change. She has several hand calculators and an old adding machine borrowed from a third-grade teacher. She also includes tubs of small objects, such as Unifix cubes, that can be sold. She is delighted to find that she now has a use for out-of-date coupons and the weekly ads from local supermarkets. The pictures and numbers make the messages understandable for customers. The store is now open for business. On opening day, workers and customers discover that Marilyn has forgotten an important component: They need money. This leads to a group project making bills and coins. (adapted from Van Hoorn, Nourot, Scales, & Alward, 1993, p. 125) ∎

Marilyn's "numeracy-enriched" store center is an excellent example of curriculum-generated play. She has designed a play setting that provides opportunities for children to recognize numbers and to count—important objectives in her kindergarten math curriculum. She uses this play center as an alternative to more traditional forms of instruction, such as direct instruction and worksheets.

Play advocates claim that play-based learning activities, such as Marilyn's store center, offer distinct advantages over more direct types of instruction. Rather than passively absorbing information and memorizing facts, children have opportunities to construct their own knowledge about mathematics, with help from their peers. Because the numbers and counting are connected with enjoyable play, children will tend to develop positive attitudes toward mathematics. No rewards or reinforcement are needed to get the children to count and to interact with numbers. Play is intrinsically motivated.

The concept of play-based education is not new. It can be traced back to the original play pioneers—Jean Jacques Rousseau (France), Johann Pestalozzi (Switzerland), and Friedrich Froebel (Germany)—who had a considerable influence on the beginnings of formal early education from the sixteenth through nineteenth centuries (Glickman, 1984). In the United States, curriculum-related play has come in and out of fashion. A number of play-based schools were established in the early 1910s, such as Carolyn Pratt's famous school in the Greenwich Village area of New York City. The trend toward play-based curriculum accelerated during the 1920s and 1930s with the rise of the child-study movement, "progressive" education, and John Dewey's experimentalist philosophy of education (Glickman, 1984; Varga, 1991). Play then faded during the general shift toward conservatism following World War II. Play-related teaching strategies came back into favor during the tumultuous 1960s, with curricula such as "inquiry-based science" and "new math," only to fade again under the onslaught of the "back-to-basics" movements during the late 1970s and early 1980s (Glickman, 1984).

Today, play is back in the center of early childhood curriculum. Two closely related factors are responsible for play's elevated status: the constructivist model of learning and concerns about developmentally appropriate practice. The *constructivist model of learning* asserts that learning is an active, social process in which children build their own understandings based on experience. Bredekamp and Copple (1997, p. 13) explain:

> Young children actively learn from observing and participating with other children and adults, including parents and teachers. Children need to form their own hypotheses and keep trying them out through social interaction, physical manipulation, and their own thought processes—observing what happens, reflecting on their findings, asking questions, and formulating answers. When objects, events, and other people challenge the working model that the child has mentally constructed, the child is forced to adjust the model or alter the mental structures to account for the new information.

Because play activities offer opportunities for this type of active, social learning to occur, play strategies are an important element in constructivist-oriented curriculums.

As defined in the influential position statement by the National Association for the Education of Young Children (NAEYC), *developmentally appropriate practice* is achieved when teachers provide learning environments and experiences based on three types of information (Bredekamp & Copple, 1997, p. 9):

1. *What is known about child development and learning*—knowledge of age-related human characteristics that permits general predictions within an age range about what activities, materials, interactions, or experiences will be safe, healthy, interesting and achievable, and also challenging to children;
2. *What is known about the strengths, interests, and needs of each individual child in the group* to be able to adapt for and be responsive to individual variation; and
3. *Knowledge of the social and cultural contexts with which the children live* to ensure that learning experiences are meaningful, relevant, and respectful for the participating children and their families.

We believe that play offers one of the best means for providing children with developmentally appropriate learning opportunities. We are not alone. One of the guiding principles in the NAEYC position statement on developmentally appropriate practice is that "play is an important vehicle for children's social, emotional, and cognitive development, as well as a reflection of their development" (Bredekamp & Copple, 1997, p. 9). The position statement urges teachers to use play as an instructional strategy and as a means for assessing children's knowledge and learning.

We begin this chapter with a discussion of the advantages of linking play and academic learning, focusing on reasons why play is a core element, or the "heart, mind, and soul" of developmentally appropriate practice. Next, we describe several ways in which play can be connected with the academic curriculum, and we provide examples of curriculum-generated play strategies that can be used in connection with language arts, mathematics, and science. This is followed by a section on play-generated curriculum and instruction in early childhood education. The chapter concludes with a discussion of some of the formidable barriers that can impede the implementation of play-based education at the preschool, kindergarten, and primary-grade levels.

ADVANTAGES OF LINKING PLAY AND ACADEMIC SUBJECTS

In Chapter 1, we discussed several traits or dispositional factors that set play apart from other behaviors, including positive affect, nonliterality, and a means-over-ends orientation (see the sidebar in that chapter, "Telltale Signs of Play?"). To this list, we add one further characteristic: Play experiences can offer a broad spectrum of learning opportunities. We believe that these basic characteristics of play (a) embody the major advantages of linking play and academic subjects, and (b) explain why play is at the heart of developmentally appropriate practice. We use several examples from one of our research projects on literacy-enriched play settings to illustrate these advantages (Enz & Christie, 1997).

POSITIVE AFFECT

Perhaps the most obvious characteristic of play is that it is fun and enjoyable. Smiles and laughter usually accompany play, signaling that play is occurring. When children incorporate academic skills and content into their play, these pleasurable feelings become associated with the academic subject area. This, in turn, can promote positive attitudes toward learning.

The enjoyment surrounding play can also supply motivation for engaging in academic activities. Children do not need to be "reinforced" or rewarded for playing. Play has its own intrinsic motivation—pleasure.

> *Joey and several of his preschool friends are playing in a post office theme center. Joey exclaims, "I'm going to write a letter!" He picks up a blank envelope and begins to write the letters of the alphabet. Before he writes each letter, he says all of the preceding letters: "A" [writes A]; "A, B" [writes B], "A, B, C" [writes C]. He continues to do this for the entire alphabet, smiling, laughing, and occasionally stopping to show his friends what he has accomplished ("Hey, look at this!"). This process is very time consuming (25 alphabet letters must be recited before writing Z), but Joey never appears to get tired or bored. Once his "letter" is completed, he delivers it to a friend and goes on to another, completely unrelated activity.*

If this alphabet writing activity had been "work" assigned by the teacher, it is highly doubtful that Joey would have persevered at this potentially boring task with such enthusiasm and interest. However, because Joey chose to do it just for "the fun of it" and could connect it with the post office play theme, the alphabet recitation/writing activity became very interesting, enjoyable, and intrinsically motivated.

NONLITERALITY

Play events are characterized by a play frame, within which personal meaning takes precedence over external reality. The usual meanings of objects are ignored, new meanings are substituted, and actions are performed differently than when they occur in nonplay settings.

> With some assistance from their preschool teacher, Noah and several friends are getting ready to take a make-believe plane trip to France. The elevated loft in the classroom has been equipped with chairs and has become the plane, and a nearby theme center has been turned into a ticket office. Noah goes into the "office," picks up a marker, and begins making scribbles on several small pieces of paper. The teacher passes by with some luggage for the trip. Noah says, "Here Kurt . . . here are some tickets." The teacher responds, "Oh great. Frequent flyer plan!" Noah then makes one more ticket for himself ("I need one, too"), using the same scribblelike script. As he leaves the center, he scribbles on a wall sign. Later, when asked what he has written, Noah explains that he wanted to let people know that he would be gone for a while.

This vignette illustrates how the nonliteral nature of play makes academic activities significant to children. The pieces of paper that Noah produced would be meaningless in most situations. Within the context of a make-believe plane trip, however, Noah's scribbles represented writing and the pieces of paper signified tickets, not just to Noah, but to the teacher and the other children, as well. This make-believe orientation enabled Noah to demonstrate his growing awareness of the practical functions of print. He showed that he knew that printed tickets can grant access to experiences such as trips and that signs can be used to leave messages for other people. In addition, the acceptance of his efforts by other players made Noah think of himself as a successful writer.

MEANS-OVER-ENDS ORIENTATION

When children play, their attention is focused on the activity itself, rather than on the goals or outcomes of the activity. In other words, means are more important than ends. This is why children often knock down block constructions right after completing them and sometimes abandon dramatizations in midstream. The act of building or dramatizing is of primary importance, not the structures being built or the stories being enacted.

This feature of play creates a low-risk environment because if outcomes are not important, then mistakes are inconsequential. There is little to lose from taking a chance and trying something new or difficult. Noah felt safe using scribble writing to construct tickets and signs. As long as these print items functioned successfully in the context of the play, they were sufficient. In nonplay situations, the tickets and signs would become much more important, decreasing the likelihood that Noah would chance using a personal form of script to construct them. Play-related literacy activities have the advantage of inviting children to experiment with emergent forms of writing and reading.

BROAD SPECTRUM OF LEARNING OPPORTUNITIES

One of the key features of developmentally appropriate practice (DAP) is that teachers should attempt to match learning activities to children's abilities, interests, and needs. Given the tremendous range of individual variation, this is a tall order when dealing with large groups of children. Traditional forms of whole-group instruction often fail to meet this criterion. The skill or concept being taught may have already been mastered by some in the group and may be too difficult or advanced for others.

Play-based learning activities often have the advantage of offering children opportunities to learn a variety of different skills and concepts (see Figure 11.1). In addition, play can provide multiple ways for children to learn these skills. This broad spectrum of learning outcomes and processes helps ensure that all children have opportunities to learn relevant skills in a developmentally appropriate manner.

Figure 11.1

Literacy-enriched play centers: A broad spectrum for learning opportunities

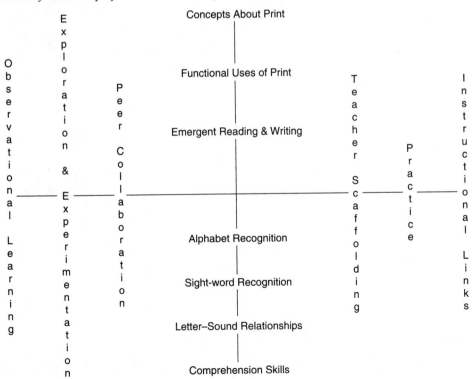

In order to illustrate this feature of linking play and academics, we use literacy-enriched play centers, a strategy described in detail later in this chapter, in the section on curriculum-generated play. This strategy involves adding theme-related reading and writing materials to sociodramatic play areas. For example, the following literacy props could be used in connection with a pizza parlor play center:

- Cardboard pizza crusts (large circles)
- Felt pizza ingredients (tomato sauce [large red circles the same size as the cardboard crusts], pepperoni, black olives, onions, etc.)
- Pencils, pens, markers
- Note pads for taking orders
- Menus
- Wall signs (e.g., "Place Your Order Here")
- Employee name tags
- Pizza boxes with company names and logos
- Cookbooks
- Blank checks
- Newspaper ads and discount coupons

Literacy-enriched play settings, such as this pizza parlor center, provide children with a broad range of opportunities to learn about reading and writing.

OPPORTUNITIES TO LEARN DIFFERENT SKILLS   The literacy-enriched pizza parlor setting provides children with opportunities to learn important *concepts about print*. At the most basic level, the literacy props illustrate that print has meaning. Children demonstrate this awareness when they point to a menu or wall sign and ask the teacher or peer, "What does that say?" These print props also provide opportunities for children to learn more advanced concepts, such as the difference between a letter and a word. Literacy terms, such as *letter* and *word* are often used by children and adults during play in print-enriched centers.

The pizza parlor setting contains many examples of the *functional uses of print*. Print is used to convey information on menus and pizza boxes. Signs, such as "Place Your Order Here" and "The Line Starts Here," illustrate the regulatory function of print.

Pizza parlors also are associated with *literacy routines*—sets of reading and writing actions that are ordinary practices of a culture (Neuman & Roskos, 1997). These routines demonstrate the instrumental functions of print and present opportunities for children to use *emergent forms of writing and reading:* Customers can read or pretend to read menus while placing orders. Waiters and counter clerks can use note pads to write down orders that will later be used by the chefs to determine which types of pizzas to bake. Chefs can consult cookbooks for information on how to prepare pizzas. Once the pizzas are baked, customers can use discount coupons from the newspaper to reduce the cost of their meals and pay their bill by writing checks.

As children have repeated exposure to print props, opportunities arise for developing *alphabet* and *sight-word recognition:* Some children may learn to recognize the letter *p* because it is the first letter in *pizza*. Others may learn to recognize entire words, such as *pepperoni, menu,* and *cheese.*

More advanced children may begin to learn about *letter–sound relationships*. For example, they may notice that *pizza, pepperoni,* and *Pepsi* all start with the letter *p* and the same sound. They may then make an association between the letter and the sound.

Opportunities also exist to learn *comprehension skills:* Neuman and Roskos (1997) have detailed how playing in print-enriched settings can lead children to develop several types of strategic knowledge that have a role in comprehending text. In a pizza parlor setting, children have opportunities to

- Seek information—A child might ask a playmate about the identity of a word on the pizza menu
- Check to see whether guesses and hypotheses are correct—A child might ask the teacher, "Is this how you spell *pizza*"?
- Self-correct errors—While writing the word "piza" on a sign, a child might exclaim, "Oops, *pizza* has two *z*'s!"

Checking and correcting are self-regulatory mechanisms that build a base for cognitive monitoring during reading.

MULTIPLE WAYS TO LEARN   The pizza parlor center presents many opportunities for *observational learning:* The center contains a variety of different types of print for children to observe and study, such as signs, menus, name tags, print on pizza boxes, and cookbooks. As players act out the literacy routines associated with pizza parlors—ordering from a menu, writing down orders, paying bills with checks—opportunities are created for other children to observe many functional uses of print.

As children act out these restaurant-related literacy routines, opportunities emerge for *exploration* and *experimentation:* Children can try out emergent versions of reading and writing and see how they work. Customers can attempt to read menus, using memory, print, and picture cues to come up with their best guesses about the contents. Waiters can write down orders using scribbles, letterlike forms, random letter streams, or invented spelling. The make-believe play frame makes it clearly permissible to use personalized script to represent writing and to pretend to read, rather than to accurately recognize every word in a text.

Much of the play in print-enriched centers is social, creating opportunities for *peer collaboration.* Research has shown that children use a variety of strategies—such as modeling, designating, and coaching—to help each other engage in play-related literacy activities (Neuman & Roskos, 1991; Stone & Christie, 1996).

As explained in Chapter 1, Vygotsky (1978) has described how adult-child interaction can create a "zone of proximal development," allowing children to engage in activities that they could not do on their own. Many opportunities for this type of *teacher scaffolding* can occur naturally in the course of play in literacy-enriched settings (Enz & Christie, 1997; Roskos & Neuman, 1993). For example, the teacher might help children make a sign for their pizza shop, assist with reading words on the menu, or supply the conventional spellings of words when children request them. This type of play-related teaching tends to be very effective because the skills are of high interest and of immediate use to children in their play activities.

Literacy-enriched play settings provide opportunities for children to *practice* literacy skills they are beginning to master. For example, a child may have begun to recognize some of the words associated with pizza parlors: *pizza, pepperoni, sausage, cheese, olives,* and *mushrooms.* This child will delight in reading these words repeatedly on menus and on orders that other children have written. This sight-recognition practice is likely to be much more meaningful than identifying a series of random words on flashcards or on a worksheet.

Finally, opportunities also exist for teachers to make *instructional links* between play and the academic curriculum. For example, if a teacher was instructing children about letter-sound relationships (phonics), links could be made to important play-related words. For example, the words *pizza* and *Pepsi* could be used to help children discover the relationship between the letter p and the sound it represents. This play linkage would create a personal connection between the child and the letter–sound relationship, probably making the rule more meaningful and easier to remember.

PLAY AND CURRICULUM

Play can have a multifaceted relationship with the academic curriculum. Van Hoorn, Nourot, Scales, and Alward (1993) have proposed several possible connections between the two, including

- *Curriculum-generated play*—Teachers provide play experiences that can enable children to learn concepts and skills from curriculum areas such as literacy, mathematics, and science. Marilyn's numeracy-enriched store center, described in the vignette at the beginning of this chapter, is a good example. Children can learn to recognize numbers and to count while playing in this center.
- *Play-generated curriculum*—Teachers organize learning experiences around themes and interests that children demonstrate in their play. For example, if children express interest in sea creatures in their play (e.g., pretending to be whales and sharks), their teacher could take advantage of this interest by designing an integrated, interdisciplinary unit focusing on fish and other things that live in the sea. In the process of learning about sea creatures, children would have opportunities to use and learn a variety of skills and concepts connected with literacy, mathematics, and science.

It is possible to have a two-way relationship between play and the academic curriculum, with the curriculum generating play experiences and children's play behavior influencing curriculum content.

CURRICULUM-GENERATED PLAY

Curriculum-generated play can serve two important functions, depending on when it occurs in relationship to instruction (see Figure 11.2):

Figure 11.2

Curriculum-generated play: Two functions

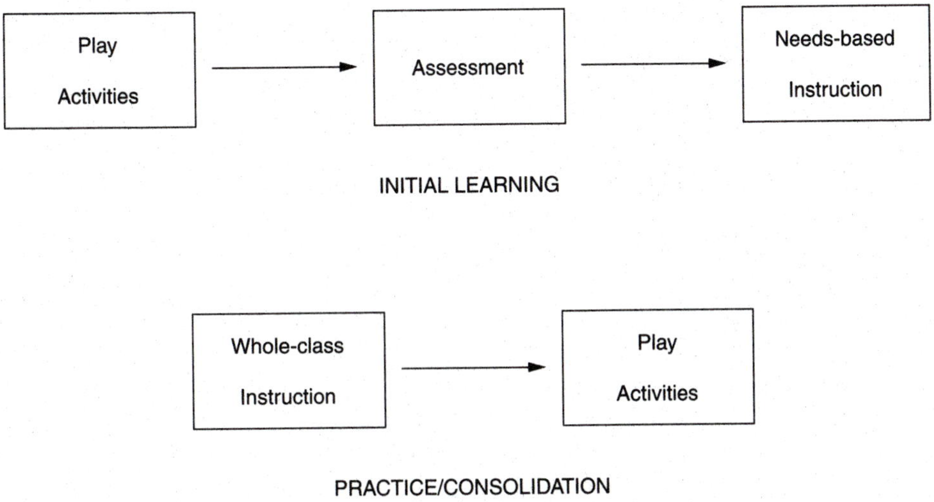

INITIAL LEARNING

PRACTICE/CONSOLIDATION

- *Initial learning*—Play activities precede instruction, providing initial opportunities for children to learn skills and concepts. After children have opportunities to play, the teacher assesses their acquisition of the target skills and provides instruction to those who did not master the skill through play.
- *Practice and consolidation*—Play follows direct instruction, providing enjoyable, meaningful opportunities to practice the skills that were taught.

The same play activity can serve either function, depending on when it occurs. Take, for example, the numeracy-enriched store center described in the vignette at the beginning of this chapter. The teacher, Marilyn, used this center as an initial opportunity for her students to learn number recognition and counting skills. As an alternative, Marilyn could have provided direct instruction on these skills first and then used the store center to provide opportunities for children to practice their numbers and counting skills.

These dual functions allow play activities to be used by teachers with diverse philosophies of learning and instruction. Teachers with constructivist beliefs, like Marilyn, can use play activities as initial learning opportunities. More traditional teachers, who rely heavily on direct instruction, can also take advantage of many of play's educational benefits, using play to provide highly motivated practice for the skills they teach.

We wish to emphasize the important role of assessment and needs-based instruction in the initial-learning function of curriculum-generated play. Play activities can offer children developmentally appropriate means for learning a broad spectrum of academic concepts and skills. However, it is important to note that opportunities for learning, no matter how rich and varied, do not guarantee that learning will occur. It is possible for children to play in Marilyn's math-enriched store center and be oblivious to the numbers and opportunities for counting that are offered in the center. For this reason, assessment is needed to determine whether children acquire the skills and concepts that curriculum-generated play experiences are intended to teach. If some children fail to learn these skills through play, then the teacher can use more direct forms of instruction to help those particular children master the skills. Note that this is *needs-based instruction* that is given only to the children who still need to learn the skills following play experiences (as opposed to *whole-class instruction* that is delivered to every student).

In the sections that follow, we present examples of several major types of curriculum-generated play activities that can be used to help children learn and practice skills in language arts, mathematics, science, and social studies. These are just a sampling of the types of curriculum-generated play that are available.

ACADEMICALLY ENRICHED PLAY CENTERS   In previous chapters, we have discussed how sociodramatic play centers can provide children with opportunities to develop oral language, cognitive, and social skills. The basic ingredients for developmentally stimulating play centers are well-arranged space for play (Chapter 9), theme-related props (Chapter 10), adequate play time (Chapter 7), and appropriate forms of teacher involvement in play (Chapter 7).

The learning potential of sociodramatic play centers can be greatly expanded by adding one more ingredient: academically related props and materials. Marilyn's numeracy-enriched store center, described in the opening vignette, is an excellent example. In addition to regular store play props, she added several types of scales, a rubber stamp with rotating numbers, hand calculators, an adding machine, coupons, and supermarket ads. The addition of these math-related props transformed the center into an ideal environment for her students to learn about numbers and counting.

Most of the research on academic-enriched play settings has focused on literacy. This is due, in large part, to the growing influence of the *emergent-literacy perspective* (McGee & Richgels, 1996; Sulzby & Teale, 1991). According to this view, written language is acquired in much the same way as oral language. Literacy learning begins very early and occurs in the context of everyday social activities. According to the emergent literacy perspective, young children's initial encounters with reading and writing should be social in nature and should focus on the practical, everyday functions of print. Literacy-enriched play centers provide an excellent means for children to have these types of experiences (Christie, 1991, 1994). The strategy is a simple one: Add theme-related reading and writing materials to play centers, creating settings that resemble the literacy environments that young children encounter at home and in their communities. The literacy-enriched pizza parlor theme center, described earlier in this chapter, is an excellent example.

Research conducted in preschool and kindergarten classrooms has shown that literacy-enriched play settings result in large increases in emergent reading and writing activity during play (Christie & Enz, 1992; Morrow & Rand, 1991; Neuman & Roskos, 1992; Vukelich, 1991). Figure 11.3 illustrates a sample of the writing that a 4-year-old did while playing in an "animal hospital" center. Jason, in the role of veterinarian, wrote a prescription for a patient's sick teddy bear. He copied one of the prescribed cures, *apple juice*, from an empty can he found in the trash. However, he wasn't able to find a model for the spelling of the other cure, penicillin. So Jason had to invent the spelling, using his knowledge of letters and words. While his spelling is not conventional, he started with the correct letter, *p*, and he did represent the fact that it was a long word with lots of letters.

In addition to increased amounts of reading and writing activity, evidence is accumulating that children learn important skills and concepts about literacy while playing in print-rich play settings. For example, Vukelich (1991) found that children gained knowledge about the functional uses of writing, and Neuman and Roskos (1997) reported that children acquired self-regulatory mechanisms, such as checking and self-correcting, that build a base for cognitive monitoring during reading.

Literacy-enriched play centers have also been found to enhance the quality of children's dramatic play. Detailed analyses of videotaped play sessions in the Neuman and Roskos (1992) study revealed that the play sequences of children who played in literacy-enriched centers were 10 times longer and much more complex than those of the control group. These effects were maintained over the entire 7 months of the study, indicating that novelty of the literacy props was not a factor.

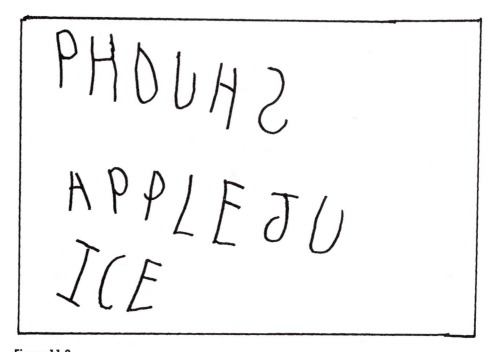

Figure 11.3

Jason's prescription for a sick teddy bear: Penicillin and apple juice.

Table 11.1 presents examples of literacy materials that can be used with a variety of dramatic-play themes. Note that most of these materials are inexpensive and easy to obtain. Converting traditional play areas into "literate" play centers requires a minimum of resources and effort. In return, children's play options are expanded, and they are presented with meaningful opportunities to experiment with emergent forms of reading and writing.

Play centers can be enriched to promote learning in other curriculum areas, such as science and social studies. Roskos (1994) helped two kindergarten teachers develop play settings that were closely connected with academic content presented in whole-group instruction. For example, during a 6-week unit on winter, the teachers taught children how to read thermometers and how to record information using symbols for degrees. To connect this content with play, the teachers provisioned the math and science lab play center with various types of thermometers; note pads and pencils for recording data; materials for an experiment measuring the temperature of water under different circumstances, lab coats for dress-up, and printed matter related to the topic.

Children's play in these instruction-related play centers was videotaped and analyzed. Results showed that a majority of the children's interactions were related to the content-oriented activity offered in the centers (e.g., using thermometers). What was more impressive, the children's attraction to the content-oriented activities was stable across the span of the play activity. That is, the children did not drift off into off-task activities such as visiting with

Table 11.1 PROPS FOR LITERACY-ENRICHED PLAY CENTERS

HOME CENTER
Pencils, pens, markers
Note pads
Post-It notes
Baby sitter instruction forms
Telephone book
Telephone message pads
Message board
Children's books
Magazines, newspapers
Cookbooks, recipe box
Product containers from
   children's homes
Junk mail

BUSINESS OFFICE
Pencils, pens, markers
Note pads
Telephone message forms
Calendar
Typewriter
Order forms
Stationery, envelopes, stamps
File folders
Wall signs

RESTAURANT
Pencils
Note pads
Menus
Wall signs ("Pay Here")
Bank checks
Cookbooks
Product containers

POST OFFICE
Pencils, pens, markers
Stationery and envelopes
Stamps
Mailboxes
Address labels
Wall signs ("Line Starts Here")

GROCERY STORE
Pencils, pens, markers
Note pads
Bank checks
Wall signs ("Supermarket")
Shelf labels for store areas ("Meat")
Product containers

VETERINARIAN'S OFFICE
Pencils, pens, markers
Appointment book
Wall signs ("Receptionist")
Labels with pets' names
Patient charts
Prescription forms
Magazines (in waiting room)

AIRPORT/AIRPLANE
Pencils, pens, markers
Tickets
Bank checks
Luggage tags
Magazines (on board plane)
Air sickness bags with
   printed instructions
Maps
Signs ("Baggage Claim Area")

LIBRARY
Pencils
Books
Shelf labels for books
   ("ABCs," "Animals")
Wall signs ("Quiet!")
Library cards
Check-out cards for books

Source: Christie, Enz, and Vukelich (1997), p. 151.

friends or other forms of play. Roskos concluded that "the combination of setting cues (e.g., the 'lab'), objects (i.e., the experiment, paper and writing tools), and opportunities for peer interaction around a common purpose appeared to create sufficient conditions for enjoyment that urged children to persist in the content-focused task as a form of play activity" (p. 10).

Jarrett (1997) describes a number of sociodramatic play centers designed to make science and mathematics concepts interesting and fun to learn. She includes lists of props for setting up a math- or science-oriented doctor's office, supermarket, zoo, and museum. Our favorite is the combined "fix-it shop" and "inventor's workshop." Suggested materials include

- Simple tools (screwdrivers, hammer, pliers, adjustable wrench)
- Fasteners (nails, nuts and bolts, glue)
- Old appliances (toasters, tape recorders, door bells, hair dryers, electric motors)
- Junk materials (egg cartons, paper cups, scraps of wood)
- Batteries and wires
- Low-voltage lightbulbs (e.g., from flashlights)

Possible activities include (a) taking apart the appliances to look for magnets and other useful components, (b) designing and building light circuits, and (c) inventing items to be used by people with disabilities. Jarrett warns teachers that this center will require more supervision than other play settings. She recommends cutting off electric cords before allowing children to play with appliances. She also warns against allowing children to disassemble television sets because of the danger of shocks, even when unplugged. The same warning applies to electronic flash units from cameras.

GAMES *Games* are activities "in which an individual or team of individuals play or compete against one another with an agreed-upon set of rules, a limited time, and a means of scoring" (Clegg, 1991). From a developmental perspective, "games are an ideal candidate for an intersection between formal school and children's play" (Fernie, 1988). Games can offer a highly enjoyable means for children to learn new academic skills and to practice skills that have already been taught.

Casberque and Kieff (1998) offer a number of examples of how traditional games, such as jacks and marbles, offer children opportunities to learn basic concepts in mathematics and science. For example, here are some of the learning opportunities that occur when children play jacks:

> When playing jacks, for example, children must toss out 10 to 12 jacks and then pick them up in successively larger groups with each turn. On the first turn, they pick up single jacks; on the second turn they pick up two at a time, and so on. . . . As children move through the steps of this game, they are constantly (while not necessarily consciously) using concepts of addition, multiplication, and division to determine which jacks to pick up. On their third turn, for instance, they see that ten jacks divided into threes yields three sets of jacks to

pick up, with one remaining to be scooped up by itself. As a cumulative effect of this play, children develop a perceptual understanding of group configurations, as well as the concept of grouping. (p. 145)

Casberque and Kieff explain that the game of dominoes focuses children's attention on one-to-one correspondence, the concept of higher and lower numbers, and basic counting skills. Marbles provide opportunities to learn basic science concepts such as trajectory and velocity. Casberque and Kieff point out that these games also promote social development by requiring children to negotiate and follow a set of rules. In order to successfully play games, children must share, take turns, cooperate, be sensitive to other players' viewpoints, and delay gratification.

In addition to traditional games, games can also be specially designed by teachers to provide opportunities to learn academic skills. Some of the best examples of instructional games are contained in the "constructivist" mathematics curricula developed by Constance Kamii (1985, 1989). Take, for example, the "The Hundred Board," a game from Kamii's (1989) second-grade mathematics program, which helps children learn about our base-10 number system and provides experience with finding numbers that are 1 more, 1 less, 10 more, or 10 less than a given number. The basic materials consist of a blank 10 × 10 grid and 100 tiles numbered 1–100. The tiles are placed upside down, and each player selects eight tiles and keeps them face up in front of her or him. One of the remaining tiles is turned up and placed in its appropriate space on the grid. For example, 68 would be placed six rows down and 8 columns to the right. The players then take turns placing tiles on the grid, which touch a side or corner of a tile already on the board. For example, if 68 is on the board, then 57, 58, 59, 67, 69, 77, 78, and 79 can be played. If a player does not have a tile that can be played, that person misses a turn and must take one of the face-down tiles. The first player to use all of her or his tiles is the winner.

Kamii and Lewis (1992, pp. 90–91) explain the advantages of using games over traditional drill-and-practice worksheets:

1. *In games the motivation to work comes from the children.* Children beg to play games. In contrast, most children complete worksheets because they are externally motivated by games or stickers or afraid of consequences such as missing recess. . . .
2. *In games children invent their own strategies and ways of achieving their goals.* If children play a board game with one die, for example, we simply introduce a second die and let them figure out what to do. . . . When worksheets are used, children repeat the same kind of calculation over and over, with only slight variations. Worksheet[s] thus promote mechanical repetition and mental passivity. . . .
3. *In games, children supervise and correct each other.* If one player takes a 3 and an 8 in Tens [a card game in which players can only use pairs of cards that make a total of 10], for example, another player is likely to object immediately. Immediate feedback from a peer is much more effective than worksheets corrected by the teacher. Worksheets are usually returned the next day, and young children cannot remember and do not care what they did yesterday.

In Kamii's curriculum, the natural activity of game playing is linked to the academic curriculum. Unfortunately, in our work-dominated elementary schools, many purportedly educational games violate basic principles of play and games. Fernie (1988, pp. 7–8) gives the following example of an academically distorted version of tic-tac-toe:

> The teacher has prepared a worksheet with a number of *tic-tac-toe* type grids. The boxes in each grid are filled with single digit numbers instead of *X*'s and *O*'s. Rows, columns, and diagonal "lines" are cleverly arranged to present sums adding to 9 in most directions. The "game" is for the individual child to find "wrong" lines (i.e., those not adding to 9) and to mark them. The teacher, of course, collects the worksheets marks the child's answers right or wrong, and grades the paper.

Another example of a pseudo game, "Math Baseball," was used unwittingly by one of the authors when he taught fourth grade. The class is divided into two teams, and four chairs are arranged like a baseball diamond. A coin is flipped to determine which team is "at bat." The teacher poses a mathematical problem (e.g., $9 \times 4 = ?$) to the first player on this team. If the player gives the correct answer, he or she moves to first base. If the question is answered incorrectly, the player is "out." The team continues to advance around the bases and score runs by crossing "home plate" until three "outs" occur. Then the other team is "at bat."

Fernie (1988) points out that these gamelike activities are not truly games because

- The rules were not negotiated or agreed upon by the players.
- Peer interaction is replaced with the solitary activity of filling in a worksheet in the first example or with a public performance in the second example.
- The playful tension on winning or losing is replaced by the serious adult standard of right and wrong answers.

It is also very doubtful that most children would find these activities to be enjoyable or that they would choose to engage in the activities on their own. King's (1979) research on children's perceptions of play revealed that kindergartners labeled this type of mathematics and spelling games as "work," even though teachers referred to them as "play."

SIMULATIONS   *Simulations* are a special type of game, based on a model of a real situation, which is designed to teach about principles that operate in that situation (Clegg, 1991). Role playing is used to increase students' personal involvement in the activity. In genuine simulation games, players act out well-defined roles and encounter decision-making situations that require them to choose from designated options. There are also less-structured simulations, which give players more control over their roles and actions.

As mentioned in Chapter 10, many high-quality computer simulation games have become available in recent years, many of which can help children learn academic skills and content. For example, *Sim City* can help students learn a variety of social-studies concepts, encompassing government and economics. Players set up their own city—buy land, build roads, set up utilities, establish businesses, confront environmental issues, conduct elections, and so on—and encounter situations that are very similar to real life.

Of course, simulations are not limited to computers. Here are examples of two traditional simulation activities:

1. "Pioneers"—In this highly structured simulation game, students become members of four wagon trains heading for Oregon in 1846 (Wesley, 1974). After choosing their family identities, students must select supplies to carry west in their wagons. Once underway, they must make a variety of important decisions. For example, when they reach a place where the trail divides into two branches, they are given information about each route and must select the best way to proceed. Fate cards are drawn by each group, to simulate uncontrollable events such as snakes, weather, and broken wagon wheels. The students also write diary entries about their experiences. Points are given based on the quality of the decisions that players make, and these points determine how quickly each wagon train moves along the trail. The first group to reach Oregon is the winner.

2. "Improvised Drama Unit"—Students pretend to be members of an indigenous tribe living in a valley where Brazilian engineers were planning to build a dam (Wagner, 1983). The children improvise a drama about their tribal life, writing about their experiences as members of the tribe. When the students began to feel like a tribe, the teacher introduces the problem facing them: Their homeland will soon be flooded because workers were blocking the river to build a dam. The children then plan and act out a drama about the conflict between the natives and the dam builders, giving rise to questions about Brazilian tribal life and the reasons for constructing dams. They then read and gather information to answer these questions. For a culminating activity, the class reenacts the life of the tribe, using the information obtained through their reading to make their improvisations more authentic and true to life.

PLAY-GENERATED CURRICULUM

One common type of play-generated curriculum occurs during free play or spontaneous play periods. In many preschool and kindergarten classrooms, play is almost synonymous with curriculum. Teachers orchestrate space, time, and materials to invite children's active participation in generating experiences and activities that are meaningful and productive for each child. The intention is to provide enriching stimulation for the whole child in a naturalistic context. Play is seen as a medium of learning and is developmentally appropriate practice par excellence.

One important criterion for evaluating the quality of play as curriculum is to determine how well the classroom environments that we create are responding to the "continuum of a child's experiences" (Cuffaro, 1995). *Continuum of experience,* a concept stemming from the educational philosophy of

John Dewey, refers to the connections among the child's familiar and remembered past, the alive and developing present, and the anticipated and unanticipated future, with all its promises and surprises. The "educational fallacy" is that we give the child experiences in free play. Experiences are had, not given. The setting should be unpressured in time and space, with appropriate social and material stimulation to afford opportunities for the child's invention and creation of curriculum and learning.

A second important criterion for high-quality educational play is *interaction*. As a child produces scripts in play, teachers need to attend to how to encourage a balanced interaction between objective and subjective factors—between reality and social constraints on the one hand, and the child's fantasies, feelings, and personal idiosyncratic needs on the other hand.

As we discussed in Chapter 7, there are numerous ways teachers can enrich play in early childhood educational settings. Teachers need to carefully observe in detail each child at play alone and when playing with others in different social contexts. Sensitive teachers can have a determining role in elevating the play process through the support and scaffolding they provide. In addition to making available appropriate time, space, and materials, teachers can assist through their suggestions, modeling, and coaching, as well as by providing themes that can be extended from one day to the next (Bodrova & Leong, 1996).

Thinking of play as a source of learning and curriculum development inevitably leads to the question of entry points. Cuffaro (1995) poses the following question: "Are there entry points for teachers in children's play? Do we introduce themes into children's play? Or do we guide/shape play primarily through questions, discussions, and trips? . . . How do we approach play in order to realize the potential of the social individual, develop a sense of community, and surface individual questions and interests?" (p. 82). Teacher choices should be based on trying to relate experience with education, following the Deweyan principles of continuity and interaction noted previously. According to Cuffaro, it is more challenging to seek out and use children's interests as the basis of play-spawned curriculum than it is to select for them, in advance, a play theme or topic.

Cuffaro (1995, p. 86) gives an example of how children and their play helped to shape the curriculum in a Bank Street kindergarten program. It was midyear, and the children's play was becoming stale and repetitive. The teacher revitalized the children's play by asking them to engage in some type of play that they had never done before. One child's idea was that the entire floor become an ocean!

TEACHER   I've been thinking—what would it be like if all the floor in the block area became a river?

YVONNE: So what do we do, swim all the time?

RICHARD: You could fish, too.

YVONNE: I don't want to fish. I want to make a school.

RICHARD: You could do that.

YVONNE: (incredulous) In the river?

TODD: Wait, Wait! I have an idea. An ocean, an ocean, all the floor an ocean.

Todd's idea was accepted by the teachers and the other children and eventually led to extended dramatic play about island life, water transportation, the birth of a hurricane, and related topics. In this example, a great deal of germane social studies subject matter emerged as the children's play evolved.

The line between play as curriculum and play-generated curriculum is often blurred, as in the preceding example. Teachers are more likely to fuse play and curriculum with younger children or when the focus is more on socioemotional goals than on intellectual and academic goals. When the focus shifts to cognitive learning, however, teachers are more likely to take ideas from free play and to use them as the basis for follow-up or related activities in adjacent time slots in the daily schedule. This is a *juxtaposition model* of play and the curriculum. Alternatively, teachers can serve as spokespersons for reality during free play itself and can try to take advantage of teachable moments (e.g., guided self-discovery). This is the *integration model* of play and the curriculum. A *segregation model* occurs when only recreational play is allowed in a program, such as during recess, and there is no attempt to have educational play.

Many teachers and programs use a combination of the integration and the juxtaposition models. They are not mutually exclusive. For example, the High/Scope Cognitively Oriented Curriculum uses a *plan–do–recall* play and learning cycle (Weikart & Schweinhart, 1993). Children think about and declare what they plan to do during free play (which play or activity center they will use), engage in their intended behaviors (with considerable latitude or leeway, in keeping with developmentally appropriate practice), and then gather at group time to recap free-play events. Planning, reconstruction, and communication skills are thereby fostered. The use of this cycle does not preclude teachers from facilitating play and learning during the *do* phase.

Additional examples of the teacher using experiences during free-play time as the basis for discussion and learning include whole-class (large circle time) discussion of problems that came up during play time. Vivian Paley (1997) recommends that the teacher should carefully observe free play and should routinely bring to the children's attention fresh problems that arise that day for group reflection and discussion. For example, perhaps one child was having trouble using a certain toy, or joining a group, or making the color brown at the easel board. For Paley, an uninvented curriculum is worse than an unexamined one (Paley, 1997). With the help and inspiration of one of her pupils (Reeny), Paley remarkably centered her whole kindergarten curriculum for the entire year on something that emerged from Reeny and classmates at play—an unfolding passion and inquisitiveness for the books and characters of author Leo Lionni.

The Projects Approach (Katz & Chard, 1993) uses free play and projects or sustained investigations in the informal part of the program. Projects emanate from children's interests, as surmised by teachers who observe the children at play. This approach also exemplifies how play can spawn curriculum and how play and learning and teaching all interconnect. Teachers and children are co–decision makers and coconstructors in this model of early childhood curriculum. The world-renowned Reggio Emilia program is another illustration akin to the Projects Approach.

Integrated or *thematic units* can also be designed to capitalize on interests that children demonstrate in their play. Readers who have an interest in this approach to curriculum planning are referred to Neuman and Roskos's (1993) discussion of child-centered activity planning and Christie, Enz, and Vukelich's (1997) directions for planning integrated, interdisciplinary curriculum activities.

BARRIERS TO SCHOOL PLAY

We have described a number of ways in which play can support and enhance the academic curriculum. Unfortunately, teachers sometimes run into roadblocks when they try to use play in their classrooms. These impediments or barriers are more common at the elementary-grade level, but many preschool and kindergarten teachers also experience difficulties implementing play-based curricula.

PRESCHOOL AND KINDERGARTEN

Early childhood education is built on a long-established tradition that play has a key role in learning and development. However, recent observational studies in England (Moyles, 1989) and in the United States (Polito, 1994) have revealed an apparent gap between rhetoric and reality concerning the role of play in some preschool and kindergarten classrooms. In these studies, teachers stated that play was valuable and had an important role in their curriculum. However, the teachers' actions often revealed that play was secondary to activities that the teachers supervise and direct.

Bennett, Wood, and Rogers (1997) conducted an extensive, yearlong study of nine early childhood teachers in British schools to investigate factors that might be contributing to this gap between rhetoric and reality. The teachers filled out preobservation questionnaires about their intended goals for play activities; next, the play activities were videotaped; and then the teachers were interviewed while they viewed the videotapes of the play.

The teachers indicated that they had a strong commitment to using play as an integral part of the curriculum. They believed that play provided ideal conditions for learning. Observation, however, revealed that in spite of their strong commitment to play, the teachers undervalued their role in play and focused their attention on more formal, worklike activities. Interviews revealed that this devaluing of play was often caused by constraints of time, space, teacher–child ratios and curriculum pressures to teach basic skills, as well as the teachers' own beliefs that adults should not intervene in play. In addition, the teachers often made unrealistic assumptions about how children would respond to play activities, over- or underestimating children's competencies or the degree of challenge presented by the play context. This further undermined the teachers' confidence in using play as a learning medium.

Bennett et al. (1997) found that the most successful play activities involved teacher participation. Teacher involvement appeared to lessen the impact of constraining factors and to promote student learning. Learning was facilitated when teachers outlined expectations for the activity and assisted children in articulating what they learned from the play. Here are some of the recommendations that Bennett et al. (1997, p. 130) made for improving the quality of play in schools:

- Integrating play into the curriculum through clearly specified aims and intentions
- Making time for high-quality interactions to enhance learning through play
- Recognizing opportunities for teaching through play, rather than relying on spontaneous learning
- Providing a structure for review time, so that children become more consciously aware of what they are doing, learning, and achieving in their play

ELEMENTARY GRADES

Barriers to play are considerably more daunting in the elementary grades. American elementary schools have a long tradition of being work oriented. Elementary schools are viewed as agencies, the main duty of which is to prepare children for their roles in adult society, with goals focusing almost exclusively on academic skills and work habits (Fernie, 1988). Direct instruction, rather than play, has been the preferred means for accomplishing these goals (Glickman, 1984). Play is regarded, at best, as a peripheral activity.

Klugman (1990) used a questionnaire to gather information about elementary-school principals' views about play. The findings highlight play's low status in the elementary grades. Eighty-nine percent of the administrators believed that play should be an integral part of the preschool curriculum, whereas only 9% responded that play should have an important role in third-grade programs. The prevailing view is that while preschools are places to play, elementary schools should focus on "real learning" (Bowman, 1990).

In addition to this general antiplay philosophy, the same factors that can impede play in early childhood settings—lack of time and adequate space, high teacher–child ratios and curriculum pressures to teach basic skills—are present in the elementary grades, often in bigger doses. For example, Goldhaber (1994) explains that elementary-school schedules are often composed of short blocks of time devoted to different curriculum areas. These short periods, coupled with interruptions for special activities—such as physical education, art, and music—make it difficult to schedule the long, uninterrupted periods of time needed for curriculum-generated play activities. In addition, many of the materials that are essential for play-based activities are absent from or forbidden in elementary classrooms. She explains that often "sand and water may be too messy, duct tape too sticky and ceiling tile struts too fragile" (p. 24).

In spite of this less than optimal environment, play does occur in American elementary schools. In her research review, King (1987) identified three types of play that are found at the elementary-grade level:

1. *Instrumental play*—This is the curriculum-generated play described previously. This play is used as means for helping children learn academic skills and knowledge.

2. *Recreational play*—This is free play that occurs outside the classroom at recess and before and after school. This play consists primarily of games (jacks, hop scotch, tag), sports (kickball, soccer, tetherball), and rough-and-tumble activity. This type of play is at odds with the work-oriented goals of the elementary school. It is not surprising, therefore, that there has been a recent movement to eliminate recess from the daily schedule (Johnson, 1998). The rationale is that by deleting useless play time, more time will be available for academic work.

3. *Illicit play*—This is play that happens behind the teacher's back. Examples include passing notes, shooting wads of paper or rubber bands, making faces, giggling, sharpening pencils needlessly, pretending to chew gum, and being intentionally late to class. Teachers try to suppress this type of play but rarely succeed. Illicit play becomes more prevalent in the upper grades, perhaps in response to reduced opportunities for recreational play (Everhart, 1987).

Recreational play is free play that occurs outside the classroom at recess and before and after school.

King (1987) contends that illicit play provides children with a sense of autonomy and control in an adult-dominated situation. The more teacher centered the curriculum, the more likely children are to engage in illicit play. This, in turn, prompts teachers to view play as "the enemy" (Perlmutter & Burrell, 1995) and encourages them to banish all forms of play from their classroom.

On the positive side, research indicates that when teachers provide opportunities for primary-grade children to engage in recreational and instrumental play in the classroom, the children respond by engaging in high-quality play. Perlmutter and Burrell (1995, p. 16) observed that the play of primary-grade children was more focused and precise than that of most younger children:

> Second graders playing in sand want to have areas clearly marked and want a purpose for all of the materials. Buildings become more complex and intricate as children's abilities expand. In dramatic play a group of the same children may maintain a complex story line over several weeks.

While playing in academically enriched play centers, primary-grade children also engage in more sophisticated literacy and mathematics activities than younger children do. For example, chapters in the book by Hall and Abbott (1991), *Play in the Primary Curriculum,* present many illustrations of the advanced writing that British primary children produced while playing in literacy-enriched centers, such as a travel agency and an airport.

Curriculum-generated play also provides opportunities for social interaction and collaborative learning—an advantage that is amplified in multi-age settings. Stone and Christie (1996) have documented how older, expert peers helped younger, novice classmates to engage in reading and writing activities in a literacy-enriched home center in a K–2 multi-age classroom.

Given all the advantages of using curriculum-generated play in the primary grades, what can educators do to counteract the antiplay forces and constraints discussed at the beginning of this section? Stone (1995) has some useful suggestions:

- Teachers need to be knowledgeable about the values of play and to be able to communicate this information to others.
- Teachers should be open advocates for play by posting the values of play in a prominent place in the classroom and by labeling play centers with specific concepts and skills children will learn.
- Teachers can involve parents by sending home a class newsletter that informs parents about the value of curriculum-generated play activities. Similarly during parent conferences, teachers can describe play experiences that document children's growth. Parents can also be asked to help plan and provision classroom play centers.

In addition, teachers can celebrate children's play performances by encouraging children to talk about their play activities during morning meetings, by having children dictate stories about dramatic play episodes, and by photographing children's play constructions (Polito, 1994).

Cohen (1997) also advocates use of extensive photographing of children at play. The cost of film and developing can be expensive, so she recommends school fund-raisers or parent contributions to help. "Play panels" with photos of children engaged in educational play can be prominently displayed in the classroom on a regular basis, especially during open house. Captions underneath the pictures should be *reader friendly* (brief and in large bold print) and should convey the nature of the play activity, explaining what children can learn from the play. Teachers, administrators, parents, and children are thereby afforded an excellent reminder of the importance of play in the curriculum. Play photo albums can also be sent home with children, giving all parents access to information about the values of play.

Teachers may also try action research on play topics in their classroom. Collaboration with other teachers, administrators, teacher educators, researchers, parents, and even the children themselves can lead to new knowledge about and appreciation for the importance of play in a program. For example, teachers could conduct surveys asking parents and children about play at home and at school, drawing out distinctions and commonalities between play in the two settings. Teacher action research can easily blend in with program assessment and evaluation and can even lead to curricular activities. By becoming producers, as well as consumers, of play research, teachers can better assimilate research into their craft knowledge, improving both their conceptual understanding and their practical know-how.

SUMMARY

This chapter began with a discussion of the advantages of linking play with the academic curriculum:

- *Positive affect*—When children incorporate academic skills and content into their play, the pleasurable feelings associated with play can become attached to the academic subject area.
- *Nonliterality*—The make-believe component of play can make academic activities meaningful and significant to children.
- *Means-over-ends orientation*—When children play, their attention is focused on the activity itself, rather than on the goals or outcomes of the activity. This feature of play creates a low-risk environment in which children are encouraged to take chances and to try something new or difficult.
- *Broad spectrum of learning opportunities*—Play-based learning activities can offer children opportunities to learn a variety of different skills and concepts. In addition, play can provide multiple ways for children to learn these skills.

Next, we gave examples of three types of curriculum-generated play that can be used to help children to learn and practice skills in literacy, mathematics, science, and social studies:

1. *Academically enriched play centers*—Teachers expand the learning potential of sociodramatic play through academically related props and materials.
2. *Games*—Traditional and academically focused games offer a highly enjoyable means for children to learn new skills and to practice skills that have already been taught.
3. *Simulations*—Simulations that involve role playing provide opportunities for children to learn complex concepts and principles by making decisions in lifelike situations.

The chapter concluded with a discussion of some of the formidable barriers that can impede the implementation of play-based education at the early childhood and primary-grade levels. Not only do teachers have to overcome negative attitudes about play, but they also must contend with factors such as lack of time and adequate space for play, high teacher–child ratios, and curriculum pressures to teach basic skills. In order to counteract these impediments, teachers need to be open advocates for play, educating parents and administrators about the academic value and uses of play.

References

Almqvist, B. (1994). *Approaching the culture of toys in Swedish child care: A literature survey and a toy inventory.* Uppsala, Sweden: Uppsala University.

American Academy of Pediatrics. (1994). *Playground safety: Guidelines for parents.* Elk Grove Village, IL: Author.

American Society for Testing and Materials. (1995). *Safety performance specifications for playground equipment for public use.* West Conshocken, PA.: Author.

Ammar, H. (1954). *Growing up in an Egyptian village.* London: Routledge & Kegan Paul.

Angell, D. (1994). Can multicultural education foster transcultural identities? In K. Borman & N. Greenman (Eds.), *Changing American Education.* Albany, NY: State University Of New York Press.

Athey, I. (1988). The relation of play to cognitive, language, and moral development. In D. Bergen (Ed.), *Play as a medium for learning and development: A handbook of theory and practice* (pp. 81–102). Portsmouth, NH: Heinemann.

Axline, V. (1947). *Play Therapy.* New York: Ballantine.

Axline, V. (1964). *Dibs: In search of self.* New York: Ballantine.

Bagley, D., & Chaille, C. (1996). Transforming play: An analysis of first-, third-, and fifth-graders play. *Journal of Research in Childhood Education, 10,* 134–142.

Bakeman, R., & Brownlee, J. (1980). The strategic use of parallel play: A sequential analysis. *Child Development, 51,* 873–887.

Barnett, L. (1990). Playfulness: Definition, design, and measurement. *Play and Culture, 3,* 319–336.

Barnett, L. (1991). Characterizing playfulness: Correlates with individual attributes and personal traits. *Play and Culture, 4,* 371–393.

Barnett, L., & Kleiber, D. (1984). Playfulness and the early play environment. *Generic Psychological Monographs, 144,* 153–164.

Barnett, L., & Storm, B. (1981). Play, pleasure, and pain: A reduction of anxiety through play. *Leisure Sciences, 4,* 161–175.

Baron-Cohen, S. (1997). Autism and symbolic play. *British Journal of Developmental Psychology, 5,* 139–148.

Bateson, G. (1955). A theory of play and fantasy. *Psychiatric Research Reports, 2,* 39–51.

Beaty, J., & Tucker, W. (1987). *The computer as paintbrush: Creative uses for the personal computer in the preschool classroom.* Columbus, OH: Merrill.

Beckwith, J. (1982). It's time for creative play. *Parks and Recreation, 17*(9), 58–62, 89.

Beizer, L., & Howes, C. (1992). Mothers and toddlers: Partners in early symbolic play: Illustrative study # 1. In C. Howes (Ed.), *The collaborative construction of pretend* (pp. 25–43). Albany, NY: State University of New York Press.

Belsky, J., & Most, R. (1981). From exploration to play: A cross-sectional study of infant free play behavior. *Developmental Psychology, 17,* 630–639.

Bennett, N., Wood, L., Rogers, S. (1997). *Teaching through play: Teacher's thinking and classroom practice.* Buckingham, United Kingdom: Open University Press.

Bergman, A., & Lefcourt, I. (1994). Self-other action play: A window into the representational world of the infant. In A. Slade & D. Wolf (Eds.), *Children at Play: Clinical and developmental approaches to meaning and representation* (pp. 133–147). New York: Oxford University Press.

Berlyne, D. (1960). *Conflict, arousal and curiosity.* New York: McGraw-Hill.

Bishop, D., & Chace, C. (1971). Parental conceptual systems, home play environment, and potential creativity in children. *Journal of Experimental Child Psychology, 12,* 318–338.

Black, B. (1989). Interactive pretense: Social and symbolic skills in preschool play groups. *Merrill-Palmer Quarterly, 35,* 379–395.

Blehar, M., Lieberman, A., & Ainsworth, M. (1977). Early face-to-face interaction and its relation to later mother-infant attachment. *Child Development, 48,* 182–194.

Bloch, M. (1989). Young boys' and girls' play at home and in the community: A cultural-ecological framework. In M. Bloch & A. Pellegrini (Eds.), *The ecological context of children's play* (pp. 120–154). Norwood, NY: Ablex.

Bloch, M., & Walsh, D. (1983, April) *Young children's activities at home: Age and sex differences in activity, location, and social context.* Paper presented at the biennial meeting of the Society for Research in Child Development, Detroit, MI.

Bodrova, E., & Leong, D. (1996). *Tools of the mind: The Vygotskian approach to early childhood education.* Englewood Cliffs, NJ: Prentice-Hall, Inc.

Bornstein, M., & O'Reilly, A. (1993). *The role of play in the development of thought. New directions for child development. No. 59.* San Fransisco: Jossey-Bass.

Bornstein, M., Vibbert, M., Tal, J., & O'Donnell, K. (1992). Toddler language and play in the second year: Stability, covariation, and influences of parenting. *First Language, 12,* 323–338.

Boutte, G., Van Scoy, I., & Hendley, S. (1996). Multicultural and nonsexist prop boxes. *Young Children, 52*(1) 34–39.

Bowman, B. (1990). Play in teacher education: The United States perspective. In E. Klugman & S. Smilansky (Eds.), *Children's play and learning: Perspectives and policy implications* (pp. 97–111). New York: Teachers College Press.

Boyatzis, C. (1985, March). *The effects of traditional playground equipment on children's play interaction.* Paper presented at meeting of The Anthropological Study of Play, Washington, DC.

Boyatzis, C. (1997). Of Power Rangers and v-chips. *Young Children, 52* (7), 74–79.

Boyd, B. (1997). Teacher response to superhero play: To ban or not to ban? *Childhood Education, 74,* 23–28.

Bradley, R. (1985). Play materials and intellectual development. In C. Brown & A. Gottfried (Eds.), *Play interactions: The role of toys and parental involvement in children's development* (pp. 129–140). Skillman, NJ: Johnson & Johnson Baby Products.

Bredekamp S., & Copple, C. (1997). *Developmentally appropriate practice in early childhood programs* (rev. ed.). Washington, DC: NAEYC.

Brett, A., Moore, R., & Provenzo, E. (1993). *The complete playground book.* Syracuse, NY: Syracuse University Press.

Bricker, D., & Criple J. (1992). *An activity based approach to early intervention.* Baltimore: Paul Brooks.

Bronson, M. (1995). *The right stuff for children birth to 8.* Washington, DC: National Association for the Education of Young Children.

Brown, N., Curry, N., & Tittnich, E. (1971). How groups of children deal with common stress through play. In N. Curry & S. Arnaud (Eds.), *Play: The child strives towards self-realization* (pp. 26–38). Washington, DC: NAEYC.

Brown, S. (1994). Animals at play. *National Geographic, 186*(6), pp. 2–35.

Bruner, J. (1972). The nature and uses of immaturity. *American Psychologist, 27,* 687–708.

Bruner, J. (1974). The nature and use of immaturity. In K. Connolly, & J. Bruner (Eds.), *The growth of competence.* London: Academic Press.

Bruner, J. (1983). Play, thought, and language. *Peabody Journal of Education, 60*(3), 60–69.

Bruner, J. (1996). *The culture of education.* Cambridge, MA: Harvard University Press.

Bruner, J., & Sherwood, V. (1976). Peekaboo and the learning of rule structures. In J. Bruner, A. Jolly, & K. Sylva (Eds.), *Play: Its role in development and evolution* (pp. 603–608). New York: Basic Books.

Bruya, L. (1985). The effect of play structure format differences on the play behavior of preschool children. In J. Frost & S. Sunderlin (Eds.), *When children play* (pp. 115–120). Wheaton, MD: Association for Childhood Education International.

Burns, S., & Brainerd, C. (1979). Effects of constructive and dramatic play on perspective taking in very young children. *Developmental Psychology, 15,* 512–521.

Buysse, V. & Bailey, D. (1993). Behavioral and developmental outcomes in young children with disabilities in integrated and segregated settings: A review of comparative studies. *Journal of Special Education, 26,* 434–461.

Caillois, R. (1961). *Man, play, and games.* New York: The Free Press.

Caldera, Y., Huston, A., & O'Brien, M. (1989). Social interactions and play patterns of parents and toddlers with feminine, masculine, and neutral toys. *Child Development, 60*(1), 70–76.

Campbell, C. (1993). Play, the fabric of elementary school counseling programs. *Elementary School Guidance and Counseling, 28,* 10–16.

Campbell, S., & Frost, J. (1985). The effects of playground type on the cognitive and social play behavior of grade two children. In J. Frost & S. Sunderlin (Eds.), *When children play* (pp. 81–89). Wheaton, MD: Association for Childhood Education International.

Caplan, F., & Caplan, T. (1974). *The power of play.* New York: Anchor Press/Doubleday.

Carlsson-Paige, N., & Levin, D. (1987). *The war play dilemma: Balancing needs and values in the early childhood classroom.* New York: Teachers College Press.

Carlsson-Paige, N., & Levin, D. (1990). *Who's calling the shots? How to respond effectively to children's fascination with war play and war toys.* Philadelphia: New Society.

Carpenter, C., Stein, A., & Baer, D. (1978). *The relation of children's activity preference to sex-type behavior.* Paper presented at the twelfth annual convention of the Association for Advancement in Behavior Theories, Chicago.

Carter, D., & Levy, D. (1988). Cognitive aspects of early sex-role development: The influence of gender schema on preschoolers' memories for sex-typed toys and activities. *Child Development, 59*(3), 782–792.

Casberque, R. & Kieff, J. (1998). Marbles, anyone? Traditional games in the classroom. *Childhood Education, 74,* 143–147.

Cazden, C. (1976). Play with language and meta-linguistic awareness: One dimension of language experience. In J. Bruner, A. Jolly, & K. Sylva (Eds.), *Play and its role in development and evolution* (pp. 603–608). New York: Basic Books.

Cheyne, J. (1982). Object play and problem-solving: Methodological problems and conceptual promise. In D. Pepler & K. Rubin (Eds.), *The play of children: Current theory and research* (pp. 79–96). Basel: Karger.

Christie, J. (1983). The effects of play tutoring on young children's cognitive performance. *Journal of Educational Research, 76,* 326–330.

Christie, J. (Ed). (1991). *Play and early literacy development.* Albany, NY: State University of New York Press.

Christie, J. (1994a). Academic play. In J. Hellendoorn, R. van der Kooij, & B. Sutton-Smith (Eds.), *Play and intervention.* Albany, NY: State University Of New York Press.

Christie, J. (1994b). Literacy play interventions: A review of empirical research. *Advances in Early Education and Day Care, 6,* 3–24.

Christie, J., & Enz, B. (1992). The effects of literacy play interventions on preschoolers' play patterns and literacy development. *Early Education and Development, 3,* 205–220.

Christie, J., Enz, B., & Vukelich, C. (1997). *Teaching language and literacy: Preschool through the elementary grades.* New York: Longman.

Christie, J., & Johnsen, P. (1983). The role of play in social-intellectual development. *Review of Educational Research, 53,* 93-115.

Christie, J., & Johnsen, P. (1985). Questioning the results of play training research. *Educational Psychologist, 20,* 7–11.

Christie, J., & Johnsen, P. (1987). Preschool play. In J. Block & N. King (Eds.), *School play* (pp. 109–142). New York: Garland.

Christie, J., Johnsen, P., & Peckover, R. (1988). The effects of play period duration on children's play patterns. *Journal of Research in Childhood Education, 3,* 123–131.

Christie, J., & Wardle, F. (1992). How much time is needed for play? *Young Children, 47*(3), 28–32.

Clegg, A., Jr. (1991). Games and simulations in social studies education. In J. Shaver (Ed.), *Handbook of research on social studies teaching and learning* (pp. 523–529). New York: MacMillan.

Clements, D., & Nastasi, B. (1993). Electronic media and early childhood education. In B. Spodek (Ed.), *Handbook of research on the education of young children* (pp. 251–275). New York: Macmillan.

Coates, S., Lord, M., & Jakabovics, E. (1975). Field dependence–independence, social–nonsocial play and sex differences in preschool children. *Perceptual and Motor Skills, 40,* 195–202.

Cohen, L. (1997, November/December). Documenting play. *Child Care Information Exchange* (Issue No. 118), 61–64.

Cohen, L., & Spenciner, L. (1994). *Assessment of young children.* White Plains, NY: Longman Publishers.

Collins, M., & Kimmel, M. (1996). *Mister Rogers' neighborhood: Children, television, and Fred Rogers.* Pittsburgh, PA: University of Pittsburgh

Connolly, J., & Doyle, A. (1984). Relation of social fantasy play to social competence in preschoolers. *Developmental Psychology, 20,* 797–806.

Connolly, J., Doyle, A., & Reznick, E. (1988). Social pretend play and social interaction in preschoolers. *Journal of Applied Developmental Psychology, 9*(3), 301–313.

Creasey, G., Jarvis, P., & Berk, L. (1998). Play and social competence. In O. Saracho and B. Spodek (Eds.), *Multiple perspectives on play in early childhood education* (pp. 116–143). Albany, NY: State University Of New York Press.

Crick, N., & Grotpeter, J. (1995). Relational aggression, gender, and social-psychological adjustment. *Child Development, 66,* 710–722.

Crosser, S. (1994). Making the most of water play. *Young Children, 49*(5), 28–32.

Cuffaro, H. (1995). *Experimenting with the world: John Dewey and the early childhood classroom.* New York: Teachers College Press.

Cunningham, C., Jones, M., & Taylor, N. (1994). The child-friendly neighborhood: Some questions and tentative answers from Australian research. *International Play Journal, 2*(2), 79–95.

Curry, N. (1971). Consideration of current basic issues on play. In N. Curry & S. Arnaud (Eds.), *Play: The child strives towards self realization.* Washington, DC: National Association for the Education of Young Children.

Damast, A., Tamis-LeMonda, S., & Bornstein, M. (1996). Mother-child play: Sequential interactions and the relation between maternal beliefs and behaviors. *Child Development, 67,* 1752–1766.

Dansky, J. & Silverman, I. (1973). Effects of play on associative fluency. *Developmental Psychology, 9,* 38–43.

Dansky, J. & Silverman, I. (1975). Play: A general facilitator of associative fluency. *Developmental Psychology, 11,* 104.

Dansky, J. (1980a). Cognitive consequences of sociodramatic play and exploration training for economically disadvantaged preschoolers. *Journal of Child Psychology and Psychiatry, 20,* 47–58.

Dansky, J. (1980b). Make-believe: A mediator of the relationship between play and creativity. *Child Development, 51,* 576–579.

Dattner, R. (1974). *Design for play.* Cambridge, MA: MIT Press.

Davidson J. (1989). *Children and computer together in the early childhood classroom.* Albany, NY: Delmar Publishers.

Dawson, G., & L., Galpert L. (1990). Mothers' use of imitative play for facilitating social responsiveness and toy play in young autistic children. *Development and Psychopathology, 2,* 151–162.

Day, D. (1983). *Early childhood education: A human ecological approach.* Glenview, IL: Scott, Foresman.

Deklyen, M., & Odom, S. (1989). Activity structure and social interactions with peers in developmentally integrated play groups. *Journal of Early Intervention, 13,* 342–352.

deMarrais, K., Nelson, P., & Baker, J. (1994). Meaning in Mud: Yup'k Eskimo girls at play. In J. Roopnarine, J. Johnson, & F. Hooper (Eds.), *Children's play in diverse cultures.* Albany, NY: State University Of New York Press.

Derman-Sparks, L. (1989). *Anti-bias curriculum: Tools for empowering young children.* Washington, DC: National Association for the Education of Young Children.

DeVries, R., & Kohlberg, L. (1987). *Constructivist early education: Overview and comparison with other programs.* Washington, DC: NAEYC.

Diamond, K., & Hestenes, L. (1996). Preschool children's conceptions of disabilities: The salience of disabilities in children's ideas about others. *Topics in Early Childhood Special Education, 16,* 458–475.

Diamond, K., LeFurgy, W., & Blass, S. (1993). Attitudes of preschool children toward their peers with disabilities: A year-long investigation in integrated classrooms. *Journal of Genetic Psychology, 154,* 215–221.

Dickinson, D. (1994). Features of early childhood classroom environments that support development and literacy. In J. Duchan, L. Hewitt, & R. Sonnenmeier (Eds.), *Pragmatics: From theory to practice* (pp. 185–201). Englewood NJ: Prentice-Hall.

Dockett, S. (1994). *Pretend play and young children's developing theories of mind.* Unpublished doctoral dissertation, University of Sydney.

Dodge, M., & Frost, J. (1986). Children's dramatic play: Influence of thematic and nonthematic settings. *Childhood Education, 62,* 166–170.

Doyle, A., Ceschin, F., Tessier, O., & Doehring, P. (1991). The relation of age and social class factors in children's social pretend play to cognitive and symbolic ability. *International Journal of Behavioral Development, 14*(4), 395–410.

Doyle, A., Connolly, J., & Rivest, L. (1980). The effect of playmate familiarity on the social interactions of young children. *Child Development, 51,* 217–223.

Doyle, P. (1977). The differential effects of multiple and single niche play activities on interpersonal relations among preschoolers. In D. Lancy and B. Tindall (Eds.), *The study of play: Problems and prospects* (pp. 199–207). West Point, NY: Leisure Press.

Doyle, P. (1978). The effect of preschool play activities on children's antisocial behavior. In M. Salter (Ed.), *Play: Anthropological Perspectives* (pp. 145–156). West Point, NY: Leisure Press.

Dunn, J., & Dale, N. (1984). I a daddy: 2-year-olds' collaboration in joint pretend with sibling and mother. In I. Bretherton (Ed.), *Symbolic play: The development of social understanding* (pp. 131–158). Orlando, FL: Academic Press.

Dunn, J., & Wooding, C. (1977). Play in the home and its implications for learning. In B. Tizard & D. Harvey (Eds.), *Biology of play.* London: Heinemann.

Dunn, L., & Herwig, J. (1992). Play behaviors and convergent and divergent thinking skills of young children attending full-day preschool. *Child Study Journal, 22*(1), 23–37.

Ebbeck, F. (1973). Learning from play in other cultures. In J. Frost (Ed.), *Revisiting early childhood education.* New York: Holt, Rinehart, & Winston.

Eddowes, A. (1993). Providing retreats for solitary activity in day care. *Day Care and Early Education, 20*(3), 27–29.

Edwards, C. (1993). Life-long learning. *Communications of the ACM, 36*(5), 76–78.

Elkind, D. (1981). *The hurried child: Growing up too fast too soon.* Menlo Park, CA: Addison-Wesley.

Elkind, D. (1994). *Ties that stress: The new family imbalance.* Cambridge, MA: Harvard University Press.

Elkind, D. (1996). Young children and technology: A cautionary note. *Young Children, 51*(6), 22–23.

El'Konin, D. (1971). Symbolics and its functions in the play of children. In R. Herron & B. Sutton-Smith (Eds.), *Child's play.* New York: Wiley.

El'Konin, D. (1978). *The psychology of play.* Moscow: Pedagogica.

Ellis, M. (1973). *Why people play.* Englewood Cliffs, NJ: Prentice-Hall.

Ellis, M. (1984). Play, novelty, and stimulus seeking. In T. Yawkey & A. Pellegrini (Eds.), *Child's play: Developmental and applied* (pp. 203–218). Hillsdale, NJ: Erlbaum.

Enz, B., & Christie, J. (1997). Teacher play interaction styles: Effects on play behavior and relationships with teacher training and experience. *International Journal of Early Childhood Education, 2,* 55–75.

Erikson, E. (1940). Studies and interpretation of play. Part I: Clinical observations of play disruption in young children. *Genetic Psychology Monograph, 22,* 557–671.

Erikson, E. (1963/1950). *Childhood and society.* New York: Norton.

Erikson, E. (1972). Play and actuality. In M. W. Piers (Ed.), *Play and development.* New York: Norton.

Erikson, E. (1977). *Toys and reasons.* New York: Norton

Erwin, E., Carpenter, E., & Kontos, S. (1993, April). *What preschool teachers do when children play.* Paper presented at the meeting of the American Educational Research Association, Atlanta.

Everhart, R. (1987). Play and the junior high adolescent. In J. Block & N. King (Eds.), *School play* (pp. 167–192). New York: Garland.

Fagot, B. (1977). Variations in density: Effect on task and social behaviors of young children. *Developmental Psychology, 13,* 166–167.

Fagot, B. (1981). Continuity and change in play styles as a function of sex of child. *International Journal of Behavioral Development, 4,* 37–43.

Fagot, B. (1983). Play styles in early childhood: Social consequences. In M. Liss (Ed.), *Social and cognitive skills: Sex roles and children's play*. New York: Academic Press.

Fagot, B., & O'Brien, M. (1994). Activity level in young children: Cross age stability, situational influences, correlates with temperament, and the perception of problem behavior. *Merrill Palmer Quarterly, 40*(3), 378–398.

Fantuzzo, J., & Sutton-Smith, B. (1994). *Play Buddy Project: A preschool-based intervention to improve the social effectiveness of disadvantaged, high-risk children*. Washington, DC: U.S. Department of Health and Human Services.

Fantuzzo, J., Sutton-Smith, B., Coolahan, K., Manz, P., Canning, S., & Debnam, D. (1995). Assessment of preschool play interaction behaviors in young low-income children: Penn Interactive Peer Play Scale. *Early Childhood Research Quarterly, 10,* 105–120.

Farran, D., Silveri, B., & Culp, A. (1991). Public school preschools and the disadvantaged. *New Directions for Child Development, 53,* 65–73.

Farver, J. (1993). Cultural differences in scaffolding pretend play: A comparison of American and Mexican mother-child and sibling-child pairs. In K. MacDonald (Ed.), *Parent-child play: Descriptions and implications* (pp. 349–366). Albany, NY: State University of New York Press.

Farver, J., Kim, Y., & Lee, Y. (1995). Cultural differences in Korean- and Anglo-American preschoolers' social interaction and play behaviors. *Child Development, 66,* 1088–1099.

Fein, G. (1975). A transformational analysis of pretending. *Developmental Psychology, 11,* 291–296.

Fein, G. (1997, April). *Play and Early Childhood Teacher Education: Discussant Remarks*. Symposium presented at the annual meeting of the Association for the Study of Play meetings, Washington, DC.

Fein, G., & Fryer, M. (1995). Maternal contributions to early symbolic play competence. *Developmental Review, 15,* 367–381.

Fein, G., Johnson, D., Kosson, N., Stork, L., & Wasserman, L. (1975). Stereotypes and preferences in the toy choices of 20-month boys and girls. *Developmental Psychology, 11,* 527–528.

Fein, G., & Stork, L. (1981). Sociodramatic play: Social class effects in integrated preschool classrooms. *Journal of Applied Developmental Psychology, 2,* 267–279.

Feitelson, D. (1959). Aspects of the social life of Kurdish Jews. *Jewish Journal of Sociology, 1,* 201–216.

Feitelson, D. (1977). Cross-cultural studies of representational play. In B. Tizard & D. Harvey (Eds.), *Biology of Play* (pp. 6–14). Philadelphia: Lippincott.

Feitelson, D., & Ross, G. (1973) The neglected factor—play. *Human Development, 16,* 202–223.

Fenson, L., Kagan, J., Kearsley, R., & Zelazo, P. (1976). The developmental progression of manipulative play in the first two years. *Child Development 47,* 232–239.

Fernald, A., & O'Neill, D. (1993). Peekaboo across cultures: How mothers play with voices, faces, and expectations. In K. MacDonald (Ed.), *Parent-child play: Descriptions and implications* (pp. 259–285). Albany, NY: State University of New York Press.

Fernie, D. (1988). Becoming a student: Messages from first settings. *Theory into Practice, 27,* 3–10.

Fewell, R., & Rich, J. (1987). Play assessment as a procedure for examining cognitive, communication, and social skills in multihandicapped children. *Journal of Psychoeducational Assessment, 2,* 107–118.

Field, T. (1980). Preschool play: Effects of teacher/child ratios and organization of classroom space. *Child Study Journal, 10,* 191–205.

Fiese, B. (1990). Playful relationships: A contextual analysis of mother-toddler interaction and symbolic play. *Child Development, 61,* 1648–1656.

File, N. (1994). Children's play, teacher-child interactions, and teacher beliefs in integrated early childhood programs. *Early Childhood Research Quarterly, 9,* 223–240.

File, N., & Kontos, S. (1993). The relationship of program quality to children's play in integrated early intervention settings. *Topics in Early Childhood Special Education, 13*(1), 1–18.

Finley, G., & Layne, O. (1971). Play behavior in young children: A cross-cultural study. *The Journal of Genetic Psychology, 119,* 202–210.

Fishbein, H., & Imai, S. (1993). Preschoolers select playmates on the basis of gender and race. *Journal of Applied Developmental Psychology, 14,* 303–316.

Fisher, E. (1992). The impact of play on development: A meta-analysis. *Play & Culture, 5,* 159–181.

Franklin, M. (1985, March). *Play and the early evolution of social life: Views of two-year-olds at school.* Paper presented at the annual meeting of the Anthropological Association for the Study of Play, Washington, DC.

Freud, S. (1961). *Beyond the pleasure principle.* New York: Norton.

Freyberg, J. (1973). Increasing the imaginative play of urban disadvantaged kindergarten children through systematic training. In J. L. Singer (Ed.), *The child's world of make-believe* (pp. 129–154). New York: Academic Press.

Friedrich, L., & Stein, A. (1975). Prosocial television and young children: The effects of verbal labeling and role playing on learning and behavior. *Child Development, 46,* 27–38.

Friend, M., & Cook, L. (1996). *Interactions: Collaboration skills for school professionals* (2nd ed.). New York: Longman.

Fromberg, D. (1995) Politics, pretend play, and pedagogy in early childhood preservice and inservice education. In E. Klugman (Ed.), *Play, policy, and practice.* St. Paul, MN: Redleaf Press.

Fromberg, D. (1997, November/December). What's new in play research? *Child Care Information Exchange.* Issue 118, 53–56.

Frost, J. (1992). *Play and playscapes.* Albany, NY: Delmar.

Frost, J., & Dreschler, N. (1995) *A parents guide to playground safety.* Wheaton, MD: Association for Childhood Education International.

Frost, J., & Klein, B. (1979). *Children's play and playgrounds.* Boston: Allyn and Bacon.

Frost, J., & Shinn, D. (in press). Physical environments and play. In B. Spodek & O. Saracho (Eds.), *Play in Early Childhood Education.* Albany, NY: State University of New York Press.

Frost, J., & Shinn, D., & Jacobs, P. (1998). Play environments and children's play. In O. Saracho & B. Spodek (Eds.), *Multiple perspective on play in early childhood education.* Albany, NY: State University of New York Press.

Garbarino, J. (1989). An ecological perspective on the role of play in child development. In M. Bloch & A. Pellegrini (Eds.), *The ecological context of children's play.* Norwood, NJ: Ablex.

Gardner, H. (1983). *Frames of mind: The theory of multiple intelligences.* New York: Basic Books.

Garvey, C. (1974). Some properties of social play. *Merrill-Palmer Quarterly, 20,* 163–180.

Garvey, C. (1977). *Play.* Cambridge, MA: Harvard University Press.

Garvey, C. (1979). An approach to the study of children's role play. *The Quarterly Newsletter of the Laboratory of Comparative Human Cognitiot 4 1(4)*, 69–73.

Garvey, C., & Berndt, R. (1977, September). *The organization of pretend play.* Paper presented at the annual meeting of the American Psychological Association, Chicago.

Gaskins, S., Miller, P., & Corsaro, W. (1992). Theoretical and methodological perspectives in the interpretive study of children. *New directions in child development, 58,* 5–23.

Gibson, M., & Ogbu, J. (Eds.) (1991). Minority status and schooling: A comparative study of immigrant and involuntary minorities. NY: Garland Publishing.

Giddings, M., & Halverson, C. (1981). Young children's use of toys in home environments. *Family Relations, 30,* 69–74.

Giffin, H. (1984). The coordination of meaning in the creation of a shared make-believe reality. In J. Bretherton (Ed.), *Symbolic play: The development of social understanding* (pp. 73–100). Orlando, FL: Academic Press.

Gilligan, C. (1982). *In a different voice: Psychological theory and women's development.* Cambridge: MA: Harvard University Press.

Gleason, T., Sebanc, A., McGinley, J., & Hartup, W. (1997). *Invisible friends and personified objects: Qualitative differences in relationships with imaginary companions.* Washington, DC: SRCD.

Glickman, C. (1984). Play in public school settings: A philosophical question. In T. Yawkey & A. Pellegrini (Eds.), *Child's play: Developmental and applied* (pp. 255–271). Hillsdale, NJ: Erlbaum.

Golden, D., & Kutner, C. (1980). *The Play Development Progress Scale.* Unpublished manuscript.

Goldhaber, J. (1992). Sticky to dry; red to purple: Exploring transformation with play dough. *Young Children, 48*(1), 26–28.

Goldhaber, J. (1994). If we call it science, then can we let the children play? *Childhood Education, 71,* 24–27.

Goldstein, J. (1992). Sex differences in aggressive play and toy preference. In K. Bjorkqvist & P. Niemela (Eds.), *Of mice and women: Aspects of female aggression.* New York: Academic Press.

Goldstein, J. (1995). Aggressive toy play. In A. Pellegrini (Ed.), *The future of play theory: Multidisciplinary inquiry into the contributions of Brian Sutton-Smith* (pp. 127–159). Albany, NY: State University of New York Press.

Golomb, C., & Cornelius, C. (1977). Symbolic play and its cognitive significance. *Developmental Psychology, 13,* 246–252.

Goltsman, S., Gilbert, T., & Wohlford, S. (1993). *The accessibility checklist: An evaluation system for buildings and outdoor settings* (2nd ed.). Berkeley, CA: MIG Communications.

Goncu, A. (1993). Development of intersubjectivity in the dynamic play of preschoolers. *Early Childhood Research Quarterly, 8,* 99–116.

Goncu, A., & Kessel, F. (1984). Children's play: A contextual-functional perspective. In F. Kessel & A. Goncu (Eds.), *Analyzing children's play dialogues* (pp. 5–22). San Francisco: Jossey-Bass.

Goodman, J. (1992). *When slow is fast enough: Educating the delayed preschool child.* New York: The Guilford Press.

Goodson, B., & Bronson, M. (1985). *Guidelines for relating children's ages to toy characteristics.* Contact No. CPSC-85-1089. Washington, DC.: U.S. Consumer Product Safety Commission.

Gould, R. (1972). *Child studies through fantasy.* New York: Quadrangle Books.

Gould, S. (1995). *Full house: The spread of excellence from Plato to Darwin.* New York: Harmony Books.

Gowen, J. (March, 1995). The early development of symbolic play. *Young Children, 50*(3) 75–81.

Greenberg, J. (1995). Making friends with the Power Rangers. *Young Children, 50*(5), 60–61.

Greenfield, P. (1984). *Mind and media: The effects of television, video games and computers.* Cambridge, MA: Harvard University Press.

Greenfield, P. (1994). Video games as cultural artifacts. *Journal of Applied Developmental Psychology, 15,* 3–12.

Greenfield, P., & Cocking, R. (Eds.) (1994), *The cross-cultural roots of minority child development.* Hillsdale, NJ: Erlbaum.

Grief, E. (1976). Sex role playing in preschool children. In J. Bruner, A. Jolly, & K. Sylva (Eds.), *Play: Its role in development and evolution.* New York: Basic Books.

Griffing, P. (1983). Encouraging dramatic play in early childhood. *Young Children, 38*(4), 13–22.

Grinder, B., & Johnson, J. (1994, April). *Gender-related teacher behavior and interventions and their consequences for preschool children at free play in day care settings: Preliminary results.* Paper presented at the annual meeting of the American Educational Research Association, New Orleans.

Guerney, L. (1983). Client-centered play therapy. In C. Schaefer & K. O'Connor (Eds.). *Handbook of Play Therapy.* New York: John Wiley & Sons.

Guerney, L. (1984). Play therapy in counseling settings. In T. Yawkey & A. Pelligrini (Eds.), *Child's play: Developmental and applied* (pp. 291–321). Hillsdale, NJ: Erlbaum.

Guralnick, M. (1990). Social competence and early intervention. *Journal of Early Intervention, 14,* 3–14.

Haight, W., & Miller, P. (1993). *Pretending at home: Early development in a sociocultural context.* Albany, NY: State University of New York Press.

Hall, N., & Abbott, L. (Eds.). (1991). *Play in the primary curriculum.* London: Hodder & Stoughton.

Hall, N., & Robinson, A. (1995). *Exploring writing and play in the early years.* London: David Fulton.

Harper, L., & Sanders, K. (1975). Preschool children's use of space: Sex differences in outdoor play. *Developmental Psychology, 11,* 119.

Harragan, B. (1977). *Games mother never taught you.* New York: Rawson Associates.

Hart, C., & Sheehan, R. (1986). Preschoolers' play behaviors in outdoor environments: Effects of traditional and contemporary playgrounds. *American Educational Research Journal, 23,* 668–678.

Hartle, L. (1996). Effects of additional materials on preschool children's outdoor play behaviors. *Journal of Research in Childhood Education, 11,* 68–81.

Hartle, L., & Johnson, J. (1993). Historical and contemporary influences of outdoor play environments. In C. Hart (Ed.), *Children on playgrounds: Research perspectives and applications* (pp. 14–42). Albany, NY: State University of New York Press.

Hartup, W. (1983). The peer system. In E.M. Hetherington (Ed.), P. Mussen (Series Ed.), *Handbook of child psychology: Vol. 4. Socialization, personality, and social development.* New York: Wiley.

Haugland, S. (1995). Classroom activities provide important support to children's computer experiences. *Early Childhood Education Journal, 23*(2), 99–100.

Haugland, S., & Shade, D. (1994). Software evaluation for young children. In J. Wright & D. Shade (Eds.), *Young Children: Active learners in a technological age* (pp. 63–76). Washington, DC: National Association for the Education of Young Children.

Haugland, S., & Wright, J. (1997). *Young children and technology: A world of discovery.* Needham Heights, MA: Allyn and Bacon.

Hay, D., Ross, H., & Goldman, B. (1979). Social games in infancy. In B. Sutton-Smith (Ed.), *Play and learning* (pp. 83–107). New York: Gardner.

Hayward, G., Rothenberg, M., & Beasley, R. (1974). Children's play and urban playground environments. *Environment and Behavior, 6,* 131–168.

Health Resources and Services Administration. (1996). *CPSC releases toy safety tips for holiday shoppers* [on-line]. Available: http://158.72.85.159/cpsc/cpsc27.htm.

Hendrickson, J., Strain, P., Tremblay, A., & Shores, R. (1981). Relationship between toy and material use and the occurrence of social interactive behaviors by normally developing preschool children. *Psychology in the Schools, 18,* 500–504.

Henniger, M. (1985). Preschool children's play behaviors in an indoor and outdoor environment. In J. Frost & S. Sunderlin (Eds.), *When children play* (pp. 145–150). Wheaton, MD: Association for Childhood Education International.

Henniger, M. (1994). Computers and preschool children's play: Are they compatible? *Journal of Computing in Childhood Education, 53*(4), 231–239.

Hill, D. (1977). *Mud, sand, and water.* Washington, DC: National Association for the Education of Young Children.

Hirsch, E. (Ed.). (1996). *The block book* (3rd ed.). Washington, DC: National Association for the Education of Young Children.

Hodapp, R., Goldfield, E., & Boyatzis, C. (1984). The use and effectiveness of maternal scaffolding in mother-infant games. *Child Development, 55,* 772–781.

Holmes, R. (1992). Play during snacktime. *Play and Culture, 5,* 295–304.

Howe, N., Moller, L., & Chambers, B. (1994). Dramatic play in day care: What happens when doctors, cooks, bakers, pirates and pharmacists invade the classroom. In H. Goelman & E. Jacobs (Eds.), *Children's play in child care settings* (pp. 102–118). Albany, NY: State University of New York Press.

Howe, N., Moller, L., Chambers, B., & Petrakos, H. (1993). The ecology of dramatic play centers and children's social and cognitive play. *Early Childhood Research Quarterly, 8,* 235–252.

Howes, C. (1980). Peer play scale as an index of complexity of peer interaction. *Developmental Psychology, 16,* 371–372.

Howes, C. (1988). Peer interaction of young children. *Monographs of the Society for Research in Child Development, 53* (Serial No. 217).

Howes, C., & Clements, D. (1994). Adult socialization of children's play in child care. In H. Goelman & E. Jacobs (Eds.), *Children's play in child care settings.* Albany, NY: State University of New York Press.

Howes, C., & Matheson, C. (1992). Sequences in the development of competent play with peers: Social and social pretend play. *Developmental Psychology, 28,* 961–974.

Howes, C. & Smith, E. (1995). Relations among child care quality, teacher behavior, children's play activities, emotional security, and cognitive activity in child care. *Early Childhood Research Quarterly, 10,* 381–404.

Howes, C., Unger, O., & Seidner, L. (1989). Social pretend play in toddlers: Parallels with social play and solitary pretend. *Child Development 60,* 77–84.

Hughes, M., & Hutt, C. (1979). Heart-rate correlates of childhood activities: Play, exploration, problem-solving and day dreaming. *Biological Psychology, 8,* 253–263.

Humphreys, A., & Smith, P. (1984). Rough-and-tumble play in preschool and play-ground. In P. Smith (Ed.), *Play in animals and humans,* (pp. 241-270). London: Blackwell.

Hutt, C. (1966). Exploration and play in children. In *Play, exploration and territory in mammals. Symposia of the zoological society of London, 18,* 61–81.

Hutt, C. (1971). Exploration and play in children. In R. Herron & B. Sutton-Smith (Eds.), *Child's play* (pp. 231–251). New York: Wiley.

Hutt, C., & Vaizey, M. (1966). Differential effects of group density on social behaviour. *Nature, 209,* 1371–1372.

Hutt, S., Tyler, S., Hutt, C., & Christopherson, H. (1989). *Play, exploration, and learning: A natural history of the pre-school.* London: Routledge.

Hyun, E., & Marshall, D. (1997). Theory of multiple/multiethnic perspective-taking ability for teachers' developmentally and culturally appropriate practice (DCAP). *Journal of Research in Childhood Education,* 11(2), 188–198.

Irwin, D., & Bushnell, M. (1980). *Observation strategies for child study.* New York: Holt, Rinehart and Winston.

Isaacs, S. (1930). *Intellectual growth in young children.* London: Routledge & Kegan Paul.

Isenberg, J., & Jalongo, M. (1997). *Creative expression and play in early childhood* (2nd ed.). Columbus, OH: Merrill.

Istomina, Z. (1977). The development of voluntary memory in preschool-age children. In M. Cole (Ed.), *Soviet developmental psychology.* White Plains, NY: Sharpe. (Original work published in 1948.)

Jackowitz, E. & Watson, M. (1980). The development of object transformations in early pretend play. *Developmental Psychology, 16,* 543–549.

Jacobson, J. (1981). The role of inanimate objects in early peer interaction. *Child Development, 52,* 618–626.

Jarrett, O. (1997). Science and math through role-play centers in the elementary classroom. *Science Activities, 34*(2), 13–19.

Jeffree, D., & McConkey, R. (1976). An observation scheme for recording children's imaginative doll play. *Journal of Child Psychology and Psychiatry, 17,* 189–197.

Jennings, K. (1975). People versus object orientation, social behavior, and intellectual abilities in preschool children. *Developmental Psychology, 11,* 511–519.

Jipson, J. (1991), Developmentally appropriate practices: Culture, curriculum, connections. *Early Education and Development, 2,* 120–136.

Johnson, J. (1978). Mother-child interaction and imaginative behavior of preschool children. *Journal of Psychology, 100,* 123–129.

Johnson, J. (1983). Context effects on preschool children's symbolic behavior. *Journal of Genetic Psychology, 143,* 259–268.

Johnson, J. (1986). Attitudes toward play and beliefs about development. In B. Mergen (Ed.), Association for the Study of Play, *Cultural dimensions of play, games, and sport* (Vol. 10, pp. 98–102), Champaign, IL: Human Kinetic Publishers.

Johnson, J. (1990). The role of play in cognitive development. In E. Klugman & S. Smilansky (Eds.), *Children's play and learning: Perspectives and policy implications* (pp. 213–234). New York: Teachers College Press.

Johnson, J. (1998). Sequence and stages of play development: Ages four to eight. In D. Fromberg & D. Bergen (Eds.), *Play from birth to twelve: Contexts, perspectives, meanings.* New York: Garland.

Johnson, J., Ershler, J., & Bell, C. (1980). Play behavior in a discovery-based and a formal education preschool program. *Child Development, 51,* 271–274.

Johnson, J., Ershler, J., & Lawton, J. (1982). Intellective correlates of preschoolers' spontaneous play. *Journal of General Psychology, 106,* 115–122.

Johnson, J., & Hoffman, T. (1984, November). *Incorporating microcomputers into the early childhood curriculum.* Paper presented at the annual meeting of the National Association for the Education of Young Children, Los Angeles.

Johnson, J., & Roopnarine, J. L. (1983). The preschool classroom and sex differences in children's play. In M. Liss (Ed.), *Social and cognitive skills: Sex roles and children's play.* New York: Academic Press.

Johnson, M. (1935). The effect on behavior of variation in the amount of play equipment. *Child Development, 6,* 52–68.

Jones, E. & Reynolds, G. (1992). *The play's the thing: Teacher's role in pretend play.* New York: Teacher's College Press.

Kamii, C. (1985). *Young children reinvent arithmetic.* New York: Teachers College Press.

Kamii, C. (1989). *Young children continue to reinvent arithmetic, 2nd grade: Implications of Piaget's theory.* New York: Teachers College Press.

Kamii, C., & Lewis, B. (1992). Primary arithmetic: The superiority of games over worksheets. In V. Dimidjian (Ed.), *Play's place in public education for young children* (pp. 85–103). Washington, DC: National Education Association.

Katz, L. & Chard, S. (1989). *Engaging children's minds: The project approach.* Norwood, NJ: Ablex.

Katz, L. & Chard, S.(1993). *Engaging children's minds: The project approach.* Norwood, NJ: Ablex.

King, N. R. (1979). Play: The kindergartners' perspective. *Elementary School Journal, 80,* 81–87.

King, N. R. (1982). Work and play in the classroom. *Social Education, 46,* 110–113.

King, N. (1986). When educators study play in school. *Journal of Curriculum and Supervision, 1*(3), 223–246.

King, N. (1987). Elementary school play: Theory and research. In J. Block & N. King (Eds.), *School play* (pp. 143–165). New York: Garland.

Kinsman, C., & Berk, L. (1979). Joining the block and housekeeping areas: Changes in play and social behavior. *Young Children, 35*(1), 66–75.

Kitson, N. (1994). "Please Miss Alexander: Will you be the robber?" Fantasy play: A case for adult intervention. In J. Moyles (Ed.), *The excellence of play* (pp. 88–98). Buckingham, United Kingdom: Open University Press.

Klugman, E. (1990). Early childhood moves into the public schools: Mix or meld. In E. Klugman & S. Smilansky (Eds.), *Children's play and learning: Perspectives and policy implications* (pp. 188–209). New York: Teachers College Press.

Kostelnick, M., Whiren, A., & Stein, L. (1986). Living with He-Man: Managing superhero fantasy play. *Young Children, 41,* 3–9.

Kritchevsky, S., & Prescott, E. (1997). *Planning environments for young children: Physical space* (2nd ed.). Washington, DC: National Association for the Education of Young Children.

LaFreniere, P., Strayer, F., & Gauthier, R. (1984). The emergence of same-sex affiative preferences among preschool peers: A developmental ethnological perspective. *Child Development, 55,* 1958–1965.

Lamb, M. E. (1977). The development of parental preferences in the first two years of life. *Sex Roles, 3,* 495–497.

Lamb, M. E., Easterbrooks, A., & Holden, G. (1980). Reinforcement and punishment among preschoolers: Characteristics, effects, and correlates. *Child Development, 51,* 1230–1236.

Lamorey, S., & Bricker, D. (1993). Integrating programs: Effects on young children and their parents. In C. Peck, S. Odom, & D. Bricker (Eds.). *Integrating young children with disabilities into community programs* (pp. 249–270). Baltimore: Paul H. Brookes.

Landreth, G. (1993). Child-entered play therapy. *Elementary School Guidance and Counseling, 28,* 17–29.

Lasater, C. & Johnson, J. (1994). Culture, play, and early childhood education. In J. Roopnarine, J. Johnson, & F. Hooper (Eds.), *Children's play in diverse cultures.* Albany, NY: SUNY.

Leslie, A. (1987). Pretense and representation: The origins of "theory of mind." *Psychological Review, 94,* 412–426.

Levin, D. (1995). Media, culture, and the undermining of play in the United States. In E. Klugman (Ed.), *Play, policy, and practice.* St. Paul, MN: Redleaf.

Levin, D., & Carlsson-Paige, N. (1994). Developmentally appropriate television: Putting children first. *Young Children, 49,* 38–44.

Levin, H., & Wardell, E. (1971). The research uses of doll play. In R. E. Herron & B. Sutton-Smith (Eds.), *Child's play* (pp. 145–184). New York: Wiley.

Levine, R. & Levine, A. (1963). Nyansongo: A Gusii community in Kenya. In B. Whiting (Ed.), *Six cultures: Studies in child rearing* (pp. 190–202). New York: Wiley.

Levy, A., Wolfgang, C., & Koorland, M. (1992). Sociodramatic play as a method for enhancing language performance of kindergarten age students. *Early Childhood Research Quarterly, 7,* 245–262.

Liddell, C., & Kruger, P. (1989). Activity and social behavior in a crowded South African township nursery: A follow-up study on the effects of crowding at home. *Merrill Palmer Quarterly, 35,* 209–226.

Liebermann, J. (1977). *Playfulness: Its relationship to imagination and creativity.* New York: Academic Press.

Lillard, A. (1998). Playing with a theory of mind. In O. Saracho and B. Spodek (Eds.), *Multiple perspectives on play in early childhood education* (pp. 11–33). Albany, NY: SUNY Press.

Linder, T. (1990). *Transdisciplinary play-based assessment.* Baltimore: Paul H. Brookes.

Lindquist, T., Lind, J., & Harvey, D. (1977). Play in hospital. In B. Tizard & D. Harvey (Eds.), *Biology of play.* Philadelphia: Lippincott.

Liss, M. B. (1981). Patterns of toy play: An analysis of sex differences. *Sex Roles, 7,* 1143–1150.

Loo, C. (1972). The effects of spatial density on the social behavior of children. *Journal of Applied Social Psychology, 2,* 372–381.

Lowe, M. (1975). Trends in the development of representational play in infants from one to three years: An observational study. *Journal of Child Psychology and Psychiatry, 16,* 33–47.

Maccoby, E. (1990). Gender and relationship: A developmental account. *American Psychologist, 45* (4) 513–520.

Maccoby, E., & Jacklin, C. N. (1974). *The psychology of sex differences.* Stanford, CA: Stanford University Press.

MacDonald, K. (1987). Parent-child play with rejected, neglected, and popular boys. *Developmental Psychology, 23,* 705–711.

Malone, T. (1984). Toward a theory of intrinsically motivating instruction. In D. Walker & R. Hess (Eds.), *Instructional software: Principles of design and use.* Belmont, CA: Wadsworth.

Maltz, D. & Borker, R. (1982). A cultural approach to male-female miscommunication. In J. Gumperz (Ed.), *Language and social identity* (pp. 196–216). New York: Cambridge University Press.

Manning, K., & Sharp, A. (1977). *Structuring play in the early years at school.* London: Ward Lock Educational.

Marston, D. (1996). A comparison of inclusion only, pull-out only, and combined service models for students with mild disabilities. *Journal of Special Education, 30,* 121–132.

Martin, P. & Caro, T. (1985). On the functions of play and its role in behavioral development. In J. Rosenblatt, C. Beer, M. Busnel, & P. Slater (Eds.), *Advances in the study of behavior* (Vol. 15, 59–103). New York: Academic Press.

Matthews, W. S. (1977). Modes of transformation in the initiation of fantasy play. *Developmental Psychology, 12,* 211–236.

Matthews, W. S. (1981). Sex-role perception, portrayal, and preferences in the fantasy play of young children. *Sex Roles, 1* (10), 979–987.

McChesney Johnson, K. (1994). *Teacher directiveness in the free play of young children with diverse abilities.* Department of Curriculum and Instruction. Unpublished doctoral dissertation: The Pennsylvania State University.

McClune-Nicolich, L. (1980). *A manual for analyzing free play.* New Brunswick, New Jersey: Douglas College, Rutgers University.

McConkey, R. (1994). Families at play: Intervention for children with developmental handicaps. J. Hellendoorn, R. van der Kooij, and B. Sutton-Smith (Eds.), *Play and Intervention* (pp. 123–132). Albany, NY: SUNY Press.

McCormick, L., & Feeny, S. (1995). Modifying and expanding activities for children with disabilities. *Young Children, 50*(4), 10–17.

McGee, L., & Richgels, D. (1996). *Literacy's beginnings: Supporting young readers and writers* (2nd ed.). Boston: Allyn & Bacon.

MCHD Online. (1996). *Toy safety guidelines released at Indianapolis SAFE KIDS coalition event* [on-line]. Available: http://www.mchd.com/toy2.htm.

McLane, J. (1984). *Lekotek evaluation.* Chicago: Erikson Institute, Loyola University.

McLean, S. (1995). Creating the learning environment: Context for living and learning. In J. Moyer (Ed.), *Selecting educational equipment and materials for school and home* (pp. 5–13). Wheaton, MD: Association for Childhood Education International.

McLoyd, V. C. (1980). Verbally expressed modes of transformation in the fantasy play of black preschool children. *Child Development, 51,* 1133–1139.

McLoyd, V. (1982). Social class differences in sociodramatic play: A critical review. *Developmental Review, 2,* 1–30.

McLoyd, V. (1983). The effects of the structure of play objects on the pretend play of low-income preschool children. *Child Development, 54,* 626–635.

McLoyd, V., Morrison, B., & Toler, B. (1979). *The effects of adult presence vs. absence on children's pretend play.* Paper presented at Hampton-Michigan Research Exchange, Hampton Institute, Hampton, VA.

McLoyd, V. (1990). Minority children: Introduction to the special issue. *Child Development, 61,* 263–266.

McNeilly-Choque, M., Hart, C., Robinson, C., Nelson, L. & Olsen, S. (1996). Overt and relational aggression on the playground: Correspondence among different informants. *Journal of Research in Childhood Education, 11,* 47–67.

Mead, M. (1975). Children's play style: Potentialities and limitations of its use as a cultural indicator. *Anthropological Quarterly, 48,* 157–181.

Meisels, S. (in press). Charting the continuum of assessment and interventions. In S. Meisels & E. Fenichel (Eds.), *New visions for the developed assessment of infants and young children*. Washington, DC: Zero to Three: National Center for Infants, Toddlers, and Families.

Mergen, B. (1982). *Play and playthings: A reference guide*. Westport, CT: Greenwood Press.

Miller, B. C., & Gerald, D. (1979, July). Family influences on the development of creativity in children: An integrative review. *The Family Coordinator, 295–312.*

Miller, S., Fernie, D., & Kantor, R. (1992). Distinctive literacies in different preschool play contexts. *Play and Culture, 5,* 107–119.

Monigham-Nourot, P., Scales, B., Van Hoorn, J., & Almy, M. (1987). *Looking at children's play: A bridge between theory and practice*. New York: Teachers College Press.

Monighan-Nourot, P. (1995). Play across curriculum and culture: Strengthening early primary education in California. In E. Klugman (Ed.) *Play, Policy, and Practice*. St. Paul, MN: Redleaf Press.

Montagner, H. [as reported by Maya Pines] (1984, December). Children's winning ways. *Psychology Today,* 59–65.

Moore, G. (1986). Effects of the spatial definition of behavior settings on children's behavior: A quasi-experimental study. *Journal of Environmental Psychology, 6,* 205–231.

Moore, G. (1987). The physical environment and cognitive development in child-care centers. In C. Weinstein & T. David (Eds.), *Spaces for children: The built environment and child development* (pp. 41–72). New York: Plenum.

Moore, N. V., Evertson, C. M., & Brophy, J. E. (1974). Solitary play: Some functional reconsiderations. *Developmental Psychology, 10,* 830–834.

Morrow, L., & Rand, M. (1991). Preparing the classroom environment to promote literacy during play. In J. Christie (Ed.), *Play and early literacy development* (pp. 141–165). Albany, NY: State University of New York Press.

Moyer, J. (Ed.). (1995). *Selecting educational equipment and materials for school and home*. Wheaton, MD: Association for Childhood Education International.

Moyles, J. (1989). *Just playing? The role and status of play in early childhood education*. Milton Keynes, England: Open University Press.

Mueller, E., & Lucas, T. (1975). A developmental analysis of peer interaction among toddlers. In M. Lewis & L. Rosenblum (Eds.), *Friendship and peer relations*. New York: Wiley, 1975.

Murphy, L. (1972). Infants' play and cognitive development. In M. Piers (Ed.), *Play and development*. New York: W. W. Norton.

National Association for the Education of Young Children. (1996). Playgrounds: *Keeping outdoor learning safe*. Washington, DC: Author.

National Association for the Education of Young Children. (1996). Position statement: Technology and young children—ages three through eight. *Young Children, 51*(6), 11–16.

National Council on Disability (1993). *Study on the functioning of assistive technology devices and services for individuals with disabilities*. A report to the President and the Congress of the United States. Washington, DC.

National Program for Playground Safety. (1995). *So Andrew can go out to play*. Cedar Falls, IA: Author.

Naylor, H. (1985). Outdoor play and play equipment. *Early Child Development and Care, 19,* 109–130.

Neill, S. (1982). Experimental alterations in playroom layout and their effect on staff and child behaviour. *Educational Psychology, 2,* 103–119.

Nelson, C. A., & Bloom, F. E. (1997). Child development and neurosciences. *Child Development.*

Nelson, R. (1996). *Play in child life programs.* Unpublished manuscript. The Pennsylvania State University, University Park, PA.

Neuman, S., & Roskos, K. (1991). Peers as literacy informants: A description of young children's literacy conversations in play. *Early Childhood Research Quarterly, 6,* 233–248.

Neuman, S., & Roskos, K. (1992). Literacy objects as cultural tools: Effects on children's literacy behaviors during play. *Reading Research Quarterly, 27,* 203–223.

Neuman, S., & Roskos, K. (1993). *Language and learning in the early years: An integrated approach.* New York: Harcourt Brace.

Neuman, S., & Roskos, K. (1997). Literacy knowledge in practice: Contexts of participation for young writers and readers. *Reading Research Quarterly, 32,* 10–32.

Nicholson, S. (1974). The theory of loose parts. In G. Coates (Ed.), *Alternative learning environments* (pp. 370–381). Stroudsburgh, PA: Dowden, Hutchinson, and Ross.

Nourot, P. (1997). Playing with play in four dimensions In J. Isenberg & M. Jalongo (Eds.), *Major trends and issues in early childhood education: Challenges, controversies, and insights.* New York: Teachers College Press.

Novick, R. (1993). Activity-based intervention and developmentally appropriate practice: Points of convergence. *Topics in early childhood special education 13*(4), 403–417.

O'Connell, B., & Bretherton, I. (1984). Toddler's play alone and with mother: The role of maternal guidance. In I. Bretherton (Ed.), *Symbolic Play* (pp. 337–366). Orlando, FL: Academic Press.

Odom, S. & Brown, W. (1993). Social interaction skills intervention for young children with disabilities in integrated settings. In C. Peck, S. Odom, & D. Bricker (Eds.), *Integrating young children with disabilities into community programs* (pp. 39–64). Baltimore: Paul H. Brookes.

Ogbu, J. (1991). Immigrant and involuntary minorities in comparative perspective. In M. Gibson & J. Ogbu (Eds.), *Minority status and schooling: A comparative study of immigrant and involuntary minorities.* New York: Garland.

Olszewski, P., & Fuson, K. C. (1982). Verbally expressed fantasy play of preschoolers as a function of toy structure. *Developmental Psychology, 18,* 57–61.

Olweus, D. (1993). Bullies on the playground: The role of victimization. In C. Hart (Ed.), *Children on playgrounds: Research perspectives and applications* (pp. 85–128). Albany, NY: State University of New York Press.

Orellana, M. (1994). Appropriating the voice of the superheroes: Three preschoolers bilingual language use in play. *Early Childhood Research Quarterly, 9,* 171–193.

Ostrosky, M. M. & Kaiser, A. P. (1991). Preschool classroom environments that promote communication, *Teaching Exceptional Children, 23*(4), 6–10.

Paley, V. (1984). *Boys and girls: Superheroes in the doll corner.* Chicago: University of Chicago Press.

Paley, V. (1990). *The boy who would be a helicopter: The uses of story telling in the classroom.* Cambridge, MA: Harvard University Press.

Paley, V. (1992). *You can't say you can't play.* Cambridge, MA: Harvard University Press.

Paley, V. (1997). *The girl with the brown crayon.* Cambridge: Harvard University Press.

Pan, H. (1994). Children's play in Taiwan. In J. Roopnarine, J. Johnson, & F. Hooper (Eds.), *Children's play in diverse cultures.* Albany, NY: SUNY.

Papert, S. (1993). *The children's machine: Rethinking school in the age of the computer.* New York: Basic Books.

Papert, S. (1996). *The connected family: Bridging the digital generation gap*. Atlanta, GA: Longstreet.

Parten, M. B. (1932). Social participation among preschool children. *Journal of Abnormal and Social Psychology, 27*, 243–269.

Parten, M. B. (1933). Social play among preschool children. *Journal of Abnormal and Social Psychology, 28*, 136–147.

Partington, J. T. & Grant, C. (1984). Imaginary companions. In P. Smith (Ed.), *Play in animals and humans* (pp. 217–240). New York: Harper & Row.

Peck, C., Carlson, P., & Helnstetter, E. (1992). Parent and teacher perceptions of outcomes for nonhandicapped children enrolled in integrated early child programs: A statewide study. *Journal of Early Intervention, 16*, 53–63.

Pellegrini, A. (1980). The relationship between kindergartners' play and achievement in prereading, language, and writing. *Psychology in the Schools, 17*, 530–535.

Pellegrini, A. (1984). The effects of classroom ecology on preschoolers' functional uses of language. In A. Pellegrini & T. Yawkey (Eds.), *The development of oral and written language in social contexts* (pp. 129–141). Norwood, NJ: Ablex.

Pellegrini, A. (1991). A longitudinal study of popular and rejected children's rough and tumble play. *Early Education and Development, 2(3)*, 205–213.

Pellegrini, A. (1995a). Boys' rough-and-tumble play and social competence: Contemporaneous and longitudinal relations. In A. Pellegrini (Ed.), *The future of play research* (pp. 107–126). Albany, NY: SUNY Press.

Pelligrini, A. (1995b). *School recess and playground behavior*. Albany, NY: State University of New York Press.

Pellegrini, A. (1996). *Observing children in their natural worlds: A methodological primer*. Mahwah, NJ: Erlbaum.

Pellegrini, A. & Galda, L. (1982). The effects of thematically fantasy play training on the development of children's story comprehension. *American Educational Research Journal, 19*, 443–452.

Pellegrini, A. & Galda, L. (1993). Ten years after: A reexamination of symbolic play and literacy research. *Reading Research Quarterly, 28(2)*, 162–177.

Pellegrini, A., Galda, L., Dresden, J., & Cox, S. (1991). A longitudinal study of the predictive relations among symbolic play, linguistic verbs, and early literacy. *Research in the Teaching of English, 25*(2), 219–235.

Pellegrini, A. & Jones, I. (1994). Play, toys, and language. In J. Goldstein (Ed.), *Play, toys and child development* (pp. 27–45). New York: Cambridge University Press.

Peller, L. (Ed.). Models of children's play. *Mental Hygiene, 36*, 66–83.

Pepler, D., & Ross, H. (1981). Effects of play on convergent and divergent problem solving. *Child Development, 52*, 1202–1210.

Perlmutter, J., & Burrell, L. (1995). Learning through "play" as well as "work" in the primary grades. *Young Children, 50(5)*, 14–21.

Petrakos, H., & Howe, N. (1996). The influence of the physical design of the dramatic play center on children's play. *Early Childhood Research Quarterly, 11*, 63–77.

Phillips, A. (Ed.) (1996). *Topics in early childhood education: Playing for keeps*. Vol. 2. St. Paul., MN: Redleaf.

Piaget, J. (1962). *Play, dreams and imitation in childhood*. New York: Norton.

Polito, T. (1994). How play and work are organized in a kindergarten classroom. *Journal of Research in Childhood Education, 9*, 47–57.

Powlishta, K., Serbin, L., & Moller, L. (1993). The stability of individual differences in gender typing: Implications for understanding gender segregation. *Sex Roles, 28* (11–12), 723–737.

Pulaski, M. (1973). Toys and imaginative play. In J. Singer (Ed.), *The child's world of make-believe: Experimental studies of imaginative play* (pp. 74–103). New York: Academic Press.

Pulaski, M. A. (1970). Play as a function of toy structure and fantasy predisposition. *Child Development, 41*, 531–537.

Ramsey, P. (1995). Changing social dynamics in early childhood classrooms. *Child Development, 66* (3), 764–773.

Rheingold, H., & Cook, K. (1975). The contents of boy's and girl's rooms as an index of parents' behavior. *Child Development, 46*, 920–927.

Rhodes, L., & Nathenson-Mejia, S. (1992). Anecdotal records: A powerful tool for ongoing literacy assessment. *The Reading Teacher, 45*, 502–509.

Rivkin, M. (1995). *The great outdoors: Restoring children's right to play outside.* Washington, DC: National Association for the Education of Young Children.

Robinson, C., & Jackson, R. (1987). The effects of varying toy detail within a prototypical play object on the solitary pretend play of preschool children. *Journal of Applied Developmental Psychology, 8*, 209–220.

Roopnarine, J., Johnson, J., & Hooper, F. (Eds.), (1994). *Children's play in diverse cultures.* Albany, NY: SUNY Press.

Roper, R., & Hinde, R. (1978). Social behavior in a play group: Consistency and complexity. *Child Development, 49*, 570–579.

Rosen, C. E. (1974). *The effects of sociodramatic play on problem-solving behavior among culturally disadvantaged preschool children. Child Development, 45*, 920–927.

Rosenblatt, D. (1977). Developmental trends in infant play. In B. Tizard & O. Harvey (Eds.), *The biology of play.* Philadelphia: Lippincott.

Roskos, K. (1994, April). *Connecting academic work and play at school: Preliminary observations of young children's content-oriented interaction and talk under conditions of play in kindergarten.* Paper presented at the meeting of the American Educational Research Association, New Orleans.

Roskos, K. (in press). Through the bioecological lens: Some observations of literacy in play as a proximal process. In K. Roskos & J. Christie (Eds.), *Literacy and play in the early years: Cognitive, ecological, and sociocultural perspectives.* Mahwah, NJ: Erlbaum.

Roskos, K., & Neuman, S. (1993). Descriptive observations of adults' facilitation of literacy in play. *Early Childhood Research Quarterly, 8*, 77–97.

Roskos, K. & Newman, S. (1998). Play as an opportunity for literacy. In O. Saracho and B. Spodek (Eds.), *Multiple perspectives on play in early childhood education* (pp. 100–115). Albany, NY: SUNY Press.

Roskos, K., Vukelich, C., Christie, J., Enz, B., & Neuman, S. (1995). *Linking literacy and play: Facilitator's guide.* Newark, DE: International Reading Association.

Ross, H. S., Goldman, B. D., & Hay, D. F. (1979). Features and functions of infant games. In B. Sutton Smith (Ed.), *Play and learning.* New York: Gardner Press.

Ross, H. & Lollis, S. (1987). Communication within infant social games. *Developmental Psychology, 23*, 241–248.

Rubin, K. (1977). The social and cognitive value of preschool toys and activities. *Canadian Journal of Behavioral Science, 9*, 382–385.

Rubin, K. (1980). Fantasy play: Its role in the development of social skills and social cognition. In K. H. Rubin (Ed.), *Children's play* (pp. 69–84). San Francisco: Jossey-Bass.

Rubin, K. H. (1982). Nonsocial play in preschoolers: Necessarily evil? *Child Development, 53*, 651–657.

Rubin, K. H., Fein, G. G., & Vandenberg, B. (1983). Play. In P. H. Mussed (Ed.), *Handbook of child psychology: Vol. 4, Socialization, personality, and social development* (4th ed., pp. 693–774). New York: Wiley.

Rubin, K. H., & Hayvern, M. (1981). The social and cognitive play of preschool-aged children differing with regard to sociometric status. *Journal of Research and Development in Education, 14,* 116–122.

Rubin, K. & Maioni, T. (1975). Play preferences and its relation to egocentrism, popularity, and classification skills in preschoolers. *Merrill Palmer Quarterly 21,* 171–179.

Rubin, K. H., Maioni, T. L., & Hornung, M. (1976). Free play behaviors in middle- and lower-class preschoolers: Parten and Piaget revisited. *Child Development, 47,* 414–419.

Rubin, I., Provenzano, F., & Luria, Z. (1974). The eyes of the beholder: Parents' views of sex of newborns. *American Journal of Orthopsychiatry, 44,* 512–519.

Rubin, K., & Seibel, C. (1979, April). *The effects of ecological setting on the cognitive and social play behaviors of preschoolers.* Paper presented at the annual meeting of the American Educational Research Association, San Francisco.

Rubin, K., Watson, K., & Jambor, T. (1978). Free play behavior in preschool and kindergarten children. *Child Development, 49,* 534–536.

Russell, B. (1967). *The problems of philosophy.* New York: Oxford University Press. (Original work published 1912)

Sachs, J. (1987). Preschool boys' and girls' language use in pretend play. In S. Philips, S. Steele, & C. Tanz (Eds.), *Language, gender, and sex in comparative perspective* (pp. 178–188). New York: Cambridge University Press.

Sackett, G., Sameroff, A., Cairns, R. & Suomi, S. (1981). Continuity in behavioral development: Theoretical and empirical issues. In K. Immelmann, G. Barrow, L. Petrinovich, and M. Main (Eds.), *Behavioral development* (pp. 23–57). New York: Cambridge University Press.

Safford, P. (1989). *Integrate teaching in early childhood: Starting in the mainstream.* White Plains, NY: Longman.

Saltz, E., Dixon, D., & Johnson, J. (1977). Training disadvantaged preschoolers on various fantasy activities: Effects on cognitive functioning and impulse control. *Child Development, 48,* 367–380.

Saltz, E., & Johnson, J. (1974). Training for thematic-fantasy play in culturally disadvantaged children: Preliminary results. *Journal of Educational Psychology, 66,* 623–630.

Sanders, K., & Harper, L. (1976). Free-play fantasy behavior in preschool children: Relations among gender, age, season, and location. *Child Development, 47,* 1182–1185.

Sapon-Shevin, M. (1992). Cooperation activities in inclusive classrooms: Learning to become a community. *Rethinking Schools,* Jan/Feb, 18–19.

Saracho, O. (1991). Social correlates of cognitive style in young children. *Early Childhood Development and Care, 76,* 117–134.

Saracho, O. (1995). Relationship between young children's cognitive style and their play. *Early Childhood Development and Care, 113,* 77–84.

Saracho, O. (1998). What is stylish about play? In O. Saracho & B. Spodek (Eds.). *Multiple perspectives on play in early childhood education.* Albany, NY: SUNY Press.

Sawyer, R. (1997). *Pretend play as improvisation: Conversation in the preschool classroom.* Mahwah, NJ: Erlbaum.

Scali, N. (1993, Sept/Oct.). Goldilocks and the three bears. *The Writing Notebook: Visions for Learning,* 14–15.

Schaefer, C. (Ed.). (1993). *Therapeutic use of child's play.* New York: Jason Arnason.

Schaefer, C. & O'Connor, K. (Eds.) (1983). *Handbook of play therapy.* New York: John Wiley & Sons.

Schaefer, M., & Smith, P. (1996). Teachers' perceptions of play fighting and real fighting in primary school. *Educational Research, 38*, 173–181.

Schlosberg, H. (1947). The concept of play. *Psychological Review, 54*, 229–231.

Schrader, C. (1990). Symbolic play as a curricular tool for early literacy development. *Early Childhood Research Quarterly, 5*, 79–103.

Schwartzman, H. B. (1978). *Transformations: The anthropology of children's play.* New York: Plenum.

Schweder, R. (1990). "Cultural psychology—what is it?" In J. Stigler, R. Schweder, & G. Herdt (Eds.), *Cultural psychology: Essays on comparative human development.* Cambridge: Cambridge University Press.

Segal, M., & Adcock, D. (1981). *Just pretending: Ways to help children grow through imaginative play.* Englewood Cliffs, NJ: Prentice-Hall.

Segal, M., Montie, J., & Iverson, T. (1991). Observing for individual differences in the social interaction styles of preschool children. In C. Schaefer, K. Gitlin, & A. Sandgrund (Eds.), *Play diagnosis and assessment* (pp. 579–607). New York: Wiley.

Segoe, M. (1971). A comparison of children's play in six modern cultures. *Journal of School Psychology, 9*, 61–72.

Selman, R. L. (1971). The relation of role-taking to the development of moral judgment in children. *Child Development, 42*, 79–92.

Serbin, L. A., Connor, J. A., Burchardt, C. J., & Citron, C. C. (1979). Effects of peer presence on sex-typing of children's play behavior. *Journal of Experimental Child Psychology, 27*, 303–309.

Serbin, L. A., Tonick, I. J., & Sternglanz, S. H. (1977). Shaping cooperative cross-sex play. *Child Development, 48*, 924–929.

Shade, D. & Davis, B. (1997). The role of computer technology in early childhood education. In J. Isenberg & M. Jalongo (Eds.), *Major trends and issues in early childhood education: Challenges, controversies, and insights* (pp. 90–103). New York: Teachers College Press.

Sheehan, R., & Day, D. (1975). Is open space just empty space? *Day Care and Early Education, 3*, 10–13, 47.

Shell, R. & Eisenberg, N. (1990). The role of peers' gender in children's naturally occurring interest in toys. *International Journal of Behavioral Development, 13*, (1), 373–388.

Shin, D. (1994). *Preschool children's symbolic play indoors and outdoors.* Unpublished doctoral dissertation, University of Texas at Austin.

Shure, M. (1963). Psychological ecology of a nursery school. *Child Development, 34*, 979–992.

Siegle, B. (1991). Play diagnosis of autism: The ETHOS play session. In C. Schaefer, K. Gitlin, & A. Sandgrund (Eds.), *Play diagnosis and assessment* (pp. 331–365). New York: Wiley.

Silvern, S., Taylor, J., Williamson, P., Surbeck, E., & Kelley, M. (1986). Young children's story recall as a product of play, story familiarity, and adult intervention. *Merrill-Palmer Quarterly, 32*, 73–86.

Silvern, S., Williamson, P., & Countermine, T. (1983, April). *Video game playing and aggression in children.* Paper presented at the annual meeting of the American Educational Research Association, Montreal.

Silvern, S., Williamson , P., & Countermine, T. (1988). Young children's interaction with a microcomputer. *Early Child Development and Care, 32*, 23–35.

Simmons, B. (1976). Teachers, beware of sex-stereotyping. *Childhood Education, 52*, 192–195.

Simmons, D. (1996). *Play Therapy.* Unpublished manuscript. The Pennsylvania State University, University Park, PA.

Simon, T., & Smith, P. (1983). The study of play and problem solving in preschool children: Have experimenter effects been responsible for previous results? *British Journal of Developmental Psychology, 1*, 289–297.

Simon, T., & Smith, P. (1985). Play and problem-solving: A paradigm questioned. *Merrill-Palmer Quarterly, 31*, 265–277.

Singer, D., & Singer, J. (1977). *Partners in play: A step-by-step guide to imaginative play in children.* New York: Harper & Row.

Singer, D. & Singer, J. (1990). *The house of make-believe: Children's play and the developing imagination.* Cambridge, MA: Harvard University Press.

Singer, J. L. (1961). Imagination and waiting ability in young children. *Journal of Personality, 29*, 396–413.

Singer, J. L. (1973). *The child's world of make-believe: Experimental studies of imaginative play.* New York: Academic Press.

Singer, J. (1994). The scientific foundations of play therapy. In J. Hellendoorn, R. van der Kooij, & B. Sutton-Smith (Eds.), *Play and Intervention* (pp. 27–38). Albany, New York: SUNY Press.

Singer, J. (1995). Imaginative play in childhood: Precursors to subjunctive thought, daydreaming, and adult pretending games. In A. Pellegrini (Ed.), *The future of play theory* (pp. 187–219). Albany, NY: State University of New York Press.

Singer, J., & Singer, D. (1976). Can TV stimulate jissaginative play? *Journal of Communication, 26*, 74–80

Singer, J. L., & Singer, D. G. (1980). A factor analytic study of preschoolers' play behavior. *Academic Psychology Bulletin, 2*, 143–156.

Singer, J., Singer, D., Desmond, R., Hirsch, B., & Nichol, A. (1988). Family mediation and children's cognition, aggression, and comprehension of television: A longitudinal study. *Journal of Applied Developmental Psychology, 9*, 329–347.

Sinker, M. (1985). More than play: Lekotek. *Topics in Early Childhood Special Education, 5*(3), Fall, 93–100.

Slade, A. (1987). A longitudinal study of maternal involvement and symbolic play during the toddler period. *Child Development, 58*, 367–375.

Slaughter, D. & Dombrowski, J. (1989). Cultural continuities and discontinuities: Impact on social and pretend play. In M. Bloch & A. Pellegrini (Eds.), *The ecological context of children's play* (pp. 282–310). Norwood, NJ: Ablex.

Smilansky, S. (1968). *The effects of sociodramatic play on disadvantaged preschool children.* New York: Wiley.

Smilansky, S. (1988). Sociodramatic play: Its relevance to behavior and achievement in school. In E. Klugman & S. Smilansky (Eds.), *Children's play and learning: Perspectives and policy implications* (pp. 18–42). New York: Teachers College Press.

Smilansky, S. & Shefatya, L. (1979). Narrowing socioeconomic groups in achievement through kindergarten reading instruction. *Journal Studies in Education, 21*, 4–68. University of Haifa.

Smith, A. & Inder, P. (1993). Social interaction in same- and cross-gender pre-school peer groups: A participant observation study. *Educational Psychology, 13*(1), 29–42.

Smith, D. (1991). Parent-child play assessment. In C. E. Schaefer, K. Gitlin, & A. Sandgrund (Eds.), *Play diagnosis and assessment* (pp. 463–492). New York: Wiley.

Smith, P. (1978). A longitudinal study of social participation in preschool children: Solitary and parallel play reexamined. *Developmental Psychology, 14*, 512–516.

Smith, P. (1981). The impact of computerization on children's toys and games. *Journal of Children in Contemporary Society, 14*, 73–83.

Smith, P. (1997, October). *Play fighting and fighting: How do they relate?* Lisbon: ICCP.

Smith, P., & Connolly, K. (1972). Patterns of play and social interaction in preschool children. In N. Blurton-Jones (Ed.), *Ethological studies of child behaviour* (pp. 65–95). Cambridge, England: Cambridge University Press.

Smith, P. & Dodsworth, C. (1978). Social class differences in the fantasy play of preschool childrewn. *Journal of Genetic Psychology, 133,* 183–190.

Smith, P., & Thompson, D. (Eds.). (1991). *Practical approaches to bullying.* London: David Fulton.

Smith, P. & Vollstedt, R. (1985). On defining play: An empirical study of the relationship between play and various play criteria. *Child Development, 56,* 1042–1050.

Smith, P. & Whitney, S. (1987). Play and associative fluency: Experimenter effects may be responsible for previous positive findings. *Developmental Psychology, 23,* 49–53.

Smith, P. K., & Connolly, K. J. (1980). *The ecology of preschool behavior.* Cambridge, England: Cambridge University Press.

Smith, P. K., Dalgleish, M., & Herzmark, G. (1981). A comparison of the effects of fantasy play tutoring and skills tutoring in nursery classes. *International Journal of Behavioral Development, 4,* 421–441.

Smith, P. K., & Syddall, S. (1978). Play and non-play tutoring in preschool children: Is it play or tutoring which matters? *British Journal of Educational Psychology, 48,* 315–325.

Sponseller, D., & Lowry, M. (1974). Designing a play environment for toddlers. In D. Sponseller (Ed.), *Play as a learning medium* (pp. 81–106). Washington, DC: National Association for the Education of Young Children.

Spring, J. (1993, March). Seven days of play. *American Demographics,* 50–53.

Stainback, W. & Stainback S. (Eds.). (1990). *Support networks for inclusive schooling: Interdepartment integrated education.* Baltimore, MD: Paul H. Brookes.

Stone, S. (1995). Wanted: Advocates for play in the primary grades. *Young Children, 50*(6), 45–54.

Stone, S., & Christie, J. (1996). Collaborative literacy learning during sociodramatic play in a multiage (K-2) primary classroom. *Journal of Research in Childhood Education, 10,* 123–133.

Strain, P. (1990). LRE for preschool children with handicaps: What we know, what we should be doing. *Journal of Early Intervention, 14,* 291–296.

Strayer, J., Mosher, M., & Russell, C. (1981, April). *Social-cognitive skills and play behaviors of toddlers.* Paper presented to the meetings of the Society for Research in Child Development, Boston.

Stremmel, A. (1997). Diversity and the multicultural perspective. In G. Hart, D. Burts, & R. Charlesworth (Eds.), *Integrated curriculum and developmentally appropriate practices: Birth to age eight.* Albany, NY: SUNY Press.

Sulzby, E., & Teale, W. (1991). Emergent literacy. In R. Barr, M. Kamil, P. Mosenthal, & P. D. Pearson (Eds.), *Handbook of reading research* (vol. 2). New York: Longman.

Super, C. & Harkness, S. (1986). The developmental niche: A conceptualization at the interface of child and culture. *International Journal of Behavioral Development, 9,* 545–569.

Sutton-Smith, B. (1967). The role of play in cognitive development. *Young Children, 22,* 361–370.

Sutton-Smith, B. (1972). *The folkgames of children.* Austin, TX: The University of Texas Press.

Sutton-Smith, B. (1977). Towards an anthropology of play. In P. Stevens (Ed.), *Studies in the anthropology of play.* West Point, NY: Leisure Press.

Sutton-Smith, B. (1979a). Epilogue: Play as performance. In B. Sutton-Smith (Ed.), *Play and learning* (pp. 295–320).

Sutton-Smith, B. (1979b). The play of girls. In C. B. Kopp & M. Kirkpatrick (Eds.), *Becoming female: Perspectives on development*. New York: Plenum.

Sutton-Smith, B. (1980). Piaget, play and cognition revisited. In W. Overton (Ed.), *The relationship between social and cognitive development*. New York: Erlbaum.

Sutton-Smith, B. (1983). One hundred years of change in play research. *TAASP Newsletter, 9*(2), 13–17.

Sutton-Smith, B. (1985). Origins and developmental processes of play. In C. Brown & A. Gottfried (Eds.), *Play interactions: The role of toys and parental involvement in children's development* (pp. 61–66). Skillman, NJ: Johnson & Johnson Baby Products.

Sutton-Smith, B. (1986). *Toys as culture*. New York: Gardner Press.

Sutton-Smith, B. (1988). War toys and aggression. *Play and Culture, 1,* 57–69.

Sutton-Smith, B. (1990). Playfully yours. *TASP Newsletter, 16* (2), 2–5.

Sutton-Smith, B. (1998). *The ambiguity of play*. Cambridge, MA: Harvard University Press.

Sutton-Smith, B., Gerstmyer, J. & Meckly, A. (1988). Playfighting as folkplay amongst preschool children, *Western Folklore, 47,* 161–176.

Sutton-Smith, B., & Heath, S. (1981). Paradigms of pretense. *Quarterly newsletter of the Laboratory of Comparative Human Cognition, 3,* 41–45.

Sutton-Smith, B., & Sutton-Smith, S. (1974). *How to play with your child (and when not to)*. New York: Hawthorn.

Swadener, E. B. (1986). *Implementation of education that is multicultural in early childhood settings: A case study of two day care programs*. Unpublished doctoral dissertation, University of Wisconsin-Madison.

Swadener, E. B. & Johnson, J. (1988). Play in diverse social contexts: Parent and teacher roles. In M. Block and A. Pellegrini (Eds.), *Ecological contexts of play* (pp. 214–244). Norwood, NJ: Ablex Publishing.

Sylva, K., Bruner, J. S., & Genova, P. (1976). The role of play in the problem-solving of children 3–5 years old. In J. S. Bruner, A. Jolly, & K. Sylva (Eds.), *Play: Its role in development and evolution* (pp. 244–257). New York: Basic Books.

Sylva, K., Roy, C., & Painter, M. (1980). *Childwatching at playgroup & nursery school*. Ypsilanti, MI: High/Scope Press.

Tamis-LeMonda, C., & Bornstein, M. (1991). Individual variation, correspondence, stability, and change in mother and toddler play. *Infant Behavior and Development, 14,* 143–162.

Tamis-LeMonda, C., & Bornstein, M. (1993). Play and its relations to other mental functions in the child. In M. Bornstein & A. O'Reilly (Eds.), *The role of play in the development of thought: New directions in child development, Number 59,* San Francisco: Jossey-Bass, pp. 17–27.

Tarullo, L. (1994). Windows on the social worlds: Gender differences in children's play narratives. In A. Slade & D. Wolf (Eds.), *Children at Play: Clinical and developmental approaches to meaning and representation* (pp. 169–187). New York: Oxford University Press.

Taylor, M., Cartwright, B. & Carlson, S. (1993). A developmental investigation of children's imaginary companions. *Developmental Psychology, 29,* (2), 276–293.

Taylor, R. (Ed.). (1980). *The computer in the school: Tutor, tutee, tool*. New York: Teachers College Press.

Tegano, D., & Burdette, M. (1991). Length of activity period and play behaviors of preschool children. *Journal of Research in Childhood Education, 5,* 93–98.

Tegano, D., Lookabaugh, S., May, G., & Burdette, M. (1991). Constructive play and problem solving: The role of structure and time in the classroom. *Early Childhood Development and Care, 68,* 27–35.

The State of America's Children Yearbook (1997). Washington, DC: Children's Defense Fund & National Association for the Education of Young Children.

Thompson, H., & Stanford, G. (1981). *Child life in hospitals.* Springfield, IL: Charles C. Thomas Publisher.

Thompson, R. (1995). Documenting the value of play for hospitalized children: The challenge in playing the game. In E. Klugman (Ed.), *Play, policy, and practice.* St. Paul, MN: Redleaf Press.

Thornburg, H. (1979). *The bubblegum years.* Tucson: HELP Books.

Tinsworth, D., & Kramer, J. (1990). *Playground equipment related injuries and deaths.* Washington, DC: U.S. Consumer Product Safety Commission.

Tizard, B., Phelps, J., & Plewis, L. (1976). Play in preschool centres (l) Play measures and their relation to age, sex and IQ. *Journal of Child Psychology and Psychiatry, 17,* 251–264.

Tizard, B., Phelps, J., & Plewis, L. (1976). Play in preschool centres (II). Effects on play of the child's social class and of the educational orientation of the centre. *Journal of Child Psychology and Psychiatry, 17,* 265–274.

Tobin, J., Wu, D., & Davidson, S. (1989). *Preschool in three cultures.* New Haven, CT: Yale University Press.

Tomkins, S. (1962). *Affect, imagery, consciousness.* New York: Springer.

Toy Manufacturers of America. (1996). *Toy industry annual sales 1986–1995* [on-line]. Available: *http://www.toy-tma.com/STATISTICS/is chart1.html.*

Toy Manufacturers of America. (1997). *Ten toy hazards to avoid* [on-line]. Available: http://www.toy-tma/NEWA/hazards.html.

Trageton, A. (1997, October). *Play in lower primary school in Norway.* International Council for Children's Play, Lisbon.

Trawick-Smith, J. (1990). The effects of realistic versus non-realistic play materials on young children's symbolic transformation of objects. *Journal of Research in Childhood Education, 5,* 27–35.

Truhon, S. A. (1979, March). *Playfulness, play, and creativity: A path-analytic model.* Paper presented at the biennial meeting of the Society for Research in Child Development, San Francisco.

Truhon, S. A. (1982). Playfulness, play and creativity: A path-analytic model. *Journal of Genetic Psychology, 143*(1), 19–28.

Udwin, O. (1983). Imaginative play as an intervention method with institutionalized preschool children. *British Journal of Educational Psychology, 53,* 32–39.

Udwin, O., & Shmukler, D. (1981), The influence of socio-cultural economic and home background factors on children's ability to engage in imaginative play. *Developmental Psychology, 17,* 66–72.

Urberg, K. & Kaplan, M. (1989). An observational study of race-, age- and sex-heterogeneous interaction in preschoolers. *Journal of Applied Developmental Psychology, 10*(3), 299–312.

U.S. Consumer Product Safety Commission. (1991). *Public playground handbook for safety.* Washington, DC: U.S. printing office.

U.S. Consumer Product Safety Commission. (1993). *Which toy for which child: A consumer's guide for selecting suitable toys—Ages birth through five.* Washington, DC: Author.

Van Alstyne, D. (1932). *Play behavior and choice of play materials of pre-school children.* Chicago: University of Chicago Press.

Van Hoorn, J., Nourot, P., Scales, B., & Alward, K. (1993). *Play at the center of the curriculum.* New York: Macmillan.

Vance, B. (1982). Adventure playgrounds: The American experience. *Parks and Recreation, 17* (9), 67–70.

Vandenberg, B. (1990). Play and problem solving: An elusive connection. *Merrill-Palmer Quarterly, 36,* 261–272.

Vandenberg, B. (1998). Real and not real: A vital developmental dichotomy. In O. Saracho and B. Spodek (Eds.), *Multiple perspectives on play in early childhood education* (pp. 295–305). Albany, NY: SUNY Press.

van der Kooij, R. (1998). Spiel (play). In D. H. Rost (Ed.), *Handworterbuch Padagogische* [Dictionary of Educational Psychology]. Weinheim: Psychologie Verlags Union.

van der Kooij, R., & de Groot, R. (1977). *That's all in the game: Theory and research, practice and the future of children's play.* Groningen, Netherlands: Schindele-Verlag Rheinstetten.

Varga, D. (1991). The historical origins of children's play as a developmental task. *Play and Culture, 4,* 322–333.

Vukelich, C. (1991, December). *Learning about the functions of writing: The effects of three play interventions on children's development and knowledge about writing.* Paper presented at the annual meeting of the National Reading Conference, Palm Springs.

Vukelich, C. (1995). Watch me! Watch me! Understanding children's literacy knowledge. In J. Christie, K. Roskos, B. Enz, C. Vukelich, & S. Neuman (Eds.), *Readings for linking literacy and play.* Newark, DE: International Reading Association.

Vygotsky, L. S. (1976). Play and its role in the mental development of the child. In J. S. Bruner, A. Jolly, & K. Sylva (Eds.), *Play: Its role in development and evolution* (pp. 537–554). New York: Basic Books.

Vygotsky, L. (1978). *Mind in society: The development of higher mental processes.* Cambridge, MA: Harvard University Press.

Wagner, B. (1983). The expanding circle of informal classroom drama. In B. Busching & J. Schwartz (Eds.), *Integrating the language arts in the elementary school* (pp. 155–163). Urbana, IL: National Council of Teachers of English.

Walling, L. (1977). Planning an environment: A case study. In S. Kritchevsky & E. Prescott (Eds.), *Planning environments for young children: Physical space* (pp. 44–48). Washington, DC: National Association for the Education of Young Children.

Wardle, F. (1983). *Effects of complexity, age, and sex on the social and cognitive level of young children's play in an outdoor setting.* Unpublished doctoral dissertation, University of Kansas.

Wardle, F. (1987). Outdoor play: One Head Start's solution. *Children Today, 16*(2), 16–19.

Wardle, F. (1988). Is your playground physically fit? *Scholastic Pre-K Today, 27*(7), 21–26.

Wardle, F. (1990). Are we taking the fun out of playgrounds? *Daycare and Early Education, 18*(1), 30–34.

Wardle, F. (1991). Are we shortchanging boys? *Child Care Information Exchange, 79* (May/June), 48–51.

Wardle, F. (1995). Bruderhof education: Outdoor school. *Young Children, 50*(3), 68–73.

Wardle, F. (1997). *Community Playthings catalog.* Rifton, NY: Community Playthings.

Wardle, F. (1997a). Outdoor play: Designing, building and remodeling playgrounds for young children. *Early Childhood News, 9*(2), 36–42.

Wardle, F. (1997b). Playgrounds: Questions to consider when selecting materials. *Dimensions of Early Childhood*, March/April, 36–42.

Watson, M. M., & Jackowitz, E. R. (1984). Agents and recipient objects in the development of early symbolic play. *Child Development, 55,* 1091–1097.

Weikart, D. & Schweinhart, L. (1993). The High/Scope cognitively oriented curriculum in early education. In J. Roopnarine and J. Johnson (Eds.), *Approaches to early childhood education* (2nd ed.). Columbus, OH: Merrill.

Weilbacher, R. (1981). The effects of static and dynamic play environments on children's social and motor behaviors. In A. T. Cheska (Ed.), *Play as context* (pp. 248–258). West Point, NY: Leisure Press.

Weinberger, L. & Starkey, P. (1994). Pretend play by African American children in Head Start. *Early Childhood Research Quarterly, 9* (3 & 4), 327–344.

Weiner, E. & Weiner, B. (1974). Differentiation of retarded and normal children through toy-play analysis. *Multivariate behavioral research, 9,* 245–252.

Weir, R. (1962). *Language in the crib.* The Hague: Mouton.

Weisler, A., & McCall, R. B. (1976). Exploration and play: Resume and redirection. *American Psychologist, 31,* 492–508.

Wertsch, J. (1985). *Culture, communication, cognition.* New York: Cambridge University Press.

Wesley, J. (1974). *Pioneers.* Lakeside, CA: Interact Company.

Whaley, K. (1990). The emergence of social play in infancy: A proposed developmental sequence of infant-adult social play. *Early Childhood Research Quarterly, 5,* 347–358.

White, M. (1987). *The Japanese educational challenge: A commitment to children.* New York: Free Press.

Whiting, B. (Ed.) (1963). *Six cultures: Studies in child rearing.* New York: Wiley.

Whiting, B. (1980). Culture and social behavior, *Ethos, 2,* 95–116.

Wiltz, N., & Fein, G. (1996, March). Evolution of a narrative curriculum: The contributions of Vivian Gussin Paley. *Young Children,* 61–68.

Winnicott, D. W. (1971). *Playing and reality.* Harmondsworth, England: Penguin.

Winter, S., Bell, M., & Dempsey, M. (1994). Creating play environments for children with special needs. *Childhood Education, 71,* 28–32.

Witkin, H. A., Lewis, H. B., Hertzman, M., Machover, K., Meissner, P. B., & Wapner, S. (1954). *Personality through perception.* New York: Harper & Row.

Wittgenstein, L. (1958). *Philosophical investigations.* New York: Macmillan.

Wohlwill, J. (1973). *The study of behavioral development.* New York: Academic Press.

Wolf, D., & Gardner, H. (1979). Style and sequence in early symbolic play. In M. Franklin & N. Smith (Eds.), *Symbolic functioning in childhood.* Hillsdale, NJ: Erlbaum.

Wolf, D., & Grollman, S. H. (1982). Ways of playing: Individual differences in imaginative style. In D. J. Pepler & K. H. Rubin (Eds.), *The play of children: Current theory and research* (pp. 46–63). Basel, Switzerland: Karger.

Wolfberg, P., & Schuler, A. (1993, March). *A case illustrating the impact of peer play on symbolic activity in autism.* Paper presented at the Biennia Conference of the Society for Research in Child Development, New Orleans.

Wolfgang, C. (1974). An exploration of the relationship between the cognitive area of reading and selected developmental aspects of children's play. *Psychology in the Schools, 11,* 338–343.

Wood, D., McMahon, L., & Cranstoun, Y. (1980). *Working with under fives.* Ypsilanti, MI: High/Scope.

Woodard, C. (1984). Guidelines for facilitating sociodramatic play. *Childhood Education, 60,* 172–177.

Worley, M., Strain, P., & Bailey, D. (1992). Reaching potentials of children with special needs. In S. Bredekamp & T. Rosegrant (Eds.), *Reaching potentials: Appropriate curriculum and assessment for young children.* Washington, DC: NAEYC.

Wright, J. & Samaras, A. (1986). Play worlds and microworlds. In P. Campbell & G. Fein (Eds.), *Young children and microcomputers* (pp. 74–86). Englewood Cliffs, NJ: Prentice Hall.

Wright, J., Shade, D., Thouvenelle, S., & Davidson, J. (1989). New directions in software development for young children. *Journal of Computing in Childhood Education, 1* (1), 45–57.

Yawkey, T. (1986). Effects of dramatic play as a basis of a parent instructional model for home intervention programming for hispanic parents of preschool children. In B. Mergen (Ed.) *Cultural dimensions of play, games, and sport.* The Association for the Anthropological Study of Play. Vol. 10. Champaign, IL: Human Kinetics Publisher, Inc., 137–151.

Youngblade, L. & Dunn, J. (1995). Individual differences in young children's pretend play with mother and sibling: Links to relationships and understanding of other people's feelings and beliefs. *Child Development, 66,* 1472–1492.

Zimiles, H. (1993). The Bank Street Approach. In J. Roopnarine and J. Johnson (Eds.), *Approaches to Early Childhood Education* (2nd ed.) (pp. 261–274). New York: Macmillan.

INDEX